THE CRIMINAL FINANCES ACT 2017

THE CRIMINAL FINANCES ACT 2017

JONATHAN FISHER QC

ANITA CLIFFORD

informa law
from Routledge

First published 2019
by Informa Law from Routledge
2 Park Square, Milton Park, Abingdon, Oxon OX14 4RN

and by Informa Law from Routledge
52 Vanderbilt Avenue, New York, NY 10017

Informa Law from Routledge is an imprint of the Taylor & Francis Group, an informa business

© 2019 Jonathan Fisher QC and Anita Clifford

The right of Jonathan Fisher QC and Anita Clifford to be identified as authors of this work has been asserted by them in accordance with sections 77 and 78 of the Copyright, Designs and Patents Act 1988.

All rights reserved. No part of this book may be reprinted or reproduced or utilised in any form or by any electronic, mechanical, or other means, now known or hereafter invented, including photocopying and recording, or in any information storage or retrieval system, without permission in writing from the publishers.

Whilst every effort has been made to ensure that the information contained in this book is correct, neither the author nor Informa Law can accept any responsibility for any errors or omissions or any consequences arising therefrom.

Trademark notice: Product or corporate names may be trademarks or registered trademarks, and are used only for identification and explanation without intent to infringe.

British Library Cataloguing-in-Publication Data
A catalogue record for this book is available from the British Library

Library of Congress Cataloging-in-Publication Data
Names: Fisher, Jonathan, 1958– author. | Clifford, Anita, author.
Title: The Criminal Finances Act 2017 / by Jonathan Fisher QC and Anita Clifford.
Description: Abingdon, Oxon; New York, NY: Informa Law from Routledge, 2019.
Identifiers: LCCN 2018033286 | ISBN 9781138483774 (hbk) | ISBN 9781351053969 (ebk)
Subjects: LCSH: Great Britain. Criminal Finances Act 2017. | Forfeiture—Great Britain. | Money laundering—Law and legislation—Great Britain. | Crime—Finance—Law and legislation—Great Britain.
Classification: LCC KD8460. F57 2019 | DDC 345.41/0268—dc23
LC record available at https://lccn.loc.gov/2018033286

ISBN: 978-1-138-48377-4 (hbk)
ISBN: 978-1-351-05396-9 (ebk)

Typeset in Times New Roman
by Apex CoVantage, LLC

CONTENTS

Table of cases		xv
Table of legislation		xvii
	INTRODUCTION	1
CHAPTER 1	EXTENDING THE SAR MORATORIUM PERIOD	5
CHAPTER 2	MONEY LAUNDERING AND FURTHER INFORMATION ORDERS	15
CHAPTER 3	MONEY LAUNDERING AND INFORMATION SHARING	21
CHAPTER 4	UNEXPLAINED WEALTH ORDERS	27
CHAPTER 5	CHALLENGING AND RESPONDING TO AN UNEXPLAINED WEALTH ORDER	41
CHAPTER 6	SEARCH, SEIZURE, FORFEITURE AND 'GROSS HUMAN RIGHTS ABUSE'	49
CHAPTER 7	TERRORIST FINANCING AND TERRORIST PROPERTY	57
CHAPTER 8	CORPORATE FACILITATION OF TAX EVASION OFFENCES	73
CHAPTER 9	PROSECUTION AND THE REASONABLE PREVENTION PROCEDURES DEFENCE	87
	CONCLUSION	97
APPENDIX	CRIMINAL FINANCES ACT 2017	99
Index		281

DETAILED TABLE OF CONTENTS

Table of cases	xv
Table of legislation	xvii
INTRODUCTION	1
CHAPTER 1 EXTENDING THE SAR MORATORIUM PERIOD	5
Introduction	5
Criteria for making the order	7
Which court?	8
Who can apply?	8
Timing of application	8
Subsequent applications	9
Procedure – section 336B	9
Notice	9
Interested person	10
Specified information	10
Procedure – rules of court	11
The hearing	11
Application notice	11
Respondents' notice	12
The order	12
Application to withhold specified information	12
Costs	13
Tipping off	13
CHAPTER 2 MONEY LAUNDERING AND FURTHER INFORMATION ORDERS	15
Introduction	15
The order	16
The application	16
Rules of court: procedure	17
Evidential status	17
Incriminatory evidence	17
Legally privileged material	18
Appeals	18
Non-compliance	18

CHAPTER 3 MONEY LAUNDERING AND INFORMATION SHARING 21
Introduction 21
Voluntary disclosure 22
  The conditions 22
  Joint reporting 24
  Impact on the duty to report 25
  Confidentiality and privacy 25

CHAPTER 4 UNEXPLAINED WEALTH ORDERS 27
Introduction 27
Requirements 28
The respondent 29
  Politically exposed person 29
  Criminal suspects and connected persons 30
  Companies 31
Holding property 32
  Property held by a company or trust 32
  Timing 33
Insufficient means to obtain property 33
  Known sources of lawful income 33
  Trusts 34
  Market value 35
Effect of a UWO 35
  Trustee respondents 35
  Providing the explanation 36
Interim freezing 36
Non-compliance 36
Timing 37
Extra-territoriality 38

CHAPTER 5 CHALLENGING AND RESPONDING TO AN UNEXPLAINED WEALTH ORDER 41
Introduction 41
Contentious areas 41
Challenging and varying an IFO 43
Costs 44
Responding to a UWO 44
  Use of the explanation 46
Use of the new power 47

CHAPTER 6 SEARCH, SEIZURE, FORFEITURE AND 'GROSS HUMAN RIGHTS ABUSE' 49
New powers to enforcement authorities 49
  Serious Fraud Office 49
  HM Revenue & Customs 50
  Financial Conduct Authority 50
  Immigration officers 51

Offences	51
Civil cash and property forfeiture	51
Cash	51
Summary forfeiture of listed assets	52
Account freezing and forfeiture	53
Banks and building societies	53
Account freezing	54
Forfeiture	54
Expansion of 'unlawful conduct'	54
Gross human rights abuse or violation	55
CHAPTER 7 TERRORIST FINANCING AND TERRORIST PROPERTY	**57**
Introduction	57
Disclosure orders	58
Making the application	58
Terrorism	59
Terrorist property	59
Requirements to be satisfied	59
Relevant information	60
Written notice	60
Effect	61
Responding to a written notice	62
Legal privilege	62
Copies	62
Variation and discharge	62
Information sharing within the regulated sector	63
The conditions	64
Joint reporting	65
Impact on the duty to report	65
Confidentiality	65
Further information orders	66
The application	66
Condition 1	66
Condition 2	67
Effect	67
Appeals	67
Civil recovery of terrorist cash and property	67
Terrorist cash	68
Objections to administrative forfeiture	69
Application to set aside administrative forfeiture	69
Terrorist assets	69
Terrorist money in bank and building society accounts	70
Banks and building societies	70
Account freezing	70
Administrative forfeiture	71
Powers extended to financial investigators	71
Cross-border enforceability	71

DETAILED TABLE OF CONTENTS

CHAPTER 8 CORPORATE FACILITATION OF TAX EVASION OFFENCES	73
Introduction	73
Failure to prevent the facilitation of UK tax evasion	74
Relevant body	74
Person acting in the capacity of a person associated with a relevant body	75
UK tax evasion	76
UK tax evasion offence	76
Cheating the public revenue	76
Avoidance or evasion	77
The public revenue	80
Fraudulent evasion	81
Proving a UK tax evasion offence	82
Facilitation offence	83
Failure to prevent the facilitation of foreign tax evasion	83
Additional conditions for liability	84
Foreign tax evasion offence	84
Foreign tax facilitation offence	85
Jurisdiction	85
Individual liability for directors and partners	86
CHAPTER 9 PROSECUTION AND THE REASONABLE PREVENTION PROCEDURES DEFENCE	87
Introduction	87
Criminal prosecution	87
Policy	87
Companies and partnerships	88
Consent in foreign tax evasion cases	88
Consent in foreign tax evasion cases	89
Penalties	89
Prevention procedures defence	90
Guiding principles	91
Risk assessment	91
Proportionality of risk-based prevention procedures	93
Top-level commitment	94
Due diligence	94
Communication (including training)	94
Monitoring and review	95
CONCLUSION	97
APPENDIX CRIMINAL FINANCES ACT 2017	99
1 Unexplained wealth orders: England and Wales and Northern Ireland	99
362A Unexplained wealth orders	99
362B Requirements for making of unexplained wealth order	100
362C Effect of order: cases of non-compliance	102
362D Effect of order: cases of compliance or purported compliance	103

362E Offence	104
362F Statements	104
362G Disclosure of information, copying of documents, etc	105
362H Holding of property: trusts and company arrangements etc	105
362I Supplementary	106
2 Interim freezing orders	106
362J Application for interim freezing order	106
362K Variation and discharge of interim freezing order	106
362L Exclusions	108
362M Restrictions on proceedings and remedies	108
362N Receivers in connection with interim freezing orders	109
362O Powers of receivers appointed under section 362N	109
362P Supervision of section 362N receiver and variations	110
362Q Registration	111
362R Compensation	111
3 External assistance	111
362S Enforcement abroad: enforcement authority	112
362T Enforcement abroad: receiver	112
4 Unexplained wealth orders: Scotland	112
396A Unexplained wealth orders	113
396B Requirements for making of unexplained wealth order	113
396C Effect of order: cases of non-compliance	115
396D Effect of order: cases of compliance or purported compliance	116
396E Offence	117
396F Statements	117
396G Disclosure of information, copying of documents, etc	118
396H Holding of property: trusts and company arrangements etc	118
396I Supplementary	119
5 Interim freezing orders	119
396J Application for interim freezing order	119
396K Variation and recall of interim freezing order	119
396L Exclusions	121
396M Restrictions on proceedings and remedies	121
396N Arrestment of property affected by interim freezing order	121
396O Inhibition of property affected by interim freezing order	122
396P Receivers in connection with interim freezing orders	122
396Q Powers of receivers appointed under section 396P	123
396R Supervision of section 396P receiver and variations	124
396S Compensation	124
6 External assistance	125
396T Enforcement abroad: Scottish Ministers	125
396U Enforcement abroad: receiver	125
7 Disclosure orders: England and Wales and Northern Ireland	126
8 Disclosure orders: Scotland	127
9 Co-operation: beneficial ownership information	127
445A Sharing of beneficial ownership information	127

DETAILED TABLE OF CONTENTS

10 Power to extend moratorium period	128
336A Power of court to extend the moratorium period	129
336B Proceedings under section 336A: supplementary	130
336C Extension of moratorium period pending determination of proceedings etc	131
336D Sections 336A to 336C: interpretation	132
11 Sharing of information within the regulated sector	133
339ZB Voluntary disclosures within the regulated sector	133
339ZC Section 339ZB: disclosure requests and required notifications	134
339ZD Section 339ZB: effect on required disclosures under section 330 or 331	134
339ZE Limitations on application of section 339ZD(2) and (3)	136
339ZF Section 339ZB: supplementary	137
339ZG Sections 339ZB to 339ZF: interpretation	137
12 Further information orders	138
339ZH Further information orders	138
339ZI Statements	139
339ZJ Appeals	140
339ZK Supplementary	140
13 Unlawful conduct: gross human rights abuses or violations	141
241A "Gross human rights abuse or violation"	141
14 Forfeiture of cash	143
15 Forfeiture of certain personal (or moveable) property	144
303B "Listed asset"	144
303C Searches	145
303D Searches: supplemental provision	146
303E Prior approval	146
303F Report on exercise of powers	148
303G Code of practice: Secretary of State	149
303H Code of practice: Scotland	149
303I Code of practice: Northern Ireland	150
303J Seizure of listed assets	150
303K Initial detention of seized property	151
303L Further detention of seized property	151
303M Testing and safekeeping of property seized under section 303J	153
303N Release of detained property	153
303O Forfeiture	154
303P Associated and joint property	155
303Q Agreements about associated and joint property	156
303R Associated and joint property: default of agreement	157
303S Sections 303O to 303R: appeals	159
303T Realisation of forfeited property	159
303U Proceeds of realisation	160
303V Victims and other owners	160
303W Compensation	161
303X Powers for prosecutors to appear in proceedings	162

DETAILED TABLE OF CONTENTS

	303Y "The minimum value"	163
	303Z Financial investigators	163
16	Forfeiture of money held in bank and building society accounts	163
	303Z1 Application for account freezing order	163
	303Z2 Restrictions on making of application under section 303Z1	164
	303Z3 Making of account freezing order	165
	303Z4 Variation and setting aside of account freezing order	165
	303Z5 Exclusions	166
	303Z6 Restriction on proceedings and remedies	166
	303Z7 "Bank"	167
	303Z8 "The minimum amount"	167
	303Z9 Account forfeiture notice	167
	303Z10 Giving of account forfeiture notice	168
	303Z11 Lapse of account forfeiture notice	169
	303Z12 Application to set aside forfeiture	170
	303Z13 Application of money forfeited under account forfeiture notice	170
	303Z14 Forfeiture order	170
	303Z15 Continuation of account freezing order pending appeal	171
	303Z16 Appeal against decision under section 303Z14	172
	303Z17 Application of money forfeited under account forfeiture order	172
	303Z18 Compensation	173
	303Z19 Powers for prosecutors to appear in proceedings	174
17	Serious Fraud Office	174
18	Her Majesty's Revenue and Customs: removal of restrictions	175
19	Her Majesty's Revenue and Customs: new powers	175
20	Financial Conduct Authority	176
21	Immigration officers	176
22	Search and seizure warrants: assault and obstruction offences	177
	356A Certain offences in relation to execution of search and seizure warrants	177
23	Assault and obstruction offence in relation to SFO officers after section 453A of the proceeds of Crime Act 2002 insert – 453B certain offences in relation to SFO officers	178
24	External requests, orders and investigations	179
25	Obstruction offence in relation to immigration officers	179
	453C Obstruction offence in relation to immigration officers	179
26	Seized money: England and Wales	180
27	Seized money: Northern Ireland	181
28	Seized money	182
	131ZA Seized money	182
29	Recovery orders relating to heritable property	184
	245ZA Notice to local authority: Scotland	184
	269A Leases and occupancy rights: Scotland	185
30	Money received by administrators	186
31	Accredited financial investigators	186
32	Reconsideration of discharged orders	187

DETAILED TABLE OF CONTENTS

33 Confiscation investigations: determination of the available amount	188
34 Confiscation orders and civil recovery: minor amendments	188
35 Disclosure orders	190
36 Sharing of information within the regulated sector	190
21CA Voluntary disclosures within the regulated sector	190
21CB Section 21CA: disclosure requests and notifications	191
21CC Section 21CA: effect on disclosures under section 21A	192
21CD Limitations on application of section 21CC(2) and (3)	194
21CE Section 21CA: supplementary	195
21CF Sections 21CA to 21CE: interpretation	195
37 Further information orders	196
22B Further information orders	196
22C Statements	198
22D Appeals	199
22E Supplementary	199
38 Forfeiture of terrorist cash	199
39 Forfeiture of certain personal (or moveable) property	205
40 Forfeiture of money held in bank and building society accounts	205
41 Extension of powers to financial investigators	205
63F Counter-terrorism financial investigators	205
42 Offences in relation to counter-terrorism financial investigators	208
120BOffences in relation to counter-terrorism financial investigators	208
43 Enforcement in other parts of United Kingdom	209
120C Enforcement of orders in other parts of United Kingdom	210
44 Meaning of relevant body and acting in the capacity of an associated person	210
45 Failure to prevent facilitation of UK tax evasion offences	211
46 Failure to prevent facilitation of foreign tax evasion offences	212
47 Guidance about preventing facilitation of tax evasion offences	213
48 Offences: extra-territorial application and jurisdiction	214
49 Consent to prosecution under section 46	214
50 Offences by partnerships: supplementary	215
51 Consequential amendments	215
52 Interpretation of Part 3	216
53 Minor and consequential amendments	216
54 Power to make consequential provision	217
55 Section 54: procedural requirements	217
56 Financial provision	218
57 Extent	218
58 Commencement	220
59 Short title	221
454A Serious Fraud Office	225
37A Disclosure orders in relation to terrorist financing investigations	225
412A Power to vary monetary amounts	275
Index	281

TABLE OF CASES

A v ACC [2017] EWHC 301 (QB) 5.13

Ensign Tankers (Leasing) Ltd v Stokes [1992] 1 AC 655..8.21

Gogitidze & Others v Georgia [2015] ECHR 536 ....5.2

Hitch v Stone (Inspector of Taxes) [2001] EWCA Civ 63..8.18
Hussein v Chong Fook Kam [1970] AC 942 ....4.15

Lush v Coles [1967] 1 WLR 685..8.31

NCA v Simkus & Others [2016] EWHC 255 (Admin)..........................7.23, 7.24, 7.35
New South Wales Crime Commission v Arthur Calvert [2017] NSWSC 13 ....4.15
New South Wales Crime Commission v Elskaf [2017] NSWSC 681 ....4.28
New South Wales Crime Commission v Susan Nehme [2016] NSWSC 1410..............5.16
Nuttall & Anor v NCA [2016] EWHC 1911 (Admin) 7.8, 7.35, 7.37

Perry v SOCA [2012] UKSC 35 ....4.47
Propaye v HMRC (2011) UK FTT 136 TC 001010...4.28

R (on the application of Inland Revenue Commissioners) v Kingston Crown
    Court [2001] STC 1615..8.22
R (on the application of Raeside) v Crown Court at Luton [2012] 1 WLR 2777.........1.12
R v Charlton [1996] STC 1418 ....8.18
R v Dimsey & Allen [2002] 1 AC 509 ....8.18
R v Director of Public Prosecutions, *ex parte* Kebilene [2000] 2 AC 326 ....9.14
R v Foggon [2003] EWCA Crim 270 ....8.18
R v GH [2015] 2 Cr App R 12 ....9.6
R v Hunt [1994] STC 819..8.17, 8.18
R v IRC, *ex parte* Mead [1993] 1 All ER 772...8.18
R v Khanani [2009] EWCA Crim 276 ....9.6
R v Lane & Letts [2018] UKSC 36..7.10
R v Leaf [2007] EWCA Crim 802 ....8.18
R v Lunn [2017] EWCA Crim 34 ....8.18
R v Manchester Crown Court, *ex parte* McDonald [1999] 1 WLR 841.....................1.12
R v MK; R v Gega (also known as Maione) [2018] EWCA Crim 667........................9.14
R v Norwich Crown Court, *ex parte* Stiller [1992] COD 310 ....1.12

xv

TABLE OF CASES

R v Perrin [2012] EWCA Crim 1729; [2012] EWCA Crim 1730 ....8.24
R v Rogers [2014] EWCA Crim 1680 ....4.48
R v Stannard [2005] EWCA Crim 2717 ....8.18
R v Tonner [1985] 1 WLR 344 ....8.31
R v Webb & Simpson, 23 October 2000, Court of Appeal (Criminal Division),
 unreported..8.18

Snook v London & West Riding Investments [1967] 2 QB 786..8.18
SOCA v Azam [2013] EWCA Civ 970...5.10
SOCA v Matthews [2009] EWHC 1544 (Admin) 6.34
Stanford International Bank, Re [2011] Ch33 ....1.10

Tesco Supermarkets Limited v Natrass [1971] UKHL 1 ....4.17

Wiese v UK Border Agency [2012] EWHC 2019 (Admin) 5.17

TABLE OF LEGISLATION

The main text is referenced to paragraph numbers, the text summary and Criminal Finances Act 2017 to page numbers.

Accessories and Abettors Act 1861 —
   s. 8 .... 7.68
Administrative Forfeiture of Terrorist Cash and Terrorist Money Held in Bank and Building Society Accounts (Cash and Account Forfeiture Notices) Regulations 2017 (SI 2017 No. 1226) 7.73
Anti-Terrorism, Crime and Security Act (ACTSA) 2001 (c. 24) 6.15, 7.3, 205, 206, 260
   Pts. 1–4 .... 7.70, 7.86
   Pt. 1 .... 7.68
   s. 1 .... 7.68, 260
   s. 1(1)(a) ..233, 236, 237, 240, 246, 247, 249, 253, 260
   s. 1(1)(b) 233, 236, 237, 240, 246, 247, 249, 253
   s. 1(2) 260
   Pt. 4A 7.70, 7.86, 260
   Pt. 4B 7.70, 260
   Sch. 1 ...7.69, 7.71, 7.97, 199, 201, 202, 207, 232, 245, 246, 259, 260
   Sch. 1, Pt. 1 260
   para. 1(1) 260
   para. 1(2) 200
   para. 1(2)(e)-(h), (4), (5)(a)-(c), (6), (7) ..200
   para. 1(5) 200
   Sch. 1, Pt. 2 .... 7.74, 260
   para. 2(2) 201
   para. 3 204
   para. 3(1A) 203
   para. 3(2) 188, 189, 201–204
   para. 3(2)(a) 201
   para. 3(3A)(a) 260
   para. 3(6)-(9) 201
   para. 5 201
   para. 5(1), (4) 260
   Sch. 1, Pt. 2A 7.72–7.74, 7.82, 201, 202, 260
   para. 5A 188, 189
   para. 5A(2) 201
   para. 5A(3) 204
   para. 5A(4)(d) 202
   para. 5A(10) 204
   para. 5B 189, 203, 204
   para. 5B(3) 203, 204
   para. 5B(4) 189, 202
   para. 5C 203, 204
   para. 5C(4) 203
   para. 5D 7.81, 202, 204
   para. 5D(1) 203
   para. 5D(3) 204
   para. 5E(2) 203
   para. 5F(5) 204
   Sch. 1, Pt. 3 260
   para. 6 .... 202, 204, 260
   para. 6(2) 188, 189
   para. 7(4) 204
   para. 8 261
   para. 8(1) 260
   para. 8A 261
   Sch. 1, Pt. 4 260
   para. 9 260
   para. 9(3)-(6) 204
   para. 9A 189
   para. 9A(a), (b) 260
   para. 10 232
   para. 10(1) 261
   para. 10(4) 7.83

para. 10(7), (7A)(a)(i), (ii), (b) 207
Sch. 1, Pt. 4A 7.84, 232, 236, 237, 240, 242–44
para. 10A..7.85, 245
para. 10A(1), (2) 233
para. 10B.................234, 235, 239, 241, 243
para. 10B(1)..233
para. 10B(2).............................233, 235, 237
para. 10C..235, 244
para. 10C(1)..233
para. 10D..236, 244
para. 10D(1)......................188, 189, 234, 235
para. 10G 237–45
para. 10G(2)...... 188, 189, 236–38, 240, 241
para. 10G(3).....................................236, 240, 243
para. 10G(4).....................................236, 240, 243
para. 10G(5)...240
para. 10G(5)(c) 237, 239
para. 10G(7) 189, 236, 237
para. 10G(9)...237
para. 10H(1)...238
para. 10H(1)(c) 237, 238
para. 10H(2)...239
para. 10H(2)(c) 238
para. 10I 237, 238, 240, 242, 244, 245
para. 10I(1) 189, 239, 240
para. 10I(1)(b)...238
para. 10I(2) 239
para. 10I(3) 238, 239
para. 10I(6) 239, 240, 242
para. 10I(7) 239, 240
para. 10I(11) 239
para. 10J................. 237, 238, 243–45
para. 10J(1)(a)........................237, 240, 242
para. 10J(1)(b) 237, 240, 241, 242
para. 10J(3) 188, 189, 240
para. 10J(4) 240, 243
para. 10J(5) 243
para. 10J(6) 241
para. 10J(7) 241, 242
para. 10J(9) 241, 243
para. 10J(11) 241, 243
para. 10K 243
para. 10K(1)(c), (d), (4) 242
para. 10L 242
para. 10M 243
para. 10M(1)...243
para. 10N 236
para. 10N(1)(c) 243
para. 10O 236, 245

para. 10O(1)..243
para. 10O(5), (6) 244
para. 10P 241, 245
para. 10P(1) 244
Sch. 1, Pt. 4B 7.87, 7.89, 246, 249, 256
para. 10Q 247
para. 10Q(1)...246
para. 10Q(4)...7.92
para. 10Q(4)(a), (b), (7) 256
para. 10R 246, 256
para. 10R(1), (2) 247
para. 10S 258
para. 10S(2) 188, 189
para. 10S(3) 247, 251
para. 10T 247, 251
para. 10T(1) 248
para. 10U 7.93, 246
para. 10U(4)..248
para. 10U(6)..249
para. 10V(1)..249
para. 10W 188, 189
para. 10W(2)...249
para. 10W(3)...256
para. 10W(4)(c) 250
para. 10W(6)(a), (b)..................................252
para. 10W(6)(c) 247
para. 10Y..250
para. 10Y(1)(a) 251
para. 10Y(2)-(7)..247
para. 10Y(3)..251
para. 10Y(3)(a), (b).............................247, 251
para. 10Y(6), (7) 251
para. 10Y(9)..254
para. 10Z..250, 252
para. 10Z(1), (3)..252
para. 10Z(6)(a)...252
para. 10Z2 ....250–252, 254, 255, 258
para. 10Z2(2) 253, 254
para. 10Z2(3) 188, 189, 253, 254
para. 10Z2(4) 253
para. 10Z2(6) 247, 251
para. 10Z2(7) 247
para. 10Z2(7)(a) 254
para. 10Z2(7)(b)..253
para. 10Z2(8) 247, 253
para. 10Z3 ....247, 253
para. 10Z3(1)(a), (b), (3) 254
para. 10Z4 ....254, 255
para. 10Z4(1), (2), (5) 254
para. 10Z5..254

TABLE OF LEGISLATION

para. 10Z7 209
Sch. 1, Pt. 4C 209
para. 10Z8 261
para. 10Z8(1), (2), (3)(a), (4)(a) 209
Sch. 1, Pt. 4D 261
para. 10Z9 261
para. 10Z9(2)(1) 261
Sch. 1, Pt. 6 —
para. 19 256
para. 19(1) 204, 245, 256
para. 19(1)(i), (ii) 208
para. 19(6), (7) 256

Banking and Financial Dealings Act 1971 .... 107, 120, 133, 151, 170, 234, 251
Bankruptcy and Diligence etc. (Scotland) Act 2007 (asp. 3) 279
s. 214(1) 279
s. 214(2)(1), (2)(j), (k) 280
s. 216(1)(a), (1A)(a), (b) 280
s. 218(2), (3) 280
Betting, Gaming, Lotteries and Amusements (Northern Ireland) Order 1985 (S.I. 1985 No. 1204) (N.I. 11) 200
Art. 2 .... 143, 200
Art. 170 .... 144, 201
Bribery Act 2010 .... 9.18, 97
s. 7 .... 8.4, 8.5
British Nationality Act 1981 130
British Nationality (Hong Kong) Act 1997 ... 130
British Overseas Territories Act 2002 130
Building Societies Act 1986 .... 6.32, 7.90, 164, 180, 182, 183, 186, 246
s. 5 .... 6.32, 7.90

Civil Jurisdiction and Judgments Act 1982 (c. 27) —
s. 18(2)(f), (g), (3) 257
s. 18(4ZA), (4ZB) 257, 258
s. 18(5)(d)(i)-(v) 258
Civil Partnership Act 2004 —
Pt. 3, Ch. 3 185
Civil Recovery Proceedings Practice Direction (2018 update) —
s. III 4.7, 5.1
para. 12.1A 5.1
para. 12.1G 5.12
Commissioners for Revenue & Customs Act 2005 —
Sch. 1 .... 6.9

Consolidated Fund Act 1816, 56 Geo. 3, c. 98 .... 8.31
Copyright, Designs and Patents Act 1988 —
s. 4(1)(a) 144, 233
Corporation Tax Act 2010 —
s. 1122 .... 4.11, 4.14, 4.17, 102, 115
Crime and Courts Act 2013 —
section 48 .... 4.47
Sch. 17 .... 9.9
Sch. 17, Pt. 2, paras. 26A, 26B 216
Criminal Finances Act 2017 .... 1.1, 1.4, 1.5, 1.38, 3.26, 4.1, 4.2, 4.18, 5.14, 6.1, 6.3, 6.5, 6.8, 6.12, 6.14, 6.26, 6.28, 6.39–6.41, 7.3, 7.4, 7.17, 7.42, 7.67, 7.70, 7.72, 7.85, 7.88, 7.95, 7.99, 7.100, 8.1, 8.12, 9.1, 9.12, 97, 99, 220, 221
Explanatory Notes 8.3, 8.4, 8.12
Explanatory Notes, paras. 42, 43 .... 8.2
Explanatory Notes, paras. 45, 46 .... 8.3
Pt. 1 217
Pt. 1, Ch. 1 99
ss. 1–3 219
s. 1 .... 4.1, 99, 220, 221
s. 2 .... 106, 111, 220, 221
s. 3 .... 111, 220
ss. 4–6 119
s. 4 .... 112, 119, 221
s. 5 .... 119, 125, 220, 221
s. 6 125
s. 7 .... 7.6, 126, 219, 221
s. 8 .... 7.6, 127, 219, 221
s. 9 .... 127, 220
Ch. 2 128
s. 10 .... 1.4, 128
s. 11 .... 3.6, 133
s. 12 .... 2.1, 2.2, 138
Ch. 3 141
s. 13 .... 6.39, 141
s. 13(2)-(6) 142
s. 13(5) 257, 258
s. 14 .... 6.16, 143, 221
s. 15 .... 6.22, 144, 148, 163, 221
s. 16 .... 6.27, 163, 221
Ch. 4 174
s. 17 .... 174, 219, 221, 222
s. 18 .... 6.9, 175, 220
s. 18(4)(c) 219
s. 18(2), (3), (4)(d) 219
s. 19 .... 6.10, 175, 176, 221
s. 19(3) 219

xix

TABLE OF LEGISLATION

s. 20 .... 6.11, 176, 221
s. 20(3) 219
s. 20(4)-(6) 219, 176
s. 21 .... 6.12, 176
ss. 22–25 221
ss. 22–24 .... 6.13
s. 22 .... 177, 219
s. 23 .... 178, 179, 219
s. 24 179
s. 25 .... 179, 221
Ch. 5 180
s. 26 .... 180, 219
s. 27 .... 181, 219, 220
s. 28 .... 182, 219, 220
s. 29 .... 184, 217, 221
s. 30 .... 186, 219, 220
s. 31 186
s. 31(2) 219
s. 31(3) 219, 220
s. 32 187
s. 32(2)-(3) 219
s. 32(4)-(6) 219, 220
s. 33 .... 188, 221
s. 34 188
s. 34(2)-(9) 188
s. 34(2) 219, 262
s. 34(3), (4) 219, 220, 263
s. 34(10) 188, 221
s. 34(11) 219
Pt. 2 .... 190, 217
s. 35 .... 7.6, 190, 225
s. 36 .... 7.38, 190
s. 37 .... 7.54, 196
s. 38 .... 7.71, 199
s. 38A 7.72
s. 39 .... 205, 232
s. 40 .... 205, 245
s. 41 .... 205, 220
s. 41(2)-(5) 205
s. 41(3) 219
s. 42 .... 7.98, 208, 209, 219, 220, 261
s. 43 .... 7.99, 209
Pt. 3 .... 8.1, 8.3, 210, 220, 221
s. 44 210
s. 44(2), (3) 8.7
s. 44(4) 8.41, 216
s. 44(4)(c) 8.10, 211
s. 44(5) 8.10
s. 45 .... 8.1, 8.12, 8.24, 8.27, 8.29, 8.30, 8.33, 8.36, 8.50–8.52, 9.7–9.10, 211, 214–16
s. 45(1) 8.6, 8.41
s. 45(2) 9.3, 9.11, 211
s. 45(3) 9.11
s. 45(4) 8.8, 8.15, 8.16, 216
s. 45(4) (c) 8.11, 8.12
s. 45(5) 8.39, 8.40, 213, 216
s. 45(5)(a) 212
s. 45(6) 213, 216
s. 45(7) 8.32
s. 45(8) 9.10
s. 46 .... 8.1, 8.24, 8.27, 8.30, 8.41, 8.43, 8.46, 8.50, 8.52, 9.7–9.10, 212, 214–16
s. 46(1) 8.41
s. 46(1)(b) 212
s. 46(2) 8.42, 8.50, 212, 214, 216
s. 46(2)(b) 8.43
s. 46(3) 9.4, 9.11, 213, 216
s. 46(4) 9.11
s. 46(5) 8.44, 216
s. 46(5)(a)-(c) 8.47
s. 46(6) 8.48, 216
s. 46(6)(b) 8.49
s. 46(7) 9.10
s. 47 .... 9.13, 213
s. 47(1) 9.12, 214
s. 47(5) 214
s. 47(7) 9.12, 214
s. 48 214
s. 48(1) 8.50
s. 48(2) 8.51, 214
s. 48(3) 214
s. 49 214
s. 49(2) 9.8, 214
s. 49(3) 9.8, 214, 215
s. 49(4) 9.8
s. 49(6) 215
s. 50 215
s. 50(1) 9.7
s. 50(3) 9.7
s. 51 215
s. 51(3) 219
s. 52 216
s. 52(1) 8.32
Pt. 4 216
s. 53 .... 216, 257
ss. 54–57 220
s. 54 .... 217, 218
s. 54(1) 217
s. 54(2), (3) 217, 218
s. 54 (5) 217

s. 55 217
s. 56 218
s. 57 218
s. 57(2)-(6) 218
s. 58 220
s. 58(1)-(3) 221
s. 58(2)-(6) 220
s. 58(8)-(11) 221
s. 58(10) 221
s. 59 220
Sch. 1 .... 6.5, 6.7, 174, 189, 190, 221, 222
Sch. 1, paras. 3–6 219
Sch. 1, paras. 24, 25 219
Sch. 2 .... 7.6, 190, 225
Sch. 2, para. 3 .... 219, 229
Sch. 2, para. 4 219
Sch. 3 .... 7.84, 205, 232, 245
Sch. 4 .... 7.87, 205, 245
Sch. 5 .... 216, 219, 257
Sch. 5, para. 22 188
Sch. 5, paras. 24, 27 189
Sch. 5, para. 37 .... 1.39
Criminal Finances Act 2017 (Commencement No. 1) Regulations 2017 (SI 2017 No. 739) (C. 58) 8.1
Criminal Finances Act 2017 (Commencement No. 2 and Transitional Provisions) Regulations 2017 (SI 2017 No. 991) (C. 92) 5.14
reg. 2(a) 1.8
reg. 2(c) 2.2
Criminal Finances Act 2017 (Commencement No. 3) Regulations 2017 (SI 2017 No. 1028) (C. 94) 3.4, 3.5, 7.39
Criminal Finances Act 2017 (Commencement No. 4) Regulations 2018 (SI 2018 No. 78) (C. 11) —
reg. 2 .... 4.1
Criminal Justice Act 1925 —
s. 33 215
Criminal Justice Act 1987 (c. 38) 258
s. 1 258
s. 1(6A) 258
s. 2 .... 7.5
Pts. 2, 4, 5, 7 258
Criminal Justice Act 2003 —
s. 281(5) 177, 178, 180, 208, 209, 227
s. 282 .... 104, 227
Criminal Justice Act (Northern Ireland) 1945 (c. 15) (N.I.) —
s. 18 215

Criminal Law (Consolidation) (Scotland) Act 1995 —
s. 23A 175
s. 23A(2), (3) 175
Criminal Procedure (Amendment No. 3) Rules 2017 (SI 2017 No. 755) (the Rules) 1.5, 1.20, 1.38
r. 27.63(3) 1.26
rr. 47.62–47.65 .... 1.5
r. 47.63 .... 1.29
r. 47.63(1) 1.25, 1.26
r. 47.63(2) 1.26
r. 47.63(4), (5) 1.27
r. 47.63(6), (7) 1.28
r. 47.63(8) 1.29
r. 47.64(2) 1.30
r. 47.64(3) 1.31
r. 47.64(4) 1.32
r. 47.64(5) 1.34
r. 47.64(8) 1.35
r. 47.65(2) 1.36
r. 47.65(3), (4) 1.37
Criminal Procedure (Scotland) Act 1995 —
s. 8(2) 151, 234
s. 307 175
s. 307(1) 214
s. 307(1)(ba), (1A) 175
Criminal Procedure Rules 2015 (SI 2015 No. 1490) (L. 18) —
r. 47 .... 7.57
r. 47.5 .... 7.57
r. 47.20 .... 2.13
Criminal Recovery Act 1990 (Australia NSW) —
s. 28A(4) 4.6
Customs and Excise Management Act 1979 . 146
s. 164 146

Data Protection Act 1998 (c. 29) 259
Sch. 2(6), (7)(a), (b) 259
Sch. 3(7)(a), (b) 259
Directive 2015/849/EU on the prevention of the use of the financial system for the purposes of money laundering or terrorist financing 2015 (Anti-Money Laundering Directive) No 4 EC (4MLD) —
Art 3 .... 4.11, 101, 114
Art 3(9) 101, 114
Art 3(10) 102, 114
Art 3(11) 4.11, 102, 114
Directive 2018/843/EU (Anti-Money Laundering Directive) No 5 EC (5AMLD) 19 June 2018 .... 4.10, 97

TABLE OF LEGISLATION

Drug Trafficking Offences Act 1986............. 190

EC General Data Protection Regulation (GDPR) 2018 ....3.25
European Convention on the Protection of Human Rights and Fndamental Freedoms 1950 ....5.2
    Art 6(1) 5.2
    Art 6(2) 5.2, 9.14
    Art 6(3) 5.2
    Protocol. 1, Art. 1..............................5.2, 6.50

Finance Act 2000 —
    s. 144(1)...8.35
Finance Act 2007 —
    ss. 82, 83 175
    s. 84(3) 175
Financial Services and Markets Act 2000 —
    Pt. 4A 167, 181, 182, 184, 186, 247
    s. 38................. 167, 181, 182, 184, 186, 247
    Sch. 3, paras. 5(b), 12(1), 15 .. 167, 181, 182, 184, 186, 247
Fraud Act 2006 —
    s. 2(1) 8.16

Gambling Act 2005 .... 144, 200
    Pt. 5.. 143, 200
    s. 9(1).. 143, 200
    s. 235.. 144, 200

Homelessness etc. (Scotland) Act 2003 (asp. 10) —
    s. 11 279
    s. 11(3), (8) 184
    s. 11(5)(f), (FA)......................................279
Hong Kong Act 1985 130
Hong Kong (War Wives and Widows) Act 1996 130
Housing (Scotland) Act 1988 —
    Pt. 2... 185

Immigration Act 1971 —
    s. 26(1)(g) 179
    s. 28A(5)-(9), (10), (11) 179
Income Tax Management Act 1970 —
    s. 106A...4.16
Interpretation Act 1978 ....217, 220
Interpretation Act (Northern Ireland) 1954 —
    s. 41(3)... 148, 150
    s. 41(6)...218

Interpretation and Legislative Reform (Scotland) Act 2010 (asp 10) —
    Pt. 2...218

Justice (Northern Ireland) Act 2002 —
    s. 30(4), (7) 215
    s. 36...215

Law Reform (Miscellaneous Provisions) (Scotland) Act 1985 —
    ss. 4–7 185
Legal Aid, Sentencing and Punishment of Offenders Act 2012 —
    Pt. 1 .... 108, 166, 249
Limitation Act 1980 c. 58 —
    s. 27A...4.24, 257
    s. 27A(4), (4A), (8)(d)-(f).......................257
Limitation (Northern Ireland) Order 1989 (SI 1989 No. 1339) (N.I. 11) 258
    Art 72A(4), (4A).....................................258
Limited Partnerships Act 1907..............8.7, 211
Local Government etc. (Scotland) Act 1994 —
    s. 2... 185

Magistrates' Courts Act 1980................ 139, 197
    Sch. 3 215
Magistrates' Courts (Northern Ireland) Order 1981 (SI 1981 No 1675) (N.I. 26) ... 139, 197
    Sch. 4 215
Matrimonial Homes (Family Protection) (Scotland) Act 1981 185
Money Laundering, Terrorist Financing and Transfer of Funds (Information on the Payer) Regulations 2017 (SI 2017 No. 692) —
    reg. 35(3) 4.9
    reg. 42 ....4.34
    reg. 44(5) 4.23
    reg. 45 ....4.34

Northern Ireland Act 1998 —
    s. 4(1)...217
    ss. 6–8 .... 162, 174

Partnership Act 1890..............................8.7, 211
Perjury Act 1911 —
    s. 5.. 104, 140, 199, 228
Perjury (Northern Ireland) Order 1979 (S.I. 1979/1714) (N.I. 19)....................... 140, 199
    Art 10.. 104, 228

TABLE OF LEGISLATION

Police and Criminal Evidence Act 1984 (PACE) 226
    Code. G, para. 2.3A 4.15
Police and Criminal Evidence (Northern Ireland) Order 1989 (S.I. 1989/1341 (N.I. 12)......226
Police (Northern Ireland) Act 2000...... 161, 173, 245, 256
Police Reform and Social Responsibility Act 2011 —
    Pt. 1 .... 147, 162, 173, 186, 187, 190, 205, 245, 256
Policing and Crime Act 2009 —
    s. 62 ....4.24
    s. 65 ....6.25
Prescription and Limitation (Scotland) Act 1973 (c. 52)
    s. 19B(4), (4A).......................257
Private Housing (Tenancies) (Scotland) Act 2016 —
    Pt. 5 186
Procedure Act —
    section 211 ....183, 184
Proceeds of Crime Act 2002 (c. 29).............. 1.1, 1.24, 1.33, 1.36, 2.13, 3.4–3.6, 3.26, 4.15, 4.27, 4.42, 4.48, 4.49, 5.7, 5.23, 6.13, 6.21, 6.31, 7.4, 7.40, 7.42, 142, 143, 174–176, 184, 186–188, 222, 261
    s. 2A 6.3, 261
    s. 2A(2)(a), (b), (e)-(g)...............261
    s. 2A(3)(a)-(d).............................262
    s. 2C(2) 1.15, 132, 222, 262
    s. 2C(3) 222
    s. 2C(3A) 262
    Pt. 2 ...... 4.2, 4.32, 4.45, 5.12, 5.13, 5.19, 6.4, 6.5, 6.28, 104, 187, 222, 262
    s. 7(4)(b), (c)..............................262
    s. 21(1)(d) 187
    s. 21(7) 187
    s. 22(1)(c)...................................187
    s. 22(4) 187
    s. 24 187
    s. 24(5)-(7) 187
    s. 25 187
    s. 25(3)-(5) 187
    s. 40 ....1.10
    s. 41 107
    s. 47A(1)(b), (ba) 222
    ss. 47C-47F 178, 179
    s. 47C 222
    s. 47G 6.4, 186
    s. 47G(3)(ab), (ac) 222
    s. 47G(3)(b), (ba), (c)................186
    s. 47J 222
    s. 47M(3)(b), (ba) 222
    s. 47S(2), (2A) 222
    s. 67 180
    s. 67(1), (2)(a), (b), (2A), (3), (5), (5A), (7A, (8)...180
    s. 67(8), (9) 181
    s. 82 ....188, 262
    s. 82(2)(e), (ea) 188
    s. 82(2)(f) 262
    s. 82(3) 188
    s. 82(3)(a)...................................262
    s. 82(3)(b), (c) 188, 262
    s. 82(3)(d) 188
    Pt. 3 .... 117, 187, 263
    s. 93(4)(b), (c)............................262
    s. 106(1)(d) 187
    s. 106(6) 188
    s. 107(1)(c).................................187
    s. 107(3) 188
    s. 109 187
    s. 109(5), (6) 187
    s. 118(1) 183, 184
    s. 120 120
    s. 127C-127F 179
    s. 128 183
    s. 131 182
    s. 131ZA....................................182
    s. 131ZA(1), (5), (7), (7)(b) 183
    s. 131ZA(7).................................278
    s. 131ZA(9), (10) 184
    s. 148(2)(e), (ea) 189
    s. 148(2)(f) 263
    s. 148(3)(a).................................263
    s. 148(3)(b), (c) 189, 263
    s. 148(3)(d)-(f) 189
    Pt. 4 .... 104, 188, 222, 263
    s. 157(4)(b), (c)..........................263
    s. 171(1)(d), (7).........................188
    s. 172(1)(c).................................188
    s. 172(4) 188
    s. 174 188
    s. 174(5)-(7) 188
    s. 175 188
    s. 175(3)-(5) 188
    s. 190 107
    s. 195A(1)(b), (ba) 222
    s. 195C 178, 179, 222

ss. 195D-195F	178, 179
s. 195G	187
s. 195G(3)(ab), (ac)	222
s. 195G(3)(b), (ba)	187
s. 195G(3)(c)	263
s. 195J	222
s. 195M(3)(b), (ba)	222
s. 195S(1)(a), (c), (1A)(b), (c), (2), (2A)	223
s. 202(7)	181
s. 215	181
s. 215(1), (2)(a), (b), (2A), (3), (5), (5A), (7A)	181
s. 215(8)	181, 182
s. 215(8)(a)	181
s. 215(8)(b), (9)	182
s. 230(2)(e), (ea), (f)	189
s. 230(3)(a)	263
s. 230(3)(b), (c)	189, 263
s. 230(3)(d)-(f)	189
Pt. 5	4.2, 4.4, 4.24, 4.37, 4.39, 4.41, 4.43, 4.45, 4.47, 5.12, 5.17, 5.22, 6.1, 6.6, 6.8, 6.10, 6.12, 6.14, 6.16, 6.25, 6.28, 6.29, 6.34, 6.36, 6.40, 6.48, 6.50, 7.88, 7.93, 97, 102, 104, 115–17, 141, 144, 163, 166, 263, 265, 277
s. 240	263
s. 240(1)(b)	263
s. 241	6.39, 141
s. 241(2)	141
s. 241(2A)	6.42, 141, 142
s. 241(2A)(a)-(c)	6.42
s. 241(3)(b)	264
s. 241A	6.42, 6.43, 141
s. 241A(2)(a)	142
s. 241A(2)(a)(i), (ii)	141
s. 241A(2)(b)	142
s. 241A(5)	6.47, 142
s. 241A(5)(d)	142
s. 242	6.50
Pt. 5, Ch. 2	4.24, 4.48, 142
s. 245	184
s. 245ZA	184
s. 245ZA(2)	184, 279
s. 245A	4.37, 5.10, 108, 111, 142, 166, 248
s. 245D(1)(b)	189
s. 246	142
ss. 248, 249	111
s. 255A	120, 143
s. 256	120, 143
s. 266	185, 237, 239
s. 266(8)	185
s. 266(8ZA)	184, 185, 280
s. 267(3)(b)	185
s. 267(3)(ba)	185, 280
ss. 269, 269A	185
s. 269A(2), (3)	185
s. 278(6A)(a), (b), (7)(a), (b), (7A)	264
s. 280(2)	109, 123
s. 286A	108, 166, 248
s. 286B	108, 156, 236, 239
Pt. 5, Ch. 3	6.29, 143, 176, 265, 277, 278
s. 289	6.7, 176, 178, 179, 189, 264
s. 289(1), (1A)(a), (b), (1C), (1D)(2)-(5)	223
s. 289(5)(b)	264
s. 289(5)(ba)	175
s. 289(5A)	6.9, 175
s. 289(6)	6.16, 143
s. 289(6)(e), (7)	143
s. 289(7A)	143, 144
s. 289(7B)	143
s. 289(7C)	144
s. 290	187, 189
s. 290(4)(a)	223
s. 290(4)(aa)	189, 223
s. 290(4)(ab)	189
s. 290(4)(b), (ba)	187
s. 290(4)(c)	264
s. 290(6)	223, 264
s. 290(6A)	264
s. 291(2)	223
s. 292	176
s. 292(1), (2), (2A), (6)	224
s. 293(4)	278
s. 293A	176
s. 294	147, 175, 178, 179
s. 294(1), (2)	224
s. 294(2A)-(2C)	175
s. 294(4)	224
s. 295	266
s. 295(1)	178, 179, 224
s. 295(1B)	147
s. 295(2)	176
s. 295(4)(a)	224
s. 296(2)	224
s. 297(4)	224
s. 297A	6.25, 176, 190, 262–64
s. 297A(6)(b)	224
s. 297A(6)(ba)	190, 224
s. 297A(6)(bb)	190
s. 297D	188, 189

s. 297D(3)	224
s. 297F(4)	224
s. 298	177, 264
s. 298(1)(a)	224
s. 298(2)	262, 263
s. 298(4)	188, 189, 262, 263
s. 302(7), (7A)	224
s. 302(7B)	279
s. 302(7ZA)	190, 224
s. 302(7ZB)	190
s. 302(7A)(a)(i)	190
s. 302A	262
s. 303A	144
Pt. 5, Ch. 3A	6.22, 144, 176, 265, 266, 271, 275, 277, 278
s. 303B	144, 265
s. 303B(1)	144
s. 303B(2)	144, 278, 279
s. 303B(3)	265
s. 303C	145–50, 176, 178, 179, 278
s. 303C(1)	146
s. 303C(2)(c), (3), (6)(b)	145
s. 303C(5), (6)	145, 146
s. 303C(8)(a), (b)	146
s. 303C(9)	265
s. 303D	146
s. 303E	6.24, 146, 151, 154, 157, 176
s. 303E(6)	147, 148
s. 303F	148
s. 303F(8)	148
s. 303G	6.24, 149, 176
s. 303G(2)-(4)	149
s. 303G(5)	149, 278, 279
s. 303H	149, 176
s. 303H(1)	265
s. 303H(2)-(3)	149
s. 303H(4)	149, 278
s. 303I	147, 176
s. 303I(2)	150
s. 303I(3)	150
s. 303I(4)	150, 279
s. 303I(5)	150
s. 303J	147, 150, 151, 153, 156, 158, 160, 178, 179, 264, 278
s. 303J(1)	151
s. 303J(2)	151, 153, 155
s. 303J(3)	151
s. 303K	151, 153, 161, 178, 179, 266, 278
s. 303K(1)-(3)	151
s. 303K(5)	147, 264
s. 303L	151, 153, 160, 161, 163, 264, 266
s. 303L(1)	152, 153, 176, 262, 263
s. 303L(4)(a), (5), (6)(b)	152
s. 303L(10)(c), (12)	153
s. 303M	153
s. 303N	153
ss. 303O-303R	159
s. 303O	154–59, 161–63, 177, 264
s. 303O(1)(a)	154
s. 303O(1)(b)	265
s. 303O(2)	154
s. 303O(3)	154–56, 158, 262, 263
s. 303O(4), (5)	154, 158, 160
s. 303O(6)	158
s. 303O(6)(c)	154
s. 303O(9)	155, 262, 263
s. 303P	155
s. 303P(1)	156
s. 303P(1)(c)	155
s. 303P(2)	156
s. 303P(2)(c)	155
s. 303Q	155–57, 159, 161, 162, 264
s. 303Q(1)	156, 157, 262, 263
s. 303Q(1)(b), (3)	156
s. 303Q(6)	156, 157, 159
s. 303Q(7)	156, 157
s. 303Q(12)	156
s. 303R	155, 157, 159, 161, 162
s. 303R(1)(a), (b)	155, 158, 159
s. 303R(3)	262
s. 303R(4)	158, 160, 263
s. 303R(5)	160
s. 303R(6), (7)	158, 159
s. 303R(9)	158, 160
s. 303R(11)	159
s. 303S	159
s. 303S(1)(c), (d)	159
s. 303T	159, 160
s. 303T(1)	159
s. 303U	154, 160
s. 303U(1)(c)	160
s. 303V	160
s. 303V(1)	160
s. 303V(5)	161
s. 303V(6)	160
ss. 303W	159, 161, 177
s. 303W(1)	161
s. 303W(9)	162
s. 303W(10)	162, 278, 279
s. 303X	162, 262

TABLE OF LEGISLATION

s. 303X(1), (2) 163
s. 303Y 6.24, 163, 265
s. 303Y(1) 163
s. 303Y(2) 278, 279
s. 303Y(3) 265
s. 303Z 163
Pt. 5, Ch. 3B...6.27, 163, 176, 265, 271, 275, 277 278
s. 303Z1 163–65
s. 303Z1(1) 164
s. 303Z1(3)(a), (b) 265
s. 303Z1(6) 265
s. 303Z2 .... 163, 164
s. 303Z2(4) 165, 176, 265
s. 303Z3 .... 165, 258, 262–68, 272, 273
s. 303Z3(3) 165, 169
s. 303Z4 .... 165, 169, 264
s. 303Z5 .... 164, 166
s. 303Z5(4), (6) 166
s. 303Z6 166
s. 303Z6(1) 167
s. 303Z7 .... 6.31, 164, 167, 265
s. 303Z7(2) 167
s. 303Z8 .... 164, 167, 265
s. 303Z8(1) 167
s. 303Z8(2) 167, 278, 279
s. 303Z8(3) 265
s. 303Z9 .... 167, 262–64
s. 303Z9(2) 168
s. 303Z9(3) 265
s. 303Z9(4)(c) 169
s. 303Z9(6)(a), (b) 170
s. 303Z9(6)(c) 165
s. 303Z10 168
s. 303Z11 .... 168, 169
s. 303Z11(1)(a) 169
s. 303Z11(2)-(7) 165
s. 303Z11(3) 169
s. 303Z11(3)(a), (b), (6), (7) 169
s. 303Z11(9) 172
s. 303Z12 .... 168, 170
s. 303Z12(1), (6)(a) 170
s. 303Z14 .... 168–73, 177, 258, 264
s. 303Z14(2) 171, 172
s. 303Z14(2)(a) 171
s. 303Z14(2)(b) 265
s. 303Z14(3) 171
s. 303Z14(4) 171, 262, 263
s. 303Z14(6) 165, 169
s. 303Z14(7) 165

s. 303Z14(7)(a) 172
s. 303Z14(7)(b) 171
s. 303Z14(8) 165, 171
s. 303Z15 .... 165, 171
s. 303Z15(1)(a), (b) 172
s. 303Z15(2) 171, 172
s. 303Z15(3) 172
s. 303Z15(4) 171
s. 303Z16 172
s. 303Z16(1), (4) 172
s. 303Z17 172
s. 303Z18 .... 173, 177
s. 303Z18(9) 174
s. 303Z18(10) 174, 278, 279
s. 303Z19 .... 174, 262
s. 303Z19(1), (1) 173
s. 306(3)(c), (ca) 190
s. 308(2) 157
s. 311(2)-(2B), (3) 264
s. 311(4) 265
s. 312(2)(j)-(p) 265
s. 316 .... 6.10, 175, 176, 265
s. 316(1) 265
s. 316(1)(a), (c) 175, 176
s. 316(9) 265
Pt. 7 .... 1.4, 2.1, 4.48, 128, 138, 266, 278
ss. 327–329 .... 2.11
s. 327(1) 1.1
s. 327(2)(a) 1.1
s. 328(1) 1.1, 9.6
s. 328(2)(a) 1.1
s. 329(1) 1.1
s. 329(2)(a) 1.1
ss. 330–332 .... 2.1, 2.11
s. 330 .... 3.13, 3.14, 3.22, 134, 137
s. 330(1) 9.13
s. 330(4) 134
s. 330(5) 137
s. 330(5)(b), (c) 134
s. 330(8) 9.13
s. 331 134
s. 331(4) 134
s. 331(5) 137
s. 333A 1.40, 266
s. 333D(1) 1.40
s. 333D(1)(a) 265
s. 333D(1)(aa), (ab), (1A)(a)-(c) 266
s. 333E(5) 138
s. 335 .... 1.2, 128
s. 335(1), (2) 1.2

s. 335(2)(a) 132	s. 339ZC(3)(a), (b) 134
s. 335(4), (5) 1.2	s. 339ZD 3.18, 134, 136
s. 335(6) 1.2, 1.16, 1.19, 128, 129, 132	s. 339ZD(2), (3) 136
s. 335(6A)(a) 128	s. 339ZD(4)(c) 135
s. 335(6A)(b) 129	s. 339ZD(5) 3.19, 135
s. 335(8) 130, 132	s. 339ZD(6) 3.20
s. 336 129	s. 339ZE 3.23, 136
s. 336(8) 1.19, 129, 132	s. 339ZE(1)-(8) 135
s. 336(8A) 129	s. 339ZE(2), (3), (5)-(7) 136
s. 336(10) 130, 132	s. 339ZE(10) 135
s. 336A..1.4, 1.5, 1.15, 1.18, 1.21, 1.22, 1.40, 128–133, 266	s. 339ZF 3.7, 3.24, 137
	s. 339ZF(1) 137
s. 336A(1)-(4) 129	s. 339ZG 3.6, 137
s. 336A(1) 1.9, 1.10, 1.19	s. 339ZG(5) 138
s. 336A(2) 1.15	s. 339ZG(5)(a)-(d) 137
s. 336A(3) 1.16	s. 339ZH 2.2, 138, 266
s. 336A(5), (6) 1.19	s. 339ZH(1)-(3) 2.15
s. 336A(7) 1.18, 1.19, 131, 132	s. 339ZH(a) 2.6
s. 336A(9) 1.15, 130	s. 339ZH(2) 2.6
s. 336A(10) 1.15	s. 339ZH(3) 2.5
s. 336B 1.4, 1.5, 1.20, 1.21, 1.23, 130, 132	s. 339ZH(4) 2.8
s. 336B(1)(a), (b) 1.14	s. 339ZH(4)(c) 2.12
s. 336B(3) 1.21	s. 339ZH(5) 2.9, 139
s. 336B(4) 1.21, 130	s. 339ZH(5)(a) 2.11
s. 336B(5) 1.23, 1.36	s. 339ZH(5)(d) 2.12
s. 336B(8), (11) 1.14	s. 339ZH(6) 2.9
s. 336C 1.4, 1.5, 1.18, 129, 131, 132	s. 339ZH(7) 2.5
s. 336C(2) 1.18, 1.19, 129, 131	s. 339ZH(8) 2.19, 139
s. 336C(3) 1.18	s. 339ZH(9), (10) 2.19
s. 336C(4) 1.18, 1.19, 129, 131	s. 339ZH(12) 2.4
s. 336C(5)-(8) 1.18	s. 339ZI 2.2, 2.14, 2.15, 139
s. 336C(7) 131	s. 339ZI(1) 2.16, 140
s. 336D 1.4, 1.30, 132, 266	s. 339ZI(2) 2.16
s. 336D(2) 1.14	s. 339ZI(2)(b), (c) 140
s. 336D(3) 1.22	s. 339ZI(3) 2.16
s. 336D(7), (8) 1.15	s. 339ZJ 2.2
s. 338 .... 1.1	s. 339ZJ(1)-(4) 2.18
s. 338(1) 1.1	s. 339ZK 2.2, 140
s. 338(1)(a) 1.2	s. 339ZK(1), (2) 2.17
s. 339Z(11) 2.11	s. 339ZK(3) 2.5
s. 339ZA 133	s. 339ZK(4), (5) 2.13
ss. 339ZB-339ZF 3.6, 137	s. 340(10) 1.22
s. 339ZB 3.8, 133–35, 137, 259, 266	s. 340(11) 4.48
s. 339ZB(1) 134, 135	s. 340(11)(a)-(c) 139
s. 339ZB(3) 134, 137	s. 340(14), (15) 266
s. 339ZB(3)(a) 135	Pt. 8 .... 4.1, 6.8, 7.6, 7.16, 7.17, 7.23, 7.24, 7.28, 7.37, 175, 176, 179, 224, 266, 275, 277
s. 339ZB(3)(b) 134, 135	
s. 339ZB(4) 138	s. 341 .... 105, 118, 180, 183
s. 339ZC 3.10, 3.15, 134	s. 341(1)(c) 188
s. 339ZC(3)-(5) 133	s. 341(3)(c), (d), (3A) 266

s. 341(3B) 275	s. 362B(4) 4.8, 4.13, 4.47
s. 341(3B)(a), (b) 266, 271, 274	s. 362B(4)(a) 101
s. 341(3C) 275	s. 362B(4)(b)(ii) 102
s. 341(3C)(a) 266, 271, 275	s. 362B(5) 4.21, 4.24
s. 341(3C)(b) 267, 271, 275	s. 362B(5)(b) 4.24
s. 342(1) 267	s. 362B(6) 4.31
Pt. 8, Ch. 2 .... 99, 126	s. 362B(6)(c), (d) 4.26
s. 343(2) 267	s. 362B(7) 4.9, 4.23
s. 344 267	s. 362B(7)(a) 103
s. 345(2)(b) 267	s. 362B(9) 4.11
s. 346(2)(bb)-(bf) 267	s. 362B(e) 4.29
s. 350(5)(a) 267	s. 362C 4.39, 102
s. 351(5), (5A) 267	s. 362C(1)-(3) 102
s. 352 177-79	s. 362C(3)(b) 103
s. 352(2)(b), (5)(b), (c), (ca), (cb), (7) 268	s. 362C(4) 103, 107
s. 353 270	s. 362C(5) 4.42
s. 353(2)(bb)-(bf), (5)(a), (7B) 268	s. 362C(6)(a), (b) 103
s. 353(7C) 268	s. 362C(7) 4.41, 102
s. 353(7C)(a) 268	s. 362C(7)(b)-(d) 103
s. 353(7C)(b)-(7F)(b), (10)(b), (c), (ca), (cb), (11)(c), (ca) 269	s. 362C(8) 4.41, 102
s. 353(7D)-(7F) 268	s. 362D 102, 103
s. 355 270	s. 362D(2) 103
s. 355(1)(a) 270	s. 362D(3) 4.43, 103, 107
s. 356 .... 177, 270	s. 362D(4) 107
s. 356A 177	s. 362D(5) 4.44
s. 356A(1), (2), (3)(a) 177	s. 362D(7) 107
s. 356A(4)(a) 178	s. 362D(7)(a), (c) 104
s. 357 .... 126, 177	s. 362E 5.15, 104
s. 357(2), (2A), (3)(b), (ba), (7)(a), (b), (ba), (8), (9) 126	s. 362E(2)(b) 104
s. 357(2), (7)(b) 270	s. 362F 104
s. 358 126	s. 362F(1) 104
s. 358(2)(b), (ba) 126	s. 362F(2)(d) 105
s. 361(1)-(5) 105	s. 362G 5.19, 5.21, 105
s. 362 .... 99, 126	s. 362G(1) 5.15, 5.19
s. 362(3)(d) 4.34	s. 362H 105
s. 362(4A), (4AA) 126	s. 362H(2) 4.21, 105
s. 362(5) 4.33, 127	s. 362H(2)(b) 4.30
s. 362(6) 127	s. 362H(5) 4.18, 4.22
s. 362A 4.1, 4.32, 4.33, 99, 105, 257	s. 362I 4.1, 106
s. 362A(2)(b) 4.46	s. 362I(1) 4.5
s. 362A(3) 5.15, 100, 275	s. 362I(4) 5.1
s. 362A(4)(c) 4.35	s. 362J 4.5, 4.36, 5.11, 103, 106, 258
s. 362A(6) 102	s. 362J(2) 4.37, 4.49, 112
s. 362A(7) 275	s. 362J(3) 275
s. 362B 4.19, 100, 105	s. 362K 5.12, 106
s. 362B(2)(a) 101	s. 362K(2), (6), (9) 107
s. 362B(2)(b) 102, 275	s. 362L 5.10, 106, 108
s. 362B(3) 4.25, 4.31, 101	s. 362L(4) 108
	s. 362L(6) 5.10
	s. 362M 4.38, 108

s. 362M(3) 109	s. 391(2) 127, 274
s. 362N 4.38, 109–12	s. 391(3)(a), (aa) 127
s. 362N(2), (7) 109	s. 392 127
s. 362O 109, 111	s. 392(2)(a), (aa) 127
s. 362O(7) 110	s. 396 112
s. 362P 110	s. 396(1)(a), (3)(a) 127
s. 362P(1) 110, 111	s. 396A 113, 118, 257
s. 362P(3) 111	s. 396A(3) 113, 275
s. 362Q 111	s. 396A(6) 115
s. 362R 5.13, 111	s. 396B 113, 118
s. 362S 4.49, 112	s. 396B(2)(a) 114
s. 362S(1)(a)-(c), (2), (3), (4)(a), (b) 4.49	s. 396B(2)(b) 115, 275
s. 362T 112	s. 396B(3) 114
s. 363 .... 6.9	s. 396B(4)(a) 114
s. 363(1A) 270	s. 396B(4)(b)(ii) 115
s. 369(5), (5A), (7) 270	s. 396B(7)(a) 116
s. 370(1A) 270	s. 396B(7)(b)-(d) 115
s. 375(4) 270, 271	s. 396C 115
s. 375(4A) 270	s. 396C(1)-(3) 115
s. 375A(1), (5)(b), (ba), (bb) 271	s. 396C(3)(b) 116
s. 375B(3)(b), (ba), (bb) 271	s. 396C(4) 116, 120
s. 375C 175	s. 396C(6)(a), (b) 116
s. 377 .... 4.15	s. 396C(7), (8) 115
s. 377(1)(f), (g), (2), (2A), (3) 271	s. 396D 115, 116
s. 377A(1)(a) 224	s. 396D(2)(a), (b), (3), (4) 116
s. 378 .... 6.10, 175, 176	s. 396D(2)(a)-(c) 117
s. 378(1)(c), (ca), (2)(b), (ba) 224	s. 396D(5) 120
s. 378(3)(a)-(c) 175	s. 396D(8) 120
s. 378(3ZA)(a) 175	s. 396E 117
s. 378(3ZA)(b), (c) 176	s. 396F 117
s. 378(3A)(a), (aa), (3AA)(a), (aa) 224	s. 396F(1) 117
s. 378(3B), (3C)(a)-(d), (3D)(a), (b) 271	s. 396F(2)(d) 118
s. 378(3D)(c), (d), (3E)(a)-(d), (3F)(a)-(d) 272	s. 396G 118
	s. 396H 118
s. 378(4)(b), (ba), (6)(a), (aa) 225	s. 396H(2) 118
s. 378(8), (9)(a)(b) 176	s. 396I 119
Pt. 8, Ch. 3 .... 112, 127	s. 396J 116, 119, 258
s. 380(2), (3)(b) 272	s. 396J(2) 125
s. 381(2)(bb)-(bf) 272	s. 396J(3) 276
s. 385(4)(b) 273	s. 396K 119
s. 386(3)(b) 273	s. 396K(2), (6), (9) 120
s. 387 179	s. 396L 119, 121
s. 387(2), (3)(b) 273	s. 396M 121
s. 388(2)(bb)-(bf), (5)(a) 273	s. 396N 121
s. 388(7B), (7C)(a), (b), (7D)(a) 273	s. 396N(1), (5) 121, 122
s. 388(7D)(b), (7E)(a), (b), (7F)(a), (b) ...274	s. 396O 122
s. 390 274	s. 396O(1), (2), (5) 122
s. 390(1), (5), (6), (7) 274	s. 396P 122–125
s. 391 127	s. 396P(2) 122
s. 391(1) 127	s. 396P(7) 123

s. 396Q 123, 124
s. 396Q(4) 123
s. 396Q(8) 123, 124
s. 396R 124
s. 396R(1), (3) 124
s. 396S 124, 125
s. 396T 125
s. 396U 125
s. 397(1A) 274
s. 404(1A) 274
s. 408A(1), (5)(b), (c) 274
s. 408A(5)(d) 275
s. 408B(3)(b)-(d) 275
s. 408C 175
s. 412 .... 140, 199
s. 412(b) 275
Pt. 8, Ch. 4 .... 4.45, 275
s. 412A(1)(a), (b), (2) 275
s. 413 275
s. 414(1)(a)-(c) 4.45
s. 414(3)(za)-(a) 275
s. 416(1), (2) 275
s. 416(3), (3A), (3B), (7), (7ZA) 276
s. 435 276
s. 435(1), (2), (4)(a)-(e) 276
s. 435(4) 278
s. 435(4)(a)-(e) 276
s. 436 276
s. 436(1) 276
s. 436(5)(h), (i), (10) 277
s. 437(2)(a), (6), (7) 277
s. 438 277
s. 438(1)(a), (e), (f), (fa), (5), (10) 277
s. 439 277
s. 439(1) 277
s. 439(5)(h)(i) 278
s. 441 278
s. 441(1), (2)(a), (d), (fa), (g) 278
Pt. 11 .... 127, 179
s. 443(1)(c), (ca) 278
s. 444 179
s. 444(3)(a), (aa) 179
s. 445 .... 127, 179
s. 445(1)(b) 179
s. 445(3) 278
s. 445A 127
s. 445A(1), (5)(a), (b) 128
s. 450(1)(a) 278
s. 453 ...... 1.15, 126, 133, 146, 147, 152, 154, 164, 165, 171, 267, 270–72

s. 453A 178
s. 453A(5)(da)-(dc) 278
s. 453B 178, 179
s. 453B(1), (2) 178
s. 453B(3)(a), (4)(a) 178
s. 453C 179
s. 453C(2)(a) 180
s. 454 225
s. 454A 225
s. 459 278
s. 459(3A), (4)(a), (aza), (5)(a), (6), (6)(b), (6ZA) 278
s. 459(6ZB), (6A), (7A), (7B), (7BA), (7D) 279
s. 460(3)(a), (b) 278
Sch. 3, para. 6(1), (3), (3)(a), (4) 186
Sch. 6, para. 5 .... 110, 123
Sch. 9 .... 2.11, 138, 139
Sch. 9, para. 1(1) 137
Sch. 9, para. 1(1)(i) 138
Proceeds of Crime Act 2002 (Business in the Regulated Sector and Supervisory Authorities) Order 2007 (SI 2007 No. 3287) 2.11
Proceeds of Crime Act 2002 (Financial Threshold for Civil Recovery) Order 2003 (SI 2003 No. 175) 629
Proceeds of Crime Act 2002 (Investigations in different parts of the United Kingdom) (Amendment) Order 2017 (SI 2017 No. 1280) 1.5, 2.2
Proceeds of Crime Act 2002 (Recovery of Cash in Summary Proceedings: Minimum Amount) Order 2006 (SI 2006 No. 1699) 6.20
Prosecution of Offences Act 1985 —
  s. 22(3) 1.12

Rent (Scotland) Act 1984 —
  Pts. 2, 3 185

Sanctions and Anti-Money Laundering Act 2018 97
  Pt. 2 97
Senior Courts Act 1981 —
  s. 28 .... 1.14, 131
Serious Crime Act 2007 —
  Pt. 1 .... 102, 115
  Pt. 2 .... 8.52
  s. 2 .... 102, 115

TABLE OF LEGISLATION

s. 2A 102, 115
s. 3 .... 102, 115
Sch. 1 .... 4.14, 4.16, 5.3, 215
Sch. 1, Pt. 1, para. 8 215
Sch. 1, Pt. 1, para. 8(6) 216
Sch. 1, Pt. 1A, para. 16G 216
Sch. 1, Pt. 1A, para. 16G(5) 216
Sch. 1, Pt. 2, para. 24 216
Sch. 1, Pt. 2, para. 24(6) 216
Serious Crime Act 2015 —
  s. 8(3)(za), (a) 190
  s. 36 181
Serious Organised Crime and Police Act 2005 —
  s. 61(1)(h), (i) 215
Sheriff Courts (Scotland) Act 1907 —
  ss. 34 to 38A 185
Social Security Contributions and Benefits Act 1992 —
  Pt. 1 212
Social Security Contributions and Benefits (Northern Ireland) Act 1992 —
  Pt. 1 212
Statutory Rules (Northern Ireland) Order 1979 (S.I. 1979 No.1573) (N.I. 12) 218, 221

Taxes Management Act 1970 —
  s. 106A 8.35
Tenancy of Shops (Scotland) Act 1949 185
Terrorism Act (TACT) 2000 (c. 11) 6.15, 7.3, 7.4, 7.24, 7.33, 7.98, 205, 206, 225, 259
  s. 1 .... 7.11
  s. 1(4) 7.12
  s. 3(3)(b) 242, 255
  s. 3(8) 255
  s. 4 .... 242, 255
  s. 5 .... 242, 255
  Pt. III 198
  s. 14 .... 7.13
  ss. 15–18 ..... 7.10, 7.15, 7.45, 7.60, 196–98, 225, 226, 229, 230
  s. 17 .... 7.10
  s. 21A 7.45, 7.50, 7.53, 192, 196, 197
  s. 21C 190
  s. 21CA-CE 195
  s. 21CA 7.38, 7.41, 190–93, 195, 259
  s. 21CA(1) 192, 193
  s. 21CA(3) 196
  s. 21CA(3)(a) 193
  s. 21CA(3)(b) 191–93
  s. 21CA(4) 191–93, 196

s. 21CA(5)(a), (5)(b), (6) 192
s. 21CB 191
s. 21CB(5)-(7) 191
s. 21CB(5)(a) 191
s. 21CB(5)(b) 192
s. 21CB(7), (8) 7.44
s. 21CC 7.50, 192, 195
s. 21CC(2) 194
s. 21CC(3) 194, 195
s. 21CC(4) 7.47
s. 21CC(5) 7.48
s. 21CC(6) 7.48, 193
s. 21CC(7), (9) 7.49
s. 21CD 7.51, 194
s. 21CD(1)-(8) 193
s. 21CD(3) 7.51
s. 21CD(5)-(8) 194
s. 21CD(10) 193
s. 21CE 7.52, 195
s. 21CE(1) 195
s. 21CE(2) 7.52
s. 21CF 195
s. 21CF(2) 7.40
s. 21CF(6) 196
s. 21CF(6)(a)-(d) 196
s. 21G(1)(a), (aa) 259
s. 21H(5) 196
s. 22A 196
s. 22B 7.54, 7.56, 196
s. 22B(3) 7.53
s. 22B(5) 197
s. 22B(8) 197, 198
s. 22B(10) 198
s. 22C 198
s. 22C(1) 7.64, 198
s. 22C(2)(b) 199
s. 22C(2)(c) 198
s. 22D 7.65, 199
s. 22E 7.57, 7.64, 199
ss. 25–31 259
ss. 37, 37A 225
s. 39 .... 7.26
s. 63E 205
s. 63F 7.96, 205, 208, 260
s. 115 259
s. 120A 7.98, 208
s. 120B 7.99, 208, 209
s. 120B(1), (2), (3)(a), (4)(a) 208
s. 120C 210
s. 121 260

s. 123(5) 242, 255
s. 123(5)(b) 242, 255
Sch. 3A 7.40, 196, 198
Sch. 3A, para. 1(1) 196
Sch. 3A, para. 1(1)(b)-(i) 196
Sch. 5 ....7.54, 208, 225
Sch. 5, Pt. I 206
Sch. 5, para. 5 ....7.99, 207
Sch. 5, para. 5(1), (1A), (3)(a), (b), (5), (6)(a), (b) 206
Sch. 5, para. 6(2)(a), (b), (3), (4) 206
Sch. 5, para. 7(2)(a) 206
Sch. 5, para. 13 ....7.99, 206
Sch. 5, para. 13(1), (1A) 206
Sch. 5, para. 30 ....7.99
Sch. 5, para. 22 ....7.99
Sch. 5A 7.6, 225
Sch. 5A, Pt. 1 ....7.10, 208, 225, 228, 229
Sch. 5A, para. 9 ....7.9, 7.19, 7.99, 225
Sch. 5A, para. 9(a)-(c) 7.19
Sch. 5A, para. 9(3) 7.20
Sch. 5A, para. 9(5) 7.25
Sch. 5A, para. 10 ....7.15
Sch. 5A, para. 11 ....7.28
Sch. 5A, para. 11(1) 227, 228
Sch. 5A, para. 11(2)(a) 227
Sch. 5A, para. 11(3) 227, 228
Sch. 5A, para. 11(4)(b) 227
Sch. 5A, para. 12 ....7.29
Sch. 5A, para. 12(1), (2)(c) 228
Sch. 5A, para. 13 ....7.30
Sch. 5A, para. 13(1) 228
Sch. 5A, para. 13(4) 7.31
Sch. 5A, para. 13(5) 7.32
Sch. 5A, para. 13(7) 229

Sch. 5A, para. 14 ....7.34
Sch. 5A, Pt. 2 229
Sch. 5A, para. 19 ....7.99, 229
Sch. 5A, para. 21(1) 230, 231
Sch. 5A, paras. 21(3), (22)(1), (2)(c) 231
Sch. 6 ....7.97
Sch. 6, para. 1 ....7.99
Sch. 6, para. 1(1), (2)(a) 207
Sch. 6A 7.97
Sch. 6A, para. 1(4)(a), (aa) 207
Sch. 6A, para. 2 ....7.99
Sch. 6A, para. 3(3), (4) 207
Sch. 6A, para. 4(2), (2A) 207
Sch. 7 259
Sch. 14 260
Sch. 14, para. 1(a) 260
Terrorism Act 2000 (Enforcement in Different Parts of the United Kingdom) Order 2018 (SI 2006 No. 521) 7.102
Theft Act 1968 —
s. 17(1) 8.16
Titles to Land Consolidation (Scotland) Act 1868 —
s. 155..122
Tribunals, Courts and Enforcement Act 2007 —
Sch. 12 ....108, 189

UK Borders Act 2007 —
s. 24 ....176, 179
s. 24(1), (2)(a), (c)-(f)(i) 176
s. 24(2)(f)(ii), (g)-(h) 177
United Nations Convention Against Corruption 2003 ....4.4

Value Added Tax Act (VATA) 1994 —
s. 72(1) 8.34, 8.35

Introduction

The Criminal Finances Act 2017 introduces the most important changes to the anti-money laundering and anti-terrorist-financing regimes in the UK in over a decade. The passage of the legislation further expresses a clear intent on the part of the government to put the civil powers to freeze and forfeit cash and property derived from 'unlawful conduct' to greater use. Building on the government's 2016 *Action Plan for Anti-Money Laundering and Counter-Terrorist Finance* which earmarked the creation of 'aggressive new legal powers' and 'new capabilities' for law enforcement to enable the 'relentless disruption of criminals and terrorists' as a major priority,[1] the Act was passed on 27 April 2017 with overwhelming bipartisan support. Although the opacity of money laundering means it is notoriously difficult to quantify, the Home Office estimated in 2017 that the scale of money laundering in the UK exceeds £90 billion a year. The eye-watering figure has meant that both sides of politics have been quick to support new corporate offences, forfeiture powers as well as changes to the money laundering and counter-terrorist-financing framework. The new measures have been regarded as proportionate to the objective of protecting the UK's status as a global financial centre[2] and cleansing it – or attempting to cleanse it – from so-called 'dirty money'.

As at the time of writing, since the Act received Royal Assent, four Commencement Regulations have been made, which have brought most of the provisions in to force in England and Wales, Scotland and, to a lesser extent, Northern Ireland. Several of the provisions necessarily amount to a further inroad into the rights of the individual but the day-to-day impact of the Act is likely to be felt by companies carrying on business in the UK as well as persons, firms and individuals, in the regulated sector.

Two measures in particular have grabbed the headlines. Chapter 1 of the Act introduces the Unexplained Wealth Order (UWO), a new investigative power, into Part 8 of the Proceeds of Crime Act 2002. Two new corporate offences largely modelled on the corporate criminal liability provisions in the Bribery Act 2010 are also in force by virtue of Part 3 of the Act. The new corporate offences capture partnerships and companies that fail to prevent the facilitation of either UK tax evasion or foreign tax evasion. As at the time of writing, neither of the offences has been prosecuted but a factor may also be the availability of negotiated deferred prosecution agreements. The new offences, however, have had a noticeable impact on corporate risk management policies and procedures. Since September 2017, which is when the offences entered in to force, there has been a proliferation of anti-tax evasion and anti-tax evasion facilitation statements published online by all manner of companies, partnerships and even universities.

---

1 Page 6.
2 See comments by the Minister of State (Home Office) in Hansard 9 March 2017 column 1477, https://hansard.parliament.uk/Lords/2017-03-09/debates/294ABC93-8E53-4310-AED6-E9A83FF867DB/CriminalFinancesBill, accessed 9 July 2018.

INTRODUCTION

As for the UWO, it is a tool that has been used in Ireland and, with varied success, in Australia for several years. That said, the proposed introduction of a free-standing procedure into the Proceeds of Crime Act 2002 that compels an individual to explain the source of his wealth is a radical development in English law. This is only underscored by the ability to use the tool against a person located abroad or property located abroad. More usually, judges are required to decide upon matters relating to disclosure of information where the issue arises during civil proceedings, or where a defendant seeks to explain the legitimate origin of his or her assets in confiscation proceedings after a criminal conviction.

Notwithstanding the attention generated by UWOs and the new offences, two other measures are likely to have more of a practical impact on lawyers, estate agents, banks and other financial professionals in the regulated sector. These are the new ability for regulated persons to share information relating to a money laundering or terrorist-financing suspicion, and for a Crown Court judge to extend the moratorium or 'no action' period applying to a matter when a suspicious activity report (SAR) is filed in respect of a money laundering suspicion in discharge of the legal duty to report. Underlying both new frameworks is an intention to make the investigation of illicit funds and property or funds or property intended for an illicit purpose easier. However, when there is a descent to the detail, the open-textured nature of some of the provisions make their operation in practice uncertain.

The information-sharing framework introduced by the Criminal Finances Act 2017 is a continuation of the trend towards public/private partnerships in the fight against money laundering and terrorist financing. The Joint Money Laundering Intelligence Task Force (JMLIT), established in early 2015, was a pilot endeavour to create an information-sharing environment between private financial sector institutions and law enforcement agencies. Its success has led to a new formal channel in the Proceeds of Crime Act 2002 through which information can be shared between the wider regulated sector. The threshold for information to be shared is low but technical notification requirements attach to an information request which could make businesses, particularly those without dedicated compliance teams, recoil. Although the aim is to encourage regulated persons to collaborate over 'super SARs' leading to the delivery of more comprehensive money laundering intelligence to the National Crime Agency, the notification requirements could result in the duplication of information already in the National Crime Agency's possession.

The extended moratorium period, furthermore, presents interesting challenges for business. Prior to the Criminal Finances Act 2017, the period in which no further action on a transaction could be taken after a SAR was submitted was 31 days after the National Crime Agency's consent was withheld. The rationale behind the extension of the moratorium period is to support law enforcement agencies by providing more time to respond to information contained in SARs (e.g. compiling evidence for restraint order applications or making mutual legal assistance requests of foreign authorities). Since the passage of the Act, there is the potential for a transaction to now be delayed several months. Although use of the power is subject to procedural safeguards, the question arises whether it may cause regulated persons to think very carefully about the submission of consent SARs.

In addition to the above, the suite of new powers afforded to law enforcement includes the expanded ability to seek a disclosure order in a terrorist-financing or money laundering investigation and the new further information order enabling law enforcement to seek more detail from the submitter of a SAR. Civil powers to seize, freeze and forfeit property under

Part 5 of the Proceeds of Crime Act 2002 and Schedule 1 of the Anti-Terrorism, Crime and Security Act 2001 have also been boosted by the introduction of a new bank account freezing and forfeiture power and 'listed' asset forfeiture regime. The latter enables law enforcement to more easily seize and ultimately forfeit a small list of high-value items, from jewels to artwork, which have been identified as particularly efficient ways to move and conceal value around the world. Both closely resemble the well-established cash seizure and forfeiture provisions in the Proceeds of Crime Act 2002 enabling authorities to take action in summary proceedings. The availability of these new powers is already proving particularly valuable to law enforcement authorities. Ultimately, the emphasis of civil recovery powers in the Act suggests that the application of the criminal law will no longer be the first port of call for law enforcement authorities responding to finance-related crime in the future.

These are but some of the highlights of the Criminal Finances Act 2017. This book goes further, analysing the detail of each key new measure and distilling the implications for regulated persons as well as interested legal practitioners and individuals. Over the last two years, concerns over the UK's vulnerability to money laundering and terrorist financing have become part of mainstream public discourse. This area of law and policy in the UK is moving quickly. In such circumstances, there is always a risk that evidence-based lawmaking and careful procedural safeguards to protect the rights of the individual may become background considerations. The clear direction of travel is towards more and not less aggressive action being taken to root out suspicious property. The Criminal Finances Act 2017 is a landmark piece of legislation on this trajectory and it is hoped that this book will assist in both understanding its impact and anticipating practical issues.

CHAPTER 1

Extending the SAR moratorium period

Introduction

1.1 The most significant change to the anti-money laundering regime made by the Criminal Finances Act 2017 relates to an extension of the moratorium period. Sections 327(1), 328(1) and 329(1) of the Proceeds of Crime Act 2002 establish the principal money laundering criminal offences that are committed where a person handles criminal property or becomes concerned in facilitating another person's handling of criminal property. The handling of the property or becoming concerned in facilitating another person's handling of the criminal property, is known as 'the prohibited act'. If a prohibited act is committed a person becomes liable to a maximum period of 14 years' imprisonment. However, in respect of each of the three principal offences, there is a statutory exemption in sections 327(2)(a), 328(2)(a) and 329(2)(a) where a person 'makes an authorised disclosure under section 338 and (if the disclosure is made before he does the [prohibited] act mentioned in subsection (1)) he has the appropriate consent'.

1.2 The concept of 'appropriate consent' is defined in section 335 of the Proceeds of Crime Act 2002. Broadly speaking, appropriate consent connotes the obtaining of consent from the National Crime Agency[1] after an authorised disclosure has been made to it (section 335(1)), or the obtaining of deemed consent in accordance with the statutory provisions (section 335(2)). To be precise, a person must be treated as having received appropriate consent to proceed with the commission of a prohibited act if (a) he makes an authorised disclosure[2] to the National Crime Agency, and before the end of the notice period he does not receive notice from the National Crime Agency that consent to the doing of the act is refused. Section 335(5) defines the notice period as a period of seven working days starting with the first working day after the person makes the disclosure. If, however, the person making the authorised disclosure receives a notice from the National Crime Agency before the end of the notice period or he receives notice from a constable or customs officer that consent to the doing of the prohibited act is refused then, pursuant to section 335(4), he must wait until the expiry of what is known as 'the moratorium period' before he can proceed with the prohibited act. Under section 335(6), the moratorium period is the period of 31 days starting with the day on which the person receives notice that consent to the doing of the act is refused. The purpose of the moratorium period is to allow investigators time to gather evidence to determine whether further action, such as restraint

---

1 Technically, under the terms of the section 338(1)(a), an authorised disclosure can be made to several other law enforcement officers. In practice, the disclosure is always made to the financial intelligence unit of the National Crime Agency.

2 The meaning of an authorised disclosure is set out in section 338 of the Proceeds of Crime Act 2002. It refers to a disclosure by the person making the disclosure that he intends to handle, or become concerned in facilitating another person's handling of, criminal property.

of the funds, should take place. The operation of these provisions became known as 'the consent regime'.

1.3 The Government perceived there were serious problems with the operation of the consent regime. The key difficulty was that the moratorium period was not renewable, often does not allow sufficient time to develop the evidence, particularly where it must be sought from overseas through mutual legal assistance.

1.4 There were two solutions to the problem. Either the consent regime had to be abolished, or provision made for the extension of the moratorium period in appropriate cases.[3] In the face of opposition from the regulated sector, the Government decided to pursue the second option, and this formed the genesis of the changes made to the moratorium regime by the Criminal Finances Act 2017. Section 10 of the Criminal Finances Act 2017 amends Part 7 of the Proceeds of Crime Act 2002 by inserting new sections 336A, 336B, 336C and 336D into the Act, the effect of which is to allow a court to grant an extension of the moratorium period for a period of up to 31 days on each application, but with a long-stop limit that the moratorium period must not be extended for a period of more than 186 days from the end of the initial 31-day moratorium period.

1.5 Rules of Court have been made to govern the procedure for an application to extend the moratorium period. These are to be found in rules 47.62 to 47.65 of the Criminal Procedure (Amendment No. 3) Rules 2017 (SI 2017 No. 755) (the Rules). In addition, the Government has published a circular giving guidance to law enforcement agencies on the application of the new provisions. This is entitled Home Office Circular, Criminal Finances Act 2017, Power to Extend Moratorium Period, sections 336A to 336C, 008/2018. The Proceeds of Crime Act 2002 (Investigations in different parts of the United Kingdom) (Amendment) Order 2017 facilitates mutual recognition of orders extending the moratorium period across the different nations in the UK.

1.6 The Government expressed confidence in its impact assessment that the legislative change would deliver important benefits to law enforcement authorities in the UK. The impact assessment noted that an extended moratorium period will make better use of intelligence flowing from the reporting sector to law enforcement.[4] In referenced cases studies, the Government claimed that amounts of monies that are not restrained due to the early expiry of the moratorium period was 'in the millions':

> It is estimated from a 5-month sample of cases that failed to reach the restraint order stage due the length of the moratorium period. Over the 5-month period, £102.7 million was potentially available to use by the subjects of those requests including corrupt [Politically Exposed Persons], drug traffickers, fraudsters, and human traffickers. This is based on a sample of cases, implying the total amount that could be restrained over a 12-month period may be higher, although the actual amount recovered will depend on successful [Law Enforcement Authority] action.[5]

1.7 The impact assessment posited that there will be 173 estimated extensions of the moratorium period each year, although it recognised that '[T]here is a risk that the estimated 173 estimated extensions per annum may be larger in reality'.[6]

---

3 Home Office Action Plan for anti-money-laundering and counter-terrorist finance: consultation on legislative proposals, Government Response, October 2016, paragraph 4.2.
4 Home Office Impact Assessment, SARS Moratorium Extension, 1 November 2016.
5 Ibid, paragraph 25.
6 Ibid, paragraphs 20, 30.

1.8 Pursuant to regulation 2(a) of the Criminal Finances Act 2017 (Commencement No. 2 and Transitional Provisions) Regulations 2017, the moratorium extension provisions came into effect on 31 October 2017.

Criteria for making the order

1.9 Under section 336A(1), a court may, on an application, grant an extension of the moratorium period if four criteria have been satisfied. First, the court must be satisfied that an investigation is being carried out in relation to an authorised disclosure but has not been completed. Second, it must be satisfied that the investigation is being conducted diligently and expeditiously. Third, further time is needed for conducting the investigation. Fourth, it is reasonable in all the circumstances for the moratorium period to be extended.

1.10 If these four criteria are established, a court is not bound to grant an extension of the moratorium period. The court's power in section 336A(1) is discretionary and not mandatory. This posits the possibility that there may be other factors featuring in a case which may cause a court to reject an application. Perhaps the most obvious example is where the applicant has satisfied the criteria but failed to make full and proper disclosure of a material fact of which the court ought to have been made aware. It will be interesting to see whether a court will draw a parallel with the position in restraint orders issued under section 40 of the Proceeds of Crime Act 2002 and freezing orders in civil proceedings more generally where material non-disclosure will justify the setting aside of a court order. The reasoning in support of this approach is compelling.[7]

1.11 Also, in relation to the four criteria, a court is most likely to focus on the twin issues of diligence and expeditiousness. If an applicant can establish that notwithstanding its swift and competent work, further time to investigate the content of an authorised disclosure is required, a court is likely to view the application for an extension of the moratorium period with some sympathy.

1.12 One question that may arise is whether a lack of police resources is a matter to be taken into account considering diligence, expeditiousness and reasonableness. A significant number of cases have been decided in the context of custody time limits, which may be extended only where the prosecution can show that it has acted 'with all due diligence and expedition'.[8] The courts have indicated a reluctance to give great weight to the lack of police resource or insufficient court time to hear a matter when considering whether to extend custody time limits, stressing that the legislation requires 'expedition' as well as due diligence to be shown.[9] It remains to be seen whether the courts may be prepared to adopt a less stringent view where liberty of the individual is not involved. Common sense suggests that, as the length of the moratorium period increases, a court will become increasingly reluctant to accept that the applicant authority has acted with diligence and expeditiousness, or that a further extension is reasonable in all the circumstances.

1.13 Remembering that the application to the court is of a civil and not a criminal nature, an applicant will need to satisfy a court on a balance of probabilities that the criteria have been established. It is the civil standard of proof and not the criminal standard that will

---

7 *Re Stanford International Bank* [2011] Ch 33; *Malabu Oil and Gas Ltd v DPP* [2016] Lloyds Report FC 108.
8 See, for example, *R v Manchester Crown Court, ex parte McDonald* [1999] 1 WLR 841.
9 Prosecution of Offences Act 1985, section 22(3); *R v Norwich Crown Court, ex parte Stiller* [1992] COD 310; *R (Raeside) v Crown Court at Luton* [2012] 1 WLR 2777.

apply. A court is likely to apply the same rules which apply in an application of a criminal restraint order.

Which court?

1.14 The court to which an application to extend the moratorium period is made is, in relation to England, Wales and Northern Ireland, the Crown Court and, in relation to Scotland, the Sheriff (section 336D(2)). In England and Wales, an appeal lies on a point of law to the High Court by way of case stated (section 336B(11), and section 28 of the Senior Courts Act 1981. In Northern Ireland, an appeal on a point of law can be made to the Court of Appeal in Northern Ireland (sections 336B(8), 336B(1)(a)), and in Scotland on a point of law to the Sheriff Appeal Court (sections 336B(8), 336B(1)(b)).

Who can apply?

1.15 An application under this section may be made only by a senior officer (section 336A(2)). Pursuant to section 336D(7), in an application to the Crown Court, 'senior officer' means the Director General of the National Crime Agency, any other National Crime Agency officer authorised by the Director General (whether generally or specifically) for this purpose, a police officer of at least the rank of inspector, an officer of Revenue & Customs who is not below such grade as is designated by the Commissioners for Her Majesty's Revenue & Customs as equivalent to that rank, a member of staff of the Financial Conduct Authority who is not below such grade as is designated by the Treasury for the purposes of this Part, the Director of the Serious Fraud Office (or a member of staff of that Office authorised for the purposes of section 336A by virtue of section 2C(2)), or an accredited financial investigator who falls within a description specified in an order made for the purposes of section 336A by the Secretary of State under section 453. An immigration officer who is not below such grade as is designated by the Secretary of State as equivalent to that rank may also apply for an extension of the moratorium period, but in this case additional criteria will need to be satisfied. The court will need to be satisfied that the officer has reasonable grounds for suspecting that conduct constituting the prohibited relates to entitlement of a non-UK national to enter or travel across the UK, or relates to a nationality enactment (section 336A(9) and (10)). By section 336D(8), in the case of an application to the sheriff, 'senior officer' means a procurator fiscal.

Timing of application

1.16 An application must be made before the moratorium period in section 335(6) would otherwise end (section 336A(3)).

1.17 In addition, there are complex additional provisions to cover the situation where the moratorium period might lapse before the court has determined an application to extend, or where there is an appeal against a refusal by the Crown Court or Sheriff to make an extension order.

1.18 The general rule is that the moratorium period is extended from the time when it would otherwise end until the court determines the application or it is otherwise disposed of (section 336C(2), (4)). This is the position where an application is made to the court for the extension (or further extension) of the moratorium period under section 336A, and the period would (apart from that subsection) end before the court determines the application or it is otherwise disposed of (section 336C(3)). The moratorium period is extended from the time when it would otherwise end until the proceedings are finally determined or otherwise disposed of. But the maximum period by which the moratorium period is extended by virtue of subsection (2) or (4) is restricted to 31 days beginning with the day after the day on which the period would otherwise have ended (section 336C(5)). Where a Crown Court or Sheriff has refused to make an extension order and the initial moratorium period is due to expire, the period is extended for a period of five working days beginning with day on which the court refuses to grant the application (section 336C(6)–(8)). The restriction on the overall extension of a moratorium period mentioned in section 336A(7) applies to an extension of a moratorium period in accordance with any provision in section 336C as it applies to an extension under an order of the court. In plain English, this means that the 186-day period for the moratorium remains the long-stop, irrespective of whether the period includes any deemed extensions under the timing or appeal provisions.

Subsequent applications

1.19 Where a moratorium period is extended by the court under section 336A(1), it may be further extended by the court (on one or more occasions) on the making of another application (section 336A(5)). A moratorium period extended in accordance with subsection (2) or (4) of section 336C may also be further extended by the court on the making of an application under this section (section 336A(6)). But again, a court may not grant a further extension of a moratorium period if the effect would be to extend the period by more than 186 days (in total) beginning with the day after the end of the 31-day period mentioned in section 335(6) or (as the case may be) section 336(8) (section 336A(7)).

Procedure – section 336B

1.20 As far as the statutory amendment is concerned, the relevant procedure is set out in section 336B. But it is heavily supplemented by the provisions in the Rules, to which reference has already been made.

Notice

1.21 There is no express requirement contained in section 336B that requires notice of an application to be given to the person who made the authorised disclosure and sought consent to proceed, or the person who is the subject of the disclosure and whose affairs have been affected by the imposition of the moratorium period. It is, however, implicit from the terms of the new section that Parliament must have anticipated that service on these parties would become the default position. Section 336B(3) provides that a court may exclude from any part of the hearing of an application under section 336A 'an interested person' or 'anyone representing that person'. In addition, where an applicant for an extended moratorium order wishes to withhold 'specified information' from an interested person or anyone representing that person, it must apply to the court for an order to this effect (section 336B(4)). It is axiomatic that for an interested person or anyone representing that person to be excluded from any part of the hearing or debarred from receiving specified information, they must have known about the hearing in the first place. This was clearly the Government's intention when the impact assessment was produced. To quote directly:

> In all cases the extension hearing will be held *inter partes*. There will be a procedure under which application could be made to the Judge to exclude information to be relied upon in the proceedings from one or more of the parties and their representatives. This should also provide for the potential for one or more of the parties being excluded from any part of the hearing at which such information would be under consideration at the Hearing. We will specify the grounds on which a Judge may exercise his discretion to exclude material.[10]

Interested person

1.22 Section 336D(3) defines an interested person as 'any other person who appears to the person making the application under section 336A to have an interest in the relevant property'. The language is curious, with its reference to 'any other person', but on any view Parliament must have had in mind the person who is the subject of the authorised disclosure and whose property rights are adversely affected by the operation of the moratorium period. Presumably, the meaning of 'an interest in ... property' is governed by the meaning of 'interest' set out in section 340(10) of the Proceeds of Crime Act 2002. This provides that a person obtains property if he obtains an interest in it. References to an interest, in relation to land in England and Wales or Northern Ireland, are to any legal estate or equitable interest or power. References to an interest, in relation to land in Scotland are to any estate, interest, servitude or other heritable right in or over land, including a heritable security; and references to an interest, in relation to property other than land include references to a right (including a right to possession). The last reference to a possessory right is pivotal as far as the person making the authorised disclosure is concerned. If a bank or solicitor is holding monies suspected to constitute criminal property, the holder may not have any legal or beneficial interest in the ownership of the monies, but a possessory right is clearly established.

Specified information

1.23 There is no statutory definition of the phrase 'specified information'. It would seem to be incredibly broad, referring to any item of information which the applicant decides to specify during the making of an application to extend the moratorium period. Although the legislation does not identify the criteria to be satisfied before a person may be excluded from any part of the hearing under section 336B, Parliament has specified the requirements which must be satisfied before any specified information may be withheld section 336B(5).

1.24 Before making an order to withhold specified information, the court must be satisfied that there are reasonable grounds to believe that if the specified information were disclosed evidence of an offence would be interfered with or harmed, the gathering of information about the possible commission of an offence would be interfered with, a

---

10 Ibid, paragraph 30.

person would be interfered with or physically injured, the recovery of property under the Proceeds of Crime Act would be hindered, or national security would be put at risk.

Procedure – rules of court

The hearing

1.25 Under rule 47.63(1) of the Rules, a court may determine an application to extend the moratorium period at a hearing (which must be in private unless the court otherwise directs), and in the absence of the applicant or the respondent.

1.26 Although the court has discretion under rule 47.63(1) to determine the application without a hearing, most applications are likely to be determined at an *inter partes* hearing. This is because rule 47.63(2) restricts a court from determining an application in the applicant's absence if the applicant asks for a hearing and, more significantly, under rule 27.63(3) the court must not determine such an application in the absence of a respondent unless one of the criteria apply. The criteria are that the absentee has had at least two business days in which to make representations; or the court is satisfied that the applicant cannot identify or contact the absentee, it would prejudice the investigation if the absentee were present, it would prejudice the investigation to adjourn or postpone the application to allow the absentee to attend, or the absentee has waived the opportunity to attend.

1.27 The court officer must arrange for the court to hear an application to extend the moratorium period no sooner than two business days after notice of the application was served, unless the court directs that no hearing need be arranged, or the court gives other directions for the hearing (rule 47.63(4)). If the court directs, the parties to an application may attend a hearing by live link or telephone (rule 47.63(5)).

1.28 The court must not extend a moratorium period unless the applicant states, in writing or orally that, to the best of the applicant's knowledge and belief, the application discloses all the information that is material to what the court must decide, and the content of the application is true (rule 47.63(6)). Where this statement is made orally, the statement must be on oath or affirmation, unless the court otherwise directs, and the court must arrange for a record of the making of the statement (rule 47.63(7)).

1.29 However, the court may indulge the court officer with a degree of laxity where the case has not been heard within two business days after the application was served. The court has discretion to shorten or extend (even after it has expired) a time limit imposed by rule 47.63 or dispense with a requirement for service even after service was required, and also it may consider an application made orally instead of in writing (rule 47.63(8)).

Application notice

1.30 Notwithstanding the speed with which an application to extend the moratorium period must be made, the application process is a formal one. Under rule 47.64(2), the applicant must apply in writing before the date on which the moratorium period otherwise would end. In addition, the applicant must demonstrate that the applicant is entitled to apply as a senior officer within the meaning of section 336D of the Proceeds of Crime Act 2002. About service, the application must be served on the court officer. Notice of the application must be served on each respondent, and the application itself must be served on each respondent to such extent as the court directs.

1.31 The application must specify the authorised disclosure in respect of which the application is made, the date on which the moratorium period began, the date and period of any previous extension of that period, and the date on which that period is due to end (rule 47.64(3)).

1.32 Furthermore, the application must describe the investigation being carried out in relation to that disclosure and explain the grounds for believing that the investigation is being conducted diligently and expeditiously. In addition, the notice must record that further time is needed for conducting the investigation, and that it is reasonable in all the circumstances for the moratorium period to be extended (rule 47.64(4)).

1.33 There are prescribed forms for an application for an application to extend the moratorium period, and for a further application, available to be downloaded from the Ministry of Justice's website in the Criminal Procedure Forms page under the heading 'Proceeds of Crime Act 2002 moratorium period'.

Respondents' notice

1.34 Under rule 47.64(5), a respondent who objects to the application must serve notice of the objection on the court officer and the applicant not more than two business days after service of notice of the application. The notice must also explain the grounds of the objection.

The order

1.35 It is perhaps axiomatic that the applicant must serve any order made on each respondent (rule 47.64(8)).

Application to withhold specified information

1.36 The position for the applicant becomes slightly more complicated where there is a desire to withhold specified information from a respondent. The applicant is required to omit the specified information from any part of the application that is served on the respondent. The applicant must also mark the other part to show that, unless the court otherwise directs, it is only for the court; and in that other part, explain the grounds for believing that the disclosure of that information would have one or more of the five consequences that were foreshadowed in section 336B(5) of the statute (rule 47.65(2)). These consequences were that evidence of an offence would be interfered with or harmed, the gathering of information about the possible commission of an offence would be interfered with, a person would be interfered with or physically injured, the recovery of property under this Act would be hindered, or national security would be put at risk.

1.37 When the application is heard, the court must first determine the application to withhold information, in the respondent's absence and that of any legal representative of the respondent. If the court allows the application to withhold information, then the court must consider representations first by the applicant and then by the respondent, in the presence of both, and the court may consider further representations by the applicant in the respondent's absence and that of any legal representative of the respondent (rule 47.65(3)). If the court refuses an application to withhold information from the respondent, the applicant may withdraw the application to extend the moratorium period (rule 47.65(4)).

Costs

1.38 Neither the statutory provisions in the Criminal Finances Act 2017 nor the Rules contain any provision specifically directed to the incidence of legal costs where an application to extend the moratorium period is made. If the application is unsuccessfully opposed, the question arises as to whether the respondent will be required to bear the costs. Conversely, where an application is made and fails, either at first instance or on appeal, will a court require the applicant to suffer the loss not only of its own costs, but to pay for the costs of the successful party or parties?

Tipping off

1.39 In paragraph 37 of Schedule 5 of the Criminal Finances Act 2017, Parliament has made explicit provision to ensure that an application to extend a moratorium period does not place the person who made the report in a position whereby he breaches the prohibition against tipping-off in his dealings with the person who is the subject of the authorised disclosure in question.

1.40 A new provision in section 333D(1) provides that where an application is made to extend a moratorium period under section 336A, a person does not commit an offence under section 333A if the disclosure is made to a customer or client of the person, the customer or client appears to the person making the disclosure to have an interest in the relevant property, and the disclosure contains only such information as is necessary for the purposes of notifying the customer or client that the application under section 336A has been made.

CHAPTER 2

Money laundering and further information orders

Introduction

2.1 As an additional measure to enhance the effectiveness of the anti-money laundering regime in Part 7 of the Proceeds of Crime Act 2002, section 12 of the Criminal Finances Act 2017 establishes a new power for the National Crime Agency to request further information from any person in the regulated sector following receipt of a suspicious activity report that has been filed under sections 330–332. A similar power has been introduced in to the UK's anti-terrorist-financing legislation.

2.2 The request for further information can also be made where the National Crime Agency has been asked to provide investigative assistance from a financial intelligence unit in another country. If the information is not provided, the National Crime Agency can apply to a magistrates or sheriff's court for an order compelling the person to provide it. Failure to comply does not constitute a criminal offence but it results in a fine. Section 12 adds the new provisions as sections 339ZH, 339ZI, 339ZJ and 339ZK of the Proceeds of Crime Act 2002. On 1 February 2018, the Home Office published guidance on obtaining a further information order in Circular 010/2018. Sections 339ZH–339ZK came into force under regulation 2(c) of the Criminal Finances Act 2017 (Commencement No. 2 and Transitional Provisions) Regulations 2017 on 31 October 2017. The Proceeds of Crime Act 2002 (Investigations in different parts of the United Kingdom) (Amendment) Order 2017 facilitates mutual recognition of further information orders across the different nations in the UK.

2.3 Before the new power was introduced, if the National Crime Agency or the police received a suspicious activity report that lacked sufficient information to assess whether an investigation should be undertaken, the reporter was not obliged to respond to requests for additional information. As the Government noted in pre-legislative material, the new power to obtain information for the purposes of analysis brings the UK into full alignment with the recommendations from the Financial Action Task Force. The new power ensures that the National Crime Agency can obtain the information it needs to conduct effective intelligence analysis.[1] Inevitably, there will be costs to the regulated private sector for replying to requests for further information. The Government's impact assessment estimated the annual net direct cost to business at approximately £0.3 million per year, based on a total of 1,400 requests, each requiring 7.5 hours to respond. The Government derived this unit cost through both internal analysis of the time burden involved in due diligence

---

1 Home Office, Action Plan for anti-money laundering and counter-terrorist finance: consultation on legislative proposals, Government Response, October 2016, paragraph 5.3.

procedures, as well as an independent review of the time commitment associated with completing freedom of information requests.[2]

The order

2.4 A further information order can be sought in England, Wales and Northern Ireland only by the National Crime Agency, and only by the procurator fiscal in Scotland. The two authorities are fined as 'the relevant person' for the purpose of making the application (section 339ZH(12)).

2.5 A further information order is an order requiring the respondent to provide the information specified or described in the application for the order, or such other information as the court or sheriff making the order thinks appropriate, so far as the information is in the possession, or under the control, of the respondent (section 339ZH(3)). The order must specify how the information required under the order is to be provided, and the date by which it is to be provided (section 339ZH(7)). Information provided in pursuance of a further information order will not to be taken to breach any restriction on the disclosure of information, however imposed (section 339ZK(3)).

The application

2.6 The application must be made to a magistrates' court, or to the sheriff in Scotland (section 339ZH(a)), and the application must specify or describe the information sought under the order and specify the person from whom the information is sought. The latter person is known 'the respondent' (section 339ZH(2)).

2.7 One of two alternative conditions need to be satisfied before a further information order may be made. Condition 1 applies in domestic cases, whereas condition 2 provides the route where the information is required by a foreign authority where mutual investigatory assistance is sought.

2.8 Condition 1 is met if the information required to be given under the order would relate to a matter arising from a disclosure, the respondent is the person who made the disclosure or is otherwise carrying on a business in the regulated sector, the information would assist in investigating whether a person is engaged in money laundering or in determining whether an investigation of that kind should be started, and it is reasonable in all the circumstances for the information to be provided (section 339ZH(4)).

2.9 Condition 2 is met if the information required to be given under the order would relate to a matter arising from a disclosure made under a corresponding disclosure requirement, an external request has been made to the National Crime Agency for the provision of information in connection with that disclosure, the respondent is carrying on a business in the regulated sector, the information is likely to be of substantial value to the authority that made the external request in determining any matter in connection with the disclosure, and it is reasonable in all the circumstances for the information to be provided (section 339ZH(5)). For the purposes of subsection (5), 'external request' means a request

---

2 Government Regulatory Policy Committee, July 2017, Criminal Finances Bill – power to obtain further information Home Office RPC rating: fit for purpose.

made by an authority of a foreign country which has responsibility in that country for carrying out investigations into whether a corresponding money laundering offence has been committed (section 339ZH(6)).

2.10 In the case of both conditions 1 and 2, there is an important limitation to the exercise of the power.

2.11 A further information order can be made only where the respondent, as holder of the information, is carrying on a business in the regulated sector.[3] This is consistent with the tenor of the legislation, since an order can be made at the request of a foreign authority only where 'the information required to be given ... would relate to a matter arising from a disclosure made under a corresponding disclosure requirement' (section 339ZH(5)(a)). Here, it will be necessary to focus on the foreign law of the requesting country and whether it has 'a corresponding disclosure requirement'. Whilst in the UK sections 327–329 of the Proceeds of Crime Act 2002 provide a gateway for a person to make an authorised disclosure to obtain an exemption from liability for undertaking a prohibited act, the making of a disclosure is not a requirement, in the sense that it is not compulsory. It is only sections 330–332 that require the making of a disclosure.

2.12 Interestingly, there is a discordance in the importance of the information to an investigation between conditions 1 and 2. If the information is sought by a foreign authority, the court must be satisfied that the information 'is likely to be of substantial value' to the investigating authority (section 339ZH(5)(d)). But if the further information is sought by the National Crime Agency or procurator fiscal, it is sufficient if the information 'would assist in investigating whether a person is engaged in money laundering or in determining whether an investigation of that kind should be started' (section 339ZH(4)(c)).

Rules of court: procedure

2.13 An application for a further information order may be heard and determined in private (section 339ZK(4)). Rules of court make provision as to the practice and procedure to be followed in connection with proceedings relating to further information orders (section 339ZK(5)). The relevant Rules of Court for application to the magistrate's court are contained in rule 47.20 of the Criminal Procedure Rules 2015 as amended. There is a prescribed form for an application for a further information order available to be downloaded from the Ministry of Justice's website in the Criminal Procedure Forms page under the heading 'Proceeds of Crime Act 2002'.

Evidential status

Incriminatory evidence

2.14 The newly inserted section 339ZI addresses the issue as to whether a statement made by a person in response to a further information notice may be used in evidence against him if subsequently criminal proceedings were brought against him.

---

3 Section 339Z(11) makes clear that Schedule 9 of the Proceeds of Crime Act 2002 has effect for the purposes of determining what is a business in the regulated sector. See Proceeds of Crime Act 2002 (Business in the Regulated Sector and Supervisory Authorities) Order 2007 (SI 2007 No. 3287).

2.15 A statement made by a person in response to a further information order may not be used in evidence against the person in criminal proceedings. The raising of this issue is uncomfortable since it posits the institution of criminal proceedings against the maker of a suspicious activity report, presumably in a case where there has been a self-report of criminal conduct. But more to the point, it brings into question the scope of a further information order. The legislation clearly speaks to the provision of further information (section 339ZH(1)–(3)), which suggests that it relates to documents or data held in electronic form. There is no suggestion that the National Crime Agency or the procurator fiscal is afforded power under this provision to seek an order requiring the respondent who holds information to answer questions or to make a statement about the information he holds. Yet section 339ZI is directed to precisely this issue, namely the treatment of self-incriminatory statements which may be made by a respondent in response to a further information notice. At some future point, this aspect of the legislation will need to be judicially considered.

2.16 In an event, the general rule set out in the legislation is that a statement made by a person in response to a further information order may not be used in evidence against the person in criminal proceedings (section 339ZI(1)). However, this provision does not apply in the case of proceedings in money laundering cases, on a prosecution for perjury, or on a prosecution for some other offence where, in giving evidence, the person makes a statement inconsistent with the statement made by a person in response to a further information order (section 339ZI(2)). But a statement may not be used for this latter purpose unless evidence relating to it is adduced, or a question relating to it is asked, by or on behalf of the person in the proceedings arising out of the prosecution (section 339ZI(3)).

Legally privileged material

2.17 The legislation is clear, for the avoidance of doubt, that legally professionally privileged information cannot be the subject of a further information order. Section 339ZK(1) provides that a further information order does not confer the right to require a person to provide privileged information. 'Privileged information' is defined as information that a person would be entitled to refuse to provide on grounds of legal professional privilege in proceedings in the High Court or in Scotland (section 339ZK(2)).

Appeals

2.18 An appeal against a decision on an application for a further information order is made to the Crown Court in England and Wales, a county court in Northern Ireland, and the Sheriff Appeal Court in Scotland (section 339ZJ(1), (2) and (3)). The appeal is not specified as limited to a point of law, and the appeal court may make or discharge, or vary, a further information order as it considers appropriate (section 339ZJ(4)).

Non-compliance

2.19 If a person fails to comply with a further information order made by a magistrates' court, the court may order the person to pay an amount not exceeding £5,000 (section 339ZH(8)). This is an administrative penalty and not a criminal sanction, although for the purposes of collection by the magistrates' court it is adjudged to be paid as if it were a conviction (section 339ZH(9)). The default is a continuing one, in the sense that the respondent remains in breach of the terms of the further information order with each day that passes, but the financial penalty is not expressed as continuing at a daily rate. This means that if the respondent elects to ignore a further information order, his financial exposure will be capped at £5,000. There is power for the maximum sum to be altered to take account of changes in the value of money in due course (section 339ZH(10)).

2.20 Curiously, the penalty is not specified to apply in Scotland. The Home Office Circular 010/2018 (to which reference has already been made) indicates that in the case of Scotland, 'any breach of the order would potentially be treated as a contempt of court' (at paragraph 20).

CHAPTER 3

Money laundering and information sharing

Introduction

3.1 As financial transactions and investment opportunities become more sophisticated, so too do money laundering schemes. National boundaries are ignored and financial institutions and professional advisers from around the world may be drawn in. For the Financial Action Task Force, the peak inter-governmental body charged with setting policies to combat money laundering and terrorist financing, information sharing is critical. Its 2017 *Guidance on Private Sector Information Sharing* considers fast and comprehensive information sharing from a wide variety of sources to be necessary at the national level and also globally, both within corporate groups and between regulated persons not part of the same structure.

3.2 The development of public/private anti-money laundering partnerships is on the rise. In 2015, the Home Office conducted a review of the suspicious activity report (SAR) regime and concluded that

> the most effective way for the UK to improve its response to the threat from money laundering and terrorist finance is through stronger partnership working between the public and private sectors, and through jointly identifying and tackling those entities – individuals, companies and others – that pose the highest risk.[1]

Subsequently, in 2016, the Joint Money Laundering Intelligence Taskforce (JMLIT) was set up between UK law enforcement and vetted staff from major financial institutions. It serves as a forum for sharing information, improving a 'collective understanding of new and emerging money laundering threats' and assisting coordinated interventions by law enforcement. Between May 2016 to March 2017, it is said that JMLIT contributed to 63 arrests of individuals suspected of money laundering.[2] Although one might query whether such partnerships symbolise the growth of the outsourced private sector policeman, whether the private sector is equipped to discharge that role and what banks and other regulated entities expect in return, anti-money laundering information gateways are gaining pace.

3.3 Recommendations 18, 20, 21 of FATF's 40 recommendations which are designed to underpin national and global anti-money laundering and counter-terrorist financing policy all contemplate information sharing in some form. Further, at the 2016 London Anti-Corruption Summit, more than 20 countries expressed a commitment to developing public/private partnerships in order to combat money laundering and terrorist financing.[3] The reasons are becoming

---

1 Home Office, 'Action Plan for Anti-Money Laundering and Counter-Terrorist Financing' (April 2016) page 6.
2 National Crime Agency, Joint Money Laundering Intelligence Taskforce, www.nationalcrimeagency.gov.uk/about-us/what-we-do/economic-crime/joint-money-laundering-intelligence-taskforce-jmlit, accessed 2 June 2018.
3 As cited in RUSI, 'Occasional Paper: The Role of Financial Information-Sharing Partnerships in the Disruption of Crime' (October 2017), https://rusi.org/sites/default/files/201710_rusi_the_role_of_fisps_in_the_disruption_of_crime_maxwwell_artingstall_web_4.2.pdf, accessed 4 July 2018, see footnote 2.

increasingly familiar. More information being shared means a better level of intelligence ultimately able to be provided to enforcement authorities. For regulated entities, opportunities to confer and access more intelligence about a client or workstream means a better understanding of the attendant money laundering risk. Consequently, there is a better ability to mitigate the money laundering risk and navigate the choppy compliance waters.

3.4 Building upon the UK's public/private partnership commitment, the CFA 2017 introduces a new formal channel for the sharing of information between (1) law enforcement and the UK regulated sector and (2) members of the regulated sector. The channel appears in POCA 2002 as well as the UK's anti-terrorism legislation. Although the success of JMLIT has been the inspiration, both pieces of legislation contemplate information being shared by the wider regulated sector. The sharing of information is entirely voluntary but it is hoped that it will result in the delivery of more comprehensive anti-money laundering intelligence to the National Crime Agency in the form of joint suspicious activity reports (SARs) or 'super SARs'.[4]

3.5 The provisions entered in to force on 31 October 2017 with the issuance of the Criminal Finances Act 2017 (Commencement No. 3) Regulations 2017. In this chapter, the POCA 2002 provisions are examined. The information-sharing provisions in the UK's anti-terrorism legislation are near-identical and are discussed in Chapter 7.

Voluntary disclosure

3.6 Section 11 of the CFA 2017 inserts sections 339ZB–339ZG into POCA 2002 enabling:

- regulated persons in the UK to request and share information with their regulated peers;
- a UK enforcement authority to request that a regulated person share information with another regulated person.

3.7 Insulation from resulting claims of breach of confidence or contravention of data protection laws is ensured by section 339ZF, which provides that a relevant disclosure 'made in good faith' does not breach any duties of confidence or 'any other restriction on the disclosure of information, howsoever imposed'.

The conditions

3.8 Although it is a voluntary framework, information may be shared only if all of the following conditions, set out in section 339ZB POCA 2002, are met:

- A National Crime Agency officer or a person, B, has requested another person, A, make a disclosure.
- Where B is requesting the disclosure, before B makes the request, they have notified the National Crime Agency.

---

4 See, for instance, Explanatory Note to Criminal Finances Act 2017 (Commencement No. 3) Regulations 2017.

- A is carrying on business in the regulated sector, the information to be disclosed by A came to A in the course of that business and the person to whom the information is to be disclosed, B, is also in the regulated sector.
- Before A makes the disclosure, B has notified the National Crime Agency that a disclosure request has been made and complied with the notification requirements.
- A is satisfied that the disclosure 'will or may assist in determining any matter in connection with a suspicion that a person is engaged in money laundering'.

3.9 The final condition is striking in that it is a low bar for information to be shared either with the National Crime Agency or another in the regulated sector. The information that is requested 'does need not to be probative of even the suspicion. Instead, it must merely have the ability to assist in determining something connected to such a suspicion.'[5] It is a matter for A as to whether they consider that it 'will or may assist'. The test is subjective but will be easily satisfied.

3.10 The notification requirements also bear examination. The detail is located in section 339ZC POCA 2002. For a voluntary regime, the technicality of the provisions is surprising. Where a regulated person is requesting the information, the National Crime Agency is to be kept informed from the outset. Certain information must be provided including, amongst other matters, reasons why the information request is being made and the nature of the information that is sought before any request is even sent.

3.11 The disclosure request itself must then set out, amongst other matters, the grounds for the suspicion that a person is engaged in money laundering and specify the information sought.

3.12 Then, so that the recipient of the notice can comply with the request, the National Crime Agency must be notified. This is known as a 'required notification' and it must be made before any information is disclosed. Where it is the National Crime Agency who has made the request, the regulated person must notify it that it is about to disclose information. Where it is a regulated person who has made the request, that regulated person must notify the National Crime Agency that the information is to be disclosed.

3.13 The requirements of the 'required notification' are prescribed by legislation. The National Crime Agency must be provided with all of the following information before any such sharing of information takes place:

the required notification must –

(a) state that a disclosure request has been made,
(b) specify the person to whom the request was made,
(c) identify any person (if known) suspected of being engaged in money laundering in connection with whom the request was made, and
(d) provide all such other information that the person giving the notification would be required to give if making the required disclosure for the purposes of section 330 . . . .

---

5 Ailsa McKeon, 'Money Laundering: Information Sharing and the Extended Moratorium Period' (September 2017), www.brightlinelaw.co.uk/images/publication-covers/2017.09.14.CompendiumMoneyLaundering. Final2.pdf, page 12.

3.14 After the required notification is provided, the information may then be voluntarily disclosed. All this seems unnecessarily complicated and potentially is also a duplication of information already in the hands of the National Crime Agency. Under section 330 POCA 2002, a person in the regulated sector is under a duty to report a suspicion that a person is engaged in money laundering 'as soon as is practicable' after it comes to him or her in the course of regulated sector business. The failure to do so is a criminal offence.

3.15 If A is requesting information from another regulated person, B, 'in connection with a suspicion' then, on one view, A has already formed a suspicion. Indeed, under the legislation, A must 'set out the grounds for a suspicion that a person is engaged in money laundering' in the disclosure request: section 339ZC POCA 2002. This, combined with the reporting duty, would suggest that A would have already submitted a SAR to the National Crime Agency. Accordingly, for A to provide this information again in the form of the 'required notification' is to deliver unnecessary information that still needs to be processed by the National Crime Agency. In simple terms, it is a 'doubling up'.

3.16 Whilst keeping the National Crime informed throughout ensures a level of oversight and militates against confidential information being shared for inappropriate or non-AML reasons, the requirement for the National Crime Agency to be notified before information is disclosed and, indeed, before there is any collaboration over a joint SAR, seems at odds with the object of encouraging better quality intelligence.

3.17 Separately, the question arises as to the incentive for a regulated person to request information bearing on a money laundering suspicion if they have already submitted a SAR and discharged their legal duty. On the one hand, there is a compelling argument that requesting more information after a SAR has been submitted enables the regulated person to form a clearer picture of the attendant money laundering risk and to confer with regulated peers with an interest in the same matter. On the other, the cumbersome procedure that must be followed before any information can be disclosed – the costs of which are absorbed by the regulated person – undermines the attractiveness of the framework.

Joint reporting

3.18 Notwithstanding the above, where information is shared pursuant to a request, the regime contemplates a subsequent joint SAR: section 339ZD POCA. In practical terms, this is where the nominated officers appointed by the person or persons who requested the disclosure and the person who received the disclosure request collaborate over a SAR.

3.19 The requirements of a joint SAR are prescribed. It must explain the 'extent to which there are continuing grounds for suspicion', identify the relevant property or person, set out the grounds for the suspicion and provide any other relevant information: section 339ZD(5) POCA 2002.

3.20 Unless the period is lengthened by the National Crime Agency, a joint SAR is to be submitted within 84 days of the required notification: section 339ZD(6) POCA 2002. This is substantially longer than the 28-day period that applies when information is shared in the context of a terrorist-financing suspicion. Notably, if there has been a required notification and a joint SAR is not to be made, the person who made the required notification (A) must notify the National Crime Agency.

Impact on the duty to report

3.21 The 'required notification' affects more than the timing of the joint SAR.

3.22 Notably, the making of a 'required notification' by the person who requests the information (A) will satisfy both A's duty, the duty on the recipient of the request (B) and the duty on any other regulated person to whom A passes the information (C) to report a suspicion that a person is engaged in money laundering. In other words, if A were to request information from B in connection with a terrorist-financing suspicion and were to pass it to C, A, B and C would be protected if they had not yet submitted a SAR in discharge of the duty to report a suspicion under section 330 POCA 2002.

3.23 However, there is a limit to the cover afforded to A, B and C. Persons are protected only where the suspicion is formed because of the required notification and knowledge, suspicion or belief about matters has come about as a result of the disclosure request: section 339ZE POCA 2002. The protection does not extend to a situation where a suspicion that a person is engaged in money laundering is reasonably supported by something else, for example, a piece of information which is not the subject of the disclosure request. In such cases, the duty to report remains and a SAR based on this separate information would have to be made.

Confidentiality and privacy

3.24 As indicated at the outset, concerns over the sharing of confidential information pertaining to a client are addressed by the legislation. Where information is shared in good faith, there will not be a breach of any obligation of confidence or other restriction however imposed: section 339ZF POCA 2002.

3.25 Still, at a broader level, an inherent tension exists between expectations that the private sector will share information and the emphasis of data protection, particularly in the wake of the European Union's General Data Protection Regulation (GDPR) which entered in to force in May 2018.

3.26 The regime that has been introduced by the CFA 2017 deftly skirts around the tension by providing absolute legal cover to regulated entities that disclose information. But an expectation that regulated entities will share information with each other relating to individual matters seems at odds with the ever-growing protections applicable to the storage and handling of personal data and wider discussion of an evolving right to be forgotten. Notably, the UK's new information-sharing framework in POCA does not contain any reference to the age or type of the information that a regulated entity can now request from another in the regulated sector.

3.27 It is not inconceivable that sharing information which may assist in determining any matter in connection with a money laundering suspicion could lead to the sharing of certain private information obtained in the course of performing Customer Due Diligence. Such information could identify a person's political opinions or sensitive personal relationship with a politically prominent person. The information may also extend to a person's financial history or that of his or her family, or personal background such as the geographical locations in which they have worked or done business in the past. According to the Financial Action Task Force guidance, these privacy issues bear consideration. In certain jurisdictions, they could pose a challenge to the introduction of private sector information-sharing frameworks.

CHAPTER 4

Unexplained wealth orders

Introduction

4.1 On 31 January 2018, a new tool directed at the investigation of illicit wealth entered into force in England and Wales and Scotland.[1] Situated between sections 362A and 362I Proceeds of Crime Act 2002 (POCA 2002), the provisions for an unexplained wealth order (UWO) were introduced by section 1 of the Criminal Finances Act 2017 (CFA 2017), which amends Part 8 POCA 2002. Their arrival makes the UK one of the few common law jurisdictions to have a UWO framework, alongside Ireland and Australia who were early adopters. The provisions mark an important development in the law of the UK. Typically, courts determine matters relating to disclosure once a civil or criminal investigation has developed, during the course of civil proceedings, or where a defendant seeks to explain the legitimate origin of their assets in confiscation proceedings following criminal conviction. However, a UWO does not require any civil or criminal proceedings to have commenced and may be sought as a first step in an investigation.

4.2 The broad rationale of the framework is to assist enforcement agencies in gathering evidence to support civil proceedings in the High Court for the freezing and forfeiture of recoverable property under Part 5 POCA 2002. In its impact assessment report on UWOs issued in June 2017, the Home Office noted that the new tool

> reflects the concern about those involved in grand corruption overseas laundering the proceeds of crime in the UK; and the fact that it may be difficult for law enforcement agencies to satisfy any evidential standard at the outset of such an investigation given that all relevant information may be outside of the jurisdiction.

Fundamentally, a UWO compels a person to explain the provenance of specific property to an enforcement agency within a time frame. The person does not necessarily have to be the subject of any criminal investigation. The veracity of the explanation and any documents provided is then assessed by the enforcement agency with a view to forfeiture proceedings in the High Court. Unlike a confiscation order under Part 2 POCA 2002, a forfeiture order under Part 5 POCA 2002 can occur in the absence of a criminal conviction. Where a person is deceased or outside of the jurisdiction or much of the evidence that would support a criminal prosecution is abroad, it is particularly attractive. Evidentially, it requires the court to be satisfied to the civil standard that the property is derived from a type of unlawful conduct. Subject to certain safeguards, the property can be followed in to the hands of third parties and the underlying criminal conduct need not be specified. In this sense, it is a more

---

1 The provisions entered into force on 31 January 2018 pursuant to regulation 2 of the Criminal Finances Act 2017 (Commencement No. 4) Regulations 2018. The Criminal Finances Act 2017 also introduces UWO provisions into the law of Northern Ireland but, as at the time of writing, the provisions are awaiting commencement. For this reason, strictly speaking, this chapter deals only with the position in England and Wales when referring to 'the UK'. The provisions in Scotland and, when commenced, Northern Ireland are identical in substance.

straightforward route to property confiscation. The CFA 2017 envisages that any information provided in answer to a UWO can be used against the respondent in the subsequent Part 5 POCA 2002 proceedings.

4.3 But whilst UWOs are billed as a weapon against grand international corruption,[2] their investigative value is much wider. Although the UWO is an order made in respect of property (*in rem*) as opposed to a person (*in personam*) their effect is to place a burden on a respondent to provide accurate information to the authorities about their finances at the outset. The self-incrimination privilege is preserved but the information can be put to broad use, such as to develop a criminal, civil or regulatory investigation into someone else. The failure to provide a truthful account also exposes a respondent to criminal liability.

4.4 Separately, a failure to respond at all triggers a draconian presumption that the property will be forfeited to the state under Part 5 POCA 2002. Central to the new measure is a belief that the respondent, who hitherto may not have had any adverse dealings with the authorities, has a case to answer. Once a UWO is made, the onus shifts onto the respondent to demonstrate that their property is legitimate and produce information in support to the state. Due process and privacy considerations are engaged but the provisions have been regarded by policymakers as more palatable than other ways of targeting unexplained wealth. UWOs, made by courts exercising civil jurisdiction, have been preferred in the UK over the introduction of a new offence of 'illicit enrichment'. A recommendation of the UN Convention Against Corruption,[3] to which the UK is a signatory, the offence would have exposed public officials who were unable to provide a satisfactory explanation of disproportionate wealth in their possession to criminal liability.[4] The introduction of a civil rather than criminal unexplained wealth framework suggests a limit to the tolerance of a reverse onus in the UK.

Requirements

4.5 A UWO may be made by a High Court judge on application by an enforcement authority. The civil standard applies and applicants are confined to the National Crime Agency, Her Majesty's Revenue & Customs, Financial Conduct Authority and Directors of the Serious Fraud Office and Crown Prosecution Service. A Home Office circular, issued in early 2018, clarifies that enforcement agencies that do not have the power to apply for a UWO, such as police services, may refer matters to a listed applicant agency who will determine whether an application is appropriate.[5] Without notice applications can be expected as a UWO will usually be accompanied by an application for an interim freezing order (IFO) in relation to the property in question: see sections 362I(1) and 362J POCA 2002.

---

2 See Home Office and HM Treasury, *Action Plan for Anti-Money Laundering and Counter-Terrorist Finance* (April 2016) paragraphs 2.32 and 2.33.

3 The recommendation is to undertake consultation over the introduction of the offence.

4 A proposal to introduce a new criminal offence of 'illicit enrichment' was the subject of Home Office and HM Treasury consultation which closed in June 2016, see Home Office, 'Government response to the Action Plan for anti money-laundering and counter-terrorist finance: consultation on legislative proposals' (October 2016) available at: https://assets.publishing.service.gov.uk/government/uploads/system/uploads/attachment_data/file/559958/Action_Plan_for_anti_money-laundering_and_counter-terrorist_finance_-_consultation_on_legislative_proposals__print_.pdf, accessed 12 April 2018.

5 Home Office Circular 003/2018, Unexplained Wealth Orders.

4.6 Broadly, the making of a UWO requires a High Court judge to be satisfied of three matters. First, that the person against whom a UWO is sought falls into one of the respondent categories; second, there is reasonable cause to believe they hold particular property; and, third, there is a reasonable basis to suspect their lawful income is inconsistent with the property. Unlike in Australia, the legislation does not require the satisfaction of a public interest criterion before a UWO is made.[6]

4.7 Section III of the Civil Recovery Proceedings Practice Direction, updated in early 2018, sets out the procedure for the making of a UWO application. A written application, supported by written evidence, is to be filed in the High Court. The hearing of the application shall take place in private unless otherwise directed.

The respondent

4.8 Dealing with the first of the three requirements, the court must be satisfied that the respondent to a UWO is either (1) a non-UK and non-European Economic Area (EEA) Politically Exposed Person (PEP) or (2) a suspect of serious crime or person connected to such a suspect. Section 362B(4) of the Act provides that:

> (4) The High Court must be satisfied that –
>   (a) the respondent is a politically exposed person, or
>   (b) there are reasonable grounds for suspecting that –
>   (i) the respondent is, or has been, involved in serious crime (whether in a part of the United Kingdom or elsewhere), or
>   (ii) a person connected with the respondent is, or has been, so involved.

Politically exposed person

4.9 In the context of a UWO, the definition of a PEP extends to holders of prominent political functions in a state other than the UK or other EEA state, their family members, known close associates and connected persons: section 362B(7) POCA 2002.[7] The reference to 'a State other than the UK or other EEA State' is to the country in which the prominent function is held as opposed to where the PEP happens to be located. When compared to the scope of a PEP applicable to the anti-money laundering compliance framework, there is a clear difference. PEPs, for the purposes of anti-money laundering compliance in the UK, embrace domestic and EEA PEPs. A late proposal that the UWO framework similarly apply to domestic or EEA PEPs, however, failed to gain traction when the Criminal Finances Bill was moving through Parliament.[8]

4.10 As for who is the holder of a prominent political function, this will include (amongst others) heads of state, holders of judicial office, members of parliament, members of the management of state-owned enterprises and directors, high-ranking members of the armed

---

6 The position is different in at least one jurisdiction in Australia, see section 28A(4) Criminal Recovery Act 1990 (NSW).
7 See regulation 35(3) Money Laundering, Terrorist Financing and Transfer of Funds (Information on the Payer) Regulations 2017.
8 The amendment was raised in the House of Lords by Lord Sharkey on 28 March 2017 but not moved: see https://hansard.parliament.uk/Lords/2017-03-28/debates/1FD25E98-DF29-47CF-9967-4C24F82D0965/Criminal FinancesBill.

forces, deputy directors or persons on the board of international organisations. Examples of such organisations include the International Monetary Fund, World Bank and organs of the United Nations. In future, there will be more clarity over who is a 'high-ranking' or 'prominent' official. The European Parliament and Council's Fifth Anti-Money Laundering Directive (5MLD), which was published in the European Union's *Official Journal* on 19 June 2018, will oblige states to publish a list. Although the UK will be outside of the EU by the time it is transposed into law, it can be expected to follow suit.

4.11 Whilst the scope of a PEP under the UWO provisions excludes domestic and EEA PEPs, it is still very broad. The current applicable definition in Article 3 of the European Parliament and Council's Fourth Anti-Money Laundering Directive (4MLD), casts a wide net. 'Family members' extends to spouses or equivalent, children and parents. 'Close associates' includes persons known to have joint beneficial ownership of entities with the prominent function holder or 'any other close business relations' with them.[9] The reference to 'connected persons' further widens the ambit of a PEP. Section 1122 of the Corporation Tax Act 2010, to which reference is made in section 362B(9) POCA 2002, defines a 'connected' individual as a relative, relatives of spouses or civil partners and, in turn, spouses or civil partners of those relatives. As for companies, they will be 'connected' where a person, who is either the subject individual or persons connected to the subject individual, has control. Trustees can also fall within the definition of 'connected' persons.

4.12 Importantly, where a person is a non-UK or non-EEA PEP, they do not need to be suspected of any criminal activity for a UWO to be obtained against them.

Criminal suspects and connected persons

4.13 A UWO can also be obtained against persons who are suspects of serious crime or connected to such persons. The court must be satisfied to the civil standard that there are reasonable grounds to suspect that the person is involved in serious crime or that a person connected to the respondent is or has been involved in serious crime: section 362B(4) POCA 2002.

4.14 A 'person reasonably suspected' of involvement in serious crime, past or present, in the UK or elsewhere refers to a person suspected of involvement in a crime listed in Schedule 1 Serious Crime Act 2007. The list includes but is not limited to offences of drug trafficking, modern slavery, firearms, prostitution and child exploitation, armed robbery, money laundering, fraud, tax evasion, bribery, organised crime and breach of financial sanctions. Aiding as well as attempting such an offence is covered. A suspect's 'connected persons' are, as detailed above, defined in section 1122 Corporation Tax Act 2010.

4.15 As is well established under the principles of criminal law, a criminal suspicion must be founded on a reasonable basis and is to be objectively assessed.[10] The information required to support a reasonable suspicion is of a lower standard that that required to establish a *prima facie* criminal case. Reasonable suspicion can be supported by information

---

9 Directive EU 2015/849 on the prevention of the use of the financial system for the purposes of money laundering or terrorist financing [2015], article 3(11).

10 See, for instance, paragraph [2.3A] of PACE Code G applicable to arrest without warrant on the basis that there are 'reasonable grounds to suspect' involvement in an offence.

which would not be admissible evidence.[11] Practically, on a UWO application, criminal intelligence is likely to be disclosed to the court in support of a suspicion. The Code of Practice pertaining to investigations under POCA 2002, issued pursuant to section 377 POCA 2002 in January 2018, contemplates that reasonable suspicion will be linked to current and accurate intelligence as well as information on how the individual was identified by law enforcement, previous intelligence holdings on the person, previous law enforcement involvement with the person and details of suspected links with criminal activities or organisations.[12] However, it remains to be seen quite how comprehensive the information provided in support of a criminal suspicion will be. In at least one jurisdiction in Australia, a country which has had unexplained wealth laws for several years, a court recently presiding over a UWO-related application was satisfied that there was reasonable suspicion of criminal activity where the applicant officer deposed that his suspicion was principally based on his reading of the 'fact sheet' prepared by another officer following an individual's arrest.[13]

4.16 A further point to note is that where a person is suspected of serious crime or a connected person, there is no requirement for a criminal investigation to have formally commenced in relation to the suspect or for it to have advanced to any stage. When consideration turns to the other requirements for the making of a UWO, it is apparent that satisfying the court that there is a reasonable basis for a criminal suspicion might not necessarily be all that difficult. This is because where there is information suggesting that a person's lawful income is inconsistent with particular property – another requirement of a UWO that is examined below – this of itself is likely to support a reasonable suspicion that a person is involved in a tax evasion offence. Both the offences of fraudulently evading income tax, contrary to section 106A Income Tax Management Act 1970, and cheating the revenue at common law appear in the list of serious crimes in Schedule 1 Serious Crime Act 2007.

Companies

4.17 As for companies, the UWO framework has the capacity to capture those too. Applying the definition in section 1122 Corporation Tax Act 2010, a company can be 'connected' to the holder of a prominent political function as well as 'connected' to a person suspected of serious criminal activity. Subject to the legal principles underpinning corporate criminal liability,[14] a company can also be a criminal suspect in its own right.

4.18 Interestingly, when UWOs were first proposed, paragraph [54] of the Explanatory Notes to the Criminal Finances Bill 2016, published on 22 February 2017, described them as an order 'requiring an individual to set out the nature and extent of their interest in the property'. This was somewhat curious as it would have meant that property could easily be out of the reach of a UWO where it was owned or otherwise held by a company as opposed to an individual. The position has since been clarified. The Act expressly contemplates the use of a UWO against companies and LLPs registered in the UK as well as outside of the

---

11 *Hussein v Chong Fook Kam* [1970] AC 942.
12 See paragraphs 28–31.
13 *New South Wales Crime Commission v Arthur Calvert* [2017] NSWSC 13.
14 In the UK, the 'directing mind' theory of corporate criminal liability primarily applies, *Tesco Supermarkets Limited v Natrass* [1971] UKHL 1.

UK. In the context of UWOs, section 362H(5) POCA 2002 provides that corporates can be captured:

> (5) References to a person who holds or obtains property include any body corporate, whether incorporated or formed under the law of a part of the United Kingdom or in a country or territory outside the United Kingdom.

Holding property

4.19 The second requirement for the making of a UWO relates to the person's 'holding' of the property. Section 362B POCA 2002 provides that:

> (2) The High Court must be satisfied that there is reasonable cause to believe that –
> (a) the respondent holds the property, and
> (b) the value of the property is greater than £50,000.

4.20 The definition of 'property' includes money, all forms of real or personal property and intangible property and can be located anywhere in the world: section 414 POCA 2002. As the UWO is an order in respect of property, the applicant is required to specify or describe the property in relation to which explanation is sought. More than one item of property can be specified. Notably, the value threshold applies to the entire pool of property as opposed to the value of the respondent's *interest* in the property. Evidence of property valuation will be required but, in the context of suspected serious criminality, the relatively low threshold is likely to be easily satisfied. In the early stages of the Criminal Finances Bill, the financial threshold initially proposed was £100,000. Following a recommendation by the Lords, it was halved so as to not disadvantage law enforcement agencies outside of London where conventionally property values are lower or suspected illicit proceeds are more evenly distributed.[15]

4.21 If a respondent has 'effective control' over the property, they will hold it. Practically, indicators of effective control include a person's ability to deal with the property and make decisions affecting it such as in relation to sale or use. Control can be direct or indirect and will include where a person exercises, is able to exercise control or has a right to acquire the property: section 362H(2) POCA 2002. Beneficial owners are clearly captured. Particularly relevant to real estate appearing to be inconsistent with a person's wealth, the Act recognises that property can be held by a respondent even where other persons may also hold it or have an interest in it: section 362B(5) POCA 2002.

Property held by a company or trust

4.22 As discussed, the location of the property within a corporate structure will not serve as a bar to a UWO. The same is true in relation to property that is held by a trust. In regards to trusts, the provisions clarify that property will be held by a person where they are 'the trustee of a settlement in which the property is comprised' or an 'actual or potential' beneficiary in relation to such a settlement: section 362H(5) POCA 2002.

---

15 House of Commons Hansard, 26 April 2017, Volume 624 available at: https://hansard.parliament.uk/Commons/2017-04-26/debates/35841E55-C673-4D18-B286-BF259EB27F17/CriminalFinancesBill, accessed 8 April 2018.

4.23 Notably, the reference to a 'potential' beneficiary indicates that a UWO could capture an individual who simply *could* stand to benefit from a discretionary trust and/or is one of a class of possible beneficiaries. There is also an argument that the provisions are sufficiently wide to capture an actual or potential beneficiary who is detailed in a 'letter of wishes', a non-public document created and stored separately to the trust deed which indicates the settlor's intentions.[16] Parliament's decision to include specific trust-related provisions in the legislation means that it can be expected that UWOs will be used to target property held within a trust at some point. Notwithstanding this, the ability of a UWO to penetrate opaque trust structures and bring pressure to bear on trustees and beneficiaries should not be overstated. For a UWO to be made against a corporate entity, trustee or actual or potential beneficiary, the person would still first have to fall into the category of either a non-UK or non-EEA PEP as defined in section 362B(7) POCA 2002 or a criminal suspect or person connected to one.

Timing

4.24 As for timing matters, whether the respondent obtained the property *prior* to the commencement of the provisions is irrelevant to the making of a UWO: section 362B(5)(b) POCA 2002. Conceivably, a UWO could be deployed to investigate property acquired years earlier so long as there is reasonable basis to believe that it is still held by the respondent. A UWO, however, is unlikely to be sought in relation to property obtained many years ago. UWOs have been configured as a new lever to Part 5 civil recovery proceedings in the High Court and there is another deadline to consider. At present, the limitation period for civil recovery proceedings commenced under Chapter 2, Part 5 POCA 2002 is 20 years from when the property was obtained.[17]

Insufficient means to obtain property

4.25 The third requirement for the making of a UWO is that there are reasonable grounds to suspect that the respondent's known sources of lawful income are insufficient to enable them to obtain the property: section 362B(3) POCA 2002. The suspicion is objectively assessed and must be supportable. The standard to be met, however, is lower than that of 'reasonable cause to believe' – the standard required to be met to satisfy the court that the respondent holds the property in question.

Known sources of lawful income

4.26 Section 362B(6)(d) clarifies that 'known' sources of the respondent's income are the sources of income (whether arising from employment, assets or otherwise) that are reasonably ascertainable from 'available information' at the time of making the order. 'Lawful

---

16 Regulation 44(5) of the Money Laundering, Terrorist Financing and Transfer of Funds (Information on the Payer) Regulations 2017 requires a trustee to, on request, provide information to any law enforcement authority about any other individual referred to as a 'potential beneficiary' in any document relating to a trust such as a letter of wishes.

17 Section 27A Limitation Act 1980. The limitation period was increased from 12 years in 2011 by section 62 of the Policing and Crime Act 2009.

income' refers to income obtained lawfully under the laws of the country from where it arises: section 362B(6)(c) POCA 2002.

4.27 When examining a person's known sources of lawful income, the code of practice relating to POCA 2002 investigations contemplates the use of open-source material as well as information gathered from within the UK and other jurisdictions. Aside from financial transaction records obtained from a person's known banks, the best evidence of a disparity between a person's lawful income and their property is likely to be drawn from their tax returns or other such disclosures to the state in relation to income. In terms of open-source material, corporate records showing distributions or public records of salaries of prominent function holders are also likely to assist. In several jurisdictions, public officials are under a legal duty to disclose their assets and income and the information is contained in public registers.

4.28 Presently, the depth of financial analysis required to be undertaken by the applicant enforcement authority in support of a UWO application is unclear. Certainly, the Australian experience of UWOs suggests that before an order is granted, the court will be interested in examining a person's income sources, withdrawals and expenses during the period they allegedly acquired the suspicious property to assess whether there is apparent disproportionality. In the recent case of *New South Wales Crime Commission v Elskaf*,[18] the court reproduced the detail of forensic accounting evidence highlighting an inconsistency between a person's income and expenditure in its written reasons for ordering a UWO.

Trusts

4.29 When assessing whether a person who is part of a trust has insufficient means to 'obtain' property within the settlement, the reference to 'obtaining property' is to be construed as if the respondent has already obtained direct ownership of such a share in the settled property: section 362B(e) POCA 2002. The court will look to whether there is a reasonable suspicion that the lawful income of, say, a trust beneficiary is inconsistent with their acquisition of the settled property.

4.30 In addition to actual or potential beneficiaries, trustees can also 'hold' property and therefore can be a respondent to a UWO: section 362H(2)(b) POCA 2002. The use of a UWO in relation to a trustee, however, raises an interesting practical question. Is the court to look to the trustee's known personal income streams to see whether there is an inconsistency with the property held by a trust? On the face of the legislation, where the trustee holds property, satisfaction of the third requirement would require a contrived inquiry into whether the trustee's known lawful sources of income are disproportionate to his or her 'holding' of the property that is part of a settlement. This is somewhat nonsensical since the trustee is not the person who would have incurred the costs of obtaining the property in the first place. His or her lawful income has no relationship to or bearing on the acquisition of the property. Where a trustee's known income source is, for instance, a professional salary and the trust property targeted by the UWO is high value, the requirement of 'insufficient means' will be very easily satisfied.

---

18 [2017] NSWSC 681.

Market value

4.31 When considering whether the respondent had the lawful means to obtain the property in question, it is to be assumed that the respondent obtained the property for a price corresponding to its market value: section 362B(6) POCA 2002. However, when market value should be determined is not addressed in the legislation. Is the market price, for instance, to be determined at the time of the UWO application or when it is thought that the respondent obtained the property? The latter information may not be known to the enforcement authority. Still, the key question is likely to be whether, at the time the respondent is thought to have obtained the property, they had the lawful means to afford it. In considering whether the respondent had insufficient means to afford the property, the court is required to take into account mortgages or other security that may have been reasonably available to the respondent for the purposes of obtaining the property: section 362B(3) POCA 2002.

Effect of a UWO

4.32 If a High Court judge is satisfied that each of the above three requirements are fulfilled, a UWO may be made. The language used in the legislation indicates that the court retains discretion over the making of the order and its provisions. Section 362A POCA 2002 refers to 'may' as opposed to 'must'[19] or 'shall':

(1) The High Court may, on an application made by an enforcement authority, make an unexplained wealth order in respect of any property if the court is satisfied that each of the requirements for the making of the order is fulfilled.

4.33 If the order is made, it will require the respondent to provide a statement setting out the nature and extent of their interest in the subject property, an explanation of how the property was obtained which is to include the costs incurred in obtaining it and other information 'as may be so specified': section 362A POCA 2002. Accordingly, the applicant enforcement authority can request that the order compel the respondent to provide particular details and produce documents: section 362(5) POCA 2002. The information is to be provided to the enforcement authority within the time period specified in the order.

Trustee respondents

4.34 Where the respondent is a trustee, the order will require the respondent to provide a statement 'setting out such details of the settlement as may be specified': section 362A(3)(d) POCA 2002. It can be expected that information sought about the settlement will be focused rather than general in nature since a considerable amount of information about a trust is already available to enforcement authorities. Since 26 June 2017, all UK trusts[20] and non-UK trusts with UK assets or income streams on which tax is payable have been

---

19 Contrast the provisions for the making of a restraint order in Part 2 POCA 2002.
20 For the definition of a 'UK trust' see regulation 42 of the Money Laundering, Terrorist Financing and Transfer of Funds (Information on the Payer) Regulations 2017.

obliged to provide details on the creation of the trust including where and when it was established, the names of its professional advisers, trust assets and legal and individual owners of the trust.[21] The information is recorded in the UK's trust register maintained by HMRC. As such, a UWO is likely to be used to acquire more specific information about settlements which are already known to HMRC or against trusts that are not captured by the UK's trust register.

Providing the explanation

4.35 A UWO must specify the form in which the statement is to be given, the person to whom it is to be given and the place at which it is to be given or 'if it is to be made in writing' the address to which it is to be sent: section 362A(4)(c) POCA 2002. The latter suggests that it will be possible for the order to require a statement to be made in person. The time frame for providing the statement, referred to as the 'response period', or any other requirements of the UWO will be specified in the order. Unlike in Australia where the explanation in response to a UWO is provided to the court, in the UK the statement in compliance with the UWO is provided to the applicant enforcement authority.

Interim freezing

4.36 Interim freezing orders (IFOs) may accompany a UWO, prohibiting the respondent or any other person with an interest for dealing with the property in question: section 362J POCA 2002. The application for an IFO must be made at the same time as the UWO application and the order itself can be combined in one document with the UWO.

4.37 Consistent with the making of a property freezing order pursuant to section 245A in Part 5 POCA 2002, the court may only make an IFO if it considers that it is necessary for avoiding the risk of any subsequent recovery order being frustrated: section 362J(2) POCA 2002. This is the sole consideration but factors such as the likelihood of the property being dissipated or moved to circumvent civil forfeiture and the ability to monitor the property by other means are likely to undermine the necessity of the IFO.

4.38 Once an IFO is made, the court may appoint a receiver to manage the property: section 362N POCA 2002. The court also has power to stay any action or legal process in respect of the property: section 362M POCA 2002.

Non-compliance

4.39 Unsurprisingly, severe consequences follow a failure to comply with a UWO. Being a court order, breach can expose a respondent to proceedings for contempt of court. The legislation also expressly triggers a draconian presumption that the property that is the subject of the UWO is recoverable under Part 5 POCA 2002. Once a Part 5 claim is filed by the enforcement authority in the High Court, the onus is placed on the respondent who

---

21 Regulation 45 of the Money Laundering, Terrorist Financing and Transfer of Funds (Information on the Payer) Regulations 2017.

failed to comply with the UWO to prove as part of his or her defence that the property is not recoverable. Section 362C POCA 2002 states:

(1) This section applies in a case where the respondent fails, without reasonable excuse, to comply with the requirements imposed by an unexplained wealth order in respect of any property before the end of the response period.
(2) The property is to be presumed to be recoverable property for the purposes of any proceedings taken in respect of the property under Part 5, unless the contrary is shown.

4.40 In essence, a respondent would have to show that the property has a legitimate source and is *not* derived from unlawful conduct.

4.41 Notably, the recoverability presumption will only arise where the respondent's *interest* in the property that is the subject of the UWO is more than £50,000. This is different to the financial requirement for the making of a UWO that relates to value of the entire *property* value as opposed to the value of the respondent's interest. The presumption will only apply to the respondent's interest in the property but there is one qualification. Where a recoverability presumption has been triggered, special provisions apply to UWO respondents who are only respondents by virtue of their connection with a criminal suspect or a prominent political function holder. Where a person is a respondent because of their relationship, the recoverability presumption attaches to their interest in the property as well as the interest believed to belong to the criminal suspect or prominent function holder: section 326C(7),(8) POCA 2002. Both would be defendants to the Part 5 claim.

4.42 The consequences will only arise where there has been non-compliance with a UWO without reasonable excuse. No definition is provided for 'reasonable excuse' and examples are not specified in the code of practice applicable to POCA 2002 investigations issued by the Home Office in early 2018. Notwithstanding this, it is the perspective of a prudent person that must be adopted. Whether or not non-compliance is due to unforeseeable or unusual events beyond the respondent's control is likely to be a key consideration.[22] Typical examples include illness or unexpected delays, but could well also include difficulties in obtaining documents from third parties to answer the UWO. Importantly, there will be no non-compliance where respondent has made genuine effort to comply with the UWO but may not have met all of the requirements: section 326C(5) POCA 2002.

Timing

4.43 If a freezing order, an IFO, accompanies or is part of the UWO, the enforcement authority is required to decide whether to bring further investigatory proceedings or Part 5 proceedings under POCA 2002 within 60 days of the respondent's compliance. If no such proceedings are to be brought, the High Court must be informed within the 60-day time limit: section 362D(3) POCA 2002.

4.44 Notably, if there is no IFO accompanying the UWO, the applicant enforcement authority may decide to take steps in relation to the property at any time: section 362D(5) POCA 2002.

---

22 See *Propaye v HMRC* (2011) UK FTT 136 TC 001010.

Extra-territoriality

4.45 Having examined the effect of a UWO, its reach also falls to be considered. In this respect, the UWO is striking. As with other measures available under Parts 2 and 5 POCA 2002, a UWO may be ordered against property located outside of the UK. Chapter 4 of Part 8 POCA 2002 defines key terms. 'Property' is addressed in section 414 –

> (1) Property is all property *wherever situated* and includes –
>   (a) money;
>   (b) all forms of property, real or personal, heritable or moveable;
>   (c) things in action and other intangible or incorporeal property. (emphasis added)

4.46 The person who is to respond to a UWO can also be located anywhere. Section 362A(2)(b) provides that a UWO application must:

> (b) specify the person whom the enforcement authority thinks holds the property ('the respondent') (and the person specified may include a person outside the United Kingdom).

4.47 When read together, the extra-territoriality of the UWO is clear and there are compelling policy reasons for such an approach. As recognised in 2013 when Part 5 POCA 2002 was amended to include clear extra-territorial provisions in the wake of the Supreme Court's decision in *Perry v SOCA*,[23] ill-gotten proceeds are 'rarely held in one country and are often placed in jurisdictions where recovery is difficult'.[24] Persons may also choose to keep or invest their wealth in the UK even if it derives wholly from illicit conduct that has occurred or abroad and they are not in the UK. With this in mind, the legislation also expressly recognises that where the respondent to a UWO is suspected of serious criminal activity, the conduct need not have taken place in the UK: section 362B(4) POCA 2002. Furthermore, the legislation does not contain any requirement that UWO respondents are resident, domiciled or present in the UK.

4.48 The potentially enormous reach of a UWO is in keeping with other recent legislative developments in the UK targeting suspicious wealth and financial crime. Arguably, however, the UWO goes a step further. On the face of the provisions, a nexus with the UK is not required for the tool to be used. Supplementary material, however, suggests the opposite. When POCA 2002 was first introduced, Parliament was clear that the courts should only deal with cases with 'some connection' to the UK.[25] A connection will be easily satisfied when the respondent or property is in the UK but just how strong it must be and how else it might be demonstrated – or even whether this remains the case well over a decade since POCA 2002 was enacted – is a live question. It is likely to be tough for an enforcement authority in the UK to argue that it is in the public interest to pursue a UWO in the High Court against a PEP with no connection whatsoever to the UK but the extra-territoriality of the UWO is open-textured. This is especially so in the wake of *R v Rogers*[26] where, referring to the international nature of modern banking and financial transactions, the Court of Appeal considered that the money laundering offences in Part 7 POCA 2002

---

23 [2012] UKSC 35.
24 See the Explanatory Notes to section 48 of the Crime and Courts Act 2013 which effectively overturned the Supreme Court's judgement in *Perry v SOCA* [2012] UKSC 35 which considered that orders made under Chapter 2 Part 5 POCA 2002 did not extend to property outside the jurisdiction of the court.
25 Ibid.
26 [2014] EWCA Crim 1680.

could capture conduct occurring entirely abroad and took an expansive view of 'money laundering' in section 340(11) POCA 2002.

4.49 In any event, where a respondent or the property that is the subject of a UWO is located abroad, there are express provisions for overseas enforcement. Service of persons overseas is to be dealt with according to the usual civil procedure rules for service outside the jurisdiction.[27] Furthermore, under section 362S POCA 2002, if there is a risk that a subsequent recovery order may be frustrated, the Secretary of State may request the assistance of the receiving country to secure the property that is the subject of a UWO:

(1) This section applies if –
   (a) the High Court makes an unexplained wealth order in respect of any property,
   (b) it appears to the enforcement authority that the risk mentioned in section 362J(2) applies in relation to the property, and
   (c) the enforcement authority believes that the property is in a country outside the United Kingdom (the receiving country).
(2) The enforcement authority may send a request for assistance in relation to the property to the Secretary of State with a view to it being forwarded under this section.
(3) The Secretary of State may forward the request for assistance to the government of the receiving country.
(4) A request for assistance under this section is a request to the government of the receiving country –
   (a) to secure that any person is prohibited from dealing with the property;
   (b) for assistance in connection with the management of the property, including with securing its detention, custody or preservation.

4.50 Whether the request for assistance is acceded to is, of course, a matter for the authorities of the receiving country. At least in the short term, enforcement authorities can be expected to focus on respondents with property *in* the UK. Where a respondent to a UWO is a well-connected non-EEA PEP, wider political issues may present obstacles to the enforcement of a UWO and accompanying freezing order in a foreign country. The relationship between the PEP and the political party in power is likely to be a key factor. Also foreseeable are difficulties with obtaining evidence from overseas jurisdictions in support of the UWO application. The applicant authority must gather and produce sufficient evidence to satisfy a High Court judge that the respondent meets all of the requirements for the making of a UWO. Financial evidence will be more easily gathered where there is not the need to rely on material from international counterparts. Accordingly, even though the UWO has broad extra-territorial potential, these considerations suggest that in practice UWOs will typically be deployed against property in the UK and persons with a presence in the UK.

---

27 See the Code of Practice applicable to POCA 2002 investigations at [181].

CHAPTER 5

Challenging and responding to an unexplained wealth order

Introduction

5.1 Curiously, the legislation does not contain express provisions for the variation and discharge of a UWO made in England and Wales and Scotland.[1] There are instead express provisions for the variation and discharge of IFOs. Section III of the Practice Direction applicable to Civil Recovery Proceedings, amended in March 2018, however, sets out the process for applying to discharge or vary a UWO. Paragraph 12.1A of Section III of the Practice Direction provides for applications to vary and discharge by the appropriate officer of the enforcement authority or any person affected by the order.

5.2 As for matters that may be raised on the application to discharge a UWO, it will be interesting to see whether issue is taken with the reverse onus which is at the heart of the framework in due course. The process may be draconian but the exacting criminal due process rights enshrined in Article 6(2) and (3) of the European Convention of Human Rights (ECHR), such as innocence until guilt is proven, are not engaged as a UWO is a civil order and the civil recovery regime is distinct from criminal proceedings. The right to fairness in Article 6(1) and property in Article 1 of Protocol 1 offer protection but recent decisions of the European Court of Human Rights indicate that considerable latitude is afforded to civil recovery tools. In 2015, the Fourth Section of the European Court of Human Rights in *Gogitidze & Ors v Georgia*,[2] unanimously held that a Georgian civil recovery framework with a reverse onus feature did not violate the Convention rights.

Contentious areas

5.3 The primary battleground on an application to discharge a UWO is instead likely to be whether the court can be satisfied that all three requirements for the making of a UWO have been fulfilled. A respondent may, for instance, challenge the ability for a UWO to be made against them. In the context of a criminal suspect, one way of doing so is to query the grounds upon which the 'reasonable suspicion' is founded, if at least some of that information is disclosed, or to challenge whether the suspected conduct amounts to a serious crime in Schedule I of the Serious Crimes Act 2007.

5.4 Relatedly, where a UWO has been made against a respondent because of their relationship with a prominent function holder or criminal suspect, they may challenge the existence of the connection, its nature or depth. The sufficiency and reliability of information identifying the UWO respondent as a 'close associate' of a prominent function holder – and therefore a PEP – may be open to challenge. Furthermore, in the context of

---

1 The position is different in Northern Ireland. Section 362I(4) POCA 2002 expressly states that the High Court in Northern Ireland may discharge or vary the order.
2 [2015] ECHR 536.

PEPs with alleged unexplained wealth, the issue of immunity could arise. Whilst corrupt kleptocrats are billed as targets of the UWO framework, a person entrusted with a prominent political function, such as former or present heads of state, government ministers and state officials, may have the benefit of political immunity from legal proceedings. Under international law, the immunity serves as a procedural bar to legal proceedings in certain situations. Although the question of immunity was raised in the House of Lords when the Criminal Finances Bill was being considered, it was not resolved. Quite how the principles interact with and affect UWOs is uncharted territory.[3]

5.5 The relationship or lack of between the respondent and property in question could be another area of dispute. For a UWO to be ordered in relation to particular property and compel the respondent to explain themselves, the respondent must hold the property. When seeking to discharge a UWO, any distance between the respondent and the property in question provides a foundation for the respondent to contest sufficient control or interest in the property. If interest is not in issue, consideration may also turn to evidence that the property is worth less than £50,000 – the financial threshold that must be met for a UWO to be made in relation to the property.

5.6 If a UWO is to be challenged, the question arises whether there is actually a reasonable cause to believe that there is a discrepancy between lawful income and the property in question. On a discharge application, the application may, for instance, choose to explain to the court how they lawfully obtained the property and adduce evidence of sufficient means drawn from domestic and international income sources. Satisfactory explanations may turn on evidence that the property was a gift from a loved one, inheritance or a prize. Separately, a document trail of records supporting loans, property sale, salary, income from investments and tax disclosures may be relied upon. Evidence may include copies of professionally audited accounts. Although the information may serve as a basis to contest the UWO, taking such a course could well amount to prematurely providing a statement in relation to the property. Where detailed information about how the property was obtained is provided to the authorities to examine, the objective of the UWO regime will be satisfied.

5.7 Other than the three requirements, the legislation does not envisage the court considering other matters on a UWO application. Unlike in Australia, there is no public interest criteria but still, it would seem that the decision to order a UWO is discretionary. This raises the possibility of a UWO being challenged for being unnecessary or unfair. For instance, the question arises whether a UWO could be successfully discharged if it is apparent that the information could be obtained another way, without the need for such coercion. According to the code of practice applicable to POCA 2002 investigations issued by the Home Office in January 2018, the aim of a UWO is to 'access evidence that otherwise would not be available'. Although not an absolute requirement, the code considers that an applicant enforcement authority should consider alternative tools of investigation before making a UWO application.[4] Whether the information is available through the UK trusts register or other property-related registers, is already known to or accessible by the

---

3 Charlette Bunn, 'The Interaction Between Immunity Principles and UWO Proceedings' (White Collar Crime Centre, January 2017), www.brightlinelaw.co.uk/images/Unexplained_Wealth_Order_-_Briefing_Papers_Final.pdf, accessed 20 September 2017. This point was also flagged by Lord Hodgson in the Second Reading of the Criminal Finances Bill on 9 March 2017: see https://hansard.parliament.uk/Lords/2017-03-09/debates/294ABC93-8E53-4310-AED6-E9A83FF867DB/CriminalFinancesBill.

4 Paragraph 176.

enforcement authority or could be obtained by a less intrusive route such as a production order may be relevant to a discharge application.

5.8 Legal argument over the issuance of the UWO could also arise if compliance would be impossible. Destruction or loss of personal records, for example, because of age or data protection requirements could cast doubt over the fairness of an order requiring a respondent to provide property information or produce certain documentation. Similarly, fairness considerations may be engaged where personal records are not accessible because of the closure of businesses or a lack of co-operation by third parties located abroad. A lack of records may render it impossible for a respondent to ever detail the lawful provenance of the property that is the subject of the UWO.

5.9 As for variation, any person affected by a UWO may apply to vary it. The sufficiency of the response period will be an issue to consider. A respondent's need to request documents from third parties – taking into account timeframes for subject access requests and gathering information that may be held overseas – may lead to the variation of the UWO's response period.

Challenging and varying an IFO

5.10 An IFO may be varied so as to enable the frozen property to be dealt with or to exclude property for the purposes of allowing a respondent reasonable living, business expenses and/or legal expenses: section 362L POCA 2002. In regards to the latter, the desirability of legal representation is an express consideration for the court: section 362L(6) POCA 2002. The conditions applicable to the legal expenses exclusion are the same as those applying to a property freezing order under section 245A POCA 2002. The procedure is also identical, requiring a statement of assets to be produced by the person seeking reasonable legal expenses and an estimate of costs for each stage of legal work. An application for reasonable legal expenses is unlikely to be successful where there is evidence that the respondent can fund legal representation by other means, such as by property not captured by the UWO, or rely on others to provide funding.[5]

5.11 As for the discharge of an IFO, if the UWO is successfully discharged an IFO relating to the property which forms part of the UWO or which is in force in parallel will also fall away. Conceivably, however, an application could be made to discharge an IFO even where a UWO is in force. The critical consideration for an IFO, as discussed, is whether it is 'necessary' for the purposes of 'avoiding a risk of frustrating a recovery order': section 362J POCA 2002. If the property can be monitored another way or there is no appreciable risk of it being moved or dissipated, the IFO could well be challenged.

5.12 The court has the discretion to discharge an IFO at any time. Under the legislation, it will be mandatory in two instances. The first is where: (1) the 60-day time limit for the making of a decision to institute Part 5 proceedings or take a further investigatory step has passed; and (2) a further 48 hours has passed and either a 'relevant application' has not been made by the enforcement authority or has been disposed of. A 'relevant application' refers to a restraint order under Part 2 POCA 2002 or a property freezing order or interim receiving order under Part 5 POCA 2002. The second instance is where the enforcement

---

5 See *SOCA v Azam* [2013] EWCA Civ 970.

authority has notified the court that no further proceedings will be brought: section 362K POCA 2002. Orders for the variation or discharge of an IFO may be made by a master or district judge where all parties consent.[6]

5.13 Any person affected by an IFO which has been discharged may apply to the court for compensation: section 362R POCA 2002. The application for compensation must be made within three months of the discharge date. The court's ability to make a compensation order is strictly limited to situations where it is satisfied that applicant has suffered loss and that there has been 'serious default' by the enforcement authority such that, without the default, the IFO would not have been made. The position is similar to that under Part 2 POCA 2002 concerning compensation for restraint and conviction-based confiscation orders. Enforcement authorities are afforded a wide berth.[7] In the context of the unexplained wealth laws, grave negligence or dishonesty that has had a decisive impact on the making of the IFO is required before compensation will be ordered. In the event that a compensation order is made, the compensation is payable by the enforcement authority who applied for the IFO: section 362R POCA 2002.

Costs

5.14 As to the issue of costs on a UWO-related application, the standard civil procedure rules will apply. A late proposal to include in the CFA 2017 a provision for mandatory costs capping orders in relation to all UWO applications was ultimately unsuccessful.[8]

Responding to a UWO

5.15 To properly respond to a UWO, the respondent must truthfully explain the provenance of the property that is the subject of it. They must set out the nature and extent of their interest in the property that is the subject of the UWO and explain how it was obtained 'including, in particular, how any costs incurred in obtaining it were met': section 362A(3) POCA 2002. Although a person is not required to waive legal and professional privilege, the need to provide information about the property expressly trumps any other disclosure restriction 'however imposed': section 362G(1) POCA 2002. This would include confidentiality clauses or duties. The legislation also introduces a new criminal offence of making a statement that the person knows is false or misleading in a 'material particular' or recklessly making such a statement: section 362E POCA 2002. On indictment, the offence is punishable by two years' imprisonment. In reality, it is highly questionable how many UWO respondents who, for example, have invested the proceeds of tax evasion in specific property would choose to be frank about their conduct. Theoretically, however, the UWO regime compels the respondent to be transparent about their wealth, including its dubious origins.

5.16 Typically, the respondent will provide information about the property and how it was funded in the form of a witness statement. On the face of the legislation, the extent to which a person should detail how the funds used to acquire the property were generated is not clear. In

---

6 See paragraph 12.1G of the Civil Recovery Proceedings Practice Direction.
7 See, for instance, *A v ACC* [2017] EWHC 301 (QB) which concerned compensation under Part 2 POCA 2002.
8 https://publications.parliament.uk/pa/bills/cbill/2016-2017/0097/amend/criminal_rm_rep_0207.pdf.

other jurisdictions with UWOs, such as New South Wales, a full description of the property interest including the nature, name of the person or firm possessing the title documents, date of acquisition and the source of the funds used to acquire the property will be necessary.[9] But just how far back should a person go when explaining their source of funds and producing supporting financial analysis and material? Presumably, if a luxury flat in central London was bought with the proceeds from the sale of shares in a company, a respondent will be expected in a witness statement to go into some detail about how and when the shares were first acquired and then sold. Evidence in support of the sale of the shares would be provided along with, where available, an audit trail of documents to support wider lawful income production.

5.17 The explanation, the property and all documents produced in support will be assessed by the enforcement authority with a view to commencing civil recovery proceedings under Part 5 POCA 2002 where appropriate. As to what will constitute a satisfactory explanation of the property is entirely unknown. It is axiomatic that the respondent's explanation will be carefully scrutinised but the extent to which the enforcement authority will be able to poke holes in it is bound to be case-specific. In cases which solely concern domestic income sources and assets, a considerable amount of material will be available to cross-check against the person's explanation. But where, for example, a respondent explains that property in the UK was acquired using funds in whole or in part lawfully generated from a business or businesses abroad, or other legitimate income sources abroad, and produces documents in support, the enforcement authority assessing the explanation in the UK will likely require the assistance of overseas counterparts to verify the information or obtain material which refutes it. Receiving assistance from overseas enforcement authorities is not always a straightforward process. The UK, for instance, lacks close, cooperative relationships with countries such as Iran and Russia. In circumstances where the enforcement authority is unable to gather information from abroad to refute the person's explanation of his or her foreign income sources, it is hard to see how any challenge to the explanation can be sustained. Additionally, the absence of an audit trial in support of an explanation should not necessarily mean that an explanation is unsatisfactory. The reasonableness of the explanation is dependent on the circumstances. In *Wiese v UK Border Agency*,[10] a claim for the recovery of half a million pounds of bundled cash at an airport, under Part 5 POCA 2002, the court was satisfied that the funds were not obtained through unlawful conduct even though an audit trail was not provided.

5.18 Further, disputing a respondent's explanation that their seemingly inconsistent wealth is traceable to a gift or derived from gambling has posed difficulties in other jurisdictions with UWOs. In Australia, the explanation of how the property was obtained is provided to the court along with the enforcement authority. Gambling winnings and gifts are not tax assessable and not required to be disclosed to the tax authority. Notably, in the absence of any records to the contrary, a respondent's explanation that property is derived from a gambling win or a gift has been held to be adequate in Australia.[11] The question arises as to whether similar explanations in response to a UWO could be accepted in the UK. Whilst there is greater awareness of the intersection of gambling and money laundering, certain wealth, including gambling wins and some financial gifts, are also not tax assessed in the UK.

---

9 *New South Wales Crime Commission v Susan Nehme* [2016] NSWSC 1410.
10 [2012] EWHC 2019 (Admin).
11 Booz, Allen & Hamilton, *Comparative Evaluation of Unexplained Wealth Orders* (Washington, DC: Department of Justice, January 2012), 79.

Use of the explanation

5.19 The UWO impact assessment report, published in November 2016 by the Home Office, noted that, 'if evidence is provided, it could be used by the investigative agency to further develop their case against the individual in a civil recovery investigation'. The evidence cannot be used in criminal proceedings against the respondent subject to a small handful of exceptions which include confiscation proceedings under Part 2 POCA 2002 and the criminal offence of failing to comply with a UWO. Section 362G POCA 2002 otherwise preserves the self-incrimination privilege:

> (1) A statement made by a person in response to a requirement imposed by an unexplained wealth order may not be used in evidence against that person in criminal proceedings.

5.20 The prohibition on the use of the response in criminal proceedings only applies to criminal proceedings against the respondent. This is an entirely conventional but important safeguard in any coercive investigation framework. It is also, on close examination of the legislation, the main qualification on the use of a UWO explanation. Aside from in criminal proceedings against the respondent, information and documents provided in response to a UWO can be put to wide use.

5.21 Section 362G POCA 2002 expressly authorises the enforcement authority to copy any documents provided in response to a UWO and to retain any documents if it is contemplated that they may need to be produced *'for the purposes of any legal proceedings'* and might be otherwise unavailable. The legislation is silent on the destruction of information and the use of the documents that are provided in answer to a UWO. Consequently, the provision highlights the broad investigative value of a UWO and potential for the derivative use of any information provided.

5.22 Aside from furthering civil recovery proceedings under Part 5 POCA 2002, information and documents provided in response to a UWO could be used to develop a criminal investigation into persons other than the UWO respondent. It is readily conceivable that when seeking to satisfy the enforcement authority of the legitimate provenance of their property, a person might provide full details of their assets, transactions, financial institutions, professional advisers, business partners and knowledge of corporate entities and trusts. In so doing, they are offering up lines of inquiry in relation to money flow, persons of interest and suspicious structures. Although the information may not be used against the person in criminal proceedings, there is nothing to stop it being used in this way against other individuals and corporate entities.

5.23 Subject to the information gateways, the information may also be shared with other enforcement authorities – including those abroad – for the purposes of criminal enforcement action against other individuals and corporate entities. So long as a legal basis is identified, the code of practice applicable to POCA 2002 investigations recognises that information that arises in the course of an investigation can be shared with the NCA, police, HMRC and other departments and agencies.[12] Seen this way, there is potential for UWOs to be used to develop or strengthen a criminal case against a person who is far more significant than the UWO respondent. This is particularly so when it is considered that the financial threshold for the making of a UWO is relatively low and that a person can be a respondent because

---

12 Paragraph 64.

of their relationship with either a prominent function holder or criminal suspect. A typical example is where a UWO is sought in relation to property held by the spouse of a PEP or the spouse of a criminal suspect. Another is where a UWO is sought in relation to a person who is either a suspect himself or herself or an associate of a suspect but is very much on the periphery of a criminal organisation. Notably, the code of practice is silent on the use of UWOs in this strategic manner.

5.24 The value of a UWO is also not limited to civil recovery or broader criminal investigations. The information provided in response could trigger an investigation into the conduct of financial institutions and regulated professional advisers, such as lawyers and estate agents, in a regulatory or civil context. If a person is on the receiving end of a UWO, their financial institutions and professional advisers must also be at risk of having their risk-management processes and dealings with the UWO respondent scrutinised.

Use of the new power

5.25 In February 2018, fewer than four weeks after the powers entered into force, the first two UWOs were obtained by the NCA. Both orders concerned super-prime real estate in London and south-east England.[13] The respondent in question hails from a Commonwealth of Independent States (CIS) state. Amidst the rising political concern over money laundering in the UK, the Home Office's original estimate that just 20 UWOs a year would be obtained 'after an initial year of no cases' is in need of revision following announcements that more are underway. Given the UWO's ability to serve as the first step in an investigation and potential for the response to be used in a variety of ways, it is of little surprise. The effect of a UWO is to coerce a respondent who may not necessarily even be a criminal suspect to explain how they generated their wealth and produce a supporting audit trail to be pored over. Whilst the reverse onus may be unfamiliar in the UK and what will constitute a satisfactory wealth explanation is unclear, UWOs are a coup for enforcement authorities. The financial information provided in answer to a UWO might otherwise have taken longer to gather or may not have been obtained at all, particularly if overseas assistance was required. A complication, however, could arise if evidence that would have supported the respondent's explanation of their wealth is no longer accessible. Such a scenario would engage concerns about the fairness of the UWO remaining in force.

5.26 Separately, another issue could arise when it is time for the enforcement authority to assess the UWO response. Although case-specific, it is likely that enforcement authorities in the UK will still have to turn to their overseas counterparts for assistance to verify or dispute an explanation that hinges on income, gifts or assets overseas. Where there is no evidence to the contrary, the rejection of a person's explanation of their wealth will be difficult to sustain. This, in practice, may mean there is a limit to the value of UWOs after all.

---

13 National Crime Agency, 'NCA Secures First Unexplained Wealth Orders' (28 February 2018), www.nationalcrimeagency.gov.uk/news/1297-nca-secures-first-unexplained-wealth-orders, accessed 7 June 2018.

CHAPTER 6

Search, seizure, forfeiture and 'gross human rights abuse'

6.1 On an initial review of the CFA 2017, one could be forgiven for thinking that the high-water mark of the changes are the new unexplained wealth orders and the new corporate offence. Certainly, both developments have generated the most attention. Even so, there are several other provisions that have been introduced by the CFA 2017 that are likely to have a greater impact on the day-to-day work of regulated professionals and lawyers alike. They include:

- new powers given to HM Revenue & Customs, the Serious Fraud Office, Financial Conduct Authority and immigration officers
- wider ability to forfeit property following civil proceedings and, in relation to cash and money held in accounts, administratively
- expansion of the definition of 'unlawful conduct' in Part 5 of the Proceeds of Crime Act 2002 (POCA 2002).

6.2 This chapter considers the implications of each of the above.

New powers to enforcement authorities

6.3 The extension of powers under the CFA 2017 not only ensures consistency between enforcement authorities in the UK but suggests that the use of non-conviction-based confiscation powers (otherwise known as the 'civil recovery' of property) will only increase in the future. Indeed, government guidance issued in January 2018 in respect of HM Revenue & Customs, the Serious Fraud Office, National Crime Agency, Financial Conduct Authority and Crown Prosecution Service, urges that 'asset recovery and financial investigation should be considered at an early stage in every case, including consideration of the non-conviction-based powers of forfeiture, civil recovery and taxation action'.[1]

Serious Fraud Office

6.4 Part 2 POCA 2002 provides for the restraint of assets and confiscation of a criminal benefit after a criminal conviction. Enforcement authorities are afforded search and seizure of property powers where a confiscation has been made or may be made against them. The rationale for the power is that unless the property is seized, it may otherwise diminish in value or be unavailable when it is time for the confiscation order to be satisfied. The ability

---

1 Guidance issued under section 2A Proceeds of Crime Act 2002, available at: https://assets.publishing.service.gov.uk/government/uploads/system/uploads/attachment_data/file/678293/2018_01_s2A_Guidance.pdf.

to search and seize is subject to obtaining appropriate approval from a justice of the peace or, if not reasonably practicable, a senior officer: section 47G POCA 2002.

6.5 Prior to the CFA 2017, Part 2 POCA 2002 search and seizure powers could only be exercised by an officer of HM Revenue & Customs, a police constable, immigration officer or an accredited financial investigator. The position was somewhat incoherent since the Serious Fraud Office, responsible for the most complex of financial crime cases, is a 'prosecutor' for the purposes of Part 2 restraint and confiscation orders. Schedule 1 of CFA 2017 amends Part 2 POCA 2002 to give staff of the Serious Fraud Office the search and seizure power.

6.6 Part 5 POCA 2002 establishes the regime for non-conviction-based seizure and forfeiture of cash in the magistrates' court, and the freezing and civil recovery of property in the High Court. Central to Part 5 POCA 2002 is the need for the cash or property to have been obtained by or intended for use in unlawful conduct.

6.7 Under section 289, select enforcement authorities have the power to search premises for recoverable cash. The cash may then be seized and detained by order of a justice of the peace or magistrate, and forfeited either administratively or following a magistrates' court hearing. Schedule 1 of CFA 2017 opens up the cash search and seizure powers, as well as the power to seek forfeiture of cash to staff of the Serious Fraud Office.

HM Revenue & Customs

6.8 Before the CFA 2017, HM Revenue & Customs was restricted in its use of the criminal financing investigation powers under Part 5 and Part 8 POCA 2002.

6.9 Powers, including the cash search and seizure powers detailed above, the ability to seek a production order compelling a person to produce documents in connection with a money laundering or property confiscation investigation or apply for a bank account monitoring order or customer information order,[2] were not available to HM Revenue & Customs when they related to 'excluded matters'. These, in brief, concerned certain taxes and allowances specified in Schedule 1 of the Commissioners for Revenue & Customs Act 2005: section 289(5A) POCA 2002. Section 18 of CFA 2017 lifts these restrictions, suggesting that HM Revenue & Customs will be more aggressive in future investigations.

6.10 The above prediction is only underscored by HM Revenue & Customs' new ability to commence a civil recovery investigation and proceedings for recovery of property in the High Court under Part 5 POCA 2002. The power is conferred by section 19 CFA 2017, which amends sections 316 and 378 POCA 2002.

Financial Conduct Authority

6.11 The power to commence a civil recovery investigation and proceedings in the High Court is also conferred on the Financial Conduct Authority, by virtue of section 20 CFA 2017. The new power further encourages the FCA to be highly strategic in its criminal

---

2 This is an order compelling a financial institution to provide any such information about a customer who is subject to a confiscation, civil recovery or money laundering investigation as specified by law enforcement: see section 363 of the Proceeds of Crime Act 2002.

prosecution of financial market wrongdoing as, in the absence of a criminal prosecution, illicit proceeds can still be targeted.

Immigration officers

6.12 In addition to the above, the CFA 2017 introduces several new provisions aimed at making it easier for immigration officers to seize and forfeit unlawful cash at immigration borders. Section 21 CFA 2017 extends the cash civil recovery powers, available under Part 5 POCA 2002, to immigration officers.

Offences

6.13 The criminal offences of assault and obstruction in the exercise of powers conferred by POCA 2002 have been amended to take into account the wider use of these powers by HM Revenue & Customs, immigration officers and officers of the Serious Fraud Office: sections 22–24 CFA 2017.

Civil cash and property forfeiture

6.14 The emphasis of civil recovery proceedings in the CFA 2017 is further reflected by the expansion of the definition of 'cash' vulnerable to seizure and forfeiture under Part 5 POCA 2002, the introduction of a new ability to recover in summary proceedings a 'listed asset' as well as to forfeit money in bank and building society accounts.

6.15 The provisions are replicated in the Terrorism Act 2000 (TACT 2000) and the Anti-Terrorism, Crime and Security Act 2001 (ACTSA 2001).

Cash

6.16 Section 14 CFA 2017 amends section 289(6) POCA 2002 to close a loophole in the definition of 'cash'. The definition is critical to the search, seizure, detention and forfeiture powers in Part 5 POCA 2002.

6.17 Previously, where suspected illicit funds had been converted into gambling tokens they could not be seized and summarily forfeited. Now, 'cash' includes, alongside notes and coins and banker's drafts:

- gaming vouchers, which are vouchers physically issued by a gaming machine representing a right to be paid the amount stated on it
- fixed-value casino tokens, representing the right to be paid the amount stated on it
- betting receipts, representing a physical receipt which gives a person the right to be paid the amount stated on it.

6.18 The expanded definition of 'cash' does not extend to cryptoassets or cryptocurrency.

6.19 The common feature is the need for any gambling document to state an amount and to represent a right to be paid that amount. As such, documents such as betting slips, which do not confer any right to be paid, fall outside the scope.

6.20 'Cash' that has been seized and detained is vulnerable to forfeiture either administratively upon the issuance of a forfeiture notice by the relevant enforcement authority or following successful forfeiture proceedings in the magistrates' court. The powers may only be used where the financial threshold, £1,000, has been met.[3]

Summary forfeiture of listed assets

6.21 A new framework for the forfeiture of certain high-value assets in the magistrates' court has also been introduced into the Proceeds of Crime Act 2002 to complement the cash forfeiture regime.

6.22 Chapter 3A of Part 5 POCA 2002 has been inserted by section 15 CFA 2017, enabling a constable, officer of HM Revenue & Customs, an SFO officer or accredited financial investigator to search for, seize and ultimately seek the detention and forfeiture of certain high-value 'listed assets' believed to have been obtained through unlawful conduct or to be intended for use in unlawful conduct. According to the 2017 Home Office impact assessment, which explains the rationale for the new regime, the following assets have been identified as being particularly susceptible to be used by criminals to store and move value both domestically and across international borders:

- precious metals (gold, silver or platinum only)
- precious stones
- watches
- artistic works
- face-value vouchers
- postage stamps.

6.23 These are the assets that fall within the category of 'listed assets' in new Chapter 3A and therefore, are vulnerable to being seized and eventually forfeited.

6.24 There are several procedural safeguards within the new regime that replicate those applicable to cash seizure. For example, exercise of the search and seizure powers is subject to approval first being obtained from a judicial officer (justice of the peace) or, if not practicable, a senior officer: section 303E POCA 2002. Enforcement authorities are guided in the exercise of the new powers over listed assets by a detailed code of practice, which was issued pursuant to section 303G POCA 2002 on 16 April 2018.[4] There is also (limited) provision for compensation and for victims of detained property to seek release. The powers, furthermore, are only available where the 'listed asset' has a minimum value of £1,000: section 303Y POCA 2002.

6.25 There is, however, one striking difference between the listed asset regime and the cash regime in Part 5 POCA 2002. Administrative forfeiture is not available for 'listed assets' whereas it is for seized cash in relation to which a justice of the peace or magistrate has authorised detention. The power of law enforcement to administratively forfeit

---

[3] Proceeds of Crime Act 2002 (Recovery of Cash in Summary Proceedings: Minimum Amount) Order 2006 (SI 2006 No. 1699).

[4] Home Office, *Code of Practice issued under 303G POCA 2002 Recovery of Listed Assets: Search Powers* (April 2018).

detained cash pursuant to section 297A POCA 2002 was introduced by section 65 of the Policing and Crime Act 2000 which came in to force in 2014. Whilst forfeiture of property without judicial oversight is a highly draconian feature of any legal system and is vulnerable to criticism, the slight difference in the approach to illicit cash and illicit mobile high-value assets does seem incoherent.

6.26 In 2017, the Home Office estimated that the number of 'listed asset' forfeiture cases would be 150–200 a year. It is projected that, on average, the value of the asset will be between £5,000 to £8,000.[5]

Account freezing and forfeiture

6.27 Law enforcement powers are further enhanced by the new ability to freeze and forfeit funds held in bank and building society accounts. Section 16 CFA 2017 introduces new Chapter 3B into Part 5 POCA 2002. Chapter 3B aligns closely with the cash forfeiture provisions and new 'listed asset' forfeiture provisions detailed above. The impact of this new power, however, should not be underestimated.

6.28 Prior to the CFA 2017, law enforcement were able to obtain bank account monitoring orders and identify suspicious accounts from suspicious activity reports (SARs) submitted by the regulated sector; but the route to freezing and ultimately forfeiting money in bank accounts was not straightforward. Freezing and forfeiture depended on the use of either Part 2 POCA 2002 powers (restraint and conviction-based confiscation) or Part 5 POCA 2002 powers (civil recovery).

6.29 Use of Part 5 powers presented several challenges. Axiomatically, money held in bank accounts is not 'cash'. Consequently, the ability to summarily forfeit the funds under Chapter 3 Part 5 POCA 2002 was not open. Further, although de-risking banks voluntarily suspend bank accounts because of suspicious activity, the subsequent recovery of the funds depended on the enforcement authority commencing civil recovery proceedings in the High Court. Quite apart from the time, money and investigative resources required to pursue High Court proceedings, the property in question must meet the £10,000 value threshold.[6]

6.30 According to the Home Office in its impact assessment of the new bank account freezing and forfeiture provisions, it is estimated that between £30 million and £50 million is sitting in accounts that have been suspended by banks and building societies in the UK. The new power presents a clear route to the recovery of the funds, so long as the court is satisfied that on that they have been obtained through unlawful conduct or are intended for use by any person in unlawful conduct. The power is open to HM Revenue & Customs, police, the National Crime Agency, Serious Fraud Office and accredited financial investigators.

Banks and building societies

6.31 As for what is a 'bank account' or a 'building society account', a bank is defined as an 'authorised deposit taker' that has its head office or a branch in the UK: section 303Z7

---

5 Home Office, Criminal Finances Act – Overarching Impact Assessment (20 June 2017), https://assets.publishing.service.gov.uk/government/uploads/system/uploads/attachment_data/file/621192/Impact_Assessment_-_CF_Act_Overarching.pdf, accessed 7 June 2018, paragraph 89.
6 Proceeds of Crime Act 2002 (Financial Threshold for Civil Recovery) Order 2003.

POCA 2002. The Act is silent on whether the account to be frozen must actually be maintained by a UK branch.

6.32 'Building society' is as defined in the Building Societies Act 1986. A building society is a society incorporated under that Act for the purpose of making loans secured on residential property and funded substantially by its members which has its principal office in the UK: section 5 Building Societies Act 1986.

6.33 Consistent with the regime for cash and listed asset forfeiture, there is a minimum financial threshold. The account must contain at least £1,000.

Account freezing

6.34 Where an enforcement officer has reasonable grounds for suspecting that money held in a bank or building society account is 'recoverable' (obtained through unlawful conduct) or intended for use in unlawful conduct, he or she may apply to the magistrates' court for an account freezing order. As the court in *SOCA v Matthews*[7] clarified, there is no need to identify a particular offence to satisfy 'unlawful conduct' for the purposes of Part 5 POCA 2002 proceedings. The unlawful conduct need not to take place in the UK.

6.35 Prior to the making of the application, the applicant must have obtained approval from a senior officer within his or her enforcement authority. The application will be successful where the court is satisfied that there are reasonable grounds for suspecting that all or part of the funds have been obtained through unlawful conduct or are intended for use in unlawful conduct. Once it is made, the order prohibits the making of withdrawals or payments from the account. All persons affected by the order must be given notice of it.

6.36 The framework contains provisions for the variation and discharge of the order and replicates the provisions elsewhere in Part 5 POCA 2002 for the exclusion of property for the purposes of reasonable living or business expenses and legal expenses.

Forfeiture

6.37 Forfeiture of money held in bank or building society accounts is available two ways:

- administratively by the enforcement authority on the issuance of an account forfeiture notice
- by order of a magistrates' court.

6.38 The provisions are identical to those applicable to cash forfeiture. For the funds to be forfeited, the decision maker must be satisfied on the balance of probabilities that the funds are recoverable property or intended for use in unlawful conduct.

Expansion of 'unlawful conduct'

6.39 In addition to the above, the advent of the CFA 2017 marks an expansion of the definition of 'unlawful conduct' in section 241 of Part 5 POCA 2002 to expressly include a gross human rights abuse or violation. The amendment to the definition is introduced by section 13 CFA 2017 and entered into force on 31 January 2018.

---

7 [2009] EWHC 1544 (Admin).

6.40 The purpose of the amendment, as explained by the Home Office, is to ensure that proceeds derived from gross human rights abuses overseas may be frozen and recovered under Part 5 POCA 2002. Underscoring the *in terrorem* effect, the government's overarching impact assessment of the CFA 2017, published in June 2017, records, '[the measure] demonstrates that the UK is a hostile environment for those who commit human rights abuses or violations abroad, and for the proceeds of these crimes if they are brought to the UK'.[8]

6.41 Prior to the CFA 2017, the definition of 'unlawful conduct' was subject to a dual criminality requirement. Proceeds could not be recovered in the UK if the underlying conduct, though regarded illegal under UK law, was considered legal in the country in which it took place. An impediment to civil forfeiture could particularly arise where proceeds were obtained through or derived from human rights abuse and yet, in the country in which the abuse took place, the conduct was legal, considered justified or 'state-sanctioned' by the government in power.

6.42 With this in mind, section 241(2A) contains the following provision which removes the dual criminality requirement in the context of a gross human rights abuse:

> (2A) Conduct which –
> (a) occurs in a country or territory outside the United Kingdom,
> (b) constitutes, or is connected with, the commission of a gross human rights abuse or violation (see section 241A), and
> (c) if it occurred in a part of the United Kingdom, would be an offence triable under the criminal law of that part on indictment only or either on indictment or summarily, is also unlawful conduct.

Gross human rights abuse or violation

6.43 New section 241A POCA 2002 goes on to define 'gross human rights abuse or violation' by reference to three conditions.

6.44 The first condition is that there has been the torture or cruel, inhuman and degrading treatment of a person who has 'sought to expose illegal activity carried out by a public official' or person acting in that capacity or who has sought to 'obtain, exercise or defend' human rights. The breadth of this term is likely to attract future judicial consideration. Conceivably, persons captured could include campaigners, political dissidents, investigative journalists as well as whistleblowers who have sought to expose grand corruption and civilians seeking to exercise, for instance, freedom of expression or worship.

6.45 The second condition is that the 'conduct', namely the torture or cruel, inhuman and degrading treatment, against the person has been carried out in consequence of the person having sought to expose the illegal activity or obtain, exercise or defend human rights.

6.46 The third condition is that the 'conduct' has been carried out by a public official or person acting in that capacity, or with the consent or acquiescence of such a person.

6.47 Subject to these conditions being satisfied, the unlawful conduct could also comprise of acting as agent in the commission of the gross human rights abuse or violation, directing or sponsoring such activities, materially assisting such activities, directing such activities or profiting from such activities: section 241A(5) POCA 2002. 'Material assistance' includes providing goods and services that assists the activities or providing financial or technological support.

---

8 Paragraph 51.

6.48 To fall into the category of 'unlawful conduct' for the purposes of Part 5 POCA 2002, all of the conditions must be satisfied to the civil standard. Gathering sufficient evidence is likely to be challenging but, even so, the amendment potentially exposes individuals as well as companies who deal in, receive, invest or profit from funds derived from abusive regimes to civil recovery proceedings in the UK.

6.49 The government's overarching impact assessment, published in June 2017, contains an example of how the new expanded definition could benefit law enforcement in practice. By way of illustration, the provision could be relied on where a government official participated in or was the architect of a state-sanctioned regime of abuse in an internment camp and had moved some of his salary into a UK bank account and purchased property in the UK. Under the previous framework, even if the abuse of, say, political campaigners and dissidents was well documented, civil proceedings for the recovery of funds in the official's bank account or UK property could not commence because it would not meet the dual criminality test. The amendment removes the impediment.

6.50 The question arises whether the provision could be relied on where a link between gross human rights abuse and funds or property is identifiable but less direct than in the scenario above. For property to be 'recoverable' under Part 5 POCA 2002, it must be obtained 'through' unlawful conduct, which means 'by or in return': section 242 POCA 2002. Axiomatically, a person's property rights under Article 1 Protocol 1 to the European Convention on Human Rights are at stake. However, in the context of concerns over the UK being a final resting place for so-called 'dirty money', how widely – or narrowly – this term will be interpreted by the courts remains to be seen.

CHAPTER 7

Terrorist financing and terrorist property

Introduction

7.1 As the UK's 2017 national risk assessment recognises, tackling financial activity and making greater use of financial intelligence is a major priority for law enforcement in the fight against domestic and global terrorism. Between October 2014 and September 2015, just 1,899 of the 381,882 suspicious activity reports (SARs) received by the National Crime Agency (NCA) were linked to terrorism.[1] This is perhaps because large-scale, coordinated terrorist financing is not the norm in the UK. Instead, financial support of terrorism is varied and typically low-level,[2] making it all the more difficult to detect. The movement of funds may be directed at supporting a small group planning on joining terrorist groups abroad. Recent experiences also show they may be directed at supporting a low-cost unsophisticated domestic attack perpetrated by just one or two individuals.

7.2 In the UK at least, a common method of terrorist fundraising is not identifiable.[3] Funds intended to be used to support terrorism may have been legitimately earned or may constitute personal savings. Equally, they may constitute the proceeds of a fraud orchestrated to raise funds to aid terrorism or comprise some of the profits of an organised criminal activity, such as drug trafficking, which seems unrelated to terrorist aims. Whilst the movement of terrorist funds can and does involve large financial institutions, depending on the end destination money may also be routed through money service businesses (MSBs) and personal couriers.

7.3 Against this backdrop, the CFA 2017 introduces several amendments to the Terrorism Act 2000 (TACT 2000) and the Anti-Terrorism, Crime and Security Act 2001 (ATCSA 2001) directed at further combating terrorist financing. The key measures comprise:

- disclosure orders
- an information-sharing framework for persons in the regulated sector
- further information orders
- expanded provisions for the civil recovery of terrorist property
- powers to freeze and forfeit money held in bank accounts.

7.4 The suite of new terrorist-financing measures will be discussed in this chapter. Several are identical in substance to others in the CFA 2017 that amend the Proceeds of Crime

---

1 Home Office, Criminal Finances Bill – Factsheet – Part 2 – Terrorist Finance (2016), https://assets.publishing.service.gov.uk/government/uploads/system/uploads/attachment_data/file/564477/CF_Bill_-_Factsheet_8_-_Terrorist_Finance.pdf, accessed 7 January 2018.
2 Paragraph 3.3.
3 HM Treasury and Home Office, *National Risk Assessment of Money Laundering and Terrorist Financing 2017* (2017), paragraph 3.5.

Act 2002 (POCA 2002) and apply to money laundering and civil recovery of property more generally. Consequently, the changes bring consistency to the legal framework targeting terrorist financing and criminal proceeds in the UK. However, there is one noticeable difference that reflects the prioritisation of the terrorist threat by policymakers and law enforcement in the UK. The CFA amends the TACT so that certain court orders made in connection with the investigation of terrorist financing, such as disclosure orders, account monitoring orders and production orders, are enforced throughout the UK. This is unique as there is not yet provision for cross-border enforceability of similar investigation orders made in the context of a money laundering or property recovery investigation.

Disclosure orders

7.5 Originally only used in property civil recovery and confiscation investigations,[4] a disclosure order is an order permitting law enforcement to issue any person considered to have information relevant to the investigation with a written notice compelling them to answer questions, disclose specified information and produce specific documents. The order is made by a Crown Court judge.

7.6 Section 35, together with Schedule 2, of the CFA 2017 introduce a framework for the making of a disclosure order in the context of a terrorist-financing investigation. The provisions entered into force on 31 January 2018. Appearing in Schedule 5A of the TACT 2000, the framework is very similar to the provisions for a disclosure order in a property confiscation investigation or, since the entry into force of sections 7 and 8 of CFA 2017, which was also on 31 January 2018, a money laundering investigation in Part 8 POCA.

Making the application

7.7 On application to a Crown Court judge, a disclosure order may be made in the context of a terrorist-financing investigation against *any* person. Applications may be made by a constable or counter-terrorism financial investigator subject to the authorisation of a senior police officer with the minimum rank of superintendent. Almost always they will be made 'on the papers' or without notice to a judge in chambers.

7.8 Where an order is made on the papers, there is no legal duty on the court to give reasons.[5]

7.9 In terms of procedural requirements of the application, the applicant must state in the application that a person or property is subject to a 'terrorist-financing investigation' and the order is sought for the purposes of the investigation: Schedule 5A(9) TACT 2000. The person against whom the disclosure order is sought need not be the subject or a subject of the investigation.

7.10 Part 1 of Schedule 5A of the TACT 2000 defines a 'terrorist-financing investigation' as an investigation into:

- the commission, preparation or instigation of an offence under sections 15–18 of the TACT, namely offences of terrorist fundraising, possession of funds or property for

---

4 A similar power is available to the Serious Fraud Office under section 2 of the Criminal Justice Act 1987.
5 *Nuttall & Anor v NCA* [2016] EWHC 1911 (Admin).

the purposes of terrorism, being concerned in an arrangement for the purposes of terrorism, payments under an insurance contract for the purposes of terrorism, and being concerned in an arrangement to facilitate terrorist property; and
- the identification of terrorist property or its movement or use.[6]

Terrorism

7.11 The definition of 'terrorism' is found in section 1 of the TACT 2000. It has, in essence, three strands:

- use of action or a threat to use action which involves serious violence against a person, serious damage to property, endangering of another person's life, serious risk to the health or safety of the public or a section of the public or which is designed to seriously interfere with or disrupt an electronic system;
- such use of action or threat of action is designed to influence the government, an international governmental organisation or to intimidate the public or a section of the public; and
- such use or threat is made for the purpose of advancing a political, religious, racial or ideological cause.

7.12 The 'action' includes that outside of the UK. Similarly, the reference to 'public' and 'government' is not UK-specific: section 1(4) TACT 2000.

Terrorist property

7.13 As for 'terrorist property', this is defined broadly in section 14 of the TACT 2000 and comprises money or other property likely to be used for the purposes of terrorism, proceeds of acts of terrorism and proceeds of acts carried out for the purposes of terrorism.

7.14 Proceeds can include any property that wholly or partly represents the proceeds of an act of terrorism, including payments or other rewards.

Requirements to be satisfied

7.15 The making of a disclosure order for the purposes of a terrorist-financing investigation is subject to the Crown Court judge being satisfied of the following four cumulative requirements appearing in Schedule 5A(10) of the TACT 2000:

Requirements for making of disclosure order

(1) These are the requirements for the making of a disclosure order.
(2) There must be reasonable grounds for suspecting that a person has committed an offence under any of sections 15 to 18 or that the property specified in the application is terrorist property.
(3) There must be reasonable grounds for believing that information which may be provided in compliance with a requirement imposed under the order is likely to be of substantial value (whether or not by itself) to the terrorist financing investigation concerned.

---

6 In *R v Lane & Letts* [2018] UKSC 36 the Court recently clarified that the *mens rea* of the offence contrary to section 17 TACT 2000 requires an objective, as opposed to subjective, suspicion that funds will or may be used for terrorist purposes.

(4) There must be reasonable grounds for believing that it is in the public interest for the information to be provided, having regard to the benefit likely to accrue to the investigation if the information is obtained.

7.16 The requirements are identical in substance to those applicable to the making of disclosure orders under Part 8 POCA 2002. The criminal suspicion is objectively assessed and can be based on information or intelligence that is not in the form of admissible evidence. A higher standard – reasonable grounds for belief as opposed to suspicion – must be met in relation to the matters of substantial value to the investigation and benefit to the public interest if the information is obtained.

7.17 The public interest criterion is striking when it is considered that it does not apply to the making of an unexplained wealth order, another coercive investigative tool available under Part 8 POCA 2002 which has been introduced by the CFA 2017. Although unexplained wealth orders can be sought against persons who are criminal suspects, like the disclosure order, they can also be sought in relation to people who are not and yet no such public interest consideration appears in the legislation.

Relevant information

7.18 Notwithstanding the importance of the 'public interest' safeguard, judicial consideration of the notice that is served on a person pursuant to a disclosure order is limited.

7.19 The four requirements apply to the making of the disclosure order only and the order itself does not necessarily impose requirements on any person. Instead, under Schedule 5A(9) of the TACT 2000, where the four requirements are met and a disclosure order is made, it authorises

> an appropriate officer to give to any person the officer considers has relevant information *notice in writing requiring the person to do any or all of the following* with respect to any matter relevant to the terrorist financing investigation concerned –
>
> (a) answer questions, either at a time specified in the notice or at once, at a place so specified;
> (b) provide information specified in the notice, by a time and in a manner so specified;
> (c) produce documents, or documents of a description, specified in the notice, either at or by a time so specified or at once, and in a manner so specified. (emphasis added)

7.20 Somewhat circularly, a person will be considered to have 'relevant information' where the officer concerned considers it to be relevant: Schedule 5A(9)(3) TACT 2000. Where this is the case, the officer may serve them with a notice. The respondent could be an individual or legal person.

Written notice

7.21 Typically, the written notice served by the appropriate officer specifying the information sought from the person will not be considered by the court. The court therefore will not turn its mind to whether or not a particular person has 'relevant information' or descend to the detail of the information sought from them. There are clear reasons for this. At the time of the making of a disclosure order, an indeterminate range of people, from professional advisers, banks, money service businesses, family members and individual associates might hold information relevant to a terrorist-financing investigation. The nature of the information required and the persons who have been identified as potentially being able to assist is also likely to change as it develops over time. Information that is disclosed may lead to new persons being identified. New lines of inquiry may surface.

7.22 A disclosure order is valuable as, once it is made, it remains force for the duration of an investigation and empowers law enforcement to issue notices where they consider appropriate throughout the life of the investigation. Further applications are not necessary, sparing enforcement authorities – and the court – time and resources.

7.23 However, the efficiency of the process does give rise to potential issues. In *NCA v Simkus & Ors*,[7] which concerned a disclosure order under Part 8 POCA 2002, the court observed that 'the level of judicial oversight over the operation of the order is quite limited'.[8] There are neither provisions in the legislation which prevent repeat written notices to disclose information being served on the same person nor provisions which limit the number of written notices being served in total.

7.24 As for the scope of a written notice issued pursuant to a disclosure order, it could also be directed at seeking information that goes beyond the property or person specified in the disclosure order. Such a view was taken in *Simkus* (cited above) after the court engaged in statutory construction of the disclosure order provisions in Part 8 POCA 2002. At paragraph [63], the court noted that: 'A power to investigate only what is known is a very limited and unusual investigative power. Investigations are usually conducted in order to discover that which is not known'. In the context of a civil recovery of property investigation, it was appropriate for notices issued pursuant to a disclosure order under Part 8 POCA 2002 to be directed at seeking information about further recoverable property.[9] A similarly wide view of the disclosure order powers under the TACT 2000 can be expected to be taken.

Effect

7.25 Once a written notice is served, the effect of it is to compel the person to truthfully provide the information specified or submit to an interview at a place and time specified. The person served, however, is not obliged to comply unless evidence of the authority to give the written notice is produced to him or her: Schedule 5A(9)(5) TACT 2000. In practice, the disclosure order will be served with the written notice. Unsurprisingly, however, the evidence relied upon in support of the disclosure order will not be.

7.26 Typically, disclosure orders will be used during the course of a covert investigation. The target may not learn of the disclosure order and any other investigative measure taken until many months later. As such, the written notice is likely to contain a warning to the recipient against doing anything to alert the target to the terrorist-financing investigation or which would amount to 'tipping off'. It is an offence, under section 39 of the TACT 2000, for a person to disclose to another anything which is likely to prejudice a terrorism investigation or interfere with material that is likely to be relevant to the investigation.

---

7 [2016] EWHC 255 (Admin).
8 Paragraph [14].
9 Paragraph [63].

Responding to a written notice

7.27 There is no requirement in the legislation as to the format for information provision.

7.28 The experience of written notices issued pursuant to Part 8 POCA 2000 disclosure orders is that unless it is specified that the person is to attend an interview, the information will be provided to the enforcement authority in written form. It is not necessary for the information to be provided in a witness statement or affidavit. However, as is conventional with the increasingly prevalent coercive investigative orders in the UK, a person will commit an offence if they knowingly or recklessly make a statement that is false or misleading in a material particular: Schedule 5A(11) TACT 2000. Triable either way, the offence exposes a person to a period of two years' imprisonment if resolved on indictment.

7.29 The protection against self-incrimination applies to any statement given in answer to disclosure order notice: Schedule 5A(12) TACT 2000. This, however, is subject to a small handful of exceptions such as 'false statement' prosecutions or where the person is prosecuted and adduces evidence of or is asked a question about information provided in response to a disclosure order notice: Schedule 5A(12) TACT 2000. Axiomatically, the protection does not prevent the use of the information within the statement in aid of a criminal investigation and eventual prosecution of another. It also does not prevent the use of the information to develop a civil or regulatory investigation into the person who provided it as well as any others. This is a consideration likely to weigh on the minds of firms in receipt of a disclosure order notice.

Legal privilege

7.30 A person served with a disclosure order notice is not required to provide information or documents that are privileged: Schedule 5A(13) TACT 2000. The privilege will not extend to the name and address of a client.

7.31 Subject to this above, the notice will take primacy over restrictions on the dissemination of information however imposed: Schedule 5A(13)(4) TACT 2000. This, for instance, would include general duties of client confidentiality or data protection requirements.

Copies

7.32 Any documents produced in answer to a disclosure order notice may be copied and retained by the enforcement authority who sought the order: Schedule 5A(13)(5) TACT 2000. The documents may be retained for the duration of the terrorist-financing investigation but there is provision to retain them for longer if they may have a bearing on other legal proceedings.

Variation and discharge

7.33 The disclosure order framework in the TACT 2000 contains express statutory provisions for the variation and discharge of a disclosure order.

7.34 Applications for variation and discharge may be made to the Crown Court by the person who applied for the order as well as any person affected by it: Schedule 5A(14) TACT 2000. The latter would include the target of the investigation – once the disclosure order is made known – or a person served with a written notice who is seeking to discharge the application of the order to themselves.

7.35 To properly challenge the making of the disclosure order, a person is entitled to be served with the evidence relied on in support of the order.[10] Any redactions of the evidence are to be properly reasoned.[11]

7.36 In challenging a disclosure order made in the context of a terrorist-financing investigation, whether or not the four requirements have been met is likely to be a key issue. Within this, whether or not the information sought to be obtained by the disclosure order notice is available via another less intrusive route is a matter for consideration. If the information requested in the written notice is known to police already or readily accessible, the proposition that the disclosure order is in the public interest because of the benefit to the investigation, one of the four requirements, will be undermined.

7.37 Further, a person who has been served with a written notice may also seek to discharge its application in relation to them on the basis that they simply do not hold information 'relevant' to the investigation. A separate issue may arise where a notice is issued long after the disclosure order was made or repeat written notices are served on one person, probing slightly different issues each time. These issues have occasionally arisen in practice in relation to disclosure orders under Part 8 POCA 2002. There is at least an argument that the public interest is not served by law enforcement taking its time to pursue an investigation or repeatedly using a coercive investigative tool against a person to seek information in a piecemeal fashion. Depending on the facts, the use of the powers in this manner could amount to an abuse of process. The complexity and magnitude of the investigation will be balanced against such arguments.[12] In any event, where a delay or repeated issuance of written notices has occurred, there may be a basis to challenge the application of the disclosure order.

Information sharing within the regulated sector

7.38 Section 36 of CFA 2017 introduces a formal channel for the sharing of information relating to terrorist financing or terrorist property within the regulated sector. The framework appears in section 21CA TACT 2000 and contemplates information being shared between (1) persons in the regulated sector and (2) a person in the regulated sector and law enforcement. The framework aligns with the Financial Action Task Force's encouragement of timely and effective private sector information sharing.[13] Sharing information is to be regarded as a cornerstone of a well-functioning anti-money laundering and counter-terrorist financing regime.

7.39 The provisions entered in to force on 31 October 2017 with the issuance of the Criminal Finances Act 2017 (Commencement No. 3) Regulations 2017. The sharing of information is entirely voluntary and the process can be initiated by a request from a person in the regulated sector or a constable.

7.40 References to 'regulated sector' are construed in accordance with Schedule 3A TACT 2000 and mirror those in POCA 2002. All references to a 'constable' in the framework include a police constable as well as an equivalent authorised officer of the National Crime Agency: section 21CF(2) TACT 2000. However, before any information can be shared, several conditions must be met.

---

10 *Nuttall & Anor v NCA* [2016] EWHC 1911 (Admin) at [5].
11 *NCA v Simkus & Ors* [2016] EWHC 255 (Admin) at [50].
12 *Nuttall & Anor v NCA* [2016] EWHC 1911 (Admin).
13 Financial Action Task Force, *FATF Guidance – Private Sector Information Sharing* (2017).

The conditions

7.41 In the context of terrorist financing, a person in the regulated sector may voluntarily share information subject to the meeting of the following conditions set out in section 21CA TACT 2000:

- A constable or a person, B, has requested another person, A, make a disclosure.
- Where B is requesting the disclosure, before B makes the request, they have notified a constable.
- A is carrying on business in the regulated sector, the information to be disclosed by A came to A in the course of that business and the person to whom the information is to be disclosed, B, is also in the regulated sector.
- Before A makes the disclosure, B has notified a constable that a disclosure request has been made and complied with the notification requirements.
- A is satisfied that the disclosure 'will or may assist in determining any matter in connection with a suspicion that a person is involved in a terrorist financing offence or the identification of terrorist property or of its movement or use'.

7.42 The framework mirrors the new provisions for information sharing in the context of anti-money laundering that have also been introduced by the CFA 2017. The consistency, however, means that the framework suffers from the same unnecessarily complicated features as the framework that appears in POCA 2002. For a voluntary regime, the technicality of the provisions is surprising.

7.43 Chief amongst these complicated features are the notification requirements that must be met before any information is actually shared. Although the objective of the framework is to enhance the quality of terrorist-financing intelligence received in the form of a suspicious activity report (SAR) by encouraging regulated persons to share information, the procedure itself is technical. The police, in essence, must be informed of the process throughout. Certain information must be provided including, amongst other matters, reasons why the information request is being made and the nature of the information that is sought before any request is even sent.

7.44 Then, so that the recipient of the notice can comply with the request, the person requesting the information must notify the police that a disclosure request has been made. This is known as the 'required notification'. In so far as it is known, they must detail the person suspected to be involved in terrorist financing or, where the request is made in connection with terrorist property, detail the property and person who holds it: section 21CB(7), (8) TACT 2000.

7.45 Arguably, the information to be provided at the 'required notification' stage is a duplication of what would already be in the possession of the police or the NCA.

Under section 21A TACT 2000 a person in the regulated sector is under a duty to report a suspicion that a terrorist-financing offence between sections 15–18 TACT 2000 has been committed or has been attempted 'as soon as is practicable after it comes to him'. The failure to do so is a criminal offence.

7.46 It follows that if a person, A, is requesting information from another regulated person, B, 'in connection with a suspicion' then, on one view, A has already formed a suspicion. A SAR containing the basis for the suspicion and details of the relevant property and person would already have been submitted by A in discharge of A's reporting duty. In these circumstances, one might query the incentive for a regulated person to go the extra mile, work through the technical procedure, and request that another regulated person share information that may further support the suspicion.

Joint reporting

7.47 Notwithstanding the above, where information is shared pursuant to a request, the regime contemplates a subsequent joint SAR: section 21CC(4) TACT 2000. In practical terms, this is where the nominated officers appointed by the person or persons who requested the disclosure and the person who received the disclosure request collaborate over a SAR.

7.48 The requirements of a joint SAR are prescribed. It must explain the 'extent to which there are continuing grounds for suspicion', identify the relevant property or person, set out the grounds for the suspicion and provide any other relevant information: section 21CC(5), (6) TACT 2000.

7.49 Unless the period is lengthened by the police, a joint SAR is to be submitted within 28 days of the required notification: section 21CC(7) TACT 2000. Notably, if information has been shared and a joint SAR is not to be made, the person who made the required notification (A) must notify a constable: section 21CC(9) TACT 2000.

Impact on the duty to report

7.50 The 'required notification' affects more than the timing of the joint SAR. Notably, the making of a 'required notification' by the person who requests the information (A) will satisfy both A's duty, the duty on the recipient (B) and the duty on any other regulated person to whom A passes the information (C) to report a suspicion that a terrorist financing has been committed or attempted: section 21CC TACT 2000. In other words, if A were to request certain information from B in connection with a terrorist-financing suspicion and were to pass it to C, A, B and C would be protected if they had not yet submitted a SAR in discharge of the duty to report a suspicion under section 21A TACT 2000.

7.51 However, there is a limit to the cover afforded to A, B and C. Persons are protected only where the suspicion arises because of the required notification and knowledge, suspicion or belief about matters has come about as a result of the disclosure request: section 21CD TACT 2000. The protection does not extend to a situation where suspicion is supported by something else, for example, a piece of information which is not the subject of the disclosure request. In such cases, the duty to report remains and a SAR based on this separate information would have to be made: section 21CD(3) TACT 2000.

Confidentiality

7.52 Concerns over the release of confidential information pertaining to a client are addressed by the legislation. Where information is shared in good faith, there will not be a breach of any obligation of confidence or other restriction however imposed: section 21CE TACT 2000. Regulated persons, however, must take care not to share any information that has come from an enforcement authority unless the authority has consented: section 21CE(2) TACT 2000.

Further information orders

7.53 A further information order is an order enabling law enforcement to seek more information about a SAR, made under section 21A TACT 2000, from a regulated person. The order compels the regulated person to provide the information specified or described in the order: section 22B(3) TACT 2000.

7.54 Section 22B of the TACT 2000, which has been inserted by by section 37 of CFA 2017, provides the framework for the seeking of such an order. Previously, the National Crime Agency could meet resistance from the regulated person who submitted the SAR if more information was requested. Following the discharge of the obligation to report, there was no legal duty on the regulated person to provide any further information. Similarly, there was no legal duty on other persons in the regulated sector to provide information which may expand on the suspicion contained in the SAR. Production orders, available under Schedule 5 TACT 2000, require a terrorist investigation to have formally commenced. Where the National Crime Agency had received a request from a foreign financial intelligence unit (FIU) in relation to a foreign SAR there was also no legal framework to compel a person in the UK regulated sector to assist. The provisions entered into force on 31 October 2017.

The application

7.55 A further information order is an order of a magistrates' court.

7.56 Applications are made by a law enforcement officer, namely a police constable, National Crime Agency officer or counter-terrorist financial investigator. The application must specify the information sought and the person from whom it is sought: section 22B TACT 2000.

7.57 The procedure for the making of the application and the order itself is governed by rule 47 of the Criminal Procedure Rules as amended most recently in October 2017 and April 2018. An application for a disclosure order may be heard in private: section 22E TACT 2000. It may be determined with or without a hearing, including in the absence of the applicant, the respondent or any person affected: rule 47.5 Criminal Procedure Rules as amended.

7.58 The making of the order is subject to the satisfaction of one of two alternative conditions.

7.59 The first concerns domestic SARs and the second concerns foreign SARs in relation to which a foreign FIU has requested the National Crime Agency's assistance.

Condition 1

7.60 A further information order may be made where condition 1 is satisfied. Condition 1 requires the court to be satisfied of all of the following:

- The information required relates to a matter arising from a SAR.
- The respondent is the person who either submitted the SAR or is otherwise in the regulated sector.
- The information would assist in either (1) investigating a terrorist-financing offence between sections 15–18 TACT 2000 or determining whether such an

investigation should commence or (2) identifying terrorist property, including movement and use.
- It is reasonable in all the circumstances for the information to be provided.

Condition 2

7.61 In the alternative, a further information order may be made where condition 2 is satisfied. Condition 2 requires the court to be satisfied of all of the following:

- The information required relates to a matter arising from a foreign SAR.
- An external request has been made to the National Crime Agency by a foreign authority responsible for investigating corresponding terrorist-financing offences for the provision of information in connection with that SAR.
- The respondent is in the regulated sector.
- The information is likely to be of 'substantial value' to the foreign authority making the request in 'determining any matter in connection with the disclosure'.
- It is reasonable in all the circumstances for the information to be provided.

7.62 The reference to 'substantial value' indicates that a higher bar must be met where a further information order is sought to assist a foreign enforcement authority. The reference does not appear in condition 1, which concerns domestic SARs.

Effect

7.63 Where a further information order is made, it will specify the format for the provision of the information and the deadline. Non-compliance exposes the person to a fine of up to £5,000.

7.64 Legal privilege and the protection against self-incrimination will be maintained. Subject to a small number of exceptions concerning false statements, any statement provided in response to a further information order cannot be used against the person providing it in criminal proceedings: section 22C(1) TACT 2000. A person will also not be required to provide privileged information: section 22E TACT 2000.

Appeals

7.65 Any person who was a party to the application proceedings has a right of appeal against the disclosure order: section 22D TACT 2000. Where the order is made in England and Wales, the appeal lies to the Crown Court.

7.66 On appeal, the court may make, discharge or vary the further information order.

Civil recovery of terrorist cash and property

7.67 As part of its suite of anti-terrorist financing measures, the CFA 2017 also expands the provisions for the civil recovery of terrorist cash and terrorist property. Although highly technical in nature, the amendments – which include a process for administrative forfeiture – are bound to have a substantial impact in practice and are a boon for law enforcement.

7.68 By way of background, Part 1 of ACTSA 2001 enables terrorist property to be forfeited in civil proceedings. Orders are made against the property (*in rem*) and not the person (*in personam*). Under section 1, property can be forfeited where it is one of the following:

- intended to be used for the purposes of terrorism
- consists of resources of a proscribed organisation
- is or represents property obtained through terrorism

7.69 Schedule 1 of ACTSA 2001 specifies all of the property that can be seized by law enforcement, detained and forfeited and the procedure for doing so.

7.70 Broadly, following the CFA 2017, the terrorist property that can now be seized, detained and forfeited falls into three categories – terrorist cash that is the subject of Parts 1–4, terrorist assets that are the subject of new Part 4A and terrorist money in bank and building society accounts that is the subject of new Part 4B.

Terrorist cash

7.71 The procedure for the forfeiture of terrorist cash is well established in Schedule 1 ACTSA 2001. However, section 38 CFA 2017 amends Schedule 1 ACTSA 2001 by expanding the definition of 'terrorist cash' to close a gambling-related loophole. In addition to coins and notes, postal orders, cheques and banker's drafts, gaming vouchers, fixed-value casino tokens and betting receipts found anywhere in the UK are now also vulnerable to seizure, detention and subsequent forfeiture.

7.72 Section 38A CFA 2017 further inserts a new Part 2A into Schedule 1 ACTSA 2001, which enhances the ability of law enforcement to seek the forfeiture of terrorist cash. Strikingly, the provisions permit the forfeiture of terrorist cash in the absence of a hearing or a magistrates' court order. Prior to the CFA 2017, the forfeiture of terrorist cash always required a magistrates' court order. Now, terrorist cash can be forfeited (1) administratively or (2) following forfeiture proceedings in the magistrates' court.

7.73 Although 'nonjudicial' or administrative forfeiture is a feature of American law,[14] the power of law enforcement to forfeit cash in the absence of judicial oversight is a radical development of law in the UK. The new administrative procedure is detailed in Part 2A, accompanied by the Administrative Forfeiture of Terrorist Cash and Terrorist Money Held in Bank and Building Society Accounts (Cash and Account Forfeiture Notices) Regulations 2017, which came into force on 31 January 2018.

7.74 Part 2A applies where cash has been seized by law enforcement on the basis that there are reasonable grounds for suspicion that it is terrorist cash and a justice of the peace or magistrate has subsequently authorised the detention of the cash. Detention will be authorised where further investigation or consideration of proceedings is required or where proceedings have been started but are yet to conclude: Schedule 1 Part 2 ACTSA 2001.

7.75 Following the authorisation of the cash detention, where a senior law enforcement officer is satisfied on the balance of probabilities that the cash is terrorist cash, he or she may then issue a 'cash forfeiture notice'. A senior law enforcement refers to a senior police

---

14 See for example Title 18 U.S.C. §983.

officer of at least the rank of superintendent, equivalently senior officer of HM Revenue & Customs or an equivalently senior immigration officer.

7.76 A cash forfeiture notice will be given to any person identified as affected by the cash detention order and may be posted to the person's last-known address or, where no persons are identified, published in the *London Gazette*.

7.77 A deadline for any objections to forfeiture must be included in the notice. If no objection is made within the period, the cash will be automatically forfeited.

Objections to administrative forfeiture

7.78 Importantly, the making of an objection causes the forfeiture notice to lapse. The objection must be made in writing.

7.79 Where an objection is made, law enforcement will have 48 hours in which to lodge an application for the continued detention of the cash or an application to forfeit the cash. If no such application is made, the cash must be released.

Application to set aside administrative forfeiture

7.80 Where terrorist cash has been administratively forfeited, any aggrieved person may apply to a magistrates' court for an order setting the forfeiture aside. However, there is a strict time limit. The application to set aside must be made within 30 days of the final day for lodging an objection to a forfeiture notice.

7.81 The court will only allow an aggrieved person to make an application out of time where there are 'exceptional circumstances' to explain why the applicant failed to object and failed to comply with the deadline: Schedule 1 Part 2A(5D) ACTSA 2001. The applicant should detail when the forfeiture notice first came to their attention and the circumstances.

7.82 In setting aside the administrative forfeiture, the key battleground will be whether or not there is sufficient basis for satisfaction that the cash is 'terrorist cash'. Any irregularities in complying with the detailed Part 2A procedure, however, may also merit consideration.

7.83 If an administrative forfeiture is set aside, there is limited scope for compensation. Where the detained cash is not forfeited either administratively or by way of a magistrates' court order, the court is only able to order reasonable compensation having regard to the loss suffered by the aggrieved person where it is satisfied that the circumstances are exceptional: Schedule 1 Part 4(10)(4) ACTSA 2001.

Terrorist assets

7.84 The expanded terrorist cash provisions are complemented by a new regime for the forfeiture of terrorist assets. Schedule 3 CFA 2017 introduces a new Part 4A into Schedule 1 of ACTSA 2001, which applies to terrorist property other than cash.

7.85 As observed by the Home Office impact assessment, prior to the introduction of the CFA 2017, law enforcement was only able to take action against cash, despite evidence that certain high-value property was being used by criminals to move value. As a consequence, new Part 4A(10A) of Schedule 1 defines an asset vulnerable to seizure and forfeiture, known as a 'listed asset', as precious metals (gold, silver or platinum only), precious stones, watches, artistic works, face-value vouchers and postage stamps. The Secretary of State may add to the list of assets by way of regulations.

7.86 Part 4A contains detailed provisions enabling the seizure and further detention of listed assets as well as their eventual forfeiture. The provisions mirror those applicable to the seizure, detention and forfeiture of terrorist cash in Parts 1–4 and address associated and joint property, rights of appeal, victims and compensation. There is, however, one notable omission. A 'listed asset' can only be forfeited following forfeiture proceedings in the magistrates' court and the making of a forfeiture order. Listed assets cannot be forfeited administratively.

Terrorist money in bank and building society accounts

7.87 Provisions similar to those explained above also apply to terrorist money held in a bank or building society account. A regime for the freezing and forfeiture of funds held in such accounts is contained within new Part 4B of Schedule 1 ACTSA 2001, introduced by Schedule 4 CFA 2017. The regime contemplates the freezing of accounts pending the forfeiture of funds either (1) administratively or (2) by a magistrates' court order.

7.88 According to the Home Office impact assessment on account freezing and forfeiture, published June 2017, the new regime seeks to address the issue of accounts that have been voluntarily suspended by the bank because of anti-money laundering and counter-terrorist financing risk concerns. It is estimated that the value of the suspended accounts is over £30 million but that many individual accounts are low-value and do not meet the £10,000 threshold for civil recovery proceedings in the High Court, available under Part 5 POCA 2002. Axiomatically, money in a bank account also falls outside of the cash seizure and forfeiture regime as it is not 'cash'. Prior to the CFA 2017, there was no route to forfeiture.

Banks and building societies

7.89 The definition of a 'bank' in Part 4B means an 'authorised deposit taker' that has its head office or a branch in the UK. Notably, nothing in the legislation narrows the power to funds held by an account maintained by a UK bank branch. The question arises whether an account freezing order could apply to money held in a non-UK bank account by virtue of the relevant bank having a 'branch' in the UK.

7.90 A 'building society' is as defined in the Building Societies Act 1986. A building society is a society incorporated under that Act for the purpose of making loans secured on residential property and funded substantially by its members which has its principal office in the UK: section 5 Building Societies Act 1986.

Account freezing

7.91 Where a constable or counter-terrorism financial investigator has reasonable grounds for suspecting that money held in a bank or building society account is terrorist property, he or she may apply to the magistrates' court for an account freezing order.

7.92 In terms of procedure, a senior enforcement officer is required to consult HM Treasury before any application is made unless it is not reasonably practicable: Schedule 1 Part 4B(10Q)(4) ACTSA 2001. The application itself may be made without notice. If successful, the order prohibits the making of withdrawals or payments from the account. All persons affected by the order must be given notice of it.

7.93 The framework contains provisions for the variation and discharge of the order. In line with property freezing under Part 5 POCA 2002, an account freezing order may be varied to exclude reasonable sums for living or business expenses and legal expenses. Identical principles will apply: Schedule 1 Part 4B(10U) ACTSA 2001.

Administrative forfeiture

7.94 Where a senior officer is satisfied that the money in the account is terrorist property, an account forfeiture notice may be issued. The ensuing process is identical to that discussed above in the context of the new ability of law enforcement to administratively forfeit cash.

Powers extended to financial investigators

7.95 In recognition of the important role played by civilian counter-terrorism financial investigators alongside more conventional law enforcement officers, the CFA 2017 contains a raft of new provisions applicable to such persons.

7.96 Section 41 CFA 2017 inserts new section 63F into TACT 2000 which, in essence, requires the metropolitan police force to develop a system for the monitoring and accreditation of counter-terrorism financial investigators.

7.97 The monitoring and accreditation regime is required in the light of the new investigation powers that have been given to counter-terrorism financial investigators. Powers afforded to enforcement officers in terrorist investigations under Schedules 6 and 6A TACT 2000 and Schedule 1 ACTSA 2001, such as the ability to apply for financial information orders, production orders, account monitoring orders as well as seize and forfeit terrorist cash, are now also available to counter-terrorism financial investigators.

7.98 Consistent with the new status of counter-terrorism financial investigators, section 42 CFA 2017 inserts new offence provisions into TACT 2000. All of the new offence provisions, which appear in section 120A TACT 2000, prohibit the assault or obstruction of counter-terrorism financial investigators acting in the exercise of their powers.

Cross-border enforceability

7.99 A further striking feature of the counter-terrorist measures introduced by the CFA 2017 is the new provision for cross-border enforceability. Section 43 CFA 2017 inserts section 120B into TACT 2000, which establishes that subject to the making of an Order of Council, the following investigative orders made in the course of a terrorist property investigation are enforceable throughout the UK:

- further information orders made under Schedule 6(1) TACT 2000
- disclosure orders made under Schedule 5A(9) or (19) TACT 2000
- explanation orders made under Schedule 5(13) or (30) TACT 2000
- production orders made under Schedule 5(5) or (22) TACT 2000
- financial information orders made under Schedule 6(1) TACT 2000
- account monitoring orders made under Schedule 6A(2) TACT 2000

7.100 Production orders, financial information orders and account monitoring orders were available prior to the introduction of CFA 2017.

7.101 The effect of the new provision is that orders granted in one part of the UK can be enforced in another part. The provision streamlines the investigation of terrorist financing throughout the UK.

7.102 Cross-border enforceability of the orders specified came into force on 1 June 2018, with the making of the Terrorism Act 2000 (Enforcement in Different Parts of the United Kingdom) Order 2018.

CHAPTER 8

Corporate facilitation of tax evasion offences

Introduction

8.1 Part 3 of the Criminal Finances Act 2017 creates two corporate criminal offences for cases where a person associated with a company or partnership facilitates the commission by another person of a tax evasion offence. The first offence, set out in section 45, applies where UK tax is involved. The second offence, set out in section 46, applies where foreign tax is involved. The inclusion of these offences in the Criminal Finances Act 2017 was an odd choice, since the thrust of the Act is focused on provisions that enhance the legislative response to organised crime. The two new criminal offences are more narrowly focused, directed at continuing efforts to close the gap between tax owed and tax collected, known as 'the tax gap'.[1] The legislative intention is to capture cases where tax professionals employed by banks and firms of accountants have assisted taxpayers to evade payment of tax in a manner that crosses the boundary from tax avoidance, which is a lawful activity, into the territory of tax evasion, which is unquestionably not. Pursuant to Regulation 3 of the Criminal Finances Act 2017 (Commencement No. 1) Regulations 2017, the offences came into effect on 30 September 2017.

8.2 As the Explanatory Notes record, it has always constituted a criminal offence to facilitate deliberately another person's tax evasion, and certainly a banker, an accountant or, for that matter, any other person, who deliberately facilitates a client to commit a tax evasion offence will be guilty of a criminal offence.[2] However, because of the complicated legal rules which apply to the attribution of criminal responsibility to a company or partnership that employs the banker or accountant, prior to the introduction of the two new criminal offences the company or partnership would not be criminally liable for the actions of an employee unless the employee was one of the people controlling the company or partnership activities.[3] The issue is acute for a prosecutor where a person facilitating tax evasion is employed by a large multinational company where decision making is decentralised and important decisions are taken at a level lower than the board of directors. The traditional approach to attribution of corporate criminal responsibility operates as an incentive for senior employees in a multinational company to ignore the criminal actions of its representatives, and it creates an uneven playing field in comparison to smaller businesses where the board of directors is more actively involved in the daily activities of the business.

8.3 The Explanatory Notes make clear that the purpose of the new criminal offences in Part 3 is to hold these companies and partnerships to account for the actions of their

---

1 In 2015–16, the tax gap in the UK was estimated to be £34 billion, which is 6% of tax liabilities. Tax evasion was estimated to account for £5.2 billion, which is 15% of the tax gap. *Measuring Tax Gaps 2017 edition*, Tax Gap estimates for 2015–16, HM Revenue & Customs, October 2017.
2 Explanatory Notes to the Criminal Finances Act 2017, paragraph 42.
3 Ibid, paragraph 43.

employees. But most significantly, rather than focusing on attributing the criminal act to the company, the offences concentrate on – and criminalise – the company's failure to prevent those who act for or on its behalf from criminally facilitating tax evasion when acting in that capacity.[4] Therefore, where a person acting for or on behalf of a company or partnership criminally facilitates a tax evasion offence by another person, the company or partnership will be guilty of the corporate failure to prevent the facilitation of a tax evasion offence, unless the company or partnership can show that it had in place reasonable prevention procedures (or that it was not reasonable to expect such procedures).[5]

8.4 Although the Explanatory Notes envisage the commission of the new criminal offences by bankers and accountants, the application of the legislation is much wider. All companies and partnerships have a potential liability under this legislation where an employee facilitates another person in the commission of tax evasion, and if the enforcement authorities robustly prosecute the offences, it will be difficult to delineate the boundaries of criminal responsibility in certain situations. The new offences are wider in scope than the position under section 7 of the Bribery Act 2010, which introduced a corporate criminal offence where a company failed to prevent the payment or receipt of a bribe. Unlike the position under section 7 where payment or receipt of a bribe must be made with the intention of obtaining or retaining business for the company, there is no equivalent requirement to establish corporate benefit under the new corporate tax evasion offences. An employee who facilitates the commission of another person's tax evasion may be motivated by self-enrichment, but this is another matter.

8.5 Also, under section 7 of the Bribery Act 2010, corporate criminal liability is dependent upon an employee committing the bribery, corporate criminal responsibility under the new corporate tax offences is two steps removed from the predicate criminality. There is a distinction to be drawn between a company or partnership failing to prevent an employee from committing a substantive offence and a company or partnership failing to prevent one of its employees from facilitating a criminal offence committed by another person.

Failure to prevent the facilitation of UK tax evasion

8.6 Section 45(1) provides that:

> A relevant body (B) is guilty of an offence if a person commits a UK tax evasion facilitation offence when acting in the capacity of a person associated with B.

Relevant body

8.7 For the purposes of identifying to whom the criminal offence applies, section 44(2) defines a 'relevant body' to mean 'a body corporate or partnership (wherever incorporated or formed)'. A partnership is defined in section 44(3) to mean either a partnership within the meaning of the Partnership Act 1890, a limited partnership registered under the Limited Partnerships Act 1907, or a firm or entity of a similar character formed under the law of a foreign country. It does not matter in which geographical location the company or partnership was incorporated or formed, and so, for example, a company incorporated offshore

---

4 Ibid, paragraph 45.
5 Ibid, paragraph 46.

will not be excluded from criminal liability where a person associated with it commits a UK tax evasion facilitation offence.

Person acting in the capacity of a person associated with a relevant body

8.8 It is the conduct of the person associated with the company or partnership that serves as the catalyst for the imposition of criminal liability, and careful attention needs to be paid to the meaning of the legislative language. By section 45(4):

> A person (P) acts in the capacity of a person associated with a relevant body (B) if P is –
>
> (a) an employee of B who is acting in the capacity of an employee,
> (b) an agent of B (other than an employee) who is acting in the capacity of an agent, or
> (c) any other person who performs services for or on behalf of B who is acting in the capacity of a person performing such services.

8.9 A person's status as an employee or agent of a company or partnership will be determined by an application of legal principles established in the common law. The net is sufficiently wide to capture sub-contractors, joint venture partners, consultants and subsidiary and associated companies. In each case, the relevant circumstances will need to be examined to determine whether the entity is providing services 'for or on behalf of' the company or partnership.

8.10 It is the third category of person in section 44(4)(c) which is most likely to cause difficulty because of the uncertainty surrounding the meaning of the words that the drafter has chosen to use. Principally, it is unclear when a person 'performs services for or on behalf of' a company or partnership. Is a person who contracts with a company to clean the office windows performing a service for a company? If the answer is 'yes', and a company employee pays the window cleaner in cash to facilitate the window cleaner not declaring the cash as income, is the company fixed with criminal liability because of its employee's actions? Perhaps the answer lies in the last 12 words of section 44(4)(c), which qualify the width of the provision by requiring a person performing a service to be 'acting in the capacity of a person performing such services'. But what does this mean? When a window cleaner cleans the office windows, is he not acting in the capacity of a window cleaner who is performing a window cleaning service? The qualifying words seem to add very little to narrow the scope of the provision. Section 44(5) does not shed much light on the issue either. This subsection provides that:

> For the purposes of subsection (4)(c) the question whether or not P is a person who provides services for or on behalf of B is to be determined by reference to all the relevant circumstances and not merely by reference to the nature of the relationship between P and B.

8.11 If anything, the reference to 'all the relevant circumstances' suggests that Parliament intends section 45(4)(c) to spread a wide net over anybody who provides services to a company or partnership, irrespective of the nature and duration of the services in question.

8.12 Mindful of the extensive terrain covered by section 45(4)(c), the question arises whether there needs to be a causal link between the activities of the company or partnership and the nature of tax which the taxpayer is evading. If the answer is 'no', the potential catchment area of the new corporate offence in section 45 is extremely wide, and far beyond the statutory objective articulated in the Explanatory Notes of criminalising banks and accountancy firms whose employees facilitate their customers and clients to evade tax.

The Explanatory Notes provide a steer that suggests that a causal link needs to be shown between the activities of the company or partnership and the nature of tax which the tax is evading. They note that:

> the associated person must commit the tax evasion facilitation offence in the capacity of a person associated with the relevant body. Where an employee criminally facilitates his or her partner's tax evasion in the course of their private life and as a frolic of their own, they commit a tax evasion facilitation offence but not in the capacity of a person associated with their employer. Therefore the employing relevant body does not commit the new offence. Likewise a relevant body will not commit the new offence where it contracts with another relevant body that is evading its own tax.[6]

8.13 It is hoped that a court will embrace this interpretation and reject a wide application of the offence that travels far beyond the legislative purpose.

UK tax evasion

8.14 Before a conviction can be regarded, in addition to establishing that a company or partnership has criminal responsibility because of an associated person's conduct, a prosecutor will need to prove that a UK tax evasion offence has been committed. The tax evasion offence will have been committed by a taxpayer who has been assisted in the commission of the offence by the associated person.

UK tax evasion offence

8.15 Section 45(4) defines a tax evasion offence in a straightforward manner. The phrase means –

(a) an offence of cheating the public revenue, or
(b) an offence under the law of any part of the United Kingdom consisting of being knowingly concerned in, or in taking steps with a view to, the fraudulent evasion of a tax.

8.16 There are many other criminal offences that may be committed in the context of tax evasion. For example, section 17(1) of the Theft Act 1968 establishes a criminal offence where a person makes a document that is false, misleading or deceptive in a material particular to cause gain for himself or loss to HM Revenue & Customs. It is also a criminal offence contrary to section 2(1) of the Fraud Act 2006 to make a false representation to HM Revenue & Customs. These offences were not included as a tax evasion offence for the purposes of section 45(4), presumably because it was unnecessary. The offence of cheating the revenue at common law is sufficiently wide to capture the types of conduct that would fall within these more specifically focused criminal offences.

Cheating the public revenue

8.17 Cheating the public revenue is a serious criminal offence at common law, for which the maximum sentence remains life imprisonment. The modern definition of cheating the public revenue makes clear that the offence involves fraudulent conduct which is intended

---

6 Ibid, paragraph 302. See Karl Laird, 'The Criminal Finances Act 2017 – an introduction' [2017] Cr LR 915, 933.

to deprive HM Revenue & Customs of money to which it is entitled. The Court of Appeal (Criminal Division) endorsed the formulation in *R v Hunt*[7] as follows:

> To cheat, members of the jury, is defined by the Concise Oxford Dictionary as: 'To deceive or trick a person into or out of a thing'. The common law offence of cheating the public revenue does not necessarily require a false representation either by words or conduct. Cheating can include any form of fraudulent conduct which results in diverting money from the revenue and in depriving the revenue of the money to which it is entitled. It has, of course, to be fraudulent conduct. That is to say, deliberate conduct by the defendant to prejudice, or take the risk of prejudicing, the revenue's right to the tax in question knowing that it has no right to do so.

8.18 The cheat in *R v Hunt* took the form of a false invoicing fraud, where misleading documents such as invoices, agreements and correspondence, had been produced by the defendants. The documents were false and deceptive since they purported to show that commercial transactions had been made in good faith when the transactions had not been genuine, in the sense that there was no underlying transaction taking place. In other words, the documents were sham or, to use a more contemporary word, fake. In law, a sham exists where a party says one thing and intends another, with the party to the documentation aware of the sham.[8] When a company makes a payment to satisfy a false invoice, the effect is to artificially inflate its expenditure and correspondingly reduce the level of company profit on which corporation tax is payable. HM Revenue & Customs loses its revenue, whilst the defendants who devised the false invoices enjoy the payments made on the back of the false invoices, invariably received through the establishment of an offshore company. The law reports are littered with many similar examples of this type of fraud.[9]

8.19 Tax evasion need not be so prosaic. Under the offence of cheating the public revenue, it would be sufficient for a market fruit trader to keep two sets of books, one for himself which contained income from apples and oranges, and a second set for HM Revenue & Customs in which only the sale of oranges was recorded. The maintenance of the second set of books is a form of fraudulent conduct that results in diverting money from the revenue and in depriving the revenue of the money to which it is entitled. The offence is treated in criminal law as 'a conduct offence' and not 'a result offence', so as a matter of technicality it would not be necessary for accounts based on the second set of books to be submitted to HM Revenue & Customs before the offence of cheating the public revenue is completed. The same analysis applies to the secreting of income under the floorboards, or in an offshore bank account.

Avoidance or evasion

8.20 Much more difficult, especially in the context of the two new criminal offences, is the practical application of the distinction drawn in English law between tax avoidance, which even in its most aggressive form is a lawful activity, and tax evasion, which

---

7 [1994] STC 819, per Stuart-Smith LJ at 826.

8 *Snook v London & West Riding Investments* [1967] 2 QB 786. See also *Hitch v Stone* (Inspector of Taxes) [2001] EWCA Civ 63.

9 *R v Charlton* [1996] STC 1418; *R v IRC, ex parte Mead* [1993] 1 All ER 772; *R v Webb & Simpson*, 23 October 2000, Court of Appeal (Criminal Division), unreported; *R v Dimsey & Allen* [2002] 1 AC 509; *R v Foggon* [2003] EWCA Crim 270; *R v Stannard* [2005] EWCA Crim 2717; *R v Leaf* [2007] EWCA Crim 802; *R v Lunn* [2017] EWCA Crim 34.

constitutes a criminal act. Tax evasion constitutes the criminal offence of cheating the public revenue at common law, whereas tax avoidance will not.

8.21 It is accepted under English law that a taxpayer is entitled to arrange his affairs to reduce his liability to tax, and the fact that the motive for a transaction is to avoid tax does not invalidate it unless an enactment so provides. However, if the arrangement is to be effective it is essential that the transaction has some economic or commercial substance. Lord Goff explained in *Ensign Tankers (Leasing) Ltd v Stokes*[10] that:

> Unacceptable tax avoidance typically involves the creation of complex artificial structures by which, as though by the wave of a magic wand, the taxpayer conjures out of the air a loss, or a gain, or expenditure, or whatever it may be, which otherwise would never have existed. These structures are designed to achieve an adventitious tax benefit for the taxpayer, and in truth are no more than raids on the public funds at the expense of the general body of tax payers, and as such are unacceptable.

8.22 Where the civil courts determine that tax avoidance is unacceptable, the arrangements are ineffective and the taxpayer's attempt to reduce the tax liability fails; however, the taxpayer avoids criminal liability because there is no attempt to dishonestly mislead HM Revenue & Customs in these circumstances. Rather, the taxpayer has acted in a way in which he considered, invariably on legal or accountancy advice, that he was entitled to act, albeit at the boundaries of tax law. As the High Court explained in *R (on the application of Inland Revenue Commissioners) v Kingston Crown Court*:[11]

> The distinction between lawful tax avoidance and illegal tax evasion is well-known. Tax-saving schemes that involve transactions having little or no commercial benefit apart from the scheme are a common feature of commercial life. In the absence of statutory criminal prohibitions, the transactions involved in the scheme and the scheme itself are lawful. Whether the scheme is effective depends on the provisions of the tax legislation in question. Tax-saving crosses the border from lawful to criminal when it involves the deliberate and dishonest making of false statements to the Revenue. A criminal scheme may involve the dishonest bringing into existence or use of documents evidencing transactions that never took place, or the creation and use of documents that contain some other misrepresentation of fact, such as the date when they were executed or came into effect.

8.23 Whilst the division articulated by the High Court is well known, practical application is more complex. Professor David Ormerod, a leading academic writer on criminal law topics, excoriates the distinction between tax avoidance and tax evasion, noting that 'the difficulty in distinguishing between shades of avoidance and evasion means that it is always possible for the revenue authorities to prosecute a taxpayer with the criminal offence of cheating in respect of a scheme which is alleged to be dishonest evasion but which the (non) taxpayer believes to be, at worst, an ineffective avoidance scheme'. Ormerod explains that 'even a professional tax adviser cannot state the difference between the two with precision and confidence. In reality, such schemes lie along a spectrum, with the legitimate ordering of affairs at one end and the deliberate evasion, which should no doubt be charged as an offence, at the other. The critical point along the spectrum lies between schemes classified as ineffective or unsuccessful tax avoidance where revenue law declares that tax is payable, and those classified as illegal evasion'.[12]

---

10 [1992] 1 AC 655.
11 [2001] STC 1615, per Stanley Burnton J, paragraph 2.
12 David Ormerod, 'Cheating the Public Revenue' [1998] Crim LR 627.

8.24 The implications of Professor Ormerod's analysis are startling for tax advisers since they expose the extent of their vulnerability, and more particularly of the companies and partnerships employing them, under the two new criminal offences in sections 45 and 46 of the Act. In recent years, the Crown Prosecution Service has brought several cases against taxpayers and their professional advisers for dishonestly taking advantage of tax concessions that Parliament has provided, in the context of pension fund arrangements, investment in film companies, and charitable donations.[13] Few of these cases have been brought before the Court of Appeal (Criminal Division) because ultimately the success or failure of the prosecution has depended upon the jury's assessment of the defendant's mental state and, specifically, whether he was acting dishonestly.

8.25 Jury decisions can reflect the public mood, and since the global financial crisis in 2008 and the years of public austerity that followed, the public perception towards individuals and companies who arrange their affairs to minimise their tax liability has hardened. This attitudinal change has been fostered by politicians who, in efforts to increase the level of tax paid to HM Revenue & Customs, have elided the distinction between aggressive tax avoidance schemes, which are lawful albeit sometimes ineffective, and tax evasion. With reference to a highly publicised tax avoidance arrangement made by comedian Mr Jimmy Carr, in June 2012 the former Prime Minister, David Cameron, expressed the sentiment in the following terms:

> some of these schemes we have seen are quite frankly morally wrong. People work hard, they pay their taxes, they save up to go to one of his shows. They buy the tickets. He is taking the money from those tickets and he, as far as I can see, is putting all of that into some very dodgy tax avoiding schemes.

8.26 The former Chancellor of the Exchequer, Mr George Osborne, was equally forceful in his Budget Statement on 21 March 2012:

> I regard tax evasion and – indeed – aggressive tax avoidance – as morally repugnant. We've increased both the resources and the number of staff working on evasion and avoidance at HMRC.

8.27 In the context of the elision between tax avoidance and tax evasion, if companies and partnerships are to avoid criminal liability under sections 45 and 46 for employees or other associated persons facilitating tax evasion, the words of a former Director Public Prosecutions, Sir Keir Starmer QC, need to be heeded. In a speech delivered on 23 January 2013, with reference to tax evasion masquerading as tax avoidance, Sir Keir articulated this message:

> Tax evasion has to be dealt with robustly all the time. But in a recession, when ordinary law-abiding tax payers are suffering real hardship, the need to deter, detect and prosecute those who evade tax is greater than ever … [T]onight I want to highlight an important breakthrough in another part of the prosecutorial forest, namely the ability of HM Revenue & Customs and the Crown Prosecution Service to extend the reach of the criminal law by including a further category of offender in the list of successfully prosecuted cases – namely, those who devise and operate sophisticated schemes to abuse direct tax regimes: dishonest tax avoidance schemes. These cases typically involve highly intelligent individuals, not infrequently skilled professionals with close knowledge of the tax laws, who go to great lengths to dress up a dishonest and fraudulent tax evasion scheme as a legitimate investment scheme attracting tax relief or other tax advantages. Those setting up the schemes often use extremely complex financial

---

13 *R v Perrin* [2012] EWCA Crim 1729 (conviction) and [2012] EWCA Crim 1730 (sentence).

instruments and corporate entities to create a subterfuge ... But an experienced investigator and a skilled prosecutor can spot the tell-tale signs of dishonesty, whether that be false or misleading documents, false turnover figures, hidden trading transactions, or payments that do not reflect commercial reality ...

8.28 The reference to an 'extension of the reach of the criminal law by adding a further category of offender' should not be lost. The catchment area of cheating at common law has been expanded, and companies and partnerships need to take note. Typically, fraudulent intent on the part of a taxpayer is demonstrated by evidence of collusion between the taxpayer and others, or where there is evidence that documents have been forged with intent to deceive HM Revenue & Customs. Failure to make complete disclosure during a tax investigation, and evidence that a taxpayer's previous dealings with HM Revenue & Customs have been characterised by a lack of co-operation, are also useful indicators. False invoices typically characterise cases of tax evasion involving the creation of complex artificial structures such as offshore companies and trusts, but it is only the dishonest state of the taxpayer's mind that converts a case from one of failed tax avoidance to criminal tax evasion. This is the tender area, especially where complex artificial structures have been established (a typical sign of tax avoidance) but the artificiality of the structure has been concealed from HM Revenue & Customs (a typical sign of tax evasion).

8.29 By way of example, one area that has had a convoluted history is known as an 'IR 35 fraud'. IR35 is the short name used for the 'intermediaries legislation', which is a set of tax rules that apply to a person who works for a client through an intermediary – which can be a limited company or a 'personal service company', very often established offshore. Many contractors operate in this way, with the advantage that they can sidestep the administration and expense of the PAYE scheme for employees. In many cases HMRC has been able to challenge the status of the contractors and show that they are really employees, with the tax consequences that follow. The IR 35 cases amount to tax evasion where the detail of the arrangements dishonestly misrepresent the status of the contractors and mislead HMRC, or indeed a foreign revenue authority in the jurisdiction in which the scheme is based, as to the reality of the position. If, for example, an accountant working in the UK introduces his client to a tax or payroll consultant who arranges schemes of this sort, if the scheme were to amount to tax evasion, the accountant, and more especially the company or partnership that employs him, would drift potentially into the commission of the section 45 offence.

8.30 Ultimately, with the issue of dishonesty pivotal to the determination that characterises the lawfulness or otherwise of the conduct in law, when it comes to drawing the border between tax avoidance and tax evasion, an element of subjectivity inevitably remains. As a former Chancellor of the Exchequer, the late Dennis Healey, was famously reputed to have said (presumably tongue in cheek), 'the difference between tax avoidance and tax evasion is the thickness of a prison wall'. The quip is amusing and often quoted, but it is hardly the most propitious basis on which to rest the criminal liability of companies and partnerships for tax facilitation offences under sections 45 and 46 of the Act.

The public revenue

8.31 Although the offence was traditionally used by the Inland Revenue, the expression 'the public revenue' appears to embrace all the taxes and duties now levied by HMRC,[14]

---

14 But not by local government: *Lush v Coles* [1967] 1 WLR 685.

including those formerly administered by the Board of Customs and Excise such as VAT.[15] In the absence of statutory extension, the offence presumably does not apply to frauds on the European Union. As the court explained in *Lush v Coles*:[16]

> The 'public revenue' is an ancient term of art dating at least from the year 1816 when by the statute (56 Geo. 3, c. 98) 'all the public revenues of Great Britain and Ireland were consolidated into a Consolidated Fund.' The expression 'public revenue' then became the natural way of describing all the public revenues ... The expression 'the public revenue' is also used by textbook writers to describe and, in my judgment, signifies the public revenues of the kingdom, and not the receipts or revenues of a local authority. Money which is payable by a local authority out of its funds cannot in my judgment be appropriately described as 'payable ... out of the public revenue'.

8.32 In the interests of completeness, sections 45(7) and section 52(1) should also be mentioned. Although the phrase 'UK tax evasion offence' is defined by reference to cheating the public revenue and offences of fraudulent evasion, section 45(7) makes clear that for the purposes of the offence the word 'tax' means 'a tax imposed under the law of any part of the UK, including national insurance contributions under [the social security legislation]'. Section 52(1) adds that 'tax' includes 'duty and any other form of taxation (however so described)'.

Fraudulent evasion

8.33 The second UK tax offence that catalyses section 45 of the Act is 'an offence in any part of the UK consisting of being knowingly concerned in, or in taking steps with a view to, the fraudulent evasion of a tax'. There are two statutory offences that fall into this category. In truth, the offences do not add to the application of the new criminal offence in section 45 since they reflect no more than a statutory version of the offence of cheating the public revenue at common law.

8.34 Under section 72(1) of the Value Added Tax Act 1994 (VATA 1994) a person commits an offence if he 'is knowingly concerned in, or in the taking of steps with a view to, the fraudulent evasion of VAT by him or any other person'. The offence is triable both summarily and on indictment and is punishable on conviction on indictment with seven years' imprisonment. There is an evasion of tax if tax is not paid when it should be, even if it is paid eventually. A person may be knowingly concerned in fraudulent evasion if he is not himself liable for the tax but knowingly co-operates with the person who is, for example by supplying false invoices. Suspicion is not enough, though 'wilful blindness' may perhaps be equated with knowledge. An evasion of tax may be fraudulent even if there is no deception of HMRC officers. A person may be knowingly concerned in the taking of steps with a view to fraudulent evasion even if no evasion actually occurs, for example because the fraud is detected before the false return is due to be submitted. It is a kind of inchoate offence. But it is submitted that a person is not concerned in the taking of steps with a view to fraudulent evasion unless fraudulent evasion is the purpose of the steps in which he is concerned.

8.35 Section 144(1) of the Finance Act 2000 provided that 'a person commits an offence if he is knowingly concerned in the fraudulent evasion of income tax by him or any other

---

15 *R v Tonner* [1985] 1 WLR 344.
16 [1967] 1 WLR 685, per Stamp J at 690.

person'. The section remains in force, but it has been relocated to become section 106A of the Taxes Management Act 1970. The offence is triable either way and is punishable on conviction on indictment with seven years' imprisonment. The statutory language bears a close resemblance to section 72(1) of the Value Added Tax 1994, and the authorities on that provision are likely to be relevant. The requirement of fraud implies that dishonesty must be proved. But the offence is narrower than that under section 72(1) in that it is committed only where tax is evaded, not where steps are taken with a view to evading it. This means that the tax must remain unpaid after it falls due.

Proving a UK tax evasion offence

8.36 It is the commission of a UK tax evasion facilitation offence which needs to be proved by a prosecutor to establish company or partnership liability under section 45 of the Act. Whether or not the offender who committed the underlying tax evasion which the associated person facilitated has been convicted of the predicate offence is none to the point. It will be easier for a prosecutor to establish the commission of the corporate offence where a person has been convicted for the underlying tax evasion, since this is the conduct that underpins the corporate allegation and a criminal conviction will be almost impossible to displace. If, for example, a taxpayer is convicted of cheating the public revenue after he participated in a tax evasion arrangement that was dishonestly configured to present as tax avoidance, it will not be a difficult task for HM Revenue & Customs to identify the professional person who advised him on the arrangement, and to prosecute the professional person's company or partnership for commission of the corporate offence.

8.37 However, proof of tax evasion is not necessarily dependent on the existence of a criminal conviction. There are other circumstances that would render the evidence of tax evasion equally compelling. Instead of prosecuting the miscreant taxpayer, HM Revenue & Customs might decide to offer the taxpayer a civil settlement instead of criminal prosecution, provided that the taxpayer makes a witness statement in which he admits that he was guilty of tax evasion and he was advised by his bank, accountant, or lawyer in relation to the arrangement. Frequently, this type of arrangement is embodied in a formal agreement made under HM Revenue & Customs' processes under what is known by tax practitioners as the Code of Practice 9 (COP 9). Under this investigation of fraud procedure, the recipient of COP 9 is given the opportunity to make a complete and accurate disclosure of all deliberate and non-deliberate conduct that has led to irregularities in their tax affairs. If they do so, a civil settlement will follow, and criminal prosecution will be triggered only where HM Revenue & Customs suspect that the recipient has failed to make a full disclosure of all irregularities. The key point for proof of the corporate facilitation offence is that HM Revenue & Customs has proceeded to civil settlement and in the course of the civil settlement the taxpayer has admitted in writing that he has committed tax fraud. HM Revenue & Customs is clear that it is not acceptable for a taxpayer to merely state that his deliberate conduct has brought about a loss of tax. Rather, a taxpayer's description must set out sufficient information including, but not limited to, what he did, how he did it, the involvement of other people and entities, and how he benefited from the deliberate conduct.[17]

---

17 Code of Practice 9, HMRC 06/14, June 2014.

8.38 In this way, the Code of Practice 9 mechanism perfectly sets up HM Revenue & Customs to initiate an investigation into the role of a tax professional who assisted the taxpayer, with the distinct prospect of criminally prosecuting the tax professional's company or partnership at the end of the process. The impact of the Common Reporting Standard provides fertile ground for HM Revenue & Customs. Where, for example, data about undisclosed bank accounts held by UK residents has been disclosed to HM Revenue & Customs by overseas jurisdictions such as the Crown dependencies and Overseas Territories, a tax investigation will be initiated. When HM Revenue & Customs identify a tax evader, it is likely to look back up the chain to identify the professional adviser who has facilitated the tax evasion.

Facilitation offence

8.39 The term 'tax evasion facilitation offence' is defined in section 45(5) of the Act as meaning:

an offence under the law of any part of the United Kingdom consisting of –
   (a) being knowingly concerned in, or in taking steps with a view to, the fraudulent evasion of a tax by another person,
   (b) aiding, abetting, counselling or procuring the commission of a UK tax evasion offence, or
   (c) being involved art and part in the commission of an offence consisting of being knowingly concerned in, or in taking steps with a view to, the fraudulent evasion of a tax.

8.40 It is clear from the language used in section 45(5) that an associated person must be aware that his conduct assists in the perpetration of a tax evasion. In everyday life, it is possible to facilitate somebody's conduct without appreciating the consequences that may flow from the assistance that is given. The legislation makes clear this would not be sufficient in this case. The facilitation by the associated person must be criminal under the existing law.

Failure to prevent the facilitation of foreign tax evasion

8.41 This offence broadly replicates the offence created in section 45(1) in relation to foreign taxes. It is slightly narrower in scope, in that only certain relevant bodies can commit the foreign tax offence. The rationale put forward by the government for introducing a foreign evasion facilitation offence is that it would be wrong for a UK-based company or partnership to escape criminal liability for acts which, if they were committed in relation to UK tax, would be criminal, just because the country suffering the tax loss is unable to bring a prosecution against the company or partnership within that jurisdiction's legal system. As with section 45(1), a company or partnership becomes criminally liable where a person commits a foreign tax evasion facilitation offence when acting in the capacity of a person associated with the company or partnership. The meaning of an associated person as set out in section 44(4) applies equally to the offence in section 46(1). Unlike the section 45(1) offence, the offence in section 46 is unlikely to be prosecuted very often since, even if there was sufficient probative evidence to support a criminal prosecution, the public interest in prosecuting foreign tax evasion will be very different from those pertaining where the loser is the UK taxpayer.

Additional conditions for liability

8.42 Section 46(2) of the Act states that the offence can only be committed where –

(i) A company of partnership is incorporated under the law of the UK, or
(ii) The company or partnership carries on business or part of a business from the UK, or
(iii) Any conduct constituting any part of the foreign tax evasion facilitation offence takes place in the UK.

8.43 By section 46(1)(b), Parliament made clear these conditions are not cumulative but alternatives. It follows that where a company or partnership is formed outside the UK, or no business is conducted from the UK, the section 46 foreign tax offence will not be committed.

Foreign tax evasion offence

8.44 The term 'foreign tax evasion offence' is defined in section 46(5) as meaning:

conduct which –

(a) amounts to an offence under the law of a foreign country,
(b) relates to a breach of a duty relating to a tax imposed under the law of that country, and
(c) would be regarded by the courts of any part of the United Kingdom as amounting to being knowingly concerned in, or in taking steps with a view to, the fraudulent evasion of that tax.

8.45 Here, the requirements to be satisfied are cumulative.

8.46 Determining whether a foreign tax evasion offence has been committed will present a prosecutor with multiple challenges. First, in every case an issue of foreign revenue law will be raised, and a court will need to rely upon expert evidence to determine the position. Second, a double criminality test will need to be satisfied and this is not easy where revenue law is concerned. Some criminal offences translate very easily across borders, but others do not. As the Explanatory Notes make clear:

> A foreign tax evasion offence is defined as conduct that is criminal under the foreign law in question and would also be regarded by the UK courts as amounting to an offence of being knowingly concerned in, or taking steps with a view to, the fraudulent evasion of the tax. Thus the section 46 offence cannot be committed where the acts of the associated person would not be criminal if committed in the UK, regardless of what the foreign criminal law may be.[18]

8.47 There are several unanswered questions. Are administrative tax infractions in foreign countries to be regarded as criminal offences under section 46(5)(a)? Presumably, the answer is 'no'. Is a duty requiring disclosure of information such as the location of capital to be classified as 'a duty relating to a tax imposed under the law of that country' for the purposes of section 46(5)(b)? In any event, applying section 46(5)(c), nothing short of dishonest and deliberate conduct directed at evading a tax liability will suffice for criminal liability to be engaged.

---

18 Ibid, paragraph 308.

Foreign tax facilitation offence

8.48 The phrase 'foreign tax evasion facilitation offence' is defined in section 46(6) of the Act to mean conduct that –

(1) amounts to an offence under the law of a foreign country,
(2) relates to the commission by another person of a foreign tax evasion offence under that law, and
(3) would, if the foreign tax evasion offence were a UK tax evasion offence, amount to a UK tax evasion facilitation offence.

8.49 The law used in section 46(6)(b) is far from clear. At some stage, a court will be required to determine in accordance with English law whether conduct 'relates to' the commission by another person of a foreign tax evasion offence. Arguably, this is a lower threshold that the notion of 'being knowingly concerned in' the fraudulent evasion of tax or aiding and abetting tax evasion since an associated person can commit conduct which 'relates to' the commission of tax evasion without appreciating that this is necessarily the case.

Jurisdiction

8.50 The new corporate offences have extra-territorial application, and it does not matter where any act or omission committed by an associated person takes place. This is because section 48(1) of the Act expressly provides that:

> It is immaterial for the purposes of section 45 or 46 (except to the extent provided by section 46(2)) whether -
>
> (a) any relevant conduct of a relevant body, or
> (b) any conduct which constitutes part of a relevant UK tax evasion facilitation offence or foreign tax evasion facilitation offence, or
> (c) any conduct which constitutes part of a relevant UK tax evasion offence or foreign tax evasion offence, takes place in the United Kingdom or elsewhere.

8.51 Irrespective of where the offences were committed, the criminal courts in the UK have jurisdiction to try the company or partnership, pursuant to section 48(2). As the Explanatory Notes explain, 'where a person acting in the capacity of a person associated to an overseas relevant body commits a tax evasion facilitation offence in relation to a UK taxpayer's tax evasion offence, the section 45 offence will be committed and can be tried by the courts of the United Kingdom'.[19] Therefore, where a person associated with a foreign company or partnership facilitates tax evasion abroad and HM Revenue & Customs is the loser, the company can be prosecuted in the UK for its failure to prevent the facilitation conduct. Conversely, where a person associated with a foreign company or partnership but with a business presence in the UK facilitates tax evasion and a foreign revenue authority is the loser, again, there is jurisdiction to prosecute the company or partnership in the UK for its failure to prevent the conduct in question.

---

19 Ibid, paragraph 313.

Individual liability for directors and partners

8.52 The legislation is silent on whether, in addition to company or partnership liability, criminal liability can be imposed on a director or partner for aiding and abetting, or encouraging and assisting, the company or partnership in the commission of the section 45 or 46 offences. But there is no reason in principle why criminal liability should not be imposed personally where a director or partner assists a person associated with the company or partnership to facilitate the commission by a client of conduct amounting to tax evasion. Whether indicted under section 8 of the Accessories and Abettors Act 1861 or under Part 2 of the Serious Crime Act 2007, the narrative would be the same.[20]

---

20 See Laird, ibid, 938–9.

CHAPTER 9

Prosecution and the reasonable prevention procedures defence

Introduction

9.1 The two new corporate offences introduced by the Act represent an expansion of the UK's 'failure to prevent' model of criminal liability. The offences have attracted much attention but the circumstances in which they are likely to be prosecuted merit careful consideration along with the mechanics of the single defence available to any company or partnership that is ultimately prosecuted.

9.2 In brief, where a company or partnership is prosecuted for an offence of failure to prevent the facilitation of UK tax evasion or the failure to prevent the facilitation, there is a single defence which enables the company or partnership to avoid criminal liability if the constituent elements of the offence are made out.

9.3 Under section 45(2):

> It is a defence for B to prove that, when the UK tax evasion facilitation offence was committed -
>
> (a) B had in place such prevention procedures as it was reasonable in all the circumstances to expect B to have in place, or
> (b) it was not reasonable in all the circumstances to expect B to have any prevention procedures in place.

9.4 The defence is formulated in identical terms under section 46(3), subject to the replacement of 'UK tax evasion facilitation offence' with 'foreign tax evasion facilitation offence'.

Criminal prosecution

Policy

9.5 It is HM Revenue & Customs' publicly declared policy to respond to instances of tax evasion by using civil fraud investigation procedures under COP 9 since it is more cost-effective than criminal investigation and prosecution. The latter is reserved for cases where HM Revenue & Customs needs to send a strong deterrent message or where the conduct involved is such that only a criminal sanction is appropriate. HM Revenue & Customs gives examples of the kind of circumstances in which it will generally consider starting a criminal, rather than civil investigation. Of relevance in the context of the new criminal offences are the following three circumstances:

- where an individual holds a position of trust or responsibility;
- where, pursuing an avoidance scheme, reliance is placed on a false or altered document or such reliance or material facts are misrepresented to enhance the credibility of a scheme;

- where deliberate concealment, deception, conspiracy or corruption is suspected in cases involving the use of false or forged documents.

9.6 Although legislation establishing new criminal offences is not retrospective, criminal liability could be engaged where the conduct constituting facilitation takes place before 30 September 2017 and continues after this date. A typical example could arise where an accountant or tax planner (1) devises for a taxpayer a bespoke tax arrangement scheme before 30 September 2017, (2) continues to support the taxpayer with arrangements for the scheme on or after 30 September 2017, and (3) HM Revenue & Customs subsequently alleges that that the tax arrangement constituted tax evasion masquerading as tax avoidance. The fact that the arrangement was devised before 30 September 2017 is unlikely to spare the accountant or tax planner's company or partnership from criminal liability if reasonable preventative procedures have not been put in place.[1]

Companies and partnerships

9.7 Where a prosecution is brought against a company, it is the company in its capacity as a legal person against which the criminal charge is levied and, if convicted, the conviction will be recorded against the company's names. The normal rules of criminal procedure apply where a company has been placed in administration, or where the company has been liquidated and needs to be restored to the companies' register for prosecution. The position regarding a partnership is more complicated. This is because a partnership does not have the same status as a legal person in the same way as a company. Section 50(1) of the Act provides that criminal proceedings for an offence under section 45 or 46 alleged to have been committed by a partnership must be brought in the name of the partnership and not in the name of the partners. In this way, partnerships are afforded equivalence for the purposes of criminal prosecution for the new offences. Section 50(3) stipulates that a fine imposed on a partnership must be paid of the partnership assets.

Consent in foreign tax evasion cases

9.8 There is no restriction in the legislation on the ability of the Crown Prosecution Service, any other prosecuting authority and even a private prosecutor, to initiate a criminal prosecution against a company or partnership under section 45 of the Act if the criteria regarding sufficiency of evidence is established. The position is different, however, where section 46 is involved. Here, section 49(2) and (3) of the Act provide that no criminal prosecution can be commenced without the consent of the Director of Public Prosecutions (in England, Wales and Northern Ireland) or the Director of the Serious Fraud Office. Section 49(4) requires the consent to be given personally or, where the Director is unavailable, by another person designated in writing by the Director as authorised to exercise this function. There is no need for an equivalent provision in Scotland since there prosecutions are brought by the Procurator Fiscal. The restriction on the commencement of criminal proceedings under section 46 is eminently sensible. Where foreign tax evasion is involved,

---

1 For an analogy with the offence in section 328(1) of the Proceeds of Crime Act 2002, see *R v Khanani* [2009] EWCA Crim 276; also *R v GH* [2015] 2 Cr App R 12.

the nexus with the UK may be tenuous and there may be wider public interest considerations for a senior Government official to take into account. As the Government guidance explains, it is highly unlikely that a prosecution would be taken forward where a foreign tax was in some way incompatible with the UK's legal values, such as respect for human rights. It would also be very unlikely to be in the public interest to bring a prosecution where a foreign tax was discriminatory and applied based on race, religion or gender.[2]

Consent in foreign tax evasion cases

9.9 In passing, it is interesting to note that the Director of the Serious Fraud Office is contemplated as a potential prosecutor in section 45 and 46 cases. Tax evasion can involve serious or complex fraud, but historically tax frauds have been investigated by officers from HM Revenue & Customs and, at least in recent years after the closure of the Revenue & Customs Prosecutions Office in 2006, prosecuted by the Crown Prosecution Service. It remains to be seen whether, with the enactment of the new corporate criminal offences, the Serious Fraud Office becomes more active in the prosecution of tax fraud. In this context, it should be borne in mind that almost every commercial corruption case will involve a fraud on the revenue. When funds to support a bribe are paid out by a company, invariably the withdrawal is made under cover of a false invoice. Very few companies will openly record in their books and records that a payment of its funds was made as a bribe. The false invoice will have distorted the figure shown in the company's accounts for legitimate trading expenses, with the effect that the net profit figure on which corporation tax is levied will have been artificially reduced. The recipient of a bribe rarely declares the income on his tax return, preferring to secrete the payment in a bank account operated by an offshore company with nominee directors and shareholders. Therefore, as well as a corporation tax fraud having taken place, there is also an income tax fraud that deprives the revenue authority of money to which it would otherwise have been entitled. Where a person associated with a company becomes involved in the payment or receipt of a bribe, there is a distinct possibility that the facilitation of a tax fraud may also have been committed. If one of the companies is based in the UK and another located abroad, offences under both sections 45 and 46 would be committed. Given that HM Revenue & Customs does not have an obligation to investigate foreign tax evasion, or for that matter collect foreign revenue, this may become the main deployment of the foreign tax evasion facilitation. In a case where a company has self-reported its commission of an offence contrary to section 45 or section 46, a deferred prosecution agreement could be offered by the Crown Prosecution Service or the Serious Fraud Office under Schedule 17 of the Crime and Courts Act 2013.

Penalties

9.10 On conviction on indictment for either the section 45 or 46 offence, a company or partnership is subject to the imposition of unlimited fine. In summary proceedings, the fine is limited to £5,000 (sections 45(8), 46(7)). On indictment, it is clear that a confiscation order can be made against a company and presumably also a partnership. There is power to

---

2   Ibid, 12.

make a compensation order in favour of HM Revenue & Customs or a foreign revenue authority if a tax loss has been suffered. The amount of compensation would be carved out of the monies that would otherwise be subject to the confiscation order. In cases on indictment and tried summarily, an order for costs of the prosecution can be imposed following conviction. Conviction will have additional consequences for companies and partnerships. It may require disclosure to professional regulators who may take the conviction into account when assessing an application for authorisation. Banks will be less enthusiastic to provide credit to a company or partnership that has been convicted of a section 45 or section 46 offence, and the company or partnership may be excluded from benefiting from public contracts.

Prevention procedures defence

9.11 Prevention procedures in sections 45(2) and 46(3) are defined in section 45(3) to mean 'procedures designed to prevent persons acting in the capacity of a person associated with B from committing UK tax evasion facilitation offences', and in section 46(4), from committing 'foreign tax evasion facilitation offences under the law of the foreign country concerned'.

9.12 By section 47(1), the Chancellor of the Exchequer is required 'to prepare and publish guidance about procedures that companies and partnerships can put in place to prevent persons acting in the capacity of an associated person from committing UK tax evasion facilitation offences or foreign tax evasion facilitation offences'. The Government issued guidance on 1 September 2017.[3] In addition, section 47(7) enables the Chancellor to endorse guidance prepared and published by others. It is therefore possible for guidance prepared by a trade association, for example, addressing the risks arising within that sector of industry, to be endorsed by Government. The Law Society issued guidance to solicitors on 8 September 2017 and at the time of writing endorsement from the Chancellor is awaited.[4]

9.13 It is interesting to note that Parliament does not envisage that the application of the guidance will be mandatory. Rather, the tilt is permissive, so that companies and partnerships 'can' put the guidance in place if they should wish to do so. In this sense, the legislative approach is different from that taken in the anti-money laundering legislation where, under section 330(8) of the Proceeds of Crime Act 2002, a court is obliged to consider whether a person working in the regulated sector followed guidance on anti-money laundering provisions that had been approved by HM Treasury when determining whether a criminal offence had been committed pursuant to section 330(1). There is no equivalent provision in section 47 of the Criminal Finances Act 2017.

9.14 It is quite clear from the wording of the prevention procedures defence that the obligation to prove the reasonableness of these provisions rests with the company or partnership. In this instance, the company or partnership will need to prove the reasonableness of the procedures on the balance of probabilities.[5] As the House of Lords made clear in

---

3 HM Revenue & Customs, Tackling tax evasion: Government guidance for the corporate offences of failure to prevent the criminal facilitation of tax evasion (1 September 2017).
4 Criminal Finances Act 2017, The Law Society, 8 September 2017.
5 *R v MK; R v Gega (also known as Maione)* [2018] EWCA Crim 667, paragraph 16.

R v DPP, ex parte Kebilene.[6] a statute may place the legal burden of proof of a defence on the defendant without infringing the presumption of innocence which is reflected in Article 6(2) of the European Convention on Human Rights.

9.15 The guidance provides some interesting examples that demonstrate the potential reach of the new offences. In one scenario, the guidance posits a mid-size car parts maker (UKCO) operating in the UK and Europe, which enters into a sub-contracting arrangement with a UK distributor. The senior managers of the UK distributor created a false invoicing scheme with the assistance of a purchaser, allowing the purchaser to evade UK taxes due on its purchase of the car parts in the UK. If UKCO had put procedures and processes in place to prevent its sub-contractor from evading tax, it will not have committed a criminal offence. But if it had failed to do so, criminal liability would follow.[7] It would seem to follow from this example that UKCO would not need to know that its sub-contractor was committing tax evasion; the fact that its sub-contractor, as an associated person, was complicit in the commission of the tax evasion conduct would be sufficient.

Guiding principles

9.16 In its guidance the Government indicates that prevention procedures put in place by relevant bodies to prevent tax evasion from being committed on their behalf should be informed by the six principles:

- risk assessment
- proportionality of risk-based prevention procedures
- top-level commitment
- due diligence
- communication (including training)
- monitoring and review.

9.17 These principles are not prescriptive and, in the words of the Government guidance, they are intended to be flexible and outcome focussed. Most importantly, procedures to prevent facilitation of tax evasion should be proportionate to risk.

Risk assessment

9.18 The Government guidance recommends that companies and partnerships assess the nature and extent of their exposure to the risk of those who act in the capacity of a person associated with it criminally facilitating tax evasion offences. The risk assessment must be documented and kept under review. Risk assessment procedures that allow a company or partnership to accurately identify and prioritise the risks it faces will usually reflect a few common themes. Oversight of the risk assessment by senior management is essential, with an appropriate allocation of resources to the detection and monitoring of risk. Internal and external information sources that enable the risk to be assessed and reviewed must be identified, with any gaps in the information available to the company or partnership and how these gaps might be filled. Due diligence enquiries are key, and there must be accurate

---

6   [2000] 2 AC 326.
7   Ibid, 9–10.

and appropriate documentation of the risk assessment and a clear articulation of tax evasion facilitation risks where this is considered as part of the wider risk assessment. The risk assessments need to be periodically reviewed and updated in line of changing circumstances, and companies and partnerships are expected to put in place procedures to identify emerging risks. There is an obvious commonality with the factors to be considered when preparing a risk assessment under the Bribery Act 2010, and companies and partnerships should consider from a tax evasion perspective the commonly encountered risks identified in the Government guidance on the Bribery Act 2010.[8] These risks are:

Country risk: this is evidenced by perceived high levels of secrecy or use as a tax shelter. Such countries are also unlikely to subscribe to the Common Reporting Standard and be given a low tax transparency score by the OECD.

Sectoral risk: some sectors pose a higher risk of facilitating tax evasion than others, such as financial services, tax advisory and legal sectors.

Transaction risk: certain types of transaction give rise to higher risks, for example, complex tax planning structures involving high levels of secrecy, overly complex supply chains, or transactions involving politically exposed persons.

Business opportunity risk: such risks might arise in high-value projects or with projects involving many parties, jurisdictions, or intermediaries.

Business partnership risk: certain relationships may involve higher risk, for example, the use of intermediaries in transactions, where those intermediaries are based in jurisdictions operating lower levels of transparency and disclosure. Entering into a business partnership with organisations that have no fraud prevention procedures or have known deficiencies in their fraud procedures may involve higher risk.

9.19 In addition, the following risks may also be considered for tax fraud:

Product risk: certain products and services may have a higher risk of misuse by either clients of associated persons.

Customer risk: the identification that a business unit has risks related to customers or products is highly likely to indicate that there is a greater risk of the criminal facilitation of tax evasion by an associated person.

9.20 From a tax evasion perspective, the following aspects would give rise to concern, which would need to be explored fully in enhanced customer due diligence enquiries:

- the business relationship is conducted in unusual circumstances;
- there are non-resident customers;
- legal persons or arrangements that are personal asset holding vehicles;
- companies that have nominee shareholders or shares in bearer form;
- business that are cash intensive;
- the ownership structure of the company appears unusual or excessively complex;

---

8   *The Bribery Act 2010, Guidance* (Ministry of Justice, March 2011).

- customers or transactions located in countries identified by credible sources as not having adequate anti-money laundering and counter-terrorism financing (AML/CTF) procedures;
- countries subject to sanctions, embargoes, or similar measures issued by, for example, the UN;
- countries identified by credible sources as providing support for terrorist activities, or that have designated terrorist organisations operating within their country;
- there are private banking arrangements;
- anonymous transactions (which may include cash);
- non-face-to-face business relationships or transactions;
- payment received from unknown or un-associated third parties.

9.21 That said, there are some customer-risk factors that will afford a company or partnership some comfort in terms of the level of customer due diligence that needs to be performed:

- The person with which the company or partnership is associated is subject to requirements to combat money laundering and terrorist financing consistent with Financial Action Task Force (FATF) Recommendations, and implemented these requirements.
- The person with which the company or partnership is associated is:
    - a public company listed on a stock exchange and subject to disclosure requirements that impose requirements to ensure adequate transparency of beneficial ownership;
    - a public administration or enterprise.
- The product is a life assurance policy where the premium is low; an insurance policy for a pension scheme if there is no early surrender option and the policy cannot be used as collateral; a pension, superannuation or similar scheme that provides retirement benefits to employees, where contributions are made by way of deduction from wages, and the scheme rules do not permit the assignment of a member's interest under the scheme; and a financial product or service that provides appropriately defined and limited services to certain types of customers, so as to increase access for financial inclusion purposes.

Proportionality of risk-based prevention procedures

9.22 Government guidance requires that reasonable procedures for a company or partnership to adopt to prevent persons acting in the capacity of a person associated with it from criminally facilitating tax evasion must be proportionate to the risk the relevant body faces of persons associated with it committing tax evasion facilitation offences. This will depend on the nature, scale and complexity of the relevant body's activities. The guidance recognises that the reasonableness of prevention procedures must take account of the level of control and supervision the organisation is able to exercise over a person acting on its behalf, and the proximity of the person to the company or partnership. The guidance makes the point that the new criminal offences do not require companies and partnerships to undertake excessively burdensome procedures to eradicate all risk, but they do demand more than mere lip-service to preventing the criminal facilitation of tax evasion.

Top-level commitment

9.23 Regarding top-level commitment, the management of a company or partnership must be committed to preventing persons acting in the capacity of a person associated with it from engaging in criminal facilitation of tax evasion. Management is obligated to foster a culture within the company or partnership in which activity intended to facilitate tax evasion is never acceptable. The underlying rationale is that the most senior levels of the organisation are best placed to foster a culture where actions intended to facilitate tax evasion are considered unacceptable. Senior management is encouraged to become involved in the creation and implementation of preventative procedures. It is also intended to encourage senior management involvement in the decision-making process in relation to the assessment of risk, where this is appropriate.

9.24 Typical evidence that demonstrate senior management's commitment would include board members having designated responsibility for preventative measures; a top-level endorsement of the company or partnership's preventative policy and associated publications; high-level engagement with associated persons and external bodies to help articulate the company or partnership's policies; designated responsibility for certifying the assessment of risk; designated responsibility at senior level for disciplinary procedures relating to the breach of the company or partnership's policies; and senior management's commitment to whistleblowing processes and rejecting profit by way of facilitating tax evasion.

Due diligence

9.25 In addition to the Government guidance on risk assessment, the guidance addresses as a distinct factor the importance of due diligence procedures. A company or partnership is required to apply due diligence procedures, taking an appropriate and risk-based approach, in respect of persons who perform or will perform services on behalf of the company or partnership, to mitigate identified risks. It needs to be borne in mind that due diligence procedures for the new criminal offences must be capable of identifying the risk of criminal facilitation of tax evasion by associated persons. Merely applying old procedures tailored to a different type of risk (or clients-focused procedures) will not necessarily be an adequate response to tackle the risk of tax evasion facilitation. A company or partnership may, upon conducting a risk assessment, decide that services provided to a certain group of its clients pose a higher risk of being misused to perpetrate a tax fraud. As a result, they may apply increased scrutiny over those providing services to those clients, or over those who provide those services, to address the specific risks of tax evasion facilitation identified.

Communication (including training)

9.26 It is axiomatic that, having established prevention policies and procedures, these are communicated, embedded and understood throughout the organisation, through internal and external communication, including training. Training needs to be proportionate to the risk to which the company or partnership assesses it is exposed. There must be communication across all levels within a company or partnership, and it is important that the company or partnership ensures awareness and understanding of its policies amongst those who provide services for or on its behalf. The company or partnership may feel that it is necessary to require its representatives to undertake fraud or potentially tax evasion-specific training, depending on the risks to which it is exposed. This would be to ensure that they have the skills needed to identify when they and those around them might be at risk of engaging in an illegal act and what whistle-blowing procedures should be followed if this occurs.

9.27 The nature and extent of professional training is variable. The training must be proportionate to the risk faced. Some companies and partnerships may wish to incorporate training into their existing financial crime prevention training, others may wish to introduce bespoke training to address specific tax evasion risks. Consideration should be given to the specific training needs of those in the highest risk posts, and to training required to ensure that the company or partnership representatives understand the process for referring any concerns. The effectiveness of training should be monitored and evaluated. Companies and organisations may choose either to train third party associated persons or encourage them to ensure their own arrangements are in place.

Monitoring and review

9.28 The need for a company or partnership to monitor and review its preventative procedures cannot be understated. There is no point in developing procedures that are not followed and there is a need to make improvements where necessary.

9.29 The nature of the risks faced by an organisation will change and evolve over time. This may be as a natural result of external developments, the failure to prevent an incidence of facilitation of tax evasion by an associated person, or because of changes in the organisation's activities. The organisation will therefore need to change its procedures in response to the changes in the risks that it faces.

Conclusion

At the time of writing, the robust investigative tools appearing in the Criminal Finances Act 2017 have been complemented by measures introduced by the Sanctions and Anti-Money Laundering Act 2018 which was passed on 23 May 2018. Notably, an unsuccessful amendment to the Criminal Finances Bill 2016 which would have seen that Act introduce a public register of beneficial owners of companies registered in British Overseas Territories has had a reversal of fortune. A publicly accessible offshore company register, pursuant to Part 2 of the Sanctions and Anti-Money Laundering Act 2018, shall be developed by 2020.

Parliament's Treasury Committee has also since launched an inquiry into economic crime. The scale of money laundering and terrorist financing in the UK and the means by which it is enabled is a key focus. A further Inquiry, led by the House of Lords, has commenced in relation to the Bribery Act 2010. Separately, the Law Commission of England and Wales is performing a comprehensive review of the suspicious activity report regime. Changes to the SAR framework are afoot, but it is unlikely that they will disturb any of the new powers and frameworks introduced by the Criminal Finances Act 2017.

The UK's initiatives, however, are only one piece of the broader money laundering and terrorist financing puzzle. On 19 June 2018, the European Union's Fifth Anti Money Laundering Directive (5AMLD) was published. The directive will bring cryptocurrency exchange platforms into the regulated sector and boost protection for whistleblowers who report a money laundering suspicion. By the time the 2020 transposition deadline happens, the UK will be well outside the European Union; but for the regulated sector to continue business with Europe it is inevitable that domestic anti-money laundering requirements will fall into line with 5AMLD. Previously unregulated virtual currency exchanges will find themselves subject to the legal duty to report a money laundering and terrorist-financing suspicion or risk regulatory action and potential prosecution, and on the receiving end of the further information orders, disclosure orders and information-sharing requests introduced by the Criminal Finances Act 2017. In due course, the question arises whether a forfeiture regime under Part 5 Proceeds of Crime Act 2002 applicable to cryptoassets will be discussed. Although there is a compelling argument that there are far easier and less volatile ways to conceal the profits of criminal activity, for the sophisticated criminal certain cryptoassets are attractive because they are difficult for law enforcement to identify and freeze.

Negotiation over the European Union's Sixth Anti Money Laundering Directive is also underway. The current draft proposes a standardisation of the offences across the European Union that can give rise to money laundering activity, called the 'predicate' offences. The anti-money laundering and terrorist-financing space is ever developing and what is clear is that the UK is not alone in introducing more aggressive legislation and forging new law enforcement partnerships, both with foreign counterparts and the private sector. Throughout the European Union and globally, there is a move towards greater action being taken to combat criminal finances. On 2 July 2018, for example, HM Revenue & Customs formed an alliance with counterparts from the US, Australia, Canada and the Netherlands centred on intelligence sharing to tackle tax crimes.

However, the proof of impact plainly lies in the enforcement and use of the new powers and frameworks. When legislation is passed, it is quite easy for a country to be seen to be doing something about money laundering and terrorist financing. As far as the Criminal Finances Act 2017 is concerned, it is too early to tell whether the new powers and definitions will be regularly relied upon or whether their strength is in their *in terrorem* or deterrent effect on would-be movers of illicit property through the UK. The early indication is that certain provisions will be used more than others. The new corporate offences are yet to be prosecuted but UWOs have been successfully obtained and police forces have embraced the civil power to freeze money held in bank accounts. In June 2018, in a ground-breaking case, £2.5 million in a bank account believed to be intended for unlawful use was detained by a magistrates' court.

As policy and law directed at illicit wealth develops in the UK and test cases emerge, striking a tolerable balance between tough and effective measures and fairness to the individual or company – who may not be the subject of any actual criminal investigation – will continue to be a challenge. Whilst the concealed nature of illicit wealth calls for innovative law, the need for procedural fairness to be extended to even the most suspicious of persons lies at the heart of any mature legal system. Inevitably, the width and practical operation of certain provisions in the Criminal Finances Act 2017 will attract judicial consideration.

But although this is to come, legislation like the Criminal Finances Act 2017 sends a message to the world that the UK is being more proactive about tackling money laundering and terrorist financing. It is asserting itself as a world leader in this regard. In the long term this is vital if the UK's status as a responsible and unparalleled financial centre is to be protected. The UK, however, must not only think of itself. To be a world leader in combating criminal finances, it must continue collaborating with and giving assistance to countries developing their own less mature anti-money laundering and counter-terrorist financing systems. Otherwise, for all of the UK's proactive policymaking and legislative development, there is a risk that it will have the unintended consequences of pushing illicit money elsewhere and sprouting new havens.

APPENDIX

ELIZABETH II c. **22**

Criminal Finances Act 2017

2017 CHAPTER 22

An Act to amend the Proceeds of Crime Act 2002; make provision in connection with terrorist property; create corporate offences for cases where a person associated with a body corporate or partnership facilitates the commission by another person of a tax evasion offence; and for connected purposes. [27th April 2017]

BE IT ENACTED by the Queen's most Excellent Majesty, by and with the advice and consent of the Lords Spiritual and Temporal, and Commons, in this present Parliament assembled, and by the authority of the same, as follows: –

Part 1

PROCEEDS OF CRIME

Chapter 1

INVESTIGATIONS

Unexplained wealth orders: England and Wales and Northern Ireland

1 Unexplained wealth orders: England and Wales and Northern Ireland

In Chapter 2 of Part 8 of the Proceeds of Crime Act 2002 (investigations: England and Wales and Northern Ireland), after section 362 insert –

"*Unexplained wealth orders*

362A Unexplained wealth orders
   (1) The High Court may, on an application made by an enforcement authority, make an unexplained wealth order in respect of any property if the court is satisfied that each of the requirements for the making of the order is fulfilled.

(2) An application for an order must –

(a) specify or describe the property in respect of which the order is sought, and
(b) specify the person whom the enforcement authority thinks holds the property ("the respondent") (and the person specified may include a person outside the United Kingdom).

(3) An unexplained wealth order is an order requiring the respondent to provide a statement –

(a) setting out the nature and extent of the respondent's interest in the property in respect of which the order is made,
(b) explaining how the respondent obtained the property (including, in particular, how any costs incurred in obtaining it were met),
(c) where the property is held by the trustees of a settlement, setting out such details of the settlement as may be specified in the order, and
(d) setting out such other information in connection with the property as may be so specified.

(4) The order must specify –

(a) the form and manner in which the statement is to be given,
(b) the person to whom it is to be given, and
(c) the place at which it is to be given or, if it is to be given in writing, the address to which it is to be sent.

(5) The order may, in connection with requiring the respondent to provide the statement mentioned in subsection (3), also require the respondent to produce documents of a kind specified or described in the order.

(6) The respondent must comply with the requirements imposed by an unexplained wealth order within whatever period the court may specify (and different periods may be specified in relation to different requirements).

(7) In this Chapter "enforcement authority" means –

(a) the National Crime Agency,
(b) Her Majesty's Revenue and Customs,
(c) the Financial Conduct Authority,
(d) the Director of the Serious Fraud Office, or
(e) the Director of Public Prosecutions (in relation to England and Wales) or the Director of Public Prosecutions for Northern Ireland (in relation to Northern Ireland).

362B Requirements for making of unexplained wealth order

(1) These are the requirements for the making of an unexplained wealth order in respect of any property.
(2) The High Court must be satisfied that there is reasonable cause to believe that –

(a) the respondent holds the property, and
(b) the value of the property is greater than £50,000.

APPENDIX: CRIMINAL FINANCES ACT 2017

(3) The High Court must be satisfied that there are reasonable grounds for suspecting that the known sources of the respondent's lawfully obtained income would have been insufficient for the purposes of enabling the respondent to obtain the property.

(4) The High Court must be satisfied that –

    (a) the respondent is a politically exposed person, or

    (b) there are reasonable grounds for suspecting that –

        (i) the respondent is, or has been, involved in serious crime (whether in a part of the United Kingdom or elsewhere), or

        (ii) a person connected with the respondent is, or has been, so involved.

(5) It does not matter for the purposes of subsection (2)(a) –

    (a) whether or not there are other persons who also hold the property;

    (b) whether the property was obtained by the respondent before or after the coming into force of this section.

(6) For the purposes of subsection (3) –

    (a) regard is to be had to any mortgage, charge or other kind of security that it is reasonable to assume was or may have been available to the respondent for the purposes of obtaining the property;

    (b) it is to be assumed that the respondent obtained the property for a price equivalent to its market value;

    (c) income is "lawfully obtained" if it is obtained lawfully under the laws of the country from where the income arises;

    (d) "known" sources of the respondent's income are the sources of income (whether arising from employment, assets or otherwise) that are reasonably ascertainable from available information at the time of the making of the application for the order;

    (e) where the property is an interest in other property comprised in a settlement, the reference to the respondent obtaining the property is to be taken as if it were a reference to the respondent obtaining direct ownership of such share in the settled property as relates to, or is fairly represented by, that interest.

(7) In subsection (4)(a), "politically exposed person" means a person who is –

    (a) an individual who is, or has been, entrusted with prominent public functions by an international organisation or by a State other than the United Kingdom or another EEA State,

    (b) a family member of a person within paragraph (a),

    (c) known to be a close associate of a person within that paragraph, or

    (d) otherwise connected with a person within that paragraph.

(8) Article 3 of Directive 2015/849/EU of the European Parliament and of the Council of 20 May 2015 applies for the purposes of determining –

    (a) whether a person has been entrusted with prominent public functions (see point (9) of that Article),

(b) whether a person is a family member (see point (10) of that Article), and
(c) whether a person is known to be a close associate of another (see point (11) of that Article).

(9) For the purposes of this section –

(a) a person is involved in serious crime in a part of the United Kingdom or elsewhere if the person would be so involved for the purposes of Part 1 of the Serious Crime Act 2007 (see in particular sections 2, 2A and 3 of that Act);
(b) section 1122 of the Corporation Tax Act 2010 ("connected" persons) applies in determining whether a person is connected with another.

(10) Where the property in respect of which the order is sought comprises more than one item of property, the reference in subsection (2)(b) to the value of the property is to the total value of those items.

362C Effect of order: cases of non-compliance

(1) This section applies in a case where the respondent fails, without reasonable excuse, to comply with the requirements imposed by an unexplained wealth order in respect of any property before the end of the response period.
(2) The property is to be presumed to be recoverable property for the purposes of any proceedings taken in respect of the property under Part 5, unless the contrary is shown.
(3) The presumption in subsection (2) applies in relation to property –

(a) only so far as relating to the respondent's interest in the property, and
(b) only if the value of that interest is greater than the sum specified in section 362B(2)(b).

It is for the court hearing the proceedings under Part 5 in relation to which reliance is placed on the presumption to determine the matters in this subsection.

(4) The "response period" is whatever period the court specifies under section 362A(6) as the period within which the requirements imposed by the order are to be complied with (or the period ending the latest, if more than one is specified in respect of different requirements).
(5) For the purposes of subsection (1) –

(a) a respondent who purports to comply with the requirements imposed by an unexplained wealth order is not to be taken to have failed to comply with the order (see instead section 362D);
(b) where an unexplained wealth order imposes more than one requirement on the respondent, the respondent is to be taken to have failed to comply with the requirements imposed by the order unless each of the requirements is complied with or is purported to be complied with.

(6) Subsections (7) and (8) apply in determining the respondent's interest for the purposes of subsection (3) in a case where the respondent to the unexplained wealth order –

(a) is connected with another person who is, or has been, involved in serious crime (see subsection (4)(b)(ii) of section 362B), or

(b) is a politically exposed person of a kind mentioned in paragraph (b), (c) or (d) of subsection (7) of that section (family member, known close associates etc of individual entrusted with prominent public functions).

(7) In a case within subsection (6)(a), the respondent's interest is to be taken to include any interest in the property of the person involved in serious crime with whom the respondent is connected.

(8) In a case within subsection (6)(b), the respondent's interest is to be taken to include any interest in the property of the person mentioned in subsection (7)(a) of section 362B.

(9) Where an unexplained wealth order is made in respect of property comprising more than one item of property, the reference in subsection (3)(b) to the value of the respondent's interest in the property is to the total value of the respondent's interest in those items.

362D Effect of order: cases of compliance or purported compliance

(1) This section applies in a case where, before the end of the response period (as defined by section 362C(4)), the respondent complies, or purports to comply, with the requirements imposed by an unexplained wealth order in respect of any property in relation to which the order is made.

(2) If an interim freezing order has effect in relation to the property (see section 362J), the enforcement authority must determine what enforcement or investigatory proceedings, if any, it considers ought to be taken in relation to the property.

(3) A determination under subsection (2) must be made within the period of 60 days starting with the day of compliance.

(4) If the determination under subsection (2) is that no further enforcement or investigatory proceedings ought to be taken in relation to the property, the enforcement authority must notify the High Court of that fact as soon as reasonably practicable (and in any event before the end of the 60 day period mentioned in subsection (3)).

(5) If there is no interim freezing order in effect in relation to the property, the enforcement authority may (at any time) determine what, if any, enforcement or investigatory proceedings it considers ought to be taken in relation to the property.

(6) A determination under this section to take no further enforcement or investigatory proceedings in relation to any property does not prevent such proceedings being taken subsequently (whether as a result of new information or otherwise, and whether or not by the same enforcement authority) in relation to the property.

(7) For the purposes of this section –

(a) the respondent complies with the requirements imposed by an unexplained wealth order only if all of the requirements are complied with,

(b) references to the day of compliance are to the day on which the requirements imposed by the order are complied with (or, if the requirements are complied with over more than one day, the last of those days), and

(c) where an order requires the sending of information in writing to, or the production of documents at, an address specified in the order, compliance with the order (so far as relating to that requirement) occurs when the written information is received, or the documents are produced, at that address,

and in paragraphs (a) to (c) references to compliance include purported compliance.

(8) In this section "enforcement or investigatory proceedings" means any proceedings in relation to property taken under –

(a) Part 2 or 4 (confiscation proceedings in England and Wales or Northern Ireland) (in relation to cases where the enforcement authority is also a prosecuting authority for the purposes of that Part),
(b) Part 5 (civil recovery of the proceeds of unlawful conduct), or
(c) this Chapter.

362E Offence
(1) A person commits an offence if, in purported compliance with a requirement imposed by an unexplained wealth order, the person –

(a) makes a statement that the person knows to be false or misleading in a material particular, or
(b) recklessly makes a statement that is false or misleading in a material particular.

(2) A person guilty of an offence under this section is liable –

(a) on conviction on indictment, to imprisonment for a term not exceeding 2 years, or to a fine, or to both;
(b) on summary conviction in England and Wales, to imprisonment for a term not exceeding 12 months, or to a fine, or to both;
(c) on summary conviction in Northern Ireland, to imprisonment for a term not exceeding 6 months, or to a fine not exceeding the statutory maximum, or to both.

(3) In relation to an offence committed before the coming into force of section 282 of the Criminal Justice Act 2003 (increase in maximum sentence on summary conviction of offence triable either way), the reference in subsection (2)(b) to 12 months is to be read as a reference to 6 months.

362F Statements
(1) A statement made by a person in response to a requirement imposed by an unexplained wealth order may not be used in evidence against that person in criminal proceedings.
(2) Subsection (1) does not apply –

(a) in the case of proceedings under Part 2 or 4,
(b) on a prosecution for an offence under section 362E,
(c) on a prosecution for an offence under section 5 of the Perjury Act 1911 or Article 10 of the Perjury (Northern Ireland) Order 1979 (S.I. 1979/1714 (N.I. 19)) (false statements), or
(d) on a prosecution for some other offence where, in giving evidence, the person makes a statement inconsistent with the statement mentioned in subsection (1).

(3) A statement may not be used by virtue of subsection (2)(d) against a person unless –

    (a) evidence relating to it is adduced, or
    (b) a question relating to it is asked,

by the person or on the person's behalf in proceedings arising out of the prosecution.

362G Disclosure of information, copying of documents, etc

(1) An unexplained wealth order has effect in spite of any restriction on the disclosure of information (however imposed).
(2) But subsections (1) to (5) of section 361 (rights in connection with privileged information, questions and material) apply in relation to requirements imposed by an unexplained wealth order as they apply in relation to requirements imposed under a disclosure order.
(3) The enforcement authority may take copies of any documents produced by the respondent in connection with complying with the requirements imposed by an unexplained wealth order.
(4) Documents so produced may also be retained for so long as it is necessary to retain them (as opposed to a copy of them) in connection with an investigation of a kind mentioned in section 341 in relation to the property in respect of which the unexplained wealth order is made.
(5) But if the enforcement authority has reasonable grounds to believe that the documents –

    (a) may need to be produced for the purposes of any legal proceedings, and
    (b) might otherwise be unavailable for those purposes, they

may be retained until the proceedings are concluded.

362H Holding of property: trusts and company arrangements etc

(1) This section applies for the purposes of sections 362A and 362B.
(2) The cases in which a person (P) is to be taken to "hold" property include those where –

    (a) P has effective control over the property;
    (b) P is the trustee of a settlement in which the property is comprised;
    (c) P is a beneficiary (whether actual or potential) in relation to such a settlement.

(3) A person is to be taken to have "effective control" over property if, from all the circumstances, it is reasonable to conclude that the person –

    (a) exercises,
    (b) is able to exercise, or
    (c) is entitled to acquire,

direct or indirect control over the property.

(4) Where a person holds property by virtue of subsection (2) references to the person obtaining the property are to be read accordingly.
(5) References to a person who holds or obtains property include any body corporate, whether incorporated or formed under the law of a part of the United Kingdom or in a country or territory outside the United Kingdom.

APPENDIX: CRIMINAL FINANCES ACT 2017

(6) For further provision about how to construe references to the holding of property, see section 414.

362I Supplementary

(1) An application for an unexplained wealth order may be made without notice.
(2) Rules of court may make provision as to the practice and procedure to be followed in connection with proceedings relating to unexplained wealth orders before the High Court in Northern Ireland.
(3) An application to the High Court in Northern Ireland to discharge or vary an unexplained wealth order may be made by –

    (a) the enforcement authority, or
    (b) the respondent.

(4) The High Court in Northern Ireland –

    (a) may discharge the order;
    (b) may vary the order."

2 Interim freezing orders

After section 362I of the Proceeds of Crime Act 2002 (inserted by section 1 above) insert –

"Unexplained wealth orders: interim freezing of property

362J Application for interim freezing order

(1) This section applies where the High Court makes an unexplained wealth order in respect of any property.
(2) The court may make an interim freezing order in respect of the property if the court considers it necessary to do so for the purposes of avoiding the risk of any recovery order that might subsequently be obtained being frustrated.
(3) An interim freezing order is an order that prohibits the respondent to the unexplained wealth order, and any other person with an interest in the property, from in any way dealing with the property (subject to any exclusions under section 362L).
(4) An interim freezing order –

    (a) may be made only on the application of the enforcement authority that applied for the unexplained wealth order to which the interim freezing order relates,
    (b) must be made in the same proceedings as those in which the unexplained wealth order is made, and
    (c) may be combined in one document with the unexplained wealth order.

(5) If an application for an unexplained wealth order in respect of any property is made without notice, an application for an interim freezing order in respect of the property must also be made without notice.

362K Variation and discharge of interim freezing order

(1) The High Court may at any time vary or discharge an interim freezing order.
(2) The High Court must discharge an interim freezing order, so far as it has effect in relation to any property, in each of the following three cases.

(3) The first case is where –

(a) the applicable 48 hour period has ended, and
(b) a relevant application has not been made before the end of that period in relation to the property concerned.

(4) The second case is where –

(a) a relevant application has been made before the end of the applicable 48 hour period in relation to the property concerned, and
(b) proceedings on the application (including any on appeal) have been determined or otherwise disposed of.

(5) The third case is where the court has received a notification in relation to the property concerned under section 362D(4) (notification from enforcement authority of no further proceedings).

(6) The "applicable 48 hour period" is to be read as follows –

(a) in a case where the respondent complies, or purports to comply, with the requirements imposed by an unexplained wealth order before the end of the response period, it is the period of 48 hours beginning with the day after the day with which the 60 day period mentioned in section 362D(3) ends;
(b) in any other case, it is the period of 48 hours beginning with the day after the day with which the response period ends.

(7) In calculating a period of 48 hours for the purposes of subsection (6), no account is to be taken of –

(a) any Saturday or Sunday,
(b) Christmas Day,
(c) Good Friday, or
(d) any day that is a bank holiday under the Banking and Financial Dealings Act 1971 in the part of the United Kingdom in which the interim freezing order concerned is made.

(8) Section 362D(7) applies for the purposes of subsection (6) in determining whether a person complies, or purports to comply, with the requirements imposed by an unexplained wealth order and when such compliance, or purported compliance, takes place.

(9) Before exercising power under this section to vary or discharge an interim freezing order, the court must (as well as giving the parties to the proceedings an opportunity to be heard) give such an opportunity to any person who may be affected by its decision.

(10) Subsection (9) does not apply where the court is acting as required by subsection (2).

(11) In this section –

"relevant application" means an application for –

(a) a restraint order under section 41 or 190,
(b) a property freezing order, or
(c) an interim receiving order;

"response period" has the meaning given by section 362C(4).

362L Exclusions
(1) The power to vary an interim freezing order includes (amongst other things) power to make exclusions as follows –

(a) power to exclude property from the order, and
(b) power, otherwise than by excluding property from the order, to make exclusions from the prohibition on dealing with the property to which the order applies.

(2) Exclusions from the prohibition on dealing with the property to which the order applies (other than exclusions of property from the order) may also be made when the order is made.
(3) An exclusion may (amongst other things) make provision for the purpose of enabling any person –

(a) to meet the person's reasonable living expenses, or
(b) to carry on any trade, business, profession or occupation.

(4) An exclusion may be made subject to conditions.
(5) Where the court exercises the power to make an exclusion for the purpose of enabling a person to meet legal expenses that the person has incurred, or may incur, in respect of proceedings under this Chapter, it must ensure that the exclusion –

(a) is limited to reasonable legal expenses that the person has reasonably incurred or reasonably incurs,
(b) specifies the total amount that may be released for legal expenses in pursuance of the exclusion, and
(c) is made subject to the same conditions as would be the required conditions (see section 286A) if the order had been made under section 245A (in addition to any conditions under subsection (4)).

(6) The court, in deciding whether to make an exclusion for the purpose of enabling a person to meet legal expenses in respect of proceedings under this Chapter –

(a) must have regard to the desirability of the person being represented in any proceedings under this Chapter in which the person is a participant, and
(b) must disregard the possibility that legal representation of the person in any such proceedings might, were an exclusion not made, be made available under arrangements made for the purposes of Part 1 of the Legal Aid, Sentencing and Punishment of Offenders Act 2012 or funded by the Northern Ireland Legal Services Commission.

(7) If excluded property is not specified in the order it must be described in the order in general terms.

362M Restrictions on proceedings and remedies
(1) While an interim freezing order has effect –

(a) the High Court may stay any action, execution or other legal process in respect of the property to which the order applies, and
(b) no distress may be levied, and no power to use the procedure in Schedule 12 to the Tribunals, Courts and Enforcement Act 2007 (taking control of goods)

may be exercised, against the property to which the order applies except with the leave of the High Court and subject to any terms the court may impose.

(2) If a court (whether the High Court or any other court) in which proceedings are pending in respect of any property is satisfied that an interim freezing order has been applied for or made in respect of the property, it may –

(a) stay the proceedings, or
(b) allow them to continue on any terms it thinks fit.

(3) If an interim freezing order applies to a tenancy of any premises, a right of forfeiture in relation to the premises is exercisable –

(a) only with the leave of the High Court, and
(b) subject to any terms that the court may impose.

(4) The reference in subsection (3) to a "right of forfeiture" in relation to premises is to the right of a landlord or other person to whom rent is payable to exercise a right of forfeiture by peaceable re-entry to the premises in respect of any failure by the tenant to comply with a term or condition of the tenancy.

(5) Before exercising a power conferred by this section, the court must (as well as giving the parties to any proceedings concerned an opportunity to be heard) give such an opportunity to any person who may be affected by the court's decision.

362N Receivers in connection with interim freezing orders

(1) This section applies where the High Court makes an interim freezing order on an application by an enforcement authority.
(2) The court may, on an application by the enforcement authority, by order appoint a receiver in respect of any property to which the interim freezing order applies.
(3) An application under subsection (2) may be made at the same time as the application for the interim freezing order or at any time afterwards.
(4) The application may be made without notice if the circumstances of the case are such that notice of the application would prejudice the right of the enforcement authority to obtain a recovery order in respect of any property.
(5) In its application the enforcement authority must nominate a suitably qualified person for appointment as a receiver.
(6) The person nominated may be a member of staff of the enforcement authority.
(7) The enforcement authority may apply a sum received by it under section 280(2) in making payment of the remuneration and expenses of a receiver appointed under this section.
(8) Subsection (7) does not apply in relation to the remuneration of the receiver if that person is a member of staff of the enforcement authority (but it does apply in relation to such remuneration if the receiver is a person providing services under arrangements made by the enforcement authority).

362O Powers of receivers appointed under section 362N

(1) If the High Court appoints a receiver under section 362N on an application by an enforcement authority, the court may act under this section on the application of the authority.

APPENDIX: CRIMINAL FINANCES ACT 2017

(2) The court may by order authorise or require the receiver –

  (a) to exercise any of the powers mentioned in paragraph 5 of Schedule 6 (management powers) in relation to any property in respect of which the receiver is appointed;
  (b) to take any other steps the court thinks appropriate in connection with the management of any such property (including securing the detention, custody or preservation of the property in order to manage it).

(3) The court may by order require any person in respect of whose property the receiver is appointed –

  (a) to bring the property to a place (in England and Wales or, as the case may be, Northern Ireland) specified by the receiver or to place it in the custody of the receiver (if in either case the person is able to do so);
  (b) to do anything the person is reasonably required to do by the receiver for the preservation of the property.

(4) The court may by order require any person in respect of whose property the receiver is appointed to bring any documents relating to the property which are in that person's possession or control to a place (in England and Wales or, as the case may be, Northern Ireland) specified by the receiver or to place them in the custody of the receiver.

(5) Any prohibition on dealing with property imposed by an interim freezing order does not prevent a person from complying with any requirements imposed by virtue of this section.

(6) Subsection (7) applies in a case where –

  (a) the receiver deals with property that is not property in respect of which the receiver was appointed under section 362N, but
  (b) at the time of dealing with the property the receiver believed on reasonable grounds that he or she was entitled to do so by virtue of the appointment.

(7) The receiver is not liable to any person in respect of any loss or damage resulting from the receiver's dealing with the property.

(8) But subsection (7) does not apply to the extent that the loss or damage is caused by the receiver's negligence.

362P Supervision of section 362N receiver and variations

(1) Any of the following persons may at any time apply to the High Court for directions as to the exercise of the functions of a receiver appointed under section 362N –

  (a) the receiver;
  (b) a party to the proceedings for the appointment of the receiver or the interim freezing order concerned;
  (c) a person affected by an action taken by the receiver;
  (d) a person who may be affected by an action proposed to be taken by the receiver.

(2) Before it gives directions under subsection (1) the court must give an opportunity to be heard to –

  (a) the receiver;

  (b) the parties to the proceedings for the appointment of the receiver and for the interim freezing order concerned;
  (c) a person who may be interested in the application under subsection (1).

(3) The court may at any time vary or discharge –

  (a) the appointment of a receiver under section 362N,
  (b) an order under section 362O, or
  (c) directions under this section.

(4) Before exercising a power under subsection (3) the court must give an opportunity to be heard to –

  (a) the receiver;
  (b) the parties to the proceedings for the appointment of the receiver, for the order under section 362O or (as the case may be) for the directions under this section;
  (c) the parties to the proceedings for the interim freezing order concerned;
  (d) any person who may be affected by the court's decision.

362Q Registration

Sections 248 (registration: England and Wales) and 249 (registration: Northern Ireland) apply in relation to interim freezing orders as they apply in relation to property freezing orders under section 245A.

362R Compensation

(1) Where an interim freezing order in respect of any property is discharged, the person to whom the property belongs may make an application to the High Court for the payment of compensation.

(2) The application must be made within the period of three months beginning with the discharge of the interim freezing order.

(3) The court may order compensation to be paid to the applicant only if satisfied that –

  (a) the applicant has suffered loss as a result of the making of the interim freezing order,
  (b) there has been a serious default on the part of the enforcement authority that applied for the order, and
  (c) the order would not have been made had the default not occurred.

(4) Where the court orders the payment of compensation –

  (a) the compensation is payable by the enforcement authority that applied for the interim freezing order, and
  (b) the amount of compensation to be paid is the amount that the court thinks reasonable, having regard to the loss suffered and any other relevant circumstances."

3 External assistance

After section 362R of the Proceeds of Crime Act 2002 (inserted by section 2 above) insert –

"Unexplained wealth orders: enforcement abroad

362S Enforcement abroad: enforcement authority
    (1)   This section applies if –

- (a) the High Court makes an unexplained wealth order in respect of any property,
- (b) it appears to the enforcement authority that the risk mentioned in section 362J(2) applies in relation to the property, and
- (c) the enforcement authority believes that the property is in a country outside the United Kingdom (the receiving country).

    (2)   The enforcement authority may send a request for assistance in relation to the property to the Secretary of State with a view to it being forwarded under this section.

    (3)   The Secretary of State may forward the request for assistance to the government of the receiving country.

    (4)   A request for assistance under this section is a request to the government of the receiving country –

- (a) to secure that any person is prohibited from dealing with the property;
- (b) for assistance in connection with the management of the property, including with securing its detention, custody or preservation.

362T Enforcement abroad: receiver
    (1)   This section applies if –

- (a) an interim freezing order has effect in relation to property, and
- (b) the receiver appointed under section 362N in respect of the property believes that it is in a country outside the United Kingdom (the receiving country).

    (2)   The receiver may send a request for assistance in relation to the property to the Secretary of State with a view to it being forwarded under this section.

    (3)   The Secretary of State must forward the request for assistance to the government of the receiving country.

    (4)   A request for assistance under this section is a request to the government of the receiving country –

- (a) to secure that any person is prohibited from dealing with the property;
- (b) for assistance in connection with the management of the property, including with securing its detention, custody or preservation."

Unexplained wealth orders: Scotland

4 Unexplained wealth orders: Scotland

In Chapter 3 of Part 8 of the Proceeds of Crime Act 2002 (investigations: Scotland), after section 396 insert –

APPENDIX: CRIMINAL FINANCES ACT 2017

"Unexplained wealth orders

396A Unexplained wealth orders
(1) The Court of Session may, on an application made by the Scottish Ministers, make an unexplained wealth order in respect of any property if the court is satisfied that each of the requirements for the making of the order is fulfilled.
(2) An application for an order must –
   (a) specify or describe the property in respect of which the order is sought, and
   (b) specify the person whom the Scottish Ministers think holds the property ("the respondent") (and the person specified may include a person outside the United Kingdom).
(3) An unexplained wealth order is an order requiring the respondent to provide a statement –
   (a) setting out the nature and extent of the respondent's interest in the property in respect of which the order is made,
   (b) explaining how the respondent obtained the property (including, in particular, how any costs incurred in obtaining it were met),
   (c) where the property is held by the trustees of a settlement, setting out such details of the settlement as may be specified in the order, and
   (d) setting out such other information in connection with the property as may be so specified.
(4) The order must specify –
   (a) the form and manner in which the statement is to be given,
   (b) the person to whom it is to be given, and
   (c) the place at which it is to be given or, if it is to be given in writing, the address to which it is to be sent.
(5) The order may, in connection with requiring the respondent to provide the statement mentioned in subsection (3), also require the respondent to produce documents of a kind specified or described in the order.
(6) The respondent must comply with the requirements imposed by an unexplained wealth order within whatever period the court may specify (and different periods may be specified in relation to different requirements).

396B Requirements for making of unexplained wealth order
(1) These are the requirements for the making of an unexplained wealth order in respect of any property.
(2) The Court of Session must be satisfied that there is reasonable cause to believe that –
   (a) the respondent holds the property, and
   (b) the value of the property is greater than £50,000.
(3) The Court of Session must be satisfied that there are reasonable grounds for suspecting that the known sources of the respondent's lawfully obtained income would have been insufficient for the purposes of enabling the respondent to obtain the property.

APPENDIX: CRIMINAL FINANCES ACT 2017

(4) The Court of Session must be satisfied that –

   (a) the respondent is a politically exposed person, or
   (b) there are reasonable grounds for suspecting that –

      (i) the respondent is, or has been, involved in serious crime (whether in a part of the United Kingdom or elsewhere), or
      (ii) a person connected with the respondent is, or has been, so involved.

(5) It does not matter for the purposes of subsection (2)(a) –

   (a) whether or not there are other persons who also hold the property;
   (b) whether the property was obtained by the respondent before or after the coming into force of this section.

(6) For the purposes of subsection (3) –

   (a) regard is to be had to any heritable security, charge or other kind of security that it is reasonable to assume was or may have been available to the respondent for the purposes of obtaining the property;
   (b) it is to be assumed that the respondent obtained the property for a price equivalent to its market value;
   (c) income is "lawfully obtained" if it is obtained lawfully under the laws of the country from where the income arises;
   (d) "known" sources of the respondent's income are the sources of income (whether arising from employment, assets or otherwise) that are reasonably ascertainable from available information at the time of the making of the application for the order;
   (e) where the property is an interest in other property comprised in a settlement, the reference to the respondent obtaining the property is to be taken as if it were a reference to the respondent obtaining direct ownership of such share in the settled property as relates to, or is fairly represented by, that interest.

(7) In subsection (4)(a), "politically exposed person" means a person who is –

   (a) an individual who is, or has been, entrusted with prominent public functions by an international organisation or by a State other than the United Kingdom or another EEA State,
   (b) a family member of a person within paragraph (a),
   (c) known to be a close associate of a person within that paragraph, or
   (d) otherwise connected with a person within that paragraph.

(8) Article 3 of Directive 2015/849/EU of the European Parliament and of the Council of 20 May 2015 applies for the purposes of determining –

   (a) whether a person has been entrusted with prominent public functions (see point (9) of that Article),
   (b) whether a person is a family member (see point (10) of that Article), and
   (c) whether a person is known to be a close associate of another (see point (11) of that Article).

(9) For the purposes of this section –

    (a) a person is involved in serious crime in a part of the United Kingdom or elsewhere if the person would be so involved for the purposes of Part 1 of the Serious Crime Act 2007 (see in particular sections 2, 2A and 3 of that Act);

    (b) section 1122 of the Corporation Tax Act 2010 ("connected" persons) applies in determining whether a person is connected with another.

(10) Where the property in respect of which the order is sought comprises more than one item of property, the reference in subsection (2)(b) to the value of the property is to the total value of those items.

396C Effect of order: cases of non-compliance

(1) This section applies in a case where the respondent fails, without reasonable excuse, to comply with the requirements imposed by an unexplained wealth order in respect of any property before the end of the response period.

(2) The property is to be presumed to be recoverable property for the purposes of any proceedings taken in respect of the property under Part 5, unless the contrary is shown.

(3) The presumption in subsection (2) applies in relation to property –

    (a) only so far as relating to the respondent's interest in the property, and

    (b) only if the value of that interest is greater than the sum specified in section 396B(2)(b).

It is for the court hearing the proceedings under Part 5 in relation to which reliance is placed on the presumption to determine the matters in this subsection.

(4) The "response period" is whatever period the court specifies under section 396A(6) as the period within which the requirements imposed by the order are to be complied with (or the period ending the latest, if more than one is specified in respect of different requirements).

(5) For the purposes of subsection (1) –

    (a) a respondent who purports to comply with the requirements imposed by an unexplained wealth order is not to be taken to have failed to comply with the order (see instead section 396D);

    (b) where an unexplained wealth order imposes more than one requirement on the respondent, the respondent is to be taken to have failed to comply with the requirements imposed by the order unless each of the requirements is complied with or is purported to be complied with.

(6) Subsections (7) and (8) apply in determining the respondent's interest for the purposes of subsection (3) in a case where the respondent to the unexplained wealth order –

    (a) is connected with another person who is, or has been, involved in serious crime (see subsection (4)(b)(ii) of section 396B), or

    (b) is a politically exposed person of a kind mentioned in paragraph (b), (c) or (d) of subsection (7) of that section (family member, known close associates etc of individual entrusted with prominent public functions).

(7) In a case within subsection (6)(a), the respondent's interest is to be taken to include any interest in the property of the person involved in serious crime with whom the respondent is connected.

(8) In a case within subsection (6)(b), the respondent's interest is to be taken to include any interest in the property of the person mentioned in subsection (7)(a) of section 396B.

(9) Where an unexplained wealth order is made in respect of property comprising more than one item of property, the reference in subsection (3)(b) to the value of the respondent's interest in the property is to the total value of the respondent's interest in those items.

396D Effect of order: cases of compliance or purported compliance

(1) This section applies in a case where the respondent complies, or purports to comply, with the requirements imposed by an unexplained wealth order in respect of any property in relation to which the order is made before the end of the response period (as defined by section 396C(4)).

(2) If an interim freezing order has effect in relation to the property (see section 396J), the Scottish Ministers must –

  (a) consider whether the Lord Advocate should be given an opportunity to determine what enforcement or investigatory proceedings, if any, the Lord Advocate considers ought to be taken by the Lord Advocate in relation to the property, and

  (b) determine whether they consider that any proceedings under Part 5 (civil recovery of the proceeds of unlawful conduct) or this Chapter ought to be taken by them in relation to the property.

(3) If the Scottish Ministers consider that the Lord Advocate should be given an opportunity to make a determination as mentioned in subsection (2)(a), the Lord Advocate must determine what enforcement or investigatory proceedings, if any, the Lord Advocate considers ought to be taken by the Lord Advocate in relation to the property.

(4) A determination under subsection (2)(b) or (3) must be made within the period of 60 days starting with the day of compliance.

(5) If the determinations under subsections (2)(b) and (3) are that no further proceedings under Part 5 or this Chapter and no further enforcement or investigatory proceedings ought to be taken in relation to the property, the Scottish Ministers must notify the Court of Session of the nature of the determinations as soon as reasonably practicable (and in any event before the end of the 60 day period mentioned in subsection (4)).

(6) If there is no interim freezing order in effect in relation to the property –

  (a) the Scottish Ministers may (at any time) determine whether they consider that any proceedings under Part 5 or this Chapter ought to be taken by them in relation to the property, and

  (b) the Lord Advocate may (at any time) determine what, if any, enforcement or investigatory proceedings the Lord Advocate considers ought to be taken by the Lord Advocate in relation to the property.

(7) A determination under this section to take no further proceedings under Part 5 or this Chapter or no further enforcement or investigatory proceedings in relation to any property does not prevent any such proceedings being taken subsequently (whether as a result of new information or otherwise) in relation to the property.

(8) For the purposes of this section –

   (a) the respondent complies with the requirements imposed by an unexplained wealth order only if all of the requirements are complied with,
   (b) references to the day of compliance are to the day on which the requirements imposed by the order are complied with (or, if the requirements are complied with over more than one day, the last of those days), and
   (c) where an order requires the sending of information in writing to, or the production of documents at, an address specified in the order, compliance with the order (so far as relating to that requirement) occurs when the written information is received, or the documents are produced, at that address,

   and in paragraphs (a) to (c) references to compliance include purported compliance.

(9) In this section "enforcement or investigatory proceedings" means any proceedings in relation to property taken under –

   (a) Part 3 (confiscation proceedings in Scotland), or
   (b) this Chapter.

396E Offence

(1) A person commits an offence if, in purported compliance with a requirement imposed by an unexplained wealth order, the person –

   (a) makes a statement that the person knows to be false or misleading in a material particular, or
   (b) recklessly makes a statement that is false or misleading in a material particular.

(2) A person guilty of an offence under this section is liable –

   (a) on summary conviction, to imprisonment for a term not exceeding 12 months, or to a fine not exceeding the statutory maximum, or to both, or
   (b) on conviction on indictment, to imprisonment for a term not exceeding 2 years, or to a fine, or to both.

396F Statements

(1) A statement made by a person in response to a requirement imposed by an unexplained wealth order may not be used in evidence against that person in criminal proceedings.

(2) Subsection (1) does not apply –

   (a) in the case of proceedings under Part 3,
   (b) on a prosecution for an offence under section 396E,
   (c) on a prosecution for perjury, or
   (d) on a prosecution for some other offence where, in giving evidence, the person makes a statement inconsistent with the statement mentioned in subsection (1).

(3) A statement may not be used by virtue of subsection (2)(d) against a person unless –

   (a) evidence relating to it is adduced, or
   (b) a question relating to it is asked,

   by the person or on the person's behalf in proceedings arising out of the prosecution.

396G Disclosure of information, copying of documents, etc
(1) An unexplained wealth order does not confer the right to require a person to answer any question, provide any information or produce any document which the person would be entitled to refuse to answer, provide or produce on grounds of legal privilege.
(2) An unexplained wealth order has effect in spite of any restriction on the disclosure of information (however imposed).
(3) The Scottish Ministers may take copies of any documents produced by the respondent in connection with complying with the requirements imposed by an unexplained wealth order.
(4) Documents so produced may also be retained for so long as it is necessary to retain them (as opposed to a copy of them) in connection with an investigation of a kind mentioned in section 341 in relation to the property in respect of which the unexplained wealth order is made.
(5) But if the Scottish Ministers have reasonable grounds to believe that the documents –

   (a) may need to be produced for the purposes of any legal proceedings, and
   (b) might otherwise be unavailable for those purposes, they may be retained until the proceedings are concluded.

396H Holding of property: trusts and company arrangements etc
(1) This section applies for the purposes of sections 396A and 396B.
(2) The cases in which a person (P) is to be taken to "hold" property include those where –

   (a) P has effective control over the property;
   (b) P is the trustee of a settlement in which the property is comprised;
   (c) P is a beneficiary (whether actual or potential) in relation to such a settlement.

(3) A person is to be taken to have "effective control" over property if, from all the circumstances, it is reasonable to conclude that the person –

   (a) exercises,
   (b) is able to exercise, or
   (c) is entitled to acquire,

   direct or indirect control over the property.
(4) Where a person holds property by virtue of subsection (2) references to the person obtaining the property are to be read accordingly.
(5) References to a person who holds or obtains property include any body corporate, whether incorporated or formed under the law of a part of the United Kingdom or in a country or territory outside the United Kingdom.

(6) For further provision about how to construe references to the holding of property, see section 414.

396I Supplementary
(1) An application for an unexplained wealth order may be made without notice.
(2) Provision may be made by rules of court as to the discharge and variation of unexplained wealth orders.
(3) An application to discharge or vary an unexplained wealth order may be made to the Court of Session by –

  (a) the Scottish Ministers, or
  (b) any person affected by the order.

(4) The Court of Session may –

  (a) discharge the order;
  (b) vary the order."

5 Interim freezing orders

After section 396I of the Proceeds of Crime Act 2002 (inserted by section 4 above) insert –

"Unexplained wealth orders: interim freezing of property

396J Application for interim freezing order
(1) This section applies where the Court of Session makes an unexplained wealth order in respect of any property.
(2) The court may make an interim freezing order in respect of the property if the court considers it necessary to do so for the purposes of avoiding the risk of any recovery order that might subsequently be obtained being frustrated.
(3) An interim freezing order is an order that prohibits the respondent to the unexplained wealth order, and any other person with an interest in the property, from in any way dealing with the property (subject to any exclusions under section 396L).
(4) An interim freezing order –

  (a) may be made only on the application of the Scottish Ministers,
  (b) must be made in the same proceedings as those in which the unexplained wealth order is made, and
  (c) may be combined in one document with the unexplained wealth order.

(5) If an application for an unexplained wealth order in respect of any property is made without notice, an application for an interim freezing order in respect of the property must also be made without notice.

396K Variation and recall of interim freezing order
(1) The Court of Session may at any time vary or recall an interim freezing order.
(2) The Court of Session must recall an interim freezing order, so far as it has effect in relation to any property, in each of the following three cases.

(3) The first case is where –

    (a) the applicable 48 hour period has ended, and

    (b) a relevant application has not been made before the end of that period in relation to the property concerned.

(4) The second case is where –

    (a) a relevant application has been made before the end of the applicable 48 hour period in relation to the property concerned, and

    (b) proceedings on the application (including any on appeal) have been determined or otherwise disposed of.

(5) The third case is where the court has received a notification in relation to the property concerned under section 396D(5) (notification of no further proceedings).

(6) References in this section to the "applicable 48 hour period" are to be read as follows –

    (a) in a case where the respondent complies, or purports to comply, with the requirements imposed by the unexplained wealth order before the end of the response period, it is the period of 48 hours beginning with the day after the day with which the 60 day period mentioned in section 396D(4) ends;

    (b) in any other case, it is the period of 48 hours beginning with the day after the day on which the response period ends.

(7) In calculating a period of 48 hours for the purposes of subsection (6), no account is to be taken of –

    (a) any Saturday or Sunday,

    (b) Christmas Day,

    (c) Good Friday, or

    (d) any other day that is a bank holiday under the Banking and Financial Dealings Act 1971 in Scotland.

(8) Section 396D(8) applies for the purposes of subsection (6) in determining whether a person complies, or purports to comply, with the requirements imposed by an unexplained wealth order and when such compliance, or purported compliance, takes place.

(9) Before exercising power under this section to vary or recall an interim freezing order, the court must (as well as giving the parties to the proceedings an opportunity to be heard) give such an opportunity to any person who may be affected by its decision.

(10) Subsection (9) does not apply where the court is acting as required by subsection (2).

(11) In this section –

"relevant application" means an application for –

    (a) a restraint order under section 120,

    (b) a prohibitory property order under section 255A, or

    (c) an interim administration order under section 256;

"response period" has the meaning given by section 396C(4).

396L Exclusions
(1) The power to vary an interim freezing order includes (amongst other things) power to make exclusions as follows –
  (a) power to exclude property from the order, and
  (b) power, otherwise than by excluding property from the order, to make exclusions from the prohibition on dealing with the property to which the order applies.
(2) Exclusions from the prohibition on dealing with the property to which the order applies (other than exclusions of property from the order) may also be made when the order is made.
(3) An exclusion may (amongst other things) make provision for the purpose of enabling any person –
  (a) to meet the person's reasonable living expenses, or
  (b) to carry on any trade, business, profession or occupation.
(4) An exclusion may be made subject to conditions.
(5) An exclusion may not be made for the purpose of enabling any person to meet any legal expenses in respect of proceedings under this Chapter.
(6) If excluded property is not specified in the order it must be described in the order in general terms.

396M Restrictions on proceedings and remedies
(1) While an interim freezing order has effect the Court of Session may sist any action, execution or other legal process in respect of the property to which the order applies.
(2) If a court (whether the Court of Session or any other court) in which proceedings are pending in respect of any property is satisfied that an interim freezing order has been applied for or made in respect of the property, it may –
  (a) sist the proceedings, or
  (b) allow them to continue on any terms it thinks fit.
(3) Before exercising a power conferred by this section, the court must (as well as giving the parties to any proceedings concerned an opportunity to be heard) give such an opportunity to any person who may be affected by the court's decision.

396N Arrestment of property affected by interim freezing order
(1) On the application of the Scottish Ministers the Court of Session may, in relation to moveable property to which an interim freezing order applies (whether generally or to such of it as is specified in the application), grant warrant for arrestment.
(2) An application under subsection (1) may be made at the same time as the application for the interim freezing order or at any time afterwards.
(3) A warrant for arrestment may be granted only if the property would be arrestable if the person entitled to it were a debtor.

(4) A warrant under subsection (1) has effect as if granted on the dependence of an action for debt at the instance of the Scottish Ministers against the person and may be executed, recalled, loosed or restricted accordingly.

(5) An arrestment executed under this section ceases to have effect when, or in so far as, the interim freezing order ceases to apply in respect of the property in relation to which the warrant for arrestment was granted.

(6) If an arrestment ceases to have effect to any extent by virtue of subsection (5), the Scottish Ministers must apply to the Court of Session for an order recalling or, as the case may be, restricting the arrestment.

396O Inhibition of property affected by interim freezing order

(1) On the application of the Scottish Ministers, the Court of Session may, in relation to the property mentioned in subsection (2), grant warrant for inhibition against any person specified in an interim freezing order.

(2) The property is heritable property situated in Scotland to which the interim freezing order applies (whether generally or to such of it as is specified in the application).

(3) The warrant for inhibition –

(a) has effect as if granted on the dependence of an action for debt by the Scottish Ministers against the person and may be executed, recalled, loosed or restricted accordingly, and

(b) has the effect of letters of inhibition and must forthwith be registered by the Scottish Ministers in the register of inhibitions and adjudications.

(4) Section 155 of the Titles to Land Consolidation (Scotland) Act 1868 (effective date of inhibition) applies in relation to an inhibition for which warrant is granted under subsection (1) as it applies to an inhibition by separate letters or contained in a summons.

(5) An inhibition executed under this section ceases to have effect when, or in so far as, the interim freezing order ceases to apply in respect of the property in relation to which the warrant for inhibition was granted.

(6) If an inhibition ceases to have effect to any extent by virtue of subsection (5), the Scottish Ministers must –

(a) apply for the recall or, as the case may be, the restriction of the inhibition, and

(b) ensure that the recall or restriction is reflected in the register of inhibitions and adjudications.

396P Receivers in connection with interim freezing orders

(1) This section applies where the Court of Session makes an interim freezing order on an application by the Scottish Ministers.

(2) The Court of Session may, on an application by the Scottish Ministers, by order appoint a receiver in respect of any property to which the interim freezing order applies.

(3) An application under subsection (2) may be made at the same time as the application for the interim freezing order or at any time afterwards.

(4) The application may be made without notice if the circumstances of the case are such that notice of the application would prejudice the right of the Scottish Ministers to obtain a recovery order in respect of the property.

(5) In their application the Scottish Ministers must nominate a suitably qualified person for appointment as a receiver.

(6) The person nominated may be a member of staff of the Scottish Ministers.

(7) The Scottish Ministers may apply a sum received by them under section 280(2) in making payment of the remuneration and expenses of a receiver appointed under this section.

(8) Subsection (7) does not apply in relation to the remuneration of the receiver if that person is a member of staff of the Scottish Ministers (but it does apply in relation to such remuneration if the receiver is a person providing services under arrangements made by the Scottish Ministers).

396Q Powers of receivers appointed under section 396P

(1) If the Court of Session appoints a receiver under section 396P, the court may act under this section on the application of the Scottish Ministers.

(2) The court may by order authorise or require the receiver –

(a) to exercise any of the powers mentioned in paragraph 5 of Schedule 6 (management powers) in relation to any property in respect of which the receiver is appointed;

(b) to take any other steps the court thinks appropriate in connection with the management of any such property (including securing the detention, custody or preservation of the property in order to manage it).

(3) The court may by order require any person in respect of whose property the receiver is appointed –

(a) to bring the property to a place in Scotland specified by the receiver or to place it in the custody of the receiver (if in either case the person is able to do so);

(b) to do anything the person is reasonably required to do by the receiver for the preservation of the property.

(4) The court may by order require any person in respect of whose property the receiver is appointed to bring any documents relating to the property which are in that person's possession or control to a place in Scotland specified by the receiver or to place them in the custody of the receiver.

(5) In subsection (4) "document" means anything in which information of any description is recorded.

(6) Any prohibition on dealing with property imposed by an interim freezing order does not prevent a person from complying with any requirements imposed by virtue of this section.

(7) Subsection (8) applies in a case where –

(a) the receiver deals with property that is not property in respect of which the receiver was appointed under section 396P, but

(b) at the time of dealing with the property the receiver believed on reasonable grounds that he or she was entitled to do so by virtue of his or her appointment.

APPENDIX: CRIMINAL FINANCES ACT 2017

(8) The receiver is not liable to any person in respect of any loss or damage resulting from the receiver's dealing with the property.

(9) But subsection (8) does not apply to the extent that the loss or damage is caused by the receiver's negligence.

396R Supervision of section 396P receiver and variations

(1) Any of the following persons may at any time apply to the Court of Session for directions as to the exercise of the functions of a receiver appointed under section 396P –

   (a) the receiver;
   (b) a party to the proceedings for the appointment of the receiver or the interim freezing order concerned;
   (c) a person affected by an action taken by the receiver;
   (d) a person who may be affected by an action proposed to be taken by the receiver.

(2) Before it gives directions under subsection (1), the court must give an opportunity to be heard to –

   (a) the receiver;
   (b) the parties to the proceedings for the appointment of the receiver and for the interim freezing order concerned;
   (c) any person who may be interested in the application under subsection (1).

(3) The court may at any time vary or recall –

   (a) the appointment of a receiver under section 396P,
   (b) an order under section 396Q, or
   (c) directions under this section.

(4) Before exercising a power under subsection (3) the court must give an opportunity to be heard to –

   (a) the receiver;
   (b) the parties to the proceedings for the appointment of the receiver, for the order under section 396Q or (as the case may be) for the directions under this section;
   (c) the parties to the proceedings for the interim freezing order concerned;
   (d) any person who may be affected by the court's decision.

396S Compensation

(1) Where an interim freezing order in respect of any property is recalled, the person to whom the property belongs may make an application to the Court of Session for the payment of compensation.

(2) The application must be made within the period of three months beginning with the recall of the interim freezing order.

(3) The court may order compensation to be paid to the applicant only if satisfied that –

   (a) the applicant has suffered loss as a result of the making of the interim freezing order,

(b) there has been a serious default on the part of the Scottish Ministers in applying for the order, and

(c) the order would not have been made had the default not occurred.

(4) Where the court orders the payment of compensation –

(a) the compensation is payable by the Scottish Ministers, and

(b) the amount of compensation to be paid is the amount that the court thinks reasonable, having regard to the loss suffered and any other relevant circumstances."

6 External assistance

After section 396S of the Proceeds of Crime Act 2002 (inserted by section 5 above) insert –

"Unexplained wealth orders: enforcement abroad

396T Enforcement abroad: Scottish Ministers

(1) This section applies if –

(a) the Court of Session makes an unexplained wealth order in respect of any property,

(b) it appears to the Scottish Ministers that the risk mentioned in section 396J(2) applies in relation to the property, and

(c) the Scottish Ministers believe that the property is in a country outside the United Kingdom (the receiving country).

(2) The Scottish Ministers may send a request for assistance in relation to the property to the Secretary of State with a view to it being forwarded under this section.

(3) The Secretary of State may forward the request for assistance to the government of the receiving country.

(4) A request for assistance under this section is a request to the government of the receiving country –

(a) to secure that any person is prohibited from dealing with the property;

(b) for assistance in connection with the management of the property, including with securing its detention, custody or preservation.

396U Enforcement abroad: receiver

(1) This section applies if –

(a) an interim freezing order has effect in relation to property, and

(b) the receiver appointed under section 396P in respect of the property believes that it is in a country outside the United Kingdom (the receiving country).

(2) The receiver may send a request for assistance in relation to the property to the Secretary of State with a view to it being forwarded under this section.

APPENDIX: CRIMINAL FINANCES ACT 2017

(3) The Secretary of State must forward the request for assistance to the government of the receiving country.

(4) A request for assistance under this section is a request to the government of the receiving country –

   (a) to secure that any person is prohibited from dealing with the property;
   (b) for assistance in connection with the management of the property, including with securing its detention, custody or preservation."

Disclosure orders

7 Disclosure orders: England and Wales and Northern Ireland

(1) Chapter 2 of Part 8 of the Proceeds of Crime Act 2002 (investigations: England and Wales and Northern Ireland) is amended as follows.

(2) In section 357 (disclosure orders) –

   (a) in subsection (2) omit "or a money laundering investigation";
   (b) omit subsection (2A);
   (c) in subsection (3), after paragraph (b) insert –

   "(ba) a person specified in the application is subject to a money laundering investigation which is being carried out by an appropriate officer and the order is sought for the purposes of the investigation, or";

   (d) in subsection (7) –

      (i) in paragraph (a) for "a prosecutor" substitute "an appropriate officer";
      (ii) after paragraph (b) insert –

      "(ba) in relation to a money laundering investigation, an appropriate officer, and;";

   (e) omit subsections (8) and (9).

(3) In section 358 (requirements for making a disclosure order), in subsection (2) after paragraph (b) insert –

   "(ba) in the case of a money laundering investigation, the person specified in the application for the order has committed a money laundering offence;".

(4) In section 362 (supplementary) –

   (a) for subsection (4A) substitute –

   "(4A) An application to discharge or vary a disclosure order need not be made by the same appropriate officer or (as the case may be) the same National Crime Agency officer that applied for the order (but must be made by an appropriate officer of the same description or (as the case may be) by another National Crime Agency officer).

   (4AA) If the application for the order was, by virtue of an order under section 453, made by an accredited financial investigator of a particular description, the reference in subsection (4A) to an appropriate officer of the same description is to another accredited financial investigator of that description.";

(b) after subsection (5) insert –

"(6) An appropriate officer may not make an application for a disclosure order, or an application for the discharge or variation of such an order, unless the officer is a senior appropriate officer or is authorised to do so by a senior appropriate officer."

8 Disclosure orders: Scotland

(1) Chapter 3 of Part 8 of the Proceeds of Crime Act 2002 (investigations: Scotland) is amended as follows.

(2) In section 391(disclosure orders) –

(a) in subsection (1) after "confiscation investigations" insert "or money laundering investigations";
(b) in subsection (2) omit "or a money laundering investigation";
(c) in subsection (3) after paragraph (a) insert –

"(aa) a person specified in the application is subject to a money laundering investigation and the order is sought for the purposes of the investigation, or".

(3) In section 392 (requirements for making a disclosure order), in subsection (2) after paragraph (a) insert –

"(aa) in the case of a money laundering investigation, the person specified in the application for the order has committed a money laundering offence;".

(4) In section 396 (supplementary) –

(a) in subsection (1) in paragraph (a) after "confiscation investigation" insert "or a money laundering investigation";
(b) in subsection (3) in paragraph (a) after "confiscation investigation" insert "or a money laundering investigation".

Beneficial ownership

9 Co-operation: beneficial ownership information

In Part 11 of the Proceeds of Crime Act 2002 (co-operation), after section 445 insert –

"445A Sharing of beneficial ownership information
(1) The relevant Minister must prepare a report about the arrangements in place between –

(a) the government of the United Kingdom, and
(b) the government of each relevant territory, for the sharing of beneficial ownership information.

(2) The report must include an assessment of the effectiveness of those arrangements, having regard to such international standards as appear to the relevant Minister to be relevant.

(3) The report –

   (a) must be prepared before 1 July 2019, and
   (b) must relate to the arrangements in place during the period of 18 months from 1 July 2017 to 31 December 2018.

(4) The relevant Minister must –

   (a) publish the report, and
   (b) lay a copy of it before Parliament.

(5) The reference in subsection (1) to arrangements in place for the sharing of beneficial ownership information between the government of the United Kingdom and the government of a relevant territory is to such arrangements as are set out in an exchange of notes –

   (a) for the provision of beneficial ownership information about a person incorporated in a part of the United Kingdom to a law enforcement authority of the relevant territory at the request of the authority, and
   (b) for the provision of beneficial ownership information about a person incorporated in a relevant territory to a law enforcement authority of the United Kingdom at the request of the authority.

(6) In this section –

   "beneficial ownership information" means information in relation to the beneficial ownership of persons incorporated in a part of the United Kingdom or (as the case may be) in a relevant territory;
   "exchange of notes" means written documentation signed on behalf of the government of the United Kingdom and the government of a relevant territory setting out details of the agreement reached in respect of the arrangements for the matters mentioned in subsection (5)(a) and (b);
   "relevant Minister" means the Secretary of State or the Minister for the Cabinet Office;
   "relevant territory" means any of the Channel Islands, the Isle of Man or any British overseas territory."

CHAPTER 2

MONEY LAUNDERING

10 Power to extend moratorium period

(1) Part 7 of the Proceeds of Crime Act 2002 (money laundering) is amended as follows.
(2) In section 335 (appropriate consent), after subsection (6) insert –

   "(6A) Subsection (6) is subject to –

   (a) section 336A, which enables the moratorium period to be extended by court order in accordance with that section, and

APPENDIX: CRIMINAL FINANCES ACT 2017

(b) section 336C, which provides for an automatic extension of the moratorium period in certain cases (period extended if it would otherwise end before determination of application or appeal proceedings etc)."

(3) In section 336 (nominated officer: consent), after subsection (8) insert –

"(8A) Subsection (8) is subject to –

(a) section 336A, which enables the moratorium period to be extended by court order in accordance with that section, and
(b) section 336C, which provides for an automatic extension of the moratorium period in certain cases (period extended if it would otherwise end before determination of application or appeal proceedings etc)."

(4) After section 336 insert –

336A Power of court to extend the moratorium period

(1) The court may, on an application under this section, grant an extension of a moratorium period if satisfied that –

(a) an investigation is being carried out in relation to a relevant disclosure (but has not been completed),
(b) the investigation is being conducted diligently and expeditiously,
(c) further time is needed for conducting the investigation, and
(d) it is reasonable in all the circumstances for the moratorium period to be extended.

(2) An application under this section may be made only by a senior officer.
(3) The application must be made before the moratorium period would otherwise end.
(4) An extension of a moratorium period must end no later than 31 days beginning with the day after the day on which the period would otherwise end.
(5) Where a moratorium period is extended by the court under this section, it may be further extended by the court (on one or more occasions) on the making of another application.
(6) A moratorium period extended in accordance with subsection (2) or (4) of section 336C may also be further extended by the court on the making of an application under this section.
(7) But the court may not grant a further extension of a moratorium period if the effect would be to extend the period by more than 186 days (in total) beginning with the day after the end of the 31 day period mentioned in section 335(6) or (as the case may be) section 336(8).
(8) Subsections (1) to (4) apply to any further extension of a moratorium period as they apply to the first extension of the period under this section.
(9) An application under this section may be made by an immigration officer only if the officer has reasonable grounds for suspecting that conduct constituting the prohibited act in relation to which the moratorium period in question applies –

(a) relates to the entitlement of one or more persons who are not nationals of the United Kingdom to enter, transit across, or be in, the United Kingdom (including conduct which relates to conditions or other controls on any such entitlement), or

(b) is undertaken for the purposes of, or otherwise in relation to, a relevant nationality enactment.

(10) In subsection (9) –

"prohibited act" has the meaning given by section 335(8) or (as the case may be) section 336(10);
"relevant nationality enactment" means any enactment in –

(a) the British Nationality Act 1981,
(b) the Hong Kong Act 1985,
(c) the Hong Kong (War Wives and Widows) Act 1996,
(d) the British Nationality (Hong Kong) Act 1997,
(e) the British Overseas Territories Act 2002, or
(f) an instrument made under any of those Acts.

336B Proceedings under section 336A: supplementary

(1) This section applies to proceedings on an application under section 336A.
(2) The court must determine the proceedings as soon as reasonably practicable.
(3) The court may exclude from any part of the hearing –

(a) an interested person;
(b) anyone representing that person.

(4) The person who made the application may apply to the court for an order that specified information upon which he or she intends to rely be withheld from –

(a) an interested person;
(b) anyone representing that person.

(5) The court may make such an order only if satisfied that there are reasonable grounds to believe that if the specified information were disclosed –

(a) evidence of an offence would be interfered with or harmed,
(b) the gathering of information about the possible commission of an offence would be interfered with,
(c) a person would be interfered with or physically injured,
(d) the recovery of property under this Act would be hindered, or
(e) national security would be put at risk.

(6) The court must direct that the following be excluded from the hearing of an application under subsection (4) –

(a) the interested person to whom that application relates;
(b) anyone representing that person.

(7) Subject to this section, rules of court may make provision as to the practice and procedure to be followed in connection with proceedings in relation to applications under section 336A.
(8) An appeal lies to the appropriate appeal court on a point of law arising from a decision made by the Crown Court in Northern Ireland or by the sheriff.

(9) The appropriate appeal court may on such an appeal make any order that it considers appropriate (subject to the restriction mentioned in section 336A(7)).

(10) The appropriate appeal court is –

 (a) in the case of a decision of the Crown Court in Northern Ireland, the Court of Appeal in Northern Ireland;
 (b) in the case of a decision of the sheriff, the Sheriff Appeal Court.

(11) For rights of appeal in the case of decisions made by the Crown Court in England and Wales, see section 28 of the Senior Courts Act 1981 (appeals from Crown Court and inferior courts).

336C Extension of moratorium period pending determination of proceedings etc

(1) A moratorium period is extended in accordance with subsection (2) where –

 (a) an application is made to the court under section 336A for the extension (or further extension) of the moratorium period, and
 (b) the period would (apart from that subsection) end before the court determines the application or it is otherwise disposed of.

(2) The moratorium period is extended from the time when it would otherwise end until the court determines the application or it is otherwise disposed of.

(3) A moratorium period is extended in accordance with subsection (4) where –

 (a) proceedings on an appeal in respect of a decision on an application under section 336A have been brought, and
 (b) the period would (apart from that subsection) end before the proceedings are finally determined or otherwise disposed of.

(4) The moratorium period is extended from the time when it would otherwise end until the proceedings are finally determined or otherwise disposed of.

(5) But the maximum period by which the moratorium period is extended by virtue of subsection (2) or (4) is 31 days beginning with the day after the day on which the period would otherwise have ended.

(6) A moratorium period is extended in accordance with subsection (7) where –

 (a) an application is made to the court under section 336A for an extension of the period,
 (b) the court refuses to grant the application, and
 (c) the period would (apart from that subsection) end before the end of the 5 day period.

(7) The moratorium period is extended from the time when it would otherwise end until –

 (a) the end of the 5 day period, or
 (b) if proceedings on an appeal against the decision are brought before the end of the 5 day period, the time when those proceedings are brought.

(8) The "5 day period" is the period of 5 working days beginning with the day on which the court refuses to grant the application.

(9) This restriction on the overall extension of a moratorium period mentioned in section 336A(7) applies to an extension of a moratorium period in accordance with any provision of this section as it applies to an extension under an order of the court.

336D Sections 336A to 336C: interpretation
(1) This section provides for the meaning of terms used in sections 336A to 336C (and in this section).
(2) "The court" means –

    (a) in relation to England and Wales or Northern Ireland, the Crown Court;
    (b) in relation to Scotland, the sheriff.

(3) "Interested person" means –

    (a) the person who made the relevant disclosure, and
    (b) any other person who appears to the person making the application under section 336A to have an interest in the relevant property.

(4) "Moratorium period" means the period of 31 days mentioned in section 335(6) or (as the case may be) section 336(8), or any such period as extended or further extended by virtue of an order under section 336A or in accordance with any provision of section 336C.

(5) "Relevant disclosure" means –

    (a) where the application under section 336A relates to the moratorium period mentioned in section 335(6), the authorised disclosure mentioned in section 335(2)(a);
    (b) where the application under section 336A relates to the moratorium period mentioned in section 336(8), the disclosure mentioned in section 336(4)(a).

(6) "Relevant property" means any property that would be the subject of the prohibited act (within the meaning of section 335(8) or (as the case may be) section 336(10)) in relation to which the moratorium period in question applies.

(7) In the case of an application to the Crown Court, "senior officer" means –

    (a) the Director General of the National Crime Agency,
    (b) any other National Crime Agency officer authorised by the Director General (whether generally or specifically) for this purpose,
    (c) a police officer of at least the rank of inspector,
    (d) an officer of Revenue and Customs who is not below such grade as is designated by the Commissioners for Her Majesty's Revenue and Customs as equivalent to that rank,
    (e) an immigration officer who is not below such grade as is designated by the Secretary of State as equivalent to that rank,
    (f) a member of staff of the Financial Conduct Authority who is not below such grade as is designated by the Treasury for the purposes of this Part,
    (g) the Director of the Serious Fraud Office (or a member of staff of that Office authorised for the purposes of section 336A by virtue of section 2C(2)), or

(h) an accredited financial investigator who falls within a description specified in an order made for the purposes of section 336A by the Secretary of State under section 453.

(8) In the case of an application to the sheriff, "senior officer" means a procurator fiscal.

(9) "Working day" means a day other than –

(a) a Saturday,
(b) a Sunday,
(c) Christmas Day,
(d) Good Friday, or
(e) a day which is a bank holiday under the Banking and Financial Dealings Act 1971 in the part of the United Kingdom in which the application in question under section 336A is made."

11 Sharing of information within the regulated sector

After section 339ZA of the Proceeds of Crime Act 2002 insert –

339ZB Voluntary disclosures within the regulated sector

(1) A person (A) may disclose information to one or more other persons if conditions 1 to 4 are met.

(2) Condition 1 is that –

(a) A is carrying on a business in the regulated sector as a relevant undertaking,
(b) the information on which the disclosure is based came to A in the course of carrying on that business, and
(c) the person to whom the information is to be disclosed (or each of them, where the disclosure is to more than one person) is also carrying on a business in the regulated sector as a relevant undertaking (whether or not of the same kind as A).

(3) Condition 2 is that –

(a) an NCA authorised officer has requested A to make the disclosure, or
(b) the person to whom the information is to be disclosed (or at least one of them, where the disclosure is to more than one person) has requested A to do so.

(4) Condition 3 is that, before A makes the disclosure, the required notification has been made to an NCA authorised officer (see section 339ZC(3) to (5)).

(5) Condition 4 is that A is satisfied that the disclosure of the information will or may assist in determining any matter in connection with a suspicion that a person is engaged in money laundering.

(6) A person may disclose information to A for the purposes of making a disclosure request if, and to the extent that, the person has reason to believe that A has in A's possession information that will or may assist in determining

any matter in connection with a suspicion that a person is engaged in money laundering.

339ZC Section 339ZB: disclosure requests and required notifications
(1) A disclosure request must –

    (a) state that it is made in connection with a suspicion that a person is engaged in money laundering,
    (b) identify the person (if known),
    (c) describe the information that is sought from A, and
    (d) specify the person or persons to whom it is requested that the information is disclosed.

(2) Where the disclosure request is made by a person mentioned in section 339ZB(3)(b), the request must also –

    (a) set out the grounds for the suspicion that a person is engaged in money laundering, or
    (b) provide such other information as the person making the request thinks appropriate for the purposes of enabling A to determine whether the information requested ought to be disclosed under section 339ZB(1).

(3) A required notification must be made –

    (a) in the case of a disclosure request made by an NCA authorised officer, by the person who is to disclose information under section 339ZB(1) as a result of the request;
    (b) in the case of a disclosure request made by a person mentioned in section 339ZB(3)(b), by the person who made the request.

(4) In a case within subsection (3)(a), the required notification must state that information is to be disclosed under section 339ZB(1).

(5) In a case within subsection (3)(b), the required notification must –

    (a) state that a disclosure request has been made,
    (b) specify the person to whom the request was made,
    (c) identify any person (if known) suspected of being engaged in money laundering in connection with whom the request was made, and
    (d) provide all such other information that the person giving the notification would be required to give if making the required disclosure for the purposes of section 330 (see in particular subsection (5)(b) and (c) of that section).

339ZD Section 339ZB: effect on required disclosures under section 330 or 331
(1) This section applies if in any proceedings a question arises as to whether the required disclosure has been made for the purposes of section 330(4) or 331(4) –

    (a) by a person (A) who discloses information under section 339ZB(1) as a result of a disclosure request,
    (b) by a person (B) who makes a required notification in accordance with section 339ZC(3)(b) in connection with that request, or

APPENDIX: CRIMINAL FINANCES ACT 2017

(c) by any other person (C) to whom A discloses information under section 339ZB(1) as a result of that request.

(2) The making of a required notification in good faith is to be treated as satisfying any requirement to make the required disclosure on the part of A, B and C.
This is subject to section 339ZE(1) to (8).

(3) The making of a joint disclosure report in good faith is to be treated as satisfying any requirement to make the required disclosure on the part of the persons who jointly make the report.
This is subject to section 339ZE(10).

(4) A joint disclosure report is a report to an NCA authorised officer that –

   (a) is made jointly by A and B (whether or not also jointly with other persons to whom A discloses information under section 339ZB(1)),
   (b) satisfies the requirements as to content mentioned in subsection (5),
   (c) is prepared after the making of a disclosure by A to B under section 339ZB(1) in connection with a suspicion of a person's engagement in money laundering, and
   (d) is sent to the NCA authorised officer before the end of the applicable period.

(5) The requirements as to content are that the report must –

   (a) explain the extent to which there are continuing grounds to suspect that the person mentioned in subsection (4)(c) is engaged in money laundering,
   (b) identify the person (if known),
   (c) set out the grounds for the suspicion, and
   (d) provide any other information relevant to the matter.

(6) The applicable period is –

   (a) in a case where the disclosure under section 339ZB was made as a result of a disclosure request from an NCA authorised officer by virtue of subsection (3)(a) of that section, whatever period may be specified by the officer when making the request;
   (b) in a case where the disclosure was made as a result of a disclosure request from another person by virtue of subsection (3)(b) of that section, the period of 84 days beginning with the day on which a required notification is made in connection with the request.

(7) A joint disclosure report must be –

   (a) approved by the nominated officer of each person that jointly makes the report, and
   (b) signed by the nominated officer on behalf of each such person. If there is no nominated officer the report must be approved and signed by another senior officer.

(8) References in this section to A, B or C include –

   (a) a nominated officer acting on behalf of A, B or C, and
   (b) any other person who is an employee, officer or partner of A, B or C.

APPENDIX: CRIMINAL FINANCES ACT 2017

339ZE Limitations on application of section 339ZD(2) and (3)
(1) Subsections (2) and (3) apply in a case where the required notification is made by A (notification made as a result of disclosure request received from NCA authorised officer).
(2) Section 339ZD(2) has effect in the case of A, B or C only so far as relating to –
   (a) the suspicion in connection with which the required notification is made, and
   (b) matters known, suspected or believed as a result of the making of the disclosure request concerned.
(3) Accordingly, section 339ZD(2) does not remove any requirement to make the required disclosure in relation to anything known, suspected or believed that does not result only from the making of the disclosure request.
(4) Subsections (5) to (7) apply in a case where the required notification is made by B (notification made as a result of disclosure request received from another undertaking in the regulated sector).
(5) Section 339ZD(2) has effect in the case of A or C only so far as relating to –
   (a) the suspicion in connection with which the notification by B is made, and
   (b) matters known, suspected or believed by A or C as a result of the making of that notification.
(6) Accordingly, section 339ZD(2) does not remove any requirement to make the required disclosure in relation to anything known, suspected or believed that does not result only from the making of the notification.
(7) Section 339ZD(2) has effect in the case of B only so far as relating to –
   (a) the suspicion in connection with which the notification is made, and
   (b) matters known, suspected or believed by B at the time of the making of the notification.
(8) If a joint disclosure report is not made before the end of the applicable period (whether the required notification was made by A or B), section 339ZD(2) –
   (a) has effect only so far as relating to any requirement to make the required disclosure that would have otherwise arisen within that period, and
   (b) does not remove a requirement to make the required disclosure so far as arising after the end of that period on the part of any person in respect of matters that may become known, suspected or believed by the person after the time when the required notification was made.
(9) If a joint disclosure report is not made before the end of the applicable period, the person who made the required notification must notify an NCA authorised officer that a report is not being made as soon as reasonably practicable after the period ends.
(10) Section 339ZD(3) has effect only so far as relating to –
   (a) the suspicion in connection with which the report is made, and
   (b) matters known, suspected or believed at the time of the making of the report.
(11) Terms used in this section have the same meanings as in section 339ZD.

APPENDIX: CRIMINAL FINANCES ACT 2017

339ZF Section 339ZB: supplementary
(1) A relevant disclosure made in good faith does not breach –

    (a) an obligation of confidence owed by the person making the disclosure, or
    (b) any other restriction on the disclosure of information, however imposed.

(2) But a relevant disclosure may not include information obtained from a UK law enforcement agency unless that agency consents to the disclosure.

(3) In a case where a person is acting on behalf of another ("the undertaking") as a nominated officer –

    (a) a relevant disclosure by the undertaking must be made by the nominated officer on behalf of the undertaking, and
    (b) a relevant disclosure to the undertaking must be made to that officer.

(4) Subsection (1) applies whether or not the conditions in section 339ZB were met in respect of the disclosure if the person making the disclosure did so in the reasonable belief that the conditions were met.

(5) In this section –

"relevant disclosure" means any disclosure made in compliance, or intended compliance, with section 339ZB;
"UK law enforcement agency" means –

    (a) the National Crime Agency;
    (b) a police force in England, Scotland, Northern Ireland or Wales;
    (c) any other person operating in England, Scotland, Northern Ireland or Wales charged with the duty of preventing, detecting, investigating or prosecuting offences.

339ZG Sections 339ZB to 339ZF: interpretation
(1) This section applies for the purposes of sections 339ZB to 339ZF.
(2) "Disclosure request" means a request made for the purposes of condition 2 in section 339ZB(3).
(3) "NCA authorised officer" means a person authorised for the purposes of this Part by the Director General of the National Crime Agency.
(4) "Nominated officer" means a person nominated to receive disclosures under section 330.
(5) "Relevant undertaking" means any of the following –

    (a) a credit institution;
    (b) a financial institution;
    (c) a professional legal adviser;
    (d) a relevant professional adviser;
    (e) other persons (not within paragraphs (a) to (d)) whose business consists of activities listed in paragraph 1(1) of Schedule 9.

(6) "Required disclosure" has the same meaning as in section 330(5) or (as the case may be) section 331(5).

APPENDIX: CRIMINAL FINANCES ACT 2017

(7) "Required notification" means a notification made for the purposes of condition 3 in section 339ZB(4).

(8) For the purposes of subsection (5) –

   (a) "credit institution" has the same meaning as in Schedule 9;
   (b) "financial institution" means an undertaking that carries on a business in the regulated sector by virtue of any of paragraphs to (i) of paragraph 1(1) of that Schedule;
   (c) "relevant professional adviser" has the meaning given by section 333E(5).

(9) Schedule 9 has effect for determining what is a business in the regulated sector."

12 Further information orders

After section 339ZG of the Proceeds of Crime Act 2002 (inserted by section 11 above) insert –

"Further information orders

339ZH Further information orders

(1) A magistrates' court or (in Scotland) the sheriff may, on an application made by a relevant person, make a further information order if satisfied that either condition 1 or condition 2 is met.

(2) The application must –

   (a) specify or describe the information sought under the order, and
   (b) specify the person from whom the information is sought ("the respondent").

(3) A further information order is an order requiring the respondent to provide –

   (a) the information specified or described in the application for the order, or
   (b) such other information as the court or sheriff making the order thinks appropriate,

so far as the information is in the possession, or under the control, of the respondent.

(4) Condition 1 for the making of a further information order is met if –

   (a) the information required to be given under the order would relate to a matter arising from a disclosure made under this Part,
   (b) the respondent is the person who made the disclosure or is otherwise carrying on a business in the regulated sector,
   (c) the information would assist in investigating whether a person is engaged in money laundering or in determining whether an investigation of that kind should be started, and
   (d) it is reasonable in all the circumstances for the information to be provided.

(5) Condition 2 for the making of a further information order is met if –

   (a) the information required to be given under the order would relate to a matter arising from a disclosure made under a corresponding disclosure requirement,

APPENDIX: CRIMINAL FINANCES ACT 2017

(b) an external request has been made to the National Crime Agency for the provision of information in connection with that disclosure,
(c) the respondent is carrying on a business in the regulated sector,
(d) the information is likely to be of substantial value to the authority that made the external request in determining any matter in connection with the disclosure, and
(e) it is reasonable in all the circumstances for the information to be provided.

(6) For the purposes of subsection (5), "external request" means a request made by an authority of a foreign country which has responsibility in that country for carrying out investigations into whether a corresponding money laundering offence has been committed.

(7) A further information order must specify –

(a) how the information required under the order is to be provided, and
(b) the date by which it is to be provided.

(8) If a person fails to comply with a further information order made by a magistrates' court, the magistrates' court may order the person to pay an amount not exceeding £5,000.

(9) The sum mentioned in subsection (8) is to be treated as adjudged to be paid by a conviction of the court for the purposes of the Magistrates' Courts Act 1980 or (as the case may be) the Magistrates' Courts (Northern Ireland) Order 1981 (S.I. 1981/1675 (N.I. 26)).

(10) In order to take account of changes in the value of money the Secretary of State may by regulations substitute another sum for the sum for the time being specified in subsection (8).

(11) Schedule 9 has effect for the purposes of this section in determining what is a business in the regulated sector.

(12) In this section –

"corresponding disclosure requirement" means a requirement to make a disclosure under the law of the foreign country concerned that corresponds to a requirement imposed by virtue of this Part;
"corresponding money laundering offence" means an offence under the law of the foreign country concerned that would, if done in the United Kingdom, constitute an offence specified in paragraph (a), (b) or (c) of section 340(11);
"foreign country" means a country or territory outside the United Kingdom;
"relevant person" means –

(a) in the case of an application to a magistrates' court, the Director General of the National Crime Agency or any other National Crime Agency officer authorised by the
Director General (whether generally or specifically) for this purpose, or
(b) in the case of an application to the sheriff, a procurator fiscal.

339ZI Statements
(1) A statement made by a person in response to a further information order may not be used in evidence against the person in criminal proceedings.

(2) Subsection (1) does not apply –

    (a) in the case of proceedings under this Part,
    (b) on a prosecution for perjury, or
    (c) on a prosecution for some other offence where, in giving evidence, the person makes a statement inconsistent with the statement mentioned in subsection (1).

(3) A statement may not be used by virtue of subsection (2)(c) unless –

    (a) evidence relating to it is adduced, or
    (b) a question relating to it is asked,

by or on behalf of the person in the proceedings arising out of the prosecution.

(4) In subsection (2)(b) the reference to a prosecution for perjury is –

    (a) in the case of England and Wales, a reference to a prosecution for an offence under section 5 of the Perjury Act 1911;
    (b) in the case of Northern Ireland, a reference to a prosecution for an offence under Article 10 of the Perjury (Northern Ireland) Order 1979 (S.I. 1979/1714 (N.I. 19)).

339ZJ Appeals

(1) An appeal from a decision on an application for a further information order lies to the relevant appeal court.
(2) An appeal under this section lies at the instance of any person who was a party to the proceedings on the application.
(3) The "relevant appeal court" is –

    (a) the Crown Court, in the case of a decision made by a magistrates' court in England and Wales;
    (b) a county court, in the case of a decision made by a magistrates' court in Northern Ireland;
    (c) the Sheriff Appeal Court, in the case of a decision made by the sheriff.

(4) On an appeal under this section the relevant appeal court may –

    (a) make or (as the case may be) discharge a further information order, or
    (b) vary the order.

339ZK Supplementary

(1) A further information order does not confer the right to require a person to provide privileged information.
(2) "Privileged information" is information which a person would be entitled to refuse to provide on grounds of legal professional privilege in proceedings in the High Court or, in Scotland, legal privilege as defined by section 412.
(3) Information provided in pursuance of a further information order is not to be taken to breach any restriction on the disclosure of information (however imposed).
(4) An application for a further information order may be heard and determined in private.
(5) Rules of court may make provision as to the practice and procedure to be followed in connection with proceedings relating to further information orders."

APPENDIX: CRIMINAL FINANCES ACT 2017

Chapter 3

Civil recovery

Meaning of "unlawful conduct": gross human rights abuses or violations

13 Unlawful conduct: gross human rights abuses or violations

(1) Part 5 of the Proceeds of Crime Act 2002 (civil recovery of the proceeds etc of unlawful conduct) is amended as follows.

(2) In section 241 (meaning of "unlawful conduct"), after subsection (2) insert –
"(2A) Conduct which –

(a) occurs in a country or territory outside the United Kingdom,
(b) constitutes, or is connected with, the commission of a gross human rights abuse or violation (see section 241A), and
(c) if it occurred in a part of the United Kingdom, would be an offence triable under the criminal law of that part on indictment only or either on indictment or summarily,

is also unlawful conduct."

(3) After that section insert –

241A "Gross human rights abuse or violation"

(1) Conduct constitutes the commission of a gross human rights abuse or violation if each of the following three conditions is met.

(2) The first condition is that –

(a) the conduct constitutes the torture of a person who has sought –

(i) to expose illegal activity carried out by a public official or a person acting in an official capacity, or
(ii) to obtain, exercise, defend or promote human rights and fundamental freedoms, or

(b) the conduct otherwise involves the cruel, inhuman or degrading treatment or punishment of such a person.

(3) The second condition is that the conduct is carried out in consequence of that person having sought to do anything falling within subsection (2)(a)(i) or (ii).

(4) The third condition is that the conduct is carried out –

(a) by a public official, or a person acting in an official capacity, in the performance or purported performance of his or her official duties, or
(b) by a person not falling within paragraph (a) at the instigation or with the consent or acquiescence –

(i) of a public official, or
(ii) of a person acting in an official capacity,

who in instigating the conduct, or in consenting to or acquiescing in it, is acting in the performance or purported performance of his or her official duties.

APPENDIX: CRIMINAL FINANCES ACT 2017

(5) Conduct is connected with the commission of a gross human rights abuse or violation if it is conduct by a person that involves –

   (a) acting as an agent for another in connection with activities relating to conduct constituting the commission of a gross human rights abuse or violation,
   (b) directing, or sponsoring, such activities,
   (c) profiting from such activities, or
   (d) materially assisting such activities.

(6) Conduct that involves the intentional infliction of severe pain or suffering on another person is conduct that constitutes torture for the purposes of subsection (2)(a).

(7) It is immaterial whether the pain or suffering is physical or mental and whether it is caused by an act or omission.

(8) The cases in which a person materially assists activities for the purposes of subsection (5)(d) include those where the person –

   (a) provides goods or services in support of the carrying out of the activities, or
   (b) otherwise provides any financial or technological support in connection with their carrying out."

(4) The amendments made by this section –

   (a) apply in relation to conduct, so far as that conduct constitutes or is connected with the torture of a person (see section 241A(2)(a) of the Proceeds of Crime Act 2002 as inserted by subsection (3) above), whether the conduct occurs before or after the coming into force of this section;
   (b) apply in relation to property obtained through such conduct whether the property is obtained before or after the coming into force of this section;
   (c) apply in relation to conduct, so far as that conduct involves or is connected with the cruel, inhuman or degrading treatment or punishment of a person (see section 241A(2)(b) of that Act as inserted by subsection (3) above), only if the conduct occurs after the coming into force of this section.

This is subject to subsection (5).

(5) Proceedings under Chapter 2 of Part 5 of the Proceeds of Crime Act 2002 may not be brought in respect of property obtained through unlawful conduct of the kind mentioned in section 241(2A) of the Proceeds of Crime Act 2002 (as inserted by subsection (2) above) after the end of the period of 20 years from the date on which the conduct constituting the commission of the gross human rights abuse or violation concerned occurs.

(6) Proceedings under that Chapter are brought in England and Wales or Northern Ireland when –

   (a) a claim form is issued,
   (b) an application is made for a property freezing order under section 245A of that Act, or
   (c) an application is made for an interim receiving order under section 246 of that Act,

whichever is the earliest.

APPENDIX: CRIMINAL FINANCES ACT 2017

(7) Proceedings under that Chapter are brought in Scotland when –

    (a) the proceedings are served,

    (b) an application is made for a prohibitory property order under section 255A of that Act, or

    (c) an application is made for an interim administration order under section 256 of that Act,

whichever is the earliest.

Forfeiture

14 Forfeiture of cash

(1) In section 289(6) of the Proceeds of Crime Act 2002 (meaning of cash for purposes of Chapter 3 of Part 5 of that Act), after paragraph (e) insert –

"(f) gaming vouchers,
(g) fixed-value casino tokens,
(h) betting receipts,".

(2) After section 289(7) of that Act insert – "(7A) For the purposes of subsection (6) –

    (a) "gaming voucher" means a voucher in physical form issued by a gaming machine that represents a right to be paid the amount stated on it;

    (b) "fixed-value casino token" means a casino token that represents a right to be paid the amount stated on it;

    (c) "betting receipt" means a receipt in physical form that represents a right to be paid an amount in respect of a bet placed with a person holding a betting licence.

(7B) In subsection (7A) –
"bet" –

    (a) in relation to England and Wales and Scotland, has the same meaning as in section 9(1) of the Gambling Act 2005;

    (b) in relation to Northern Ireland, has the same meaning as in the Betting, Gaming, Lotteries and Amusements

(Northern Ireland) Order 1985 (S.I. 1985/1204 (N.I. 11)) (see Article 2 of that Order);
"betting licence" –

    (a) in relation to England and Wales and Scotland, means a general betting operating licence issued under Part 5 of the Gambling Act 2005;

    (b) in relation to Northern Ireland, means a bookmaker's licence as defined in Article 2 of the Betting, Gaming, Lotteries and Amusements (Northern Ireland) Order 1985;

APPENDIX: CRIMINAL FINANCES ACT 2017

"gaming machine" –

    (a) in relation to England and Wales and Scotland, has the same meaning as in the Gambling Act 2005 (see section 235 of that Act);

    (b) in relation to Northern Ireland, has the same meaning as in the Betting, Gaming, Lotteries and Amusements (Northern Ireland) Order 1985 (see Article 2 of that Order).

(7C) In the application of subsection (7A) to Northern Ireland references to a right to be paid an amount are to be read as references to the right that would exist but for Article 170 of the Betting, Gaming, Lotteries and Amusements (Northern Ireland) Order 1985 (gaming and wagering contracts void)."

15 Forfeiture of certain personal (or moveable) property

In Part 5 of the Proceeds of Crime Act 2002 (civil recovery of the proceeds etc of unlawful conduct), after section 303A insert –

"CHAPTER 3A

RECOVERY OF LISTED ASSETS IN SUMMARY PROCEEDINGS

Definition of listed asset

303B "Listed asset"

(1) In this Chapter, a "listed asset" means an item of property that falls within one of the following descriptions of property –

    (a) precious metals;
    (b) precious stones;
    (c) watches;
    (d) artistic works;
    (e) face-value vouchers;
    (f) postage stamps.

(2) The Secretary of State may by regulations amend subsection (1) –

    (a) by removing a description of property;
    (b) by adding a description of tangible personal (or corporeal moveable) property.

(3) The Secretary of State must consult the Scottish Ministers and the Department of Justice before making regulations under subsection (2).

(4) In this section –

    (a) "precious metal" means gold, silver or platinum (whether in an unmanufactured or a manufactured state);
    (b) "artistic work" means a piece of work falling within section 4(1)(a) of the Copyright, Designs and Patents Act 1988;
    (c) "face-value voucher" means a voucher in physical form that represents a right to receive goods or services to the value of an amount stated on it.

APPENDIX: CRIMINAL FINANCES ACT 2017

Searches

303C Searches

(1) If a relevant officer is lawfully on any premises and has reasonable grounds for suspecting that there is on the premises a seizable listed asset, the relevant officer may search for the listed asset there.

(2) The powers conferred by subsection (5) are exercisable by a relevant officer if –

 (a) the relevant officer has reasonable grounds for suspecting that there is a seizable listed asset in a vehicle,
 (b) it appears to the officer that the vehicle is under the control of a person (the suspect) who is in or in the vicinity of the vehicle, and
 (c) the vehicle is in a place falling within subsection (3).

(3) The places referred to in subsection (2)(c) are –

 (a) a place to which, at the time of the proposed exercise of the powers, the public or any section of the public has access, on payment or otherwise, as of right or by virtue of express or implied permission, and
 (b) any other place to which at that time people have ready access but which is not a dwelling.

(4) But if the vehicle is in a garden or yard or other land occupied with and used for the purposes of a dwelling, the relevant officer may exercise the powers conferred by subsection (5) only if the relevant officer has reasonable grounds for believing –

 (a) that the suspect does not reside in the dwelling, and
 (b) that the vehicle is not in the place in question with the express or implied permission of a person who resides in the dwelling.

(5) The powers conferred by this subsection are –

 (a) power to require the suspect to permit entry to the vehicle;
 (b) power to require the suspect to permit a search of the vehicle.

(6) If a relevant officer has reasonable grounds for suspecting that a person (the suspect) is carrying a seizable listed asset, the relevant officer may require the suspect –

 (a) to permit a search of any article the suspect has with him or her;
 (b) to permit a search of the suspect's person.

(7) The powers conferred by subsections (5) and (6) are exercisable only so far as the relevant officer thinks it necessary or expedient.

(8) A relevant officer may –

 (a) in exercising powers conferred by subsection (5), detain the vehicle for so long as is necessary for their exercise;
 (b) in exercising powers conferred by subsection (6)(b), detain the suspect for so long as is necessary for their exercise.

(9) In this Chapter, a "relevant officer" means –

 (a) an officer of Revenue and Customs,

APPENDIX: CRIMINAL FINANCES ACT 2017

    (b)   a constable,

    (c)   an SFO officer, or

    (d)   an accredited financial investigator who falls within a description specified in an order made for the purposes of this Chapter by the Secretary of State under section 453.

(10) For the purposes of this section a listed asset is a seizable listed asset if –

    (a)   all or part of it is recoverable property or is intended by any person for use in unlawful conduct, and

    (b)   the value of the asset, or the part of it that falls within paragraph (a), is not less than the minimum value.

(11) Where a power conferred by this section is being exercised in respect of more than one seizable listed asset, this section is to apply as if the value of each asset or (as the case may be) part of an asset was equal to the aggregate value of all of those assets or parts.

303D Searches: supplemental provision

(1) The powers conferred by section 303C –

    (a)   are exercisable only so far as reasonably required for the purpose of finding a listed asset;

    (b)   include the power to carry out (or arrange for the carrying out of) tests on anything found during the course of the search for the purpose of establishing whether it is a listed asset;

    (c)   are exercisable by an officer of Revenue and Customs only if the officer has reasonable grounds for suspecting that the unlawful conduct in question relates to an assigned matter (within the meaning of the Customs and Excise Management Act 1979);

    (d)   are exercisable by an SFO officer or an accredited financial investigator only in relation to the following –

        (i)   premises in England, Wales or Northern Ireland (in the case of section 303C(1));

        (ii)   vehicles and suspects in England, Wales or Northern Ireland (in the case of section 303C(5) and (8)(a));

        (iii)   suspects in England, Wales or Northern Ireland (in the case of section 303C(6) and (8)(b)).

(2) Section 303C does not require a person to submit to an intimate search or strip search (within the meaning of section 164 of the Customs and Excise Management Act 1979).

303E Prior approval

(1) The powers conferred by section 303C may be exercised only with the appropriate approval unless, in the circumstances, it is not practicable to obtain that approval before exercising the power.

(2) The appropriate approval means the approval of a judicial officer or (if that is not practicable in any case) the approval of a senior officer.
(3) A judicial officer means –

    (a) in relation to England and Wales and Northern Ireland, a justice of the peace;
    (b) in relation to Scotland, the sheriff.

(4) A senior officer means –

    (a) in relation to the exercise of a power by an officer of Revenue and Customs, such an officer of a rank designated by the Commissioners for Her Majesty's Revenue and Customs as equivalent to that of a senior police officer;
    (b) in relation to the exercise of a power by a constable, a senior police officer;
    (c) in relation to the exercise of a power by an SFO officer, the Director of the Serious Fraud Office;
    (d) in relation to the exercise of a power by a National Crime Agency officer, the Director General of the National Crime Agency or any other National Crime Agency officer authorised by the Director General (whether generally or specifically) for this purpose;
    (e) in relation to the exercise of a power by an accredited financial investigator who is –

        (i) a member of the civilian staff of a police force in England and Wales (including the metropolitan police force), within the meaning of Part 1 of the Police Reform and Social Responsibility Act 2011,
        (ii) a member of staff of the City of London police force, or
        (iii) a member of staff of the Police Service of Northern Ireland, a senior police officer;

    (f) in relation to the exercise of a power by an accredited financial investigator who does not fall within any of the preceding paragraphs, an accredited financial investigator who falls within a description specified in an order made for this purpose by the Secretary of State under section 453.

(5) A senior police officer means a police officer of at least the rank of inspector.
(6) If the powers are exercised without the approval of a judicial officer in a case where –

    (a) no property is seized by virtue of section 303J, or
    (b) any property so seized is not detained for more than 48 hours (calculated in accordance with section 303K(5)),

the relevant officer who exercised the power must give a written report to the appointed person.

(7) But the duty in subsection (6) does not apply if, during the course of exercising the powers conferred by section 303C, the relevant officer seizes cash by virtue of section 294 and the cash so seized is detained for more than 48 hours (calculated in accordance with section 295(1B)).

(8) A report under subsection (6) must give particulars of the circumstances which led the relevant officer to believe that –

(a) the powers were exercisable, and
(b) it was not practicable to obtain the approval of a judicial officer.

(9) In this section and section 303F, the appointed person means –

(a) in relation to England and Wales, a person appointed by the Secretary of State;
(b) in relation to Scotland, a person appointed by the Scottish Ministers;
(c) in relation to Northern Ireland, a person appointed by the Department of Justice.

(10) The appointed person must not be a person employed under or for the purposes of a government department or of the Scottish Administration; and the terms and conditions of the person's appointment, including any remuneration or expenses to be paid to the person, are to be determined by the person making the appointment.

303F Report on exercise of powers
(1) As soon as possible after the end of each financial year, the appointed person must prepare a report for that year.
(2) "Financial year" means –

(a) the period beginning with the day on which section 15 of the Criminal Finances Act 2017 (which inserted this section) came into force and ending with the next 31 March (which is the first financial year), and
(b) each subsequent period of 12 months beginning with 1 April.

(3) The report must give the appointed person's opinion as to the circumstances and manner in which the powers conferred by section 303C are being exercised in cases where the relevant officer who exercised them is required to give a report under section 303E(6).
(4) In the report, the appointed person may make any recommendations he or she considers appropriate.
(5) The appointed person must send a copy of the report to whichever of the Secretary of State, the Scottish Administration or the Department of Justice appointed the person.
(6) The Secretary of State must lay a copy of any report the Secretary of State receives under this section before Parliament and arrange for it to be published.
(7) The Scottish Ministers must lay a copy of any report they receive under this section before the Scottish Parliament and arrange for it to be published.
(8) The Department of Justice must lay a copy of any report it receives under this section before the Northern Ireland Assembly and arrange for it to be published.
(9) Section 41(3) of the Interpretation Act (Northern Ireland) 1954 applies for the purposes of subsection (8) in relation to the laying of a copy of a report as it applies in relation to the laying of a statutory document under an enactment.

303G Code of practice: Secretary of State
(1) The Secretary of State must make a code of practice in connection with the exercise by officers of Revenue and Customs, SFO officers and (in relation to England and Wales) constables and accredited financial investigators of the powers conferred by section 303C.
(2) Where the Secretary of State proposes to issue a code of practice, the Secretary of State must –

   (a) publish a draft,
   (b) consider any representations made about the draft by the Scottish Ministers, the Department of Justice or any other person, and
   (c) if the Secretary of State thinks it appropriate, modify the draft in the light of any such representations.

(3) The Secretary of State must also consult the Attorney General about the draft in its application to the exercise of powers by SFO officers and the Director of the Serious Fraud Office.
(4) The Secretary of State must lay a draft of the code before Parliament.
(5) When the Secretary of State has laid a draft of the code before Parliament, the Secretary of State may bring it into operation by regulations.
(6) The Secretary of State may revise the whole or any part of the code and issue the code as revised; and subsections (2) to (5) apply to such a revised code as they apply to the original code.
(7) A failure by an officer of Revenue and Customs, an SFO officer, a constable or an accredited financial investigator to comply with a provision of the code does not of itself make him or her liable to criminal or civil proceedings.
(8) The code is admissible in evidence in criminal or civil proceedings and is to be taken into account by a court or tribunal in any case in which it appears to the court or tribunal to be relevant.

303H Code of practice: Scotland
(1) The Scottish Ministers must make a code of practice in connection with the exercise by constables in relation to Scotland of the powers conferred by section 303C.
(2) Where the Scottish Ministers propose to issue a code of practice, they must –

   (a) publish a draft,
   (b) consider any representations made about the draft, and
   (c) if they think it appropriate, modify the draft in the light of any such representations.

(3) The Scottish Ministers must lay a draft of the code before the Scottish Parliament.
(4) When the Scottish Ministers have laid a draft of the code before the Scottish Parliament, they may bring it into operation by order.
(5) The Scottish Ministers may revise the whole or any part of the code and issue the code as revised; and subsections (2) to (4) apply to such a revised code as they apply to the original code.
(6) A failure by a constable to comply with a provision of the code does not of itself make the constable liable to criminal or civil proceedings.

APPENDIX: CRIMINAL FINANCES ACT 2017

(7) The code is admissible in evidence in criminal or civil proceedings and is to be taken into account by a court or tribunal in any case in which it appears to the court or tribunal to be relevant.

303I Code of practice: Northern Ireland

(1) The Department of Justice must make a code of practice in connection with the exercise by constables and accredited financial investigators, in relation to Northern Ireland, of the powers conferred by section 303C.
(2) Where the Department of Justice proposes to issue a code of practice, it must –
   (a) publish a draft,
   (b) consider any representations made about the draft, and
   (c) if the Department of Justice thinks it appropriate, modify the draft in the light of any such representations.
(3) The Department of Justice must lay a draft of the code before the Northern Ireland Assembly.
(4) When the Department of Justice has laid a draft of the code before the Northern Ireland Assembly, the Department of Justice may bring it into operation by order.
(5) Section 41(3) of the Interpretation Act (Northern Ireland) 1954 applies for the purposes of subsections (3) and (4) in relation to the laying of a draft as it applies in relation to the laying of a statutory document under an enactment.
(6) The Department of Justice may revise the whole or any part of the code and issue the code as revised; and subsections (2) to (5) apply to such a revised code as they apply to the original code.
(7) A failure by a constable or accredited financial investigator to comply with a provision of the code does not of itself make him or her liable to criminal or civil proceedings.
(8) The code is admissible in evidence in criminal or civil proceedings and is to be taken into account by a court or tribunal in any case in which it appears to the court or tribunal to be relevant.

Seizure and detention

303J Seizure of listed assets

(1) A relevant officer may seize any item of property if the relevant officer has reasonable grounds for suspecting that –
   (a) it is a listed asset,
   (b) it is recoverable property or intended by any person for use in unlawful conduct, and
   (c) the value of it is not less than the minimum value.
(2) A relevant officer may also seize any item of property if –
   (a) the relevant officer has reasonable grounds for suspecting the item to be a listed asset,

APPENDIX: CRIMINAL FINANCES ACT 2017

- (b) the relevant officer has reasonable grounds for suspecting that part of the item is recoverable property or intended by any person for use in unlawful conduct,
- (c) the relevant officer has reasonable grounds for suspecting that the value of the part to which the suspicion relates is not less than the minimum value, and
- (d) it is not reasonably practicable to seize only that part.

(3) Where the powers conferred by this section are being exercised by a relevant officer in respect of more than one item of property, this section is to apply as if the value of each item was equal to the aggregate value of all of those items.

(4) The references in subsection (3) to the value of an item are to be read as including references to the value of part of an item where the power conferred by subsection (2) is being exercised (whether alone or in conjunction with the power conferred by subsection (1)).

(5) This section does not authorise the seizure by an SFO officer or an accredited financial investigator of an item of property found in Scotland.

303K Initial detention of seized property

(1) Property seized under section 303J may be detained for an initial period of 6 hours.

(2) Property seized under section 303J may be detained beyond the initial period of 6 hours only if its continued detention is authorised by a senior officer.

(3) If the continued detention of property seized under section 303J is authorised under subsection (2), the property may be detained for a further period of 42 hours.

(4) Subsections (1) to (3) authorise the detention of property only for so long as a relevant officer continues to have reasonable grounds for suspicion in relation to that property as described in section 303J(1) or (2) (as the case may be).

(5) In calculating a period of hours for the purposes of this section, no account shall be taken of –

- (a) any Saturday or Sunday,
- (b) Christmas Day,
- (c) Good Friday,
- (d) any day that is a bank holiday under the Banking and Financial Dealings Act 1971 in the part of the United Kingdom within which the property is seized, or
- (e) any day prescribed under section 8(2) of the Criminal Procedure (Scotland) Act 1995 as a court holiday in a sheriff court in the sheriff court district within which the property is seized.

(6) "Senior officer" has the same meaning in this section as it has in section 303E.

303L Further detention of seized property

(1) The period for which property seized under section 303J, or any part of that property, may be detained may be extended by an order made –

- (a) in England and Wales or Northern Ireland, by a magistrates' court;
- (b) in Scotland, by the sheriff.

(2) An order under subsection (1) may not authorise the detention of any property –

  (a) beyond the end of the period of 6 months beginning with the date of the order, and
  (b) in the case of any further order under this section, beyond the end of the period of 2 years beginning with the date of the first order.

(3) A justice of the peace may also exercise the power of a magistrates' court to make the first order under subsection (1) extending a particular period of detention.

(4) An application for an order under subsection (1) may be made –

  (a) in relation to England and Wales and Northern Ireland, by a person specified in subsection (5);
  (b) in relation to Scotland, by the Scottish Ministers in connection with their functions under section 303O or by a procurator fiscal.

(5) The persons referred to in subsection (4)(a) are –

  (a) the Commissioners for Her Majesty's Revenue and Customs,
  (b) a constable,
  (c) an SFO officer, or
  (d) an accredited financial investigator who falls within a description specified in an order made for the purposes of this Chapter by the Secretary of State under section 453.

(6) The court, sheriff or justice may make the order if satisfied, in relation to the item of property to be further detained, that –

  (a) it is a listed asset,
  (b) the value of it is not less than the minimum value, and
  (c) condition 1 or condition 2 is met.

(7) Subsection (6)(b) does not apply where the application is for a second or subsequent order under this section.

(8) Condition 1 is that there are reasonable grounds for suspecting that the property is recoverable property and that either –

  (a) its continued detention is justified while its derivation is further investigated or consideration is given to bringing (in the United Kingdom or elsewhere) proceedings against any person for an offence with which the property is connected, or
  (b) proceedings against any person for an offence with which the property is connected have been started and have not been concluded.

(9) Condition 2 is that there are reasonable grounds for suspecting that the property is intended to be used in unlawful conduct and that either –

  (a) its continued detention is justified while its intended use is further investigated or consideration is given to bringing (in the United Kingdom or elsewhere) proceedings against any person for an offence with which the property is connected, or

(b) proceedings against any person for an offence with which the property is connected have been started and have not been concluded.

(10) Where an application for an order under subsection (1) relates to an item of property seized under section 303J(2), the court, sheriff or justice may make the order if satisfied that –

(a) the item of property is a listed asset,
(b) condition 1 or 2 is met in respect of part of the item,
(c) the value of that part is not less than the minimum value, and
(d) it is not reasonably practicable to detain only that part.

(11) Subsection (10)(c) does not apply where the application is for a second or subsequent order under this section.

(12) Where an application for an order under subsection (1) is made in respect of two or more items of property that were seized at the same time and by the same person, this section is to apply as if the value of each item was equal to the aggregate value of all of those items.

(13) The references in subsection (12) to the value of an item are to be read as including references to the value of part of an item where subsection

(10) applies in relation to one or more of the items in respect of which the application under subsection (1) is made.

(14) An order under subsection (1) must provide for notice to be given to persons affected by it.

303M Testing and safekeeping of property seized under section 303J

(1) A relevant officer may carry out (or arrange for the carrying out of) tests on any item of property seized under section 303J for the purpose of establishing whether it is a listed asset.

(2) A relevant officer must arrange for any item of property seized under section 303J to be safely stored throughout the period during which it is detained under this Chapter.

303N Release of detained property

(1) This section applies while any property is detained under section 303K or 303L.

(2) A magistrates' court or (in Scotland) the sheriff may direct the release of the whole or any part of the property if the following condition is met.

(3) The condition is that the court or sheriff is satisfied, on an application by the person from whom the property was seized, that the conditions in section 303K or 303L (as the case may be) for the detention of the property are no longer met in relation to the property to be released.

(4) A relevant officer or (in Scotland) a procurator fiscal may, after notifying the magistrates' court, sheriff or justice under whose order property is being detained, release the whole or any part of it if satisfied that the detention of the property to be released is no longer justified.

Forfeiture

303O Forfeiture

(1) While property is detained under this Chapter, an application for the forfeiture of the whole or any part of it may be made –

    (a) to a magistrates' court by a person specified in subsection (2);
    (b) to the sheriff by the Scottish Ministers.

(2) The persons referred to in subsection (1)(a) are –

    (a) the Commissioners for Her Majesty's Revenue and Customs,
    (b) a constable,
    (c) an SFO officer, or
    (d) an accredited financial investigator who falls within a description specified in an order made for the purposes of this Chapter by the Secretary of State under section 453.

(3) The court or sheriff may order the forfeiture of the property or any part of it if satisfied that –

    (a) the property is a listed asset, and
    (b) what is to be forfeited is recoverable property or intended by any person for use in unlawful conduct.

(4) An order under subsection (3) made by a magistrates' court may provide for payment under section 303U of reasonable legal expenses that a person has reasonably incurred, or may reasonably incur, in respect of –

    (a) the proceedings in which the order is made, or
    (b) any related proceedings under this Chapter.

(5) A sum in respect of a relevant item of expenditure is not payable under section 303U in pursuance of provision under subsection (4) unless –

    (a) the person who applied for the order under subsection (3) agrees to its payment, or
    (b) the court has assessed the amount allowed in respect of that item and the sum is paid in respect of the assessed amount.

(6) For the purposes of subsection (5) –

    (a) a "relevant item of expenditure" is an item of expenditure to which regulations under section 286B would apply if the order under subsection (3) had instead been a recovery order;
    (b) an amount is "allowed" in respect of a relevant item of expenditure if it would have been allowed by those regulations;
    (c) if the person who applied for the order under subsection (3) was a constable, an SFO officer or an accredited financial investigator, that person may not agree to the payment of a sum unless the person is a senior officer or is authorised to do so by a senior officer.

(7) "Senior officer" has the same meaning in subsection (6)(c) as it has in section 303E.

(8) Subsection (3) ceases to apply on the transfer of an application made under this section in accordance with section 303R(1)(a) or (b).
(9) Where an application for the forfeiture of any property is made under this section, the property is to be detained (and may not be released under any power conferred by this Chapter) until any proceedings in pursuance of the application (including any proceedings on appeal) are concluded.
(10) Where the property to which the application relates is being detained under this Chapter as part of an item of property, having been seized under section 303J(2), subsection (9) is to be read as if it required the continued detention of the whole of the item of property.

303P Associated and joint property

(1) Sections 303Q and 303R apply if –

    (a) an application is made under section 303O in respect of property detained under this Chapter,

    (b) the court or sheriff is satisfied that the property is a listed asset,

    (c) the court or sheriff is satisfied that all or part of the property is recoverable property or intended by any person for use in unlawful conduct, and

    (d) there exists property that is associated with the property in relation to which the court or sheriff is satisfied as mentioned in paragraph (c).

(2) Sections 303Q and 303R also apply in England and Wales and Northern Ireland if –

    (a) an application is made under section 303O in respect of property detained under this Chapter,

    (b) the court is satisfied that the property is a listed asset,

    (c) the court is satisfied that all or part of the property is recoverable property, and

    (d) the property in relation to which the court is satisfied as mentioned in paragraph (c) belongs to joint tenants and one of the tenants is an excepted joint owner.

(3) In this section and sections 303Q and 303R "associated property" means property of any of the following descriptions that is not itself the forfeitable property –

    (a) any interest in the forfeitable property;

    (b) any other interest in the property in which the forfeitable property subsists;

    (c) if the forfeitable property is a tenancy in common, the tenancy of the other tenant;

    (d) if (in Scotland) the forfeitable property is owned in common, the interest of the other owner;

    (e) if the forfeitable property is part of a larger property, but not a separate part, the remainder of that property.

References to property being associated with forfeitable property are to be read accordingly.

(4) In this section and sections 303Q and 303R the "forfeitable property" means the property in relation to which the court or sheriff is satisfied as mentioned in subsection (1)(c) or (2)(c) (as the case may be).

APPENDIX: CRIMINAL FINANCES ACT 2017

303Q Agreements about associated and joint property
(1) Where –

(a) this section applies, and
(b) the person who applied for the order under section 303O (on the one hand) and the person who holds the associated property or who is the excepted joint owner (on the other hand) agree,

the magistrates' court or sheriff may, instead of making an order under section 303O(3), make an order requiring the person who holds the associated property or who is the excepted joint owner to make a payment to a person identified in the order.

(2) The amount of the payment is (subject to subsection (3)) to be the amount which the persons referred to in subsection (1)(b) agree represents –

(a) in a case where this section applies by virtue of section 303P(1), the value of the forfeitable property;
(b) in a case where this section applies by virtue of section 303P(2), the value of the forfeitable property less the value of the excepted joint owner's share.

(3) The amount of the payment may be reduced if the person who applied for the order under section 303O agrees that the other party to the agreement has suffered loss as a result of the seizure of the forfeitable property and any associated property under section 303J and its subsequent detention.

(4) The reduction that is permissible by virtue of subsection (3) is such amount as the parties to the agreement agree is reasonable, having regard to the loss suffered and any other relevant circumstances.

(5) An order under subsection (1) may, so far as required for giving effect to the agreement, include provision for vesting, creating or extinguishing any interest in property.

(6) An order under subsection (1) made by a magistrates' court may provide for payment under subsection (12) of reasonable legal expenses that a person has reasonably incurred, or may reasonably incur, in respect of –

(a) the proceedings in which the order is made, or
(b) any related proceedings under this Chapter.

(7) A sum in respect of a relevant item of expenditure is not payable under subsection (12) in pursuance of provision under subsection (6) unless –

(a) the person who applied for the order under section 303O agrees to its payment, or
(b) the court has assessed the amount allowed in respect of that item and the sum is paid in respect of the assessed amount.

(8) For the purposes of subsection (7) –

(a) a "relevant item of expenditure" is an item of expenditure to which regulations under section 286B would apply if the order under subsection (1) had instead been a recovery order;

(b) an amount is "allowed" in respect of a relevant item of expenditure if it would have been allowed by those regulations.

(9) For the purposes of section 308(2), on the making of an order under subsection (1), the forfeitable property is to be treated as if it had been forfeited.

(10) If there is more than one item of associated property or more than one excepted joint owner, the total amount to be paid under subsection (1), and the part of that amount which is to be provided by each person who holds any such associated property or who is an excepted joint owner, is to be agreed between both (or all) of them and the person who applied for the order under section 303O.

(11) If the person who applied for the order under section 303O was a constable, an SFO officer or an accredited financial investigator, that person may enter into an agreement for the purposes of any provision of this section only if the person is a senior officer or is authorised to do so by a senior officer.

"Senior officer" has the same meaning in this subsection as it has in section 303E.

(12) An amount received under an order under subsection (1) must be applied as follows –

(a) first, it must be applied in making any payment of legal expenses which, after giving effect to subsection (7), are payable under this subsection in pursuance of provision under subsection (6);

(b) second, it must be applied in payment or reimbursement of any reasonable costs incurred in storing or insuring the forfeitable property and any associated property whilst detained under this Part;

(c) third, it must be paid –

(i) if the order was made by a magistrates' court, into the Consolidated Fund;

(ii) if the order was made by the sheriff, into the Scottish Consolidated Fund.

303R Associated and joint property: default of agreement

(1) Where this section applies and there is no agreement under section 303Q, the magistrates' court or sheriff –

(a) must transfer the application made under section 303O to the relevant court if satisfied that the value of the forfeitable property and any associated property is £10,000 or more;

(b) may transfer the application made under section 303O to the relevant court if satisfied that the value of the forfeitable property and any associated property is less than £10,000.

(2) The "relevant court" is –

(a) the High Court, where the application under section 303O was made to a magistrates' court;

(b) the Court of Session, where the application under section 303O was made to the sheriff.

(3) Where (under subsection (1)(a) or (b)) an application made under section 303O is transferred to the relevant court, the relevant court may order the forfeiture of the property to which the application relates, or any part of that property, if satisfied that –

    (a) the property is a listed asset, and

    (b) what is to be forfeited is recoverable property or intended by any person for use in unlawful conduct.

(4) An order under subsection (3) made by the High Court may include provision of the type that may be included in an order under section 303O(3) made by a magistrates' court by virtue of section 303O(4).

(5) If provision is included in an order of the High Court by virtue of subsection (4) of this section, section 303O(5) and (6) apply with the necessary modifications.

(6) The relevant court may, as well as making an order under subsection (3), make an order –

    (a) providing for the forfeiture of the associated property or (as the case may be) for the excepted joint owner's interest to be extinguished, or

    (b) providing for the excepted joint owner's interest to be severed.

(7) Where (under subsection (1)(b)) the magistrates' court or sheriff decides not to transfer an application made under section 303O to the relevant court, the magistrates' court or sheriff may, as well as making an order under section 303O(3), make an order –

    (a) providing for the forfeiture of the associated property or (as the case may be) for the excepted joint owner's interest to be extinguished, or

    (b) providing for the excepted joint owner's interest to be severed.

(8) An order under subsection (6) or (7) may be made only if the relevant court, the magistrates' court or the sheriff (as the case may be) thinks it just and equitable to do so.

(9) An order under subsection (6) or (7) must provide for the payment of an amount to the person who holds the associated property or who is an excepted joint owner.

(10) In making an order under subsection (6) or (7), and including provision in it by virtue of subsection (9), the relevant court, the magistrates' court or the sheriff (as the case may be) must have regard to –

    (a) the rights of any person who holds the associated property or who is an excepted joint owner and the value to that person of that property or (as the case may) of that person's share (including any value that cannot be assessed in terms of money), and

    (b) the interest of the person who applied for the order under section 303O in realising the value of the forfeitable property.

(11) If the relevant court, the magistrates' court or the sheriff (as the case may be) is satisfied that –

    (a) the person who holds the associated property or who is an excepted joint owner has suffered loss as a result of the seizure of the forfeitable property and any associated property under section 303J and its subsequent detention, and

    (b) the circumstances are exceptional,

an order under subsection (6) or (7) may require the payment of compensation to that person.

(12) The amount of compensation to be paid by virtue of subsection (11) is the amount the relevant court, the magistrates' court or the sheriff (as the case may be) thinks reasonable, having regard to the loss suffered and any other relevant circumstances.

(13) Compensation to be paid by virtue of subsection (11) is to be paid in the same way that compensation is to be paid under section 303W.

303S Sections 303O to 303R: appeals

(1) Any party to proceedings for an order for the forfeiture of property under section 303O may appeal against –

   (a) the making of an order under section 303O;
   (b) the making of an order under section 303R(7);
   (c) a decision not to make an order under section 303O unless the reason that no order was made is that an order was instead made under section 303Q;
   (d) a decision not to make an order under section 303R(7). Paragraphs (c) and (d) do not apply if the application for the order under section 303O was transferred in accordance with section 303R(1)(a) or (b).

(2) Where an order under section 303Q is made by a magistrates' court, any party to the proceedings for the order (including any party to the proceedings under section 303O that preceded the making of the order) may appeal against a decision to include, or not to include, provision in the order under subsection (6) of section 303Q.

(3) An appeal under this section lies –

   (a) in relation to England and Wales, to the Crown Court;
   (b) in relation to Scotland, to the Sheriff Appeal Court;
   (c) in relation to Northern Ireland, to a county court.

(4) An appeal under this section must be made before the end of the period of 30 days starting with the day on which the court makes the order or decision.

(5) The court hearing the appeal may make any order it thinks appropriate.

(6) If the court upholds an appeal against an order forfeiting property, it may order the release of the whole or any part of the property.

303T Realisation of forfeited property

(1) If property is forfeited under section 303O or 303R, a relevant officer must realise the property or make arrangements for its realisation.

(2) But the property is not to be realised –

   (a) before the end of the period within which an appeal may be made (whether under section 303S or otherwise), or
   (b) if an appeal is made within that period, before the appeal is determined or otherwise disposed of.

(3) The realisation of property under subsection (1) must be carried out, so far as practicable, in the manner best calculated to maximise the amount obtained for the property.

APPENDIX: CRIMINAL FINANCES ACT 2017

303U Proceeds of realisation

(1) The proceeds of property realised under section 303T must be applied as follows –

    (a) first, they must be applied in making any payment required to be made by virtue of section 303R(9);

    (b) second, they must be applied in making any payment of legal expenses which, after giving effect to section 303O(5) (including as applied by section 303R(5)), are payable under this subsection in pursuance of provision under section 303O(4) or, as the case may be, 303R(4);

    (c) third, they must be applied in payment or reimbursement of any reasonable costs incurred in storing or insuring the property whilst detained under this Part and in realising the property;

    (d) fourth, they must be paid –

        (i) if the property was forfeited by a magistrates' court or the High Court, into the Consolidated Fund;

        (ii) if the property was forfeited by the sheriff or the Court of Session, into the Scottish Consolidated Fund.

(2) If what is realised under section 303T represents part only of an item of property seized under section 303J and detained under this Chapter, the reference in subsection (1)(c) to costs incurred in storing or insuring the property is to be read as a reference to costs incurred in storing or insuring the whole of the item of property.

Supplementary

303V Victims and other owners

(1) A person who claims that any property detained under this Chapter, or any part of it, belongs to him or her may apply for the property or part to be released.

(2) An application under subsection (1) is to be made –

    (a) in England and Wales or Northern Ireland, to a magistrates' court;

    (b) in Scotland, to the sheriff.

(3) The application may be made in the course of proceedings under section 303L or 303O or at any other time.

(4) The court or sheriff may order the property to which the application relates to be released to the applicant if it appears to the court or sheriff that –

    (a) the applicant was deprived of the property to which the application relates, or of property which it represents, by unlawful conduct,

    (b) the property the applicant was deprived of was not, immediately before the applicant was deprived of it, recoverable property, and

    (c) the property belongs to the applicant.

(5) If subsection (6) applies, the court or sheriff may order the property to which the application relates to be released to the applicant or to the person from whom it was seized.

(6) This subsection applies where –

    (a) the applicant is not the person from whom the property to which the application relates was seized,

    (b) it appears to the court or sheriff that that property belongs to the applicant,

    (c) the court or sheriff is satisfied that the release condition is met in relation to that property, and

    (d) no objection to the making of an order under subsection (5) has been made by the person from whom that property was seized.

(7) The release condition is met –

    (a) in relation to property detained under section 303K or 303L, if the conditions in section 303K or (as the case may be) 303L for the detention of the property are no longer met, and

    (b) in relation to property detained under section 303O, if the court or sheriff decides not to make an order under that section in relation to the property.

303W Compensation

(1) If no order under section 303O, 303Q or 303R is made in respect of any property detained under this Chapter, the person to whom the property belongs or from whom it was seized may make an application for compensation.

(2) An application under subsection (1) is to be made –

    (a) in England and Wales or Northern Ireland, to a magistrates' court;

    (b) in Scotland, to the sheriff.

(3) If the court or sheriff is satisfied that the applicant has suffered loss as a result of the detention of the property and that the circumstances are exceptional, the court or sheriff may order compensation to be paid to the applicant.

(4) The amount of compensation to be paid is the amount the court or sheriff thinks reasonable, having regard to the loss suffered and any other relevant circumstances.

(5) If the property was seized by an officer of Revenue and Customs, the compensation is to be paid by the Commissioners for Her Majesty's Revenue and Customs.

(6) If the property was seized by a constable, the compensation is to be paid as follows –

    (a) in the case of a constable of a police force in England and Wales, it is to be paid out of the police fund from which the expenses of the police force are met;

    (b) in the case of a constable of the Police Service of Scotland, it is to be paid by the Scottish Police Authority;

    (c) in the case of a police officer within the meaning of the Police (Northern Ireland) Act 2000, it is to be paid out of money provided by the Chief Constable of the Police Service of Northern Ireland.

(7) If the property was seized by an SFO officer, the compensation is to be paid by the Director of the Serious Fraud Office.

(8) If the property was seized by a National Crime Agency officer, the compensation is to be paid by the National Crime Agency.

(9) If the property was seized by an accredited financial investigator who was not an officer of Revenue and Customs, a constable, an SFO officer or a National Crime Agency officer, the compensation is to be paid as follows –

   (a) in the case of an investigator who was –

      (i) a member of the civilian staff of a police force (including the metropolitan police force), within the meaning of Part 1 of the Police Reform and Social Responsibility Act 2011, or
      (ii) a member of staff of the City of London police force, it is to be paid out of the police fund from which the expenses of the police force are met,

   (b) in the case of an investigator who was a member of staff of the Police Service of Northern Ireland, it is to be paid out of money provided by the Chief Constable of the Police Service of Northern Ireland,
   (c) in the case of an investigator who was a member of staff of a department of the Government of the United Kingdom, it is to be paid by the Minister of the Crown in charge of the department or by the department,
   (d) in the case of an investigator who was a member of staff of a Northern Ireland department, it is to be paid by the department,
   (e) in the case of an investigator who was exercising a function of the Welsh Revenue Authority, it is to be paid by the Welsh Revenue Authority, and
   (f) in any other case, it is to be paid by the employer of the investigator.

(10) The Secretary of State may by regulations amend subsection (9).
(11) The power in subsection (10) is exercisable by the Department of Justice (and not by the Secretary of State) so far as it may be used to make provision which could be made by an Act of the Northern Ireland Assembly without the consent of the Secretary of State (see sections 6 to 8 of the Northern Ireland Act 1998.)
(12) If an order under section 303O, 303Q or 303R is made in respect only of a part of any property detained under this Chapter, this section has effect in relation to the other part.

303X Powers for prosecutors to appear in proceedings
   (1) The Director of Public Prosecutions or the Director of Public Prosecutions for Northern Ireland may appear for a constable or an accredited financial investigator in proceedings under this Chapter if the Director –

      (a) is asked by, or on behalf of, a constable or (as the case may be) an accredited financial investigator to do so, and
      (b) considers it appropriate to do so.

   (2) The Director of Public Prosecutions may appear for the Commissioners for Her Majesty's Revenue and Customs or an officer of Revenue and Customs in proceedings under this Chapter if the Director –

      (a) is asked by, or on behalf of, the Commissioners for Her Majesty's Revenue and Customs or (as the case may be) an officer of Revenue and Customs to do so, and

(b) considers it appropriate to do so.

(3) The Directors may charge fees for the provision of services under this section.

(4) The references in subsection (1) to an accredited financial investigator do not include an accredited financial investigator who is an officer of Revenue and Customs but the references in subsection (2) to an officer of Revenue and Customs do include an accredited financial investigator who is an officer of Revenue and Customs.

303Y "The minimum value"

(1) For the purposes of this Chapter, "the minimum value" is £1,000.

(2) The Secretary of State may by regulations amend the amount for the time being specified in subsection (1).

(3) The Secretary of State must consult the Scottish Ministers and the Department of Justice before making regulations under subsection (2).

303Z Financial investigators

Where an accredited financial investigator of a particular description –

(a) applies for an order under section 303L,
(b) applies for forfeiture under section 303O, or
(c) brings an appeal under, or relating to, this Chapter,

any subsequent step in the application or appeal, or any further application or appeal relating to the same matter, may be taken, made or brought by a different accredited financial investigator of the same description."

16 Forfeiture of money held in bank and building society accounts

In Part 5 of the Proceeds of Crime Act 2002 (civil recovery of the proceeds etc of unlawful conduct), after section 303Z (inserted by section 15 above) insert –

"CHAPTER 3B

FORFEITURE OF MONEY HELD IN BANK AND BUILDING SOCIETY ACCOUNTS

Freezing of bank and building society accounts

303Z1 Application for account freezing order

(1) This section applies if an enforcement officer has reasonable grounds for suspecting that money held in an account maintained with a bank or building society –

(a) is recoverable property, or
(b) is intended by any person for use in unlawful conduct.

(2) Where this section applies (but subject to section 303Z2) the enforcement officer may apply to the relevant court for an account freezing order in relation to the account in which the money is held.

(3) For the purposes of this Chapter –

  (a) an account freezing order is an order that, subject to any exclusions (see section 303Z5), prohibits each person by or for whom the account to which the order applies is operated from making withdrawals or payments from the account;
  (b) an account is operated by or for a person if the person is an account holder or a signatory or identified as a beneficiary in relation to the account.

(4) An application for an account freezing order may be made without notice if the circumstances of the case are such that notice of the application would prejudice the taking of any steps under this Chapter to forfeit money that is recoverable property or intended by any person for use in unlawful conduct.

(5) The money referred to in subsection (1) may be all or part of the credit balance of the account.

(6) In this Chapter –

"bank" has the meaning given by section 303Z7;
"building society" has the same meaning as in the Building Societies Act 1986;
"enforcement officer" means –

  (a) an officer of Revenue and Customs,
  (b) a constable,
  (c) an SFO officer, or
  (d) an accredited financial investigator who falls within a description specified in an order made for the purposes of this Chapter by the Secretary of State under section 453;

"the minimum amount" has the meaning given by section 303Z8; "relevant court" –

  (a) in England and Wales and Northern Ireland, means a magistrates' court, and
  (b) in Scotland, means the sheriff.

303Z2 Restrictions on making of application under section 303Z1

(1) The power to apply for an account freezing order is not exercisable if the money in relation to which the enforcement officer's suspicion exists is less in amount than the minimum amount.

(2) An enforcement officer may not apply for an account freezing order unless the officer is a senior officer or is authorised to do so by a senior officer.

(3) The power to apply for an account freezing order is not exercisable by an SFO officer, or by an accredited financial investigator, in relation to an account maintained with a branch of a bank or building society that is in Scotland.

(4) For the purposes of this Chapter, a "senior officer" is –

  (a) an officer of Revenue and Customs of a rank designated by the Commissioners for Her Majesty's Revenue and Customs as equivalent to that of a senior police officer,
  (b) a senior police officer,

APPENDIX: CRIMINAL FINANCES ACT 2017

- (c) the Director of the Serious Fraud Office,
- (d) the Director General of the National Crime Agency or any other National Crime Agency officer authorised by the Director General (whether generally or specifically) for this purpose, or
- (e) an accredited financial investigator who falls within a description specified in an order made for the purposes of this Chapter by the Secretary of State under section 453.

(5) In subsection (4), a "senior police officer" means a police officer of at least the rank of inspector.

303Z3 Making of account freezing order

(1) This section applies where an application for an account freezing order is made under section 303Z1 in relation to an account.

(2) The relevant court may make the order if satisfied that there are reasonable grounds for suspecting that money held in the account (whether all or part of the credit balance of the account) –

- (a) is recoverable property, or
- (b) is intended by any person for use in unlawful conduct.

(3) An account freezing order ceases to have effect at the end of the period specified in the order (which may be varied under section 303Z4) unless it ceases to have effect at an earlier or later time in accordance with the provision made by sections 303Z9(6)(c), 303Z11(2) to (7), 303Z14(6) to (8) and 303Z15.

(4) The period specified by the relevant court for the purposes of subsection (3) (whether when the order is first made or on a variation under section 303Z4) may not exceed the period of 2 years, starting with the day on which the account freezing order is (or was) made.

(5) An account freezing order must provide for notice to be given to persons affected by the order.

303Z4 Variation and setting aside of account freezing order

(1) The relevant court may at any time vary or set aside an account freezing order on an application made by –

- (a) an enforcement officer, or
- (b) any person affected by the order.

(2) But an enforcement officer may not make an application under subsection (1) unless the officer is a senior officer or is authorised to do so by a senior officer.

(3) Before varying or setting aside an account freezing order the court must (as well as giving the parties to the proceedings an opportunity to be heard) give such an opportunity to any person who may be affected by its decision.

(4) In relation to Scotland, the references in this section to setting aside an order are to be read as references to recalling it.

303Z5 Exclusions

(1) The power to vary an account freezing order includes (amongst other things) power to make exclusions from the prohibition on making withdrawals or payments from the account to which the order applies.

(2) Exclusions from the prohibition may also be made when the order is made.

(3) An exclusion may (amongst other things) make provision for the purpose of enabling a person by or for whom the account is operated –

   (a) to meet the person's reasonable living expenses, or
   (b) to carry on any trade, business, profession or occupation.

(4) An exclusion may be made subject to conditions.

(5) Where a magistrates' court exercises the power to make an exclusion for the purpose of enabling a person to meet legal expenses that the person has incurred, or may incur, in respect of proceedings under this Part, it must ensure that the exclusion –

   (a) is limited to reasonable legal expenses that the person has reasonably incurred or that the person reasonably incurs,
   (b) specifies the total amount that may be released for legal expenses in pursuance of the exclusion, and
   (c) is made subject to the same conditions as would be the required conditions (see section 286A) if the order had been made under section 245A (in addition to any conditions imposed under subsection (4)).

(6) A magistrates' court, in deciding whether to make an exclusion for the purpose of enabling a person to meet legal expenses in respect of proceedings under this Part –

   (a) must have regard to the desirability of the person being represented in any proceedings under this Part in which the person is a participant, and
   (b) must disregard the possibility that legal representation of the person in any such proceedings might, were an exclusion not made –

      (i) be made available under arrangements made for the purposes of Part 1 of the Legal Aid, Sentencing and Punishment of Offenders Act 2012, or
      (ii) be funded by the Northern Ireland Legal Services Commission.

(7) The sheriff's power to make exclusions may not be exercised for the purpose of enabling any person to meet any legal expenses in respect of proceedings under this Part.

(8) The power to make exclusions must, subject to subsection (6), be exercised with a view to ensuring, so far as practicable, that there is not undue prejudice to the taking of any steps under this Chapter to forfeit money that is recoverable property or intended by any person for use in unlawful conduct.

303Z6 Restriction on proceedings and remedies

(1) If a court in which proceedings are pending in respect of an account maintained with a bank or building society is satisfied that an account freezing order has been

APPENDIX: CRIMINAL FINANCES ACT 2017

applied for or made in respect of the account, it may either stay the proceedings or allow them to continue on any terms it thinks fit.
(2) Before exercising the power conferred by subsection (1), the court must (as well as giving the parties to any of the proceedings concerned an opportunity to be heard) give such an opportunity to any person who may be affected by the court's decision.
(3) In relation to Scotland, the reference in subsection (1) to staying the proceedings is to be read as a reference to sisting the proceedings.

303Z7 "Bank"
(1) "Bank" means an authorised deposit-taker, other than a building society, that has its head office or a branch in the United Kingdom.
(2) In subsection (1), "authorised deposit-taker" means –
   (a) a person who has permission under Part 4A of the Financial Services and Markets Act 2000 to accept deposits;
   (b) a person who –
      (i) is specified, or is within a class of persons specified, by an order under section 38 of that Act (exemption orders), and
      (ii) accepts deposits;
   (c) an EEA firm of the kind mentioned in paragraph 5(b) of Schedule 3 to that Act that has permission under paragraph 15 of that Schedule (as a result of qualifying for authorisation under paragraph 12(1) of that Schedule) to accept deposits.
(3) A reference in subsection (2) to a person or firm with permission to accept deposits does not include a person or firm with permission to do so only for the purposes of, or in the course of, an activity other than accepting deposits.

303Z8 "The minimum amount"
(1) "The minimum amount" is £1,000.
(2) The Secretary of State may by regulations amend the amount for the time being specified in subsection (1).
(3) The Secretary of State must consult the Scottish Ministers and the Department of Justice before making regulations under subsection (2).
(4) For the purposes of this Chapter the amount of any money held in an account maintained with a bank or building society in a currency other than sterling must be taken to be its sterling equivalent, calculated in accordance with the prevailing rate of exchange.

Account forfeiture notices (England and Wales and Northern Ireland)

303Z9 Account forfeiture notice
(1) This section applies while an account freezing order made by a magistrates' court has effect.
In this section the account to which the order applies is "the frozen account".

(2) A senior officer may give a notice for the purpose of forfeiting money held in the frozen account (whether all or part of the credit balance of the account) if satisfied that the money –

    (a) is recoverable property, or
    (b) is intended by any person for use in unlawful conduct.

(3) A notice given under subsection (2) is referred to in this Chapter as an account forfeiture notice.

(4) An account forfeiture notice must –

    (a) state the amount of money held in the frozen account which it is proposed be forfeited,
    (b) confirm that the senior officer is satisfied as mentioned in subsection (2),
    (c) specify a period for objecting to the proposed forfeiture and an address to which any objections must be sent, and
    (d) explain that the money will be forfeited unless an objection is received at that address within the period for objecting.

(5) The period for objecting must be at least 30 days starting with the day after the notice is given.

(6) If no objection is made within the period for objecting, and the notice has not lapsed under section 303Z11 –

    (a) the amount of money stated in the notice is forfeited (subject to section 303Z12),
    (b) the bank or building society with which the frozen account is maintained must transfer that amount of money into an interest-bearing account nominated by an enforcement officer, and
    (c) immediately after the transfer has been made, the account freezing order made in relation to the frozen account ceases to have effect.

(7) An objection may be made by anyone (whether a recipient of the notice or not).

(8) An objection means a written objection sent to the address specified in the notice; and an objection is made when it is received at the address.

(9) An objection does not prevent forfeiture of the money held in the frozen account under section 303Z14.

303Z10 Giving of account forfeiture notice

(1) The Secretary of State must make regulations about how an account forfeiture notice is to be given.

(2) The regulations may (amongst other things) provide –

    (a) for an account forfeiture notice to be given to such person or persons, and in such manner, as may be prescribed;
    (b) for circumstances in which, and the time at which, an account forfeiture notice is to be treated as having been given.

(3) The regulations must ensure that where an account forfeiture notice is given it is, if possible, given to every person to whom notice of the account freezing order was given.

303Z11 Lapse of account forfeiture notice

(1) An account forfeiture notice lapses if –

    (a) an objection is made within the period for objecting specified in the notice under section 303Z9(4)(c),

    (b) an application is made under section 303Z14 for the forfeiture of money held in the frozen account, or

    (c) an order is made under section 303Z4 setting aside the relevant account freezing order.

(2) If an account forfeiture notice lapses under subsection (1)(a), the relevant account freezing order ceases to have effect at the end of the period of 48 hours starting with the making of the objection ("the 48- hour period").
This is subject to subsections (3) and (7).

(3) If within the 48-hour period an application is made –

    (a) for a variation of the relevant account freezing order under section 303Z4 so as to extend the period specified in the order, or

    (b) for forfeiture of money held in the frozen account under section 303Z14,

the order continues to have effect until the relevant time (and then ceases to have effect).

(4) In the case of an application of the kind mentioned in subsection (3)(a), the relevant time means –

    (a) if an extension is granted, the time determined in accordance with section 303Z3(3), or

    (b) if an extension is not granted, the time when the application is determined or otherwise disposed of.

(5) In the case of an application of the kind mentioned in subsection (3)(b), the relevant time is the time determined in accordance with section 303Z14(6).

(6) If within the 48-hour period it is decided that no application of the kind mentioned in subsection (3)(a) or (b) is to be made, an enforcement officer must, as soon as possible, notify the bank or building society with which the frozen account is maintained of that decision.

(7) If the bank or building society is notified in accordance with subsection (6) before the expiry of the 48-hour period, the relevant account freezing order ceases to have effect on the bank or building society being so notified.

(8) In relation to an account forfeiture notice –

    (a) "the frozen account" is the account in which the money to which the account forfeiture notice relates is held;

    (b) "the relevant account freezing order" is the account freezing order made in relation to the frozen account.

(9) In calculating a period of 48 hours for the purposes of this section no account is to be taken of –

    (a) any Saturday or Sunday,

    (b) Christmas Day,

(c) Good Friday, or
(d) any day that is a bank holiday under the Banking and Financial Dealings Act 1971 in the part of the United Kingdom in which the account freezing order was made.

303Z12 Application to set aside forfeiture
(1) A person aggrieved by the forfeiture of money in pursuance of section 303Z9(6)(a) may apply to a magistrates' court for an order setting aside the forfeiture of the money or any part of it.
(2) The application must be made before the end of the period of 30 days starting with the day on which the period for objecting ended ("the 30- day period").
(3) But the court may give permission for an application to be made after the 30-day period has ended if it thinks that there are exceptional circumstances to explain why the applicant –

(a) failed to object to the forfeiture within the period for objecting, and
(b) failed to make an application within the 30-day period.

(4) On an application under this section the court must consider whether the money to which the application relates could be forfeited under section 303Z14 (ignoring the forfeiture mentioned in subsection (1)).
(5) If the court is satisfied that the money to which the application relates or any part of it could not be forfeited under that section it must set aside the forfeiture of that money or part.
(6) Where the court sets aside the forfeiture of any money –

(a) it must order the release of that money, and
(b) the money is to be treated as never having been forfeited.

(7) Where money is released by virtue of subsection (6)(a), there must be added to the money on its release any interest accrued on it whilst in the account referred to in section 303Z9(6)(b).

303Z13 Application of money forfeited under account forfeiture notice
(1) Money forfeited in pursuance of section 303Z9(6)(a), and any interest accrued on it whilst in the account referred to in section 303Z9(6)(b), is to be paid into the Consolidated Fund.
(2) But it is not to be paid in –

(a) before the end of the period within which an application under section 303Z12 may be made (ignoring the possibility of an application by virtue of section 303Z12(3)), or
(b) if an application is made within that period, before the application is determined or otherwise disposed of.

Forfeiture orders

303Z14 Forfeiture order
(1) This section applies while an account freezing order has effect.

In this section the account to which the account freezing order applies is "the frozen account".

(2) An application for the forfeiture of money held in the frozen account (whether all or part of the credit balance of the account) may be made –

    (a) to a magistrates' court by a person specified in subsection (3), or

    (b) to the sheriff by the Scottish Ministers.

(3) The persons referred to in subsection (2)(a) are –

    (a) the Commissioners for Her Majesty's Revenue and Customs,

    (b) a constable,

    (c) an SFO officer, or

    (d) an accredited financial investigator who falls within a description specified in an order made for the purposes of this Chapter by the Secretary of State under section 453.

(4) The court or sheriff may order the forfeiture of the money or any part of it if satisfied that the money or part –

    (a) is recoverable property, or

    (b) is intended by any person for use in unlawful conduct.

(5) But in the case of recoverable property which belongs to joint tenants, one of whom is an excepted joint owner, an order by a magistrates' court may not apply to so much of it as the court thinks is attributable to the excepted joint owner's share.

(6) Where an application is made under subsection (2), the account freezing order is to continue to have effect until the time referred to in subsection (7)(b) or (8).

But subsections (7)(b) and (8) are subject to section 303Z15.

(7) Where money held in a frozen account is ordered to be forfeited under subsection (4) –

    (a) the bank or building society with which the frozen account is maintained must transfer that amount of money into an interest-bearing account nominated by an enforcement officer, and

    (b) immediately after the transfer has been made the account freezing order made in relation to the frozen account ceases to have effect.

(8) Where, other than by the making of an order under subsection (4), an application under subsection (2) is determined or otherwise disposed of, the account freezing order ceases to have effect immediately after that determination or other disposal.

303Z15 Continuation of account freezing order pending appeal

(1) This section applies where, on an application under subsection (2) of section 303Z14 in relation to an account to which an account freezing order applies, the court or sheriff decides –

    (a) to make an order under subsection (4) of that section in relation to part only of the money to which the application related, or

    (b) not to make an order under subsection (4) of that section.

(2) The person who made the application under section 303Z14(2) may apply without notice to the court or sheriff that made the decision referred to in subsection (1)(a) or (b) for an order that the account freezing order is to continue to have effect.

(3) Where the court or sheriff makes an order under subsection (2) the account freezing order is to continue to have effect until –

   (a) the end of the period of 48 hours starting with the making of the order under subsection (2), or
   (b) if within that period of 48 hours an appeal is brought under section 303Z16 against the decision referred to in subsection (1)(a) or (b), the time when the appeal is determined or otherwise disposed of.

(4) Subsection (9) of section 303Z11 applies for the purposes of subsection (3) as it applies for the purposes of that section.

303Z16 Appeal against decision under section 303Z14

(1) Any party to proceedings for an order for the forfeiture of money under section 303Z14 who is aggrieved by an order under that section or by the decision of the court not to make such an order may appeal –

   (a) from an order or decision of a magistrates' court in England and Wales, to the Crown Court;
   (b) from an order or decision of the sheriff, to the Sheriff Appeal Court;
   (c) from an order or decision of a magistrates' court in Northern Ireland, to a county court.

(2) An appeal under subsection (1) must be made before the end of the period of 30 days starting with the day on which the court makes the order or decision.

(3) The court hearing the appeal may make any order it thinks appropriate.

(4) If the court upholds an appeal against an order forfeiting the money, it may order the release of the whole or any part of the money.

(5) Where money is released by virtue of subsection (4), there must be added to the money on its release any interest accrued on it whilst in the account referred to in section 303Z14(7)(a).

303Z17 Application of money forfeited under account forfeiture order

(1) Money forfeited by an order under section 303Z14, and any interest accrued on it whilst in the account referred to in subsection (7)(a) of that section –

   (a) if forfeited by a magistrates' court, is to be paid into the Consolidated Fund, and
   (b) if forfeited by the sheriff, is to be paid into the Scottish Consolidated Fund.

(2) But it is not to be paid in –

   (a) before the end of the period within which an appeal under section 303Z16 may be made, or
   (b) if a person appeals under that section, before the appeal is determined or otherwise disposed of.

Supplementary

303Z18 Compensation

(1) This section applies if —

(a) an account freezing order is made, and
(b) none of the money held in the account to which the order applies is forfeited in pursuance of an account forfeiture notice or by an order under section 303Z14.

(2) Where this section applies a person by or for whom the account to which the account freezing order applies is operated may make an application to the relevant court for compensation.

(3) If the relevant court is satisfied that the applicant has suffered loss as a result of the making of the account freezing order and that the circumstances are exceptional, the relevant court may order compensation to be paid to the applicant.

(4) The amount of compensation to be paid is the amount the relevant court thinks reasonable, having regard to the loss suffered and any other relevant circumstances.

(5) If the account freezing order was applied for by an officer of Revenue and Customs, the compensation is to be paid by the Commissioners for Her Majesty's Revenue and Customs.

(6) If the account freezing order was applied for by a constable, the compensation is to be paid as follows —

(a) in the case of a constable of a police force in England and Wales, it is to be paid out of the police fund from which the expenses of the police force are met;
(b) in the case of a constable of the Police Service of Scotland, it is to be paid by the Scottish Police Authority;
(c) in the case of a police officer within the meaning of the Police (Northern Ireland) Act 2000, it is to be paid out of money provided by the Chief Constable of the Police Service of Northern Ireland.

(7) If the account freezing order was applied for by an SFO officer, the compensation is to be paid by the Director of the Serious Fraud Office.

(8) If the account freezing order was applied for by a National Crime Agency officer, the compensation is to be paid by the National Crime Agency.

(9) If the account freezing order was applied for by an accredited financial investigator who was not an officer of Revenue and Customs, a constable, an SFO officer or a National Crime Agency officer, the compensation is to be paid as follows —

(a) in the case of an investigator who was —

(i) a member of the civilian staff of a police force (including the metropolitan police force), within the meaning of Part 1 of the Police Reform and Social Responsibility Act 2011, or
(ii) a member of staff of the City of London police force, it is to be paid out of the police fund from which the expenses of the police force are met,

(b) in the case of an investigator who was a member of staff of the Police Service of Northern Ireland, it is to be paid out of money provided by the Chief Constable of the Police Service of Northern Ireland,

(c) in the case of an investigator who was a member of staff of a department of the Government of the United Kingdom, it is to be paid by the Minister of the Crown in charge of the department or by the department,

(d) in the case of an investigator who was a member of staff of a Northern Ireland department, it is to be paid by the department,

(e) in the case of an investigator who was exercising a function of the Welsh Revenue Authority, it is to be paid by the Welsh Revenue Authority, and

(f) in any other case, it is to be paid by the employer of the investigator.

(10) The Secretary of State may by regulations amend subsection (9).

(11) The power in subsection (10) is exercisable by the Department of Justice (and not by the Secretary of State) so far as it may be used to make provision which could be made by an Act of the Northern Ireland Assembly without the consent of the Secretary of State (see sections 6 to 8 of the Northern Ireland Act 1998.)

303Z19 Powers for prosecutors to appear in proceedings

(1) The Director of Public Prosecutions or the Director of Public Prosecutions for Northern Ireland may appear for a constable or an accredited financial investigator in proceedings under this Chapter if the Director –

(a) is asked by, or on behalf of, a constable or (as the case may be) an accredited financial investigator to do so, and

(b) considers it appropriate to do so.

(2) The Director of Public Prosecutions may appear for the Commissioners for Her Majesty's Revenue and Customs or an officer of Revenue and Customs in proceedings under this Chapter if the Director –

(a) is asked by, or on behalf of, the Commissioners for Her Majesty's Revenue and Customs or (as the case may be) an officer of Revenue and Customs to do so, and

(b) considers it appropriate to do so.

(3) The Directors may charge fees for the provision of services under this section.

(4) The references in subsection (1) to an accredited financial investigator do not include an accredited financial investigator who is an officer of Revenue and Customs but the references in subsection (2) to an officer of Revenue and Customs do include an accredited financial investigator who is an officer of Revenue and Customs."

CHAPTER 4

ENFORCEMENT POWERS AND RELATED OFFENCES

Extension of powers

17 Serious Fraud Office

Schedule 1 contains amendments conferring certain powers under the Proceeds of Crime Act 2002 on members of staff of the Serious Fraud Office.

APPENDIX: CRIMINAL FINANCES ACT 2017

18 Her Majesty's Revenue and Customs: removal of restrictions

(1) The following provisions, which impose restrictions on the exercise of certain powers conferred on officers of Revenue and Customs, are amended as follows.

(2) In section 23A of the Criminal Law (Consolidation) (Scotland) Act 1995 (investigation of offences by Her Majesty's Revenue and Customs), omit the following –

(a) in subsection (2), the words "Subject to subsection (3) below," and the words from "other than" to the end of the subsection;

(b) subsection (3).

(3) In section 307 of the Criminal Procedure (Scotland) Act 1995 (interpretation), omit the following –

(a) in subsection (1), in paragraph (ba) of the definition of "officer of law", the words "subject to subsection (1A) below,";

(b) subsection (1A).

(4) In the Proceeds of Crime Act 2002 omit the following –

(a) in section 289 (searches), subsections (5)(ba) and (5A);

(b) in section 294 (seizure of cash), subsections (2A), (2B) and (2C);

(c) section 375C (restriction on exercise of certain powers conferred on officers of Revenue and Customs);

(d) section 408C (restriction on exercise of certain powers conferred on officers of Revenue and Customs).

(5) In the Finance Act 2007, in section 84 (sections 82 and 83: supplementary), omit subsection (3).

19 Her Majesty's Revenue and Customs: new powers

(1) The Proceeds of Crime Act 2002 is amended as follows.

(2) In section 316 (civil recovery of the proceeds etc of unlawful conduct: general interpretation), in the definition of "enforcement authority" in subsection (1) –

(a) in paragraph (a), before "the National Crime Agency," insert "Her Majesty's Revenue and Customs,";

(b) in paragraph (c), before "the National Crime Agency," insert "Her Majesty's Revenue and Customs,".

(3) In section 378 (appropriate officers and senior appropriate officers for purposes of investigations under Part 8), for subsection (3) substitute –

"(3) In relation to a civil recovery investigation these are appropriate officers –

(a) a National Crime Agency officer;

(b) the relevant Director;

(c) an officer of Revenue and Customs.

(3ZA) In relation to a civil recovery investigation these are senior appropriate officers –

(a) a senior National Crime Agency officer;

APPENDIX: CRIMINAL FINANCES ACT 2017

(b) the Commissioners for Her Majesty's Revenue and Customs or an officer of Revenue and Customs authorised by the Commissioners (whether generally or specifically) for this purpose."

20 Financial Conduct Authority

(1) The Proceeds of Crime Act 2002 is amended as follows.

(2) In section 316 (civil recovery of the proceeds etc of unlawful conduct: general interpretation), in the definition of "enforcement authority" in subsection (1) –

  (a) in paragraph (a), after "means" insert "the Financial Conduct Authority,";
  (b) in paragraph (c), after "means" insert "the Financial Conduct Authority,".

(3) Section 378 (appropriate officers and senior appropriate officers for purposes of investigations under Part 8) is amended in accordance with subsections (4) to (6).

(4) In subsection (3) (as substituted by section 19 above), after paragraph (c) insert –

"(d) a Financial Conduct Authority officer."

(5) In subsection (3ZA) (as inserted by that section), after paragraph (b) insert – "(c) a senior Financial Conduct Authority officer."

(6) After subsection (8) insert –

"(9) For the purposes of this Part –

  (a) "Financial Conduct Authority officer" means a member of staff of the Financial Conduct Authority;
  (b) "senior Financial Conduct Authority officer" means a Financial Conduct Authority officer who is not below such grade as is designated by the Treasury for those purposes."

21 Immigration officers

(1) Section 24 of the UK Borders Act 2007 (seizure of cash) is amended as follows.

(2) For the heading substitute "Exercise of civil recovery powers by immigration officers".

(3) For subsection (1) substitute –

"(1) Chapters 3 to 3B of Part 5 of the Proceeds of Crime Act 2002 (civil recovery) apply in relation to an immigration officer as they apply in relation to a constable."

(4) In subsection (2)(a), for "section 289" substitute "sections 289 and 303C and Chapter 3B".

(5) In subsection (2)(c), for "and 297A" substitute ", 297A and 303E and in Chapter 3B (see section 303Z2(4))".

(6) In subsection (2)(d), for "section 292" substitute "sections 292 and 303G".

(7) In subsection (2)(e), for "and 293A" substitute ", 293A, 303H and 303I".

(8) In subsection (2)(f), in the words before sub-paragraph (i), after "295(2)" insert "or 303L(1)".

(9) In subsection (2)(f)(ii), after "298" insert "or (as the case may be) 303O".

(10) In subsection (2)(g), after "298" insert ", 303O or 303Z14".

(11) In subsection (2)(h), after "302" insert ", 303W or 303Z18".

Assault and obstruction offences

22 Search and seizure warrants: assault and obstruction offences

After section 356 of the Proceeds of Crime Act 2002 (and before the italic heading before section 357) insert –

356A Certain offences in relation to execution of search and seizure warrants

(1) A person commits an offence if the person assaults an appropriate person who is acting in the exercise of a power conferred by a search and seizure warrant issued under section 352.

(2) A person commits an offence if the person resists or wilfully obstructs an appropriate person who is acting in the exercise of a power conferred by a search and seizure warrant issued under section 352.

(3) A person guilty of an offence under subsection (1) is liable –

   (a) on summary conviction in England and Wales, to imprisonment for a term not exceeding 51 weeks, or to a fine, or to both;

   (b) on summary conviction in Northern Ireland, to imprisonment for a term not exceeding 6 months, or to a fine not exceeding level 5 on the standard scale, or to both.

(4) A person guilty of an offence under subsection (2) is liable –

   (a) on summary conviction in England and Wales, to imprisonment for a term not exceeding 51 weeks, or to a fine not exceeding level 3 on the standard scale, or to both;

   (b) on summary conviction in Northern Ireland, to imprisonment for a term not exceeding 1 month, or to a fine not exceeding level 3 on the standard scale, or to both.

(5) An appropriate person is –

   (a) a National Crime Agency officer, a Financial Conduct Authority officer or a member of the staff of the relevant Director, if the warrant was issued for the purposes of a civil recovery investigation;

   (b) a National Crime Agency officer, if the warrant was issued for the purposes of an exploitation proceeds investigation.

(6) In relation to an offence committed before the coming into force of section 281(5) of the Criminal Justice Act 2003 (alteration of penalties for certain summary offences: England and Wales) –

   (a) the reference in subsection (3)(a) to 51 weeks is to be read as a reference to 6 months;

APPENDIX: CRIMINAL FINANCES ACT 2017

(b) the reference in subsection (4)(a) to 51 weeks is to be read as a reference to 1 month."

23 Assault and obstruction offence in relation to SFO officers

After section 453A of the proceeds of Crime Act 2002 insert – 453B certain offences in relation to SFO officers

(1) A person commits an offence if the person assaults an SFO officer who is acting in the exercise of a relevant power.

(2) A person commits an offence if the person resists or wilfully obstructs an SFO officer who is acting in the exercise of a relevant power.

(3) A person guilty of an offence under subsection (1) is liable –

    (a) on summary conviction in England and Wales, to imprisonment for a term not exceeding 51 weeks, or to a fine, or to both;

    (b) on summary conviction in Northern Ireland, to imprisonment for a term not exceeding 6 months, or to a fine not exceeding level 5 on the standard scale, or to both.

(4) A person guilty of an offence under subsection (2) is liable –

    (a) on summary conviction in England and Wales, to imprisonment for a term not exceeding 51 weeks, or to a fine not exceeding level 3 on the standard scale, or to both;

    (b) on summary conviction in Northern Ireland, to imprisonment for a term not exceeding 1 month, or to a fine not exceeding level 3 on the standard scale, or to both.

(5) In this section "relevant power" means a power exercisable under any of the following –

    (a) sections 47C to 47F or 195C to 195F (powers to seize and search for realisable property);

    (b) section 289 (powers to search for cash);

    (c) section 294 (power to seize cash);

    (d) section 295(1) (power to detain seized cash);

    (e) section 303C (powers to search for a listed asset);

    (f) section 303J (powers to seize property);

    (g) section 303K (powers to detain seized property);

    (h) a search and seizure warrant issued under section 352.

(6) In relation to an offence committed before the coming into force of section 281(5) of the Criminal Justice Act 2003 (alteration of penalties for certain summary offences: England and Wales) –

    (a) the reference in subsection (3)(a) to 51 weeks is to be read as a reference to 6 months;

    (b) the reference in subsection (4)(a) to 51 weeks is to be read as a reference to 1 month."

24 External requests, orders and investigations

(1) Part 11 of the Proceeds of Crime Act 2002 (co-operation) is amended as follows.

(2) In section 444 (external requests and orders), in subsection (3), after paragraph

   (a) insert –

   "(aa) provision creating offences in relation to external requests and orders which are equivalent to the offences created by section 453B;".

(3) In section 445 (external investigations), in subsection (1)(b), after "Part 8" insert "and section 453B".

25 Obstruction offence in relation to immigration officers

After section 453B of the Proceeds of Crime Act 2002 (inserted by section 23 above) insert –

453C Obstruction offence in relation to immigration officers

(1) A person commits an offence if the person resists or wilfully obstructs an immigration officer who is acting in the exercise of a relevant power.

(2) A person guilty of an offence under this section is liable –

   (a) on summary conviction in England and Wales, to imprisonment for a term not exceeding 51 weeks, to a fine not exceeding level 3 on the standard scale, or to both;
   (b) on summary conviction in Scotland, to imprisonment for a term not exceeding 12 months, to a fine not exceeding level 3 on the standard scale, or to both;
   (c) on summary conviction in Northern Ireland, to imprisonment for a term not exceeding 1 month, to a fine not exceeding level 3 on the standard scale, or to both.

(3) In this section "relevant power" means a power exercisable under –

   (a) sections 47C to 47F, 127C to 127F or 195C to 195F (powers to seize and search for realisable property);
   (b) section 289 as applied by section 24 of the UK Borders Act 2007 (powers to search for cash);
   (c) section 294 as so applied (powers to seize cash);
   (d) section 295(1) as so applied (power to detain seized cash);
   (e) section 303C as so applied (powers to search for a listed asset);
   (f) section 303J as so applied (powers to seize property);
   (g) section 303K as so applied (powers to detain seized property);
   (h) a search and seizure warrant issued under section 352; or
   (i) a search and seizure warrant issued under section 387.

(4) The power conferred by subsection (5) of section 28A of the Immigration Act 1971 (arrest without warrant) applies in relation to an offence under this section as it applies in relation to an offence under section 26(1)(g) of that Act (and subsections (6) to (9), (10) and (11) of section 28A of that Act apply accordingly).

(5) In relation to an offence committed before the coming into force of section 281(5) of the Criminal Justice Act 2003 (alteration of penalties for certain summary offences: England and Wales) the reference in subsection (2)(a) to 51 weeks is to be read as a reference to 1 month."

CHAPTER 5

MISCELLANEOUS

Seized money: England and Wales and Northern Ireland

26 Seized money: England and Wales

(1) Section 67 of the Proceeds of Crime Act 2002 (seized money) is amended as follows.
(2) In subsection (2), for paragraphs (a) and (b) substitute –

"(a) has been seized under a relevant seizure power by a constable or another person lawfully exercising the power, and
(b) is being detained in connection with a criminal investigation or prosecution or with an investigation of a kind mentioned in section 341."

(3) After subsection (2) insert –

"(2A) But this section applies to money only so far as the money is free property."

(4) Omit subsection (3).
(5) In subsection (5), for "bank or building society" substitute "appropriate person".
(6) In subsection (5A), at the beginning insert "Where this section applies to money which is held in an account maintained with a bank or building society,".
(7) In subsection (7A), after "applies" insert "by virtue of subsection (1)".
(8) For subsection (8) substitute –

"(8) In this section –

"appropriate person" means –

(a) in a case where the money is held in an account maintained with a bank or building society, the bank or building society;
(b) in any other case, the person on whose authority the money is detained;

"bank" means an authorised deposit-taker, other than a building society, that has its head office or a branch in the United Kingdom;
"building society" has the same meaning as in the Building Societies Act 1986;
"relevant seizure power" means a power to seize money conferred by or by virtue of –

(a) a warrant granted under any enactment or rule of law, or
(b) any enactment, or rule of law, under which the authority of a warrant is not required."

(9) After subsection (8) insert –

"(9) In the definition of "bank" in subsection (8), "authorised deposit-taker" means –

(a) a person who has permission under Part 4A of the Financial Services and Markets Act 2000 to accept deposits;

(b) a person who –

(i) is specified, or is within a class of persons specified, by an order under section 38 of that Act (exemption orders), and

(ii) accepts deposits;

(c) an EEA firm of the kind mentioned in paragraph 5(b) of Schedule 3 to that Act that has permission under paragraph 15 of that Schedule (as a result of qualifying for authorisation under paragraph 12(1) of that Schedule) to accept deposits.

(10) A reference in subsection (9) to a person or firm with permission to accept deposits does not include a person or firm with permission to do so only for the purposes of, or in the course of, an activity other than accepting deposits."

27 Seized money: Northern Ireland

(1) Section 215 of the Proceeds of Crime Act 2002 (seized money) is amended as follows.

(2) In subsection (2), for paragraphs (a) and (b) substitute –

"(a) has been seized under a relevant seizure power by a constable or another person lawfully exercising the power, and

(b) is being detained in connection with a criminal investigation or prosecution or with an investigation of a kind mentioned in section 341."

(3) After subsection (2) insert –

"(2A) But this section applies to money only so far as the money is free property."

(4) Omit subsection (3).

(5) In subsection (5) (as it has effect before and after its amendment by section 36 of the Serious Crime Act 2015), for "bank or building society" substitute "appropriate person".

(6) In subsection (5A), at the beginning insert "Where this section applies to money which is held in an account maintained with a bank or building society,".

(7) In subsection (7A), after "applies" insert "by virtue of subsection (1)".

(8) For subsection (8) substitute –

"(8) In this section –

"appropriate chief clerk" has the same meaning as in section 202(7);
"appropriate person" means –

(a) in a case where the money is held in an account maintained with a bank or building society, the bank or building society;

APPENDIX: CRIMINAL FINANCES ACT 2017

(b) in any other case, the person on whose authority the money is detained;

"bank" means an authorised deposit-taker, other than a building society, that has its head office or a branch in the United Kingdom;

"building society" has the same meaning as in the Building Societies Act 1986;

"relevant seizure power" means a power to seize money conferred by or by virtue of –

(a) a warrant granted under any enactment or rule of law, or
(b) any enactment, or rule of law, under which the authority of a warrant is not required."

(9) After subsection (8) insert –

"(9) In the definition of "bank" in subsection (8), "authorised deposit-taker" means –

(a) a person who has permission under Part 4A of the Financial Services and Markets Act 2000 to accept deposits;
(b) a person who –
  (i) is specified, or is within a class of persons specified, by an order under section 38 of that Act (exemption orders), and
  (ii) accepts deposits;
(c) an EEA firm of the kind mentioned in paragraph 5(b) of Schedule 3 to that Act that has permission under paragraph 15 of that Schedule (as a result of qualifying for authorisation under paragraph 12(1) of that Schedule) to accept deposits.

(10) A reference in subsection (9) to a person or firm with permission to accept deposits does not include a person or firm with permission to do so only for the purposes of, or in the course of, an activity other than accepting deposits."

Miscellaneous provisions relating to Scotland

28 Seized money

After section 131 of the Proceeds of Crime Act 2002 insert –

"Seized money

131ZA Seized money
(1) This section applies to money which –
   (a) is held by a person, and
   (b) is held in an account maintained by the person with a bank or building society.

(2) This section also applies to money which is held by a person and which –

(a) has been seized under a relevant seizure power by a constable or another person lawfully exercising the power, and
(b) is being detained in connection with a criminal investigation or prosecution or with an investigation of a kind mentioned in section 341.

(3) But this section applies to money only so far as the money is free property.

(4) Subsection (5) applies if –

(a) a confiscation order is made against a person holding money to which this section applies, and
(b) an administrator has not been appointed under section 128 in relation to the money.

(5) The relevant court may order the appropriate person to pay, within such period as the court may specify, the money or a portion of it specified by the court to the appropriate clerk of court on account of the amount payable under the confiscation order.

(6) An order under subsection (5) may be made –

(a) on the application of the prosecutor, or
(b) by the relevant court of its own accord.

(7) The Scottish Ministers may by regulations amend this section so that it applies by virtue of subsection (1) not only to money held in an account maintained with a bank or building society but also to –

(a) money held in an account maintained with a financial institution of a specified kind, or
(b) money that is represented by, or may be obtained from, a financial instrument or product of a specified kind.

(8) Regulations under subsection (7) may amend this section so that it makes provision about realising an instrument or product within subsection (7)(b) or otherwise obtaining money from it.

(9) In this section –

"appropriate clerk of court", in relation to a confiscation order, means the sheriff clerk of the sheriff court responsible for enforcing the confiscation order under section 211 of the Procedure Act as applied by section 118(1);
"appropriate person" means –

(a) in a case where the money is held in an account maintained with a bank or building society, the bank or building society;
(b) in any other case, the person on whose authority the money is detained;

"bank" means an authorised deposit-taker, other than a building society, that has its head office or a branch in the United Kingdom;
"building society" has the same meaning as in the Building Societies Act 1986;

"relevant court", in relation to a confiscation order, means –

    (a)   the court which makes the confiscation order, or

    (b)   the sheriff court responsible for enforcing the confiscation order under section 211 of the Procedure Act as applied by section 118(1);

"relevant seizure power" means a power to seize money conferred by or by virtue of –

    (a)   a warrant granted under any enactment or rule of law, or

    (b)   any enactment, or rule of law, under which the authority of a warrant is not required.

(10) In the definition of "bank" in subsection (9), "authorised deposit-taker" means –

    (a)   a person who has permission under Part 4A of the Financial Services and Markets Act 2000 to accept deposits;

    (b)   a person who –

        (i)   is specified, or is within a class of persons specified, by an order under section 38 of that Act (exemption orders), and

        (ii)   accepts deposits;

    (c)   an EEA firm of the kind mentioned in paragraph 5(b) of Schedule 3 to that Act that has permission under paragraph 15 of that Schedule (as a result of qualifying for authorisation under paragraph 12(1) of that Schedule) to accept deposits.

(11) A reference in subsection (10) to a person or firm with permission to accept deposits does not include a person or firm with permission to do so only for the purposes of, or in the course of, an activity other than accepting deposits."

29 Recovery orders relating to heritable property

(1) The Proceeds of Crime Act 2002 is amended as follows.

(2) After section 245 insert –

245ZA Notice to local authority: Scotland

(1) This section applies if, in proceedings under this Chapter for a recovery order, the enforcement authority applies under section 266(8ZA) for decree of removing and warrant for ejection in relation to heritable property which consists of or includes a dwellinghouse.

(2) The enforcement authority must give notice of the application to the local authority in whose area the dwellinghouse is situated.

(3) Notice under subsection (2) must be given in the form and manner prescribed under section 11(3) of the Homelessness etc. (Scotland) Act 2003.

(4) In this section –

"dwellinghouse" has the meaning given by section 11(8) of the Homelessness etc. (Scotland) Act 2003;

"local authority" means a council constituted under section 2 of the Local Government etc. (Scotland) Act 1994; and "area", in relation to a local authority, means the local government area for which the authority is constituted."

(3) In section 266 (recovery orders), after subsection (8) insert –

"(8ZA) If the recoverable property in respect of which the Court of Session makes a recovery order includes heritable property, the Court of Session must, on the application of the enforcement authority, also grant decree of removing and warrant for ejection, enforceable by the trustee for civil recovery, in relation to any persons occupying the heritable property."

(4) In section 267(3) (functions of trustee for civil recovery), after paragraph (b) insert –

"(ba) if decree of removing and warrant for ejection is granted by the Court of Session under section 266(8ZA), to enforce the decree and warrant,".

(5) After section 269 insert –

269A Leases and occupancy rights: Scotland
(1) This section applies where, in making a recovery order, the Court of Session also grants decree of removing and warrant for ejection under section 266(8ZA) in relation to any persons occupying the heritable property.
(2) Any lease under which a person has the right to occupy the heritable property (or part of it) for residential or commercial purposes is

terminated on the granting of decree of removing and warrant for ejection.

(3) Any other right to occupy the heritable property (or part of it) which subsists immediately before the granting of decree of removing and warrant for ejection is extinguished on the granting of the decree and warrant.
(4) Subsection (3) does not apply in relation to a right under a lease to occupy or use the property other than those mentioned in subsection (2).
(5) Where the heritable property is vested in the trustee for civil recovery under the recovery order, the following enactments do not apply in relation to the heritable property –

   (a) sections 34 to 38A of the Sheriff Courts (Scotland) Act 1907 (removings, notice of termination of tenancy and notice of removal);
   (b) the Tenancy of Shops (Scotland) Act 1949;
   (c) the Matrimonial Homes (Family Protection) (Scotland) Act 1981;
   (d) Parts 2 and 3 of the Rent (Scotland) Act 1984 (security of tenure and protection against harassment and unlawful eviction);
   (e) sections 4 to 7 of the Law Reform (Miscellaneous Provisions) (Scotland) Act 1985 (termination of certain leases);
   (f) Part 2 of the Housing (Scotland) Act 1988 (rented accommodation: security of tenure etc.);
   (g) Chapter 3 of Part 3 of the Civil Partnership Act 2004 (occupancy rights and tenancies);

(h) Part 5 of the Private Housing (Tenancies) (Scotland) Act 2016 (security of tenure, termination of tenancy and eviction)."

30 Money received by administrators

(1) Paragraph 6 of Schedule 3 to the Proceeds of Crime Act 2002 (money received by administrator) is amended as follows.

(2) In sub-paragraph (1) for "an appropriate bank or institution" substitute "a bank or building society".

(3) For sub-paragraph (3) substitute –

"(3) In sub-paragraph (1) –

(a) "bank" means an authorised deposit-taker, other than a building society, that has its head office or a branch in the United Kingdom;
(b) "building society" has the same meaning as in the Building Societies Act 1986.

(4) In sub-paragraph (3)(a) "authorised deposit-taker" means –

(a) a person who has permission under Part 4A of the Financial Services and Markets Act 2000 to accept deposits;
(b) a person who –

(i) is specified, or is within a class of persons specified, by an order under section 38 of that Act (exemption orders), and
(ii) accepts deposits;

(c) an EEA firm of the kind mentioned in paragraph 5(b) of Schedule 3 to that Act that has permission under paragraph 15 of that Schedule (as a result of qualifying for authorisation under paragraph 12(1) of that Schedule) to accept deposits.

(5) A reference in sub-paragraph (4) to a person or firm with permission to accept deposits does not include a person or firm with permission to do so only for the purposes of, or in the course of, an activity other than accepting deposits."

Other miscellaneous provisions

31 Accredited financial investigators

(1) The Proceeds of Crime Act 2002 is amended as follows.

(2) In section 47G (appropriate approval for exercise of search and seizure powers in England and Wales), in subsection (3), after paragraph (b) insert –

"(ba) in relation to the exercise of a power by an accredited financial investigator who is –

(i) a member of the civilian staff of a police force in England and Wales (including the metropolitan police force), within the meaning of Part 1 of the Police Reform and Social Responsibility Act 2011, or

(ii) a member of staff of the City of London police force,

a senior police officer,".

(3) In section 195G (appropriate approval for exercise of search and seizure powers in Northern Ireland), in subsection (3), after paragraph (b) insert –

"(ba) in relation to the exercise of a power by an accredited financial investigator who is a member of staff of the Police Service of Northern Ireland, a senior police officer,".

(4) In section 290 (prior approval for exercise of search powers in relation to cash), in subsection (4), after paragraph (b) insert –

"(ba) in relation to the exercise of a power by an accredited financial investigator who is –

    (i) a member of the civilian staff of a police force in England and Wales (including the metropolitan police force), within the meaning of Part 1 of the Police Reform and Social Responsibility Act 2011,
    (ii) a member of staff of the City of London police force, or
    (iii) a member of staff of the Police Service of Northern Ireland,

a senior police officer,".

32 Reconsideration of discharged orders

(1) The Proceeds of Crime Act 2002 is amended as follows.

(2) In section 24 (inadequacy of available amount: discharge of order made under Part 2), after subsection (5) insert –

"(6) The discharge of a confiscation order under this section does not prevent the making of an application in respect of the order under section 21(1)(d) or 22(1)(c).

(7) Where on such an application the court determines that the order should be varied under section 21(7) or (as the case may be) 22(4), the court may provide that its discharge under this section is revoked."

(3) In section 25 (small amount outstanding: discharge of order made under Part 2), after subsection (3) insert –

"(4) The discharge of a confiscation order under this section does not prevent the making of an application in respect of the order under section 21(1)(d) or 22(1)(c).

(5) Where on such an application the court determines that the order should be varied under section 21(7) or (as the case may be) 22(4), the court may provide that its discharge under this section is revoked."

(4) In section 109 (inadequacy of available amount: discharge of order made under Part 3), after subsection (5) insert –

"(6) The discharge of a confiscation order under this section does not prevent the making of an application in respect of the order under section 106(1)(d) or 107(1)(c).

(7) Where on such an application the court determines that the order should be varied under section 106(6) or (as the case may be) 107(3), the court may provide that its discharge under this section is revoked."

(5) In section 174 (inadequacy of available amount: discharge of order made under Part 4), after subsection (5) insert –

"(6) The discharge of a confiscation order under this section does not prevent the making of an application in respect of the order under section 171(1)(d) or 172(1)(c).

(7) Where on such an application the court determines that the order should be varied under section 171(7) or (as the case may be) 172(4), the court may provide that its discharge under this section is revoked."

(6) In section 175 (small amount outstanding: discharge of order made under Part 4), after subsection (3) insert –

"(4) The discharge of a confiscation order under this section does not prevent the making of an application in respect of the order under section 171(1)(d) or 172(1)(c).

(5) Where on such an application the court determines that the order should be varied under section 171(7) or (as the case may be) 172(4), the court may provide that its discharge under this section is revoked."

(7) The amendments made by this section apply in relation to a confiscation order whether made before or after the day on which this section comes into force but do so only where the discharge of the order occurs after that day.

33 Confiscation investigations: determination of the available amount

In section 341(1) of the Proceeds of Crime Act 2002 (confiscation investigations), at the beginning of paragraph (c) insert "the available amount in respect of the person or".

34 Confiscation orders and civil recovery: minor amendments

(1) The Proceeds of Crime Act 2002 is amended in accordance with subsections (2) to (10).

(2) In section 82 (free property: England and Wales) –

(a) in subsection (2), after paragraph (e) insert –

"(ea) paragraph 3(2), 6(2), 10D(1), 10G(2), 10J(3), 10S(2) or 10Z2(3) of Schedule 1 to the Anti-terrorism, Crime and Security Act 2001;";

(b) in subsection (3)(b) for "or 297D" substitute ", 297D or 298(4)";

(c) after subsection (3)(c) (as inserted by paragraph 22 of Schedule 5) insert –

"(d) it has been forfeited in pursuance of a cash forfeiture notice under paragraph 5A of Schedule 1 to the Anti-terrorism, Crime and Security Act 2001 or an account forfeiture notice under paragraph 10W of that Schedule;

(e) it is detained under paragraph 5B, 5C, 9A or 10G(7) of that Schedule;

(f) it is the forfeitable property in relation to an order under paragraph 10I(1) of that Schedule."

(3) In section 148 (free property: Scotland) –

(a) in subsection (2) –

(i) omit "or" at the end of paragraph (e);

(ii) after that paragraph insert –

"(ea) paragraph 3(2), 6(2), 10D(1), 10G(2), 10J(3), 10S(2) or 10Z2(3) of Schedule 1 to the Anti- terrorism, Crime and Security Act 2001, or";

(b) in subsection (3)(b) for "or 297D" substitute ", 297D or 298(4)";

(c) after subsection (3)(c) (as inserted by paragraph 24 of Schedule 5) insert –

"(d) it has been forfeited in pursuance of a cash forfeiture notice under paragraph 5A of Schedule 1 to the Anti- terrorism, Crime and Security Act 2001 or an account forfeiture notice under paragraph 10W of that Schedule;

(e) it is detained under paragraph 5B, 5C, 9A or 10G(7) of that Schedule;

(f) it is the forfeitable property in relation to an order under paragraph 10I(1) of that Schedule."

(4) In section 230 (free property: Northern Ireland) –

(a) in subsection (2), after paragraph (e) insert –

"(ea) paragraph 3(2), 6(2), 10D(1), 10G(2), 10J(3), 10S(2) or 10Z2(3) of Schedule 1 to the Anti-terrorism, Crime and Security Act 2001;";

(b) in subsection (3)(b) for "or 297D" substitute ", 297D or 298(4)";

(c) after subsection (3)(c) (as inserted by paragraph 27 of Schedule 5) insert –

"(d) it has been forfeited in pursuance of a cash forfeiture notice under paragraph 5A of Schedule 1 to the Anti- terrorism, Crime and Security Act 2001 or an account forfeiture notice under paragraph 10W of that Schedule;

(e) it is detained under paragraph 5B, 5C, 9A or 10G(7) of that Schedule;

(f) it is the forfeitable property in relation to an order under paragraph 10I(1) of that Schedule."

(5) In section 245D (restriction on proceedings and remedies), in subsection (1)(b) after "levied" insert ", and no power to use the procedure in Schedule 12 to the Tribunals, Courts and Enforcement Act 2007 (taking control of goods) may be exercised,".

(6) In section 290 (prior approval to exercise of section 289 search powers), in subsection (4), after paragraph (aa) (inserted by Schedule 1 to this Act) insert – "(ab) in relation to the exercise of a power by a National Crime Agency officer, the Director General of the National Crime

Agency or any other National Crime Agency officer authorised by the Director General (whether generally or specifically) for this purpose,".

(7) In section 297A (forfeiture notice), in subsection (6), after paragraph (ba) (inserted by Schedule 1 to this Act, but before the "or" at the end of that paragraph) insert –

"(bb) the Director General of the National Crime Agency or any other National Crime Agency officer authorised by the Director General (whether generally or specifically) for this purpose,".

(8) In section 302 (compensation), after subsection (7ZA) (inserted by Schedule 1 to this Act) insert –

"(7ZB) If the cash was seized by a National Crime Agency officer, the compensation is to be paid by the National Crime Agency."

(9) In that section, in subsection (7A)(a)(i), for "that Part of that Act" substitute "Part 1 of the Police Reform and Social Responsibility Act 2011".

(10) In section 306 (mixing property), in subsection (3) after paragraph (c) insert – "(ca) for the discharge (in whole or in part) of a mortgage, charge or other security,".

(11) In section 8 of the Serious Crime Act 2015 (variation or discharge of confiscation orders), in subsection (3) before paragraph (a) insert –

"(za) a confiscation order made under the Drug Trafficking Offences Act 1986,".

PART 2

TERRORIST PROPERTY

Disclosures of information

35 Disclosure orders

Schedule 2 contains amendments to the Terrorism Act 2000 which enable the making of disclosure orders in connection with investigations into terrorist financing offences.

36 Sharing of information within the regulated sector

After section 21C of the Terrorism Act 2000 insert –

21CA Voluntary disclosures within the regulated sector

(1) A person (A) may disclose information to one or more other persons if –

   (a) conditions 1 to 4 are met, and
   (b) where applicable, condition 5 is also met.

(2) Condition 1 is that –

   (a) A is carrying on a business in the regulated sector as a relevant undertaking,
   (b) the information on which the disclosure is based came to A in the course of carrying on that business, and

APPENDIX: CRIMINAL FINANCES ACT 2017

(c) the person to whom the information is to be disclosed (or each of them, where the disclosure is to more than one person) is also carrying on a business in the regulated sector as a relevant undertaking (whether or not of the same kind as A).

(3) Condition 2 is that –

(a) a constable has requested A to make the disclosure, or
(b) the person to whom the information is to be disclosed (or at least one of them, where the disclosure is to more than one person) has requested A to do so.

(4) Condition 3 is that, before A makes the disclosure, the required notification has been made to a constable (see section 21CB(5) to (7)).

(5) Condition 4 is that A is satisfied that the disclosure of the information will or may assist in determining any matter in connection with –

(a) a suspicion that a person is involved in the commission of a terrorist financing offence, or
(b) the identification of terrorist property or of its movement or use.

(6) Condition 5 is that, before making the disclosure request, the person making the request (or at least one of them, where the request is made by more than one person) has notified a constable that the request is to be made.

(7) Condition 5 does not apply where the disclosure request concerned is made by a constable.

(8) A person may disclose information to A for the purposes of making a disclosure request if, and to the extent that, the person has reason to believe that A has in A's possession information that will or may assist in determining any matter of the kind mentioned in paragraph (a) or (b) of subsection (5).

21CB Section 21CA: disclosure requests and notifications

(1) A disclosure request must –

(a) state that it is made in connection with –

(i) a suspicion that a person is involved in the commission of a terrorist financing offence, or
(ii) the identification of terrorist property or of its movement or use,

(b) identify the person or property (so far as known),
(c) describe the information that is sought from A, and
(d) specify the person or persons to whom it is requested that the information is disclosed.

(2) Subsections (3) and (4) apply where the disclosure request is made by a person mentioned in section 21CA(3)(b).

(3) If the request states that it is made in connection with a suspicion that a person is involved in the commission of a terrorist financing offence, the request must also –

(a) set out the grounds for the suspicion, or

APPENDIX: CRIMINAL FINANCES ACT 2017

(b) provide such other information as the person making the request thinks appropriate for the purposes of enabling A to determine whether the information requested ought to be disclosed under section 21CA.

(4) If the request states that it is made in connection with the identification of terrorist property or of its movement or use, the request must also provide such other information as the person making the request thinks appropriate for the purposes of enabling A to determine whether the information requested ought to be disclosed under section 21CA.

(5) A required notification for the purposes of section 21CA(4) must be made –

(a) in the case of a disclosure request made by a constable, by the person who is to disclose information under section 21CA as a result of the request;
(b) in the case of a disclosure request made by a person mentioned in section 21CA(3)(b), by the person who made the request.

(6) In a case within subsection (5)(a), the required notification must state that information is to be disclosed under section 21CA.

(7) In a case within subsection (5)(b), the required notification must –

(a) state that a disclosure request has been made;
(b) specify the person to whom the request was made;
(c) where the disclosure request to which the notification relates is made in connection with a suspicion of a person's involvement in the commission of a terrorist financing offence, identify the person (so far as known);
(d) where the disclosure request to which the notification relates is made in connection with the identification of terrorist property or of its movement or use, identify the property and the person who holds it (if known).

(8) A notification for the purposes of condition 5 in subsection (6) of section 21CA must –

(a) state that a disclosure request is to be made;
(b) specify the person to whom it is to be made;
(c) describe the information to be sought in the request;
(d) explain why the request is being made.

21CC Section 21CA: effect on disclosures under section 21A

(1) This section applies if in any proceedings a question arises as to whether the required disclosure has been made –

(a) by a person (A) who discloses information under section 21CA(1) as a result of a disclosure request,
(b) by a person (B) who makes a required notification in accordance with section 21CB(5)(b), or
(c) by any other person (C) to whom A discloses information under section 21CA(1) as a result of that request.

(2) The making of a required notification in good faith is to be treated as satisfying any requirement to make the required disclosure on the part of A, B and C.

APPENDIX: CRIMINAL FINANCES ACT 2017

This is subject to section 21CD(1) to (8).

(3) The making of a joint disclosure report in good faith is to be treated as satisfying any requirement to make the required disclosure on the part of the persons who jointly make the report.
This is subject to section 21CD(10).

(4) A joint disclosure report is a report to a constable that –

(a) is made jointly by A and B (whether or not also jointly with other persons to whom A discloses information under section 21CA(1)),

(b) satisfies the requirements as to content mentioned in subsection

(5) or (as the case may be) subsection (6),

(c) is prepared after the making of a disclosure by A to B under section 21CA(1) in connection with –

(i) a suspicion of a person's involvement in the commission of a terrorist financing offence, or

(ii) the identification of terrorist property or of its movement or use, and

(d) is sent to the constable before the end of the applicable period.

(5) In the case of a joint disclosure report prepared in connection with a suspicion of a person's involvement in the commission of a terrorist financing offence, the requirements as to content are that the report must –

(a) explain the extent to which there are continuing grounds to suspect that the person is involved in the commission of the offence,

(b) identify the person (if known),

(c) set out the grounds for the suspicion, and

(d) provide any other information relevant to the matter.

(6) In the case of a joint disclosure report prepared in connection with the identification of terrorist property or of its movement or use, the requirements as to content are that the report must –

(a) explain the extent to which there are continuing grounds to suspect that the property is terrorist property,

(b) identify the property and the person who holds it (if known),

(c) provide details of its movement or use (if known), and

(d) provide any other information relevant to the matter.

(7) The applicable period is –

(a) in a case where the disclosure under section 21CA was made as a result of a request from a constable by virtue of subsection (3)(a) of that section, whatever period may be specified by the constable when making the request;

(b) in a case where the disclosure was made as a result of a request from another person by virtue of subsection (3)(b) of that section, the period of 28 days beginning with the day on which the notification is made for the purposes of condition 3 in section 21CA(4).

APPENDIX: CRIMINAL FINANCES ACT 2017

(8) A constable may vary the period of 28 days (whether by lengthening or shortening it) by giving written notice to the person who made the required notification.

(9) A joint disclosure report must be –

   (a) approved by the nominated officer of each person that jointly makes the report, and
   (b) signed by the nominated officer on behalf of each such person. If there is no nominated officer the report must be approved and signed by another senior officer.

(10) References in this section to A, B or C include –

   (a) a nominated officer acting on behalf of A, B or C, and
   (b) any other person who is an employee, officer or partner of A, B or C.

21CD Limitations on application of section 21CC(2) and (3)

(1) Subsections (2) and (3) apply in a case where the required notification is made by A (notification made as a result of disclosure request received from a constable).

(2) Section 21CC(2) has effect in the case of A, B or C only so far as relating to –

   (a) the suspicion in connection with which the required notification is made, and
   (b) matters known, suspected or believed as a result of the making of the disclosure request concerned.

(3) Accordingly, section 21CC(2) does not remove any requirement to make the required disclosure in relation to anything known, suspected or believed that does not result only from the making of the disclosure request.

(4) Subsections (5) to (8) apply in a case where the required notification is made by B (notification made as a result of disclosure request received from another undertaking in the regulated sector).

(5) Section 21CC(2) has effect in the case of A or C only so far as relating to –

   (a) the suspicion in connection with which the notification by B is made, and
   (b) matters known, suspected or believed by A or C as a result of the making of that notification.

(6) Accordingly, section 21CC(2) does not remove any requirement to make the required disclosure in relation to anything known, suspected or believed that does not result only from the making of the notification.

(7) Section 21CC(2) has effect in the case of B only so far as relating to –

   (a) the suspicion in connection with which the notification is made, and
   (b) matters known, suspected or believed by B at the time of the making of the notification.

(8) If a joint disclosure report is not made before the end of the applicable period (whether the required notification was made by A or B), section 21CC(2) –

   (a) has effect only so far as relating to any requirement to make the required disclosure that would have otherwise arisen within that period, and

APPENDIX: CRIMINAL FINANCES ACT 2017

(b) does not remove a requirement to make the required disclosure so far as arising after the end of that period on the part of any person in respect of matters that may become known, suspected or believed by the person after the time when the required notification was made.

(9) If a joint disclosure report is not made before the end of the applicable period, the person who made the required notification must notify a constable that a report is not being made as soon as reasonably practicable after the period ends.

(10) Section 21CC(3) has effect only so far as relating to –

(a) the suspicion in connection with which the report is made, and
(b) matters known, suspected or believed at the time of the making of the report.

(11) Terms used in this section have the same meanings as in section 21CC.

21CE Section 21CA: supplementary

(1) A relevant disclosure made in good faith does not breach –

(a) an obligation of confidence owed by the person making the disclosure, or
(b) any other restriction on the disclosure of information, however imposed.

(2) But a relevant disclosure may not include information obtained from a UK law enforcement agency unless that agency consents to the disclosure.

(3) In a case where a person is acting on behalf of another ("the undertaking") as a nominated officer –

(a) a relevant disclosure by the undertaking must be made by the nominated officer on behalf of the undertaking, and
(b) a relevant disclosure to the undertaking must be made to that officer.

(4) Subsection (1) applies whether or not the conditions in section 21CA were met in respect of the disclosure if the person making the disclosure did so in the reasonable belief that the conditions were met.

(5) In this section –

"relevant disclosure" means any disclosure made in compliance, or intended compliance, with section 21CA;
"UK law enforcement agency" means –

(a) the National Crime Agency;
(b) a police force in England, Scotland, Northern Ireland or Wales;
(c) any other person operating in England, Scotland, Northern Ireland or Wales charged with the duty of preventing, detecting, investigating or prosecuting offences.

21CF Sections 21CA to 21CE: interpretation

(1) This section applies for the purposes of sections 21CA to 21CE.
(2) References to a constable include references to a National Crime Agency officer authorised for those purposes by the Director General of that Agency.

(3) References to a business in the regulated sector are to be construed in accordance with Schedule 3A.
(4) "Disclosure request" means a request made for the purposes of condition 2 in section 21CA(3).
(5) "Nominated officer" means a person nominated to receive disclosures under section 21A.
(6) "Relevant undertaking" means any of the following –

   (a) a credit institution;
   (b) a financial institution;
   (c) a professional legal adviser;
   (d) a relevant professional adviser;
   (e) other persons (not within paragraphs (a) to (d)) whose business consists of activities listed in paragraph 1(1) of Schedule 3A.

(7) "Required disclosure" means a disclosure that is made –

   (a) to a constable in connection with a suspicion that a person is involved in the commission of a terrorist financing offence, and
   (b) for the purposes of avoiding the commission of an offence under section 21A by virtue of not satisfying the third condition in subsection (4) of that section.

(8) "Required notification" means a notification made for the purposes of condition 3 in section 21CA(4).
(9) For the purposes of subsection (6) –

   (a) "credit institution" has the same meaning as in Schedule 3A;
   (b) "financial institution" means an undertaking that carries on a business in the regulated sector by virtue of any of paragraphs (b) to (i) of paragraph 1(1) of that Schedule;
   (c) "relevant professional adviser" has the meaning given by section 21H(5).

(10) "Terrorist financing offence" means an offence under any of sections 15 to 18."

37 Further information orders

After section 22A of the Terrorism Act 2000 insert –

"Further information orders

22B Further information orders
   (1) A magistrates' court or (in Scotland) the sheriff may, on an application made by a law enforcement officer, make a further information order if satisfied that either condition 1 or condition 2 is met.
   (2) The application must –

      (a) specify or describe the information sought under the order, and
      (b) specify the person from whom the information is sought ("the respondent").

(3) A further information order is an order requiring the respondent to provide –

  (a) the information specified or described in the application for the order, or
  (b) such other information as the court or sheriff making the order thinks appropriate, so far as the information is in the possession, or under the control, of the respondent.

(4) Condition 1 for the making of a further information order is met if –

  (a) the information required to be given under the order would relate to a matter arising from a disclosure made under section 21A,
  (b) the respondent is the person who made the disclosure or is otherwise carrying on a business in the regulated sector,
  (c) the information would assist in –

     (i) investigating whether a person is involved in the commission of an offence under any of sections 15 to 18 or in determining whether an investigation of that kind should be started, or
     (ii) identifying terrorist property or its movement or use, and

  (d) it is reasonable in all the circumstances for the information to be provided.

(5) Condition 2 for the making of a further information order is met if –

  (a) the information required to be given under the order would relate to a matter arising from a disclosure made under a corresponding disclosure requirement,
  (b) an external request has been made to the National Crime Agency for the provision of information in connection with that disclosure,
  (c) the respondent is carrying on a business in the regulated sector,
  (d) the information is likely to be of substantial value to the authority that made the external request in determining any matter in connection with the disclosure, and
  (e) it is reasonable in all the circumstances for the information to be provided.

(6) For the purposes of subsection (5), "external request" means a request made by an authority of a foreign country which has responsibility in that country for carrying out investigations into whether a corresponding terrorist financing offence has been committed.

(7) A further information order must specify –

  (a) how the information required under the order is to be provided, and
  (b) the date by which it is to be provided.

(8) If a person fails to comply with a further information order made by a magistrates' court, the magistrates' court may order the person to pay an amount not exceeding £5,000.

(9) The sum mentioned in subsection (8) is to be treated as adjudged to be paid by a conviction of the court for the purposes of the Magistrates' Courts Act 1980 or (as the case may be) the Magistrates' Courts (Northern Ireland) Order 1981 (S.I. 1981/1675 (N.I. 26)).

APPENDIX: CRIMINAL FINANCES ACT 2017

(10) In order to take account of changes in the value of money the Secretary of State may by regulations made by statutory instrument substitute another sum for the sum for the time being specified in subsection (8).
(11) A statutory instrument containing regulations under subsection (10) is subject to annulment in pursuance of a resolution of either House of Parliament.
(12) A law enforcement officer who is a constable, a National Crime Agency officer or a counter-terrorism financial investigator may not make an application under this section unless the officer is a senior law enforcement officer or is authorised to do so by a senior law enforcement officer.
(13) Schedule 3A has effect for the purposes of this section in determining what is a business in the regulated sector.
(14) In this section –

"corresponding disclosure requirement" means a requirement to make a disclosure under the law of the foreign country concerned that corresponds to a requirement imposed by virtue of this Part;
"corresponding terrorist financing offence" means an offence under the law of the foreign country concerned that would, if done in the United Kingdom, constitute an offence under any of sections 15 to 18;
"foreign country" means a country or territory outside the United Kingdom;
"law enforcement officer" means –

(a) a constable,
(b) a National Crime Agency officer authorised for the purposes of this section by the Director General of that Agency,
(c) a counter-terrorism financial investigator, or
(d) a procurator fiscal;

"senior law enforcement officer" means –

(a) a police officer of at least the rank of superintendent;
(b) the Director General of the National Crime Agency;
(c) any other National Crime Agency officer authorised by the Director General (whether generally or specifically) for this purpose.

22C Statements

(1) A statement made by a person in response to a further information order may not be used in evidence against the person in criminal proceedings.
(2) Subsection (1) does not apply –

(a) in the case of proceedings under this Part,
(b) on a prosecution for perjury, or
(c) on a prosecution for some other offence where, in giving evidence, the person makes a statement inconsistent with the statement mentioned in subsection (1).

(3) A statement may not be used by virtue of subsection (2)(c) unless –

(a) evidence relating to it is adduced, or

(b) a question relating to it is asked, by or on behalf of the person in the proceedings arising out of the prosecution.

(4) In subsection (2)(b) the reference to a prosecution for perjury is –

(a) in the case of England and Wales, a reference to a prosecution for an offence under section 5 of the Perjury Act 1911;
(b) in the case of Northern Ireland, a reference to a prosecution for an offence under Article 10 of the Perjury (Northern Ireland) Order 1979 (S.I. 1979/1714 (N.I. 19)).

22D Appeals
(1) An appeal from a decision on an application for a further information order lies to the relevant appeal court.
(2) An appeal under this section lies at the instance of any person who was a party to the proceedings on the application.
(3) The "relevant appeal court" is –

(a) the Crown Court, in the case of a decision made by a magistrates' court in England and Wales;
(b) a county court, in the case of a decision made by a magistrates' court in Northern Ireland;
(c) the Sheriff Appeal Court, in the case of a decision made by the sheriff.

(4) On an appeal under this section the relevant appeal court may –

(a) make or (as the case may be) discharge a further information order, or
(b) vary the order.

22E Supplementary
(1) A further information order does not confer the right to require a person to provide privileged information.
(2) "Privileged information" is information which a person would be entitled to refuse to provide on grounds of legal professional privilege in proceedings in the High Court or, in Scotland, legal privilege as defined by section 412 of the Proceeds of Crime Act 2002.
(3) Information provided in pursuance of a further information order is not to be taken to breach any restriction on the disclosure of information (however imposed).
(4) An application for a further information order may be heard and determined in private.
(5) Rules of court may make provision as to the practice and procedure to be followed in connection with proceedings relating to further information orders."

Civil recovery

38 Forfeiture of terrorist cash

(1) Schedule 1 to the Anti-terrorism, Crime and Security Act 2001 (forfeiture of terrorist cash) is amended as follows.

(2) In paragraph 1 (meaning of terrorist cash) –

  (a) after sub-paragraph (2)(e) insert –

"(f) gaming vouchers,
(g) fixed-value casino tokens,
(h) betting receipts,";

  (b) after sub-paragraph (4) insert –

"(5) For the purposes of sub-paragraph (2) –

  (a) "gaming voucher" means a voucher in physical form issued by a gaming machine that represents a right to be paid the amount stated on it;
  (b) "fixed-value casino token" means a casino token that represents a right to be paid the amount stated on it;
  (c) "betting receipt" means a receipt in physical form that represents a right to be paid an amount in respect of a bet placed with a person holding a betting licence.

(6) In sub-paragraph (5) –

"bet" –

  (a) in relation to England and Wales and Scotland, has the same meaning as in section 9(1) of the Gambling Act 2005;
  (b) in relation to Northern Ireland, has the same meaning as in the Betting, Gaming, Lotteries and Amusements (Northern Ireland) Order 1985 (S.I. 1985/1204 (N.I. 11)) (see Article 2 of that Order);

"betting licence" –

  (a) in relation to England and Wales and Scotland, means a general betting operating licence issued under Part 5 of the Gambling Act 2005;
  (b) in relation to Northern Ireland, means a bookmaker's licence as defined in Article 2 of the Betting, Gaming, Lotteries and Amusements (Northern Ireland) Order 1985;

"gaming machine" –

  (a) in relation to England and Wales and Scotland, has the same meaning as in the Gambling Act 2005 (see section 235 of that Act);
  (b) in relation to Northern Ireland, has the same meaning as in the Betting, Gaming, Lotteries and Amusements (Northern Ireland) Order 1985 (see Article 2 of that Order).

(7) In the application of sub-paragraph (5) to Northern Ireland references to a right to be paid an amount are to be read as references to the right

that would exist but for Article 170 of the Betting, Gaming, Lotteries and Amusements (Northern Ireland) Order 1985 (gaming and wagering contracts void)."

(3) In paragraph 3 (detention of seized cash) –

(a) in sub-paragraph (2)(a), for "three" substitute "6";
(b) after sub-paragraph (8) insert –

"(9) Where an application for an order under sub-paragraph (2) relates to cash seized under paragraph 2(2), the court, sheriff or justice may make the order if satisfied that –

(a) the condition in sub-paragraph (6), (7) or (8) is met in respect of part of the cash, and
(b) it is not reasonably practicable to detain only that part."

(4) After paragraph 5 insert –

"PART 2A

FORFEITURE OF TERRORIST CASH WITHOUT COURT ORDER

Cash forfeiture notice

5A (1) This paragraph applies while any cash is detained in pursuance of an order under paragraph 3(2).
(2) A senior officer may give a notice for the purpose of forfeiting the cash or any part of it if satisfied that the cash or part is terrorist cash.
(3) A notice given under sub-paragraph (2) is referred to in this Schedule as a cash forfeiture notice.
(4) A cash forfeiture notice must –

(a) state the amount of cash in respect of which it is given,
(b) state when and where the cash was seized,
(c) confirm that the senior officer is satisfied as mentioned in sub-paragraph (2),
(d) specify a period for objecting to the proposed forfeiture and an address to which any objections must be sent, and
(e) explain that the cash will be forfeited unless an objection is received at that address within the period for objecting.

(5) The period for objecting must be at least 30 days starting with the day after the notice is given.
(6) The Secretary of State must by regulations made by statutory instrument make provision about how a cash forfeiture notice is to be given.
(7) The regulations may (amongst other things) provide –

(a) for a cash forfeiture notice to be given to such person or persons, and in such manner, as may be prescribed;
(b) for a cash forfeiture notice to be given by publication in such manner as may be prescribed;

APPENDIX: CRIMINAL FINANCES ACT 2017

  (c) for circumstances in which, and the time at which, a cash forfeiture notice is to be treated as having been given.

(8) The regulations must ensure that where a cash forfeiture notice is given it is, if possible, given to every person to whom notice of an order under paragraph 3(2) in respect of the cash has been given.

(9) A statutory instrument containing regulations under this paragraph is subject to annulment in pursuance of a resolution of either House of Parliament.

(10) In this Part of this Schedule –
"senior officer" means –

  (a) a senior police officer;
  (b) an officer of Revenue and Customs of a rank designated by the Commissioners for Her Majesty's Revenue and Customs as equivalent to that of a senior police officer;
  (c) an immigration officer of a rank designated by the Secretary of State as equivalent to that of a senior police officer;

"senior police officer" means a police officer of at least the rank of superintendent.

Effect of cash forfeiture notice

5B (1) This paragraph applies if a cash forfeiture notice is given in respect of any cash.

(2) The cash is to be detained until –

  (a) the cash is forfeited under this paragraph,
  (b) the notice lapses under this paragraph, or
  (c) the cash is released under a power conferred by this Schedule.

(3) If no objection is made within the period for objecting specified in the notice under paragraph 5A(4)(d), and the notice has not lapsed, the cash is forfeited (subject to paragraph 5D).

(4) If an objection is made within the period for objecting, the notice lapses.

(5) If an application is made for the forfeiture of the whole or any part of the cash under paragraph 6, the notice lapses.

(6) If the cash or any part of it is released under a power conferred by this Schedule, the notice lapses or (as the case may be) lapses in relation to that part.

(7) An objection may be made by anyone (whether a recipient of the notice or not).

(8) An objection means a written objection sent to the address specified in the notice; and an objection is made when it is received at the address.

(9) An objection does not prevent forfeiture of the cash under paragraph 6.

(10) Nothing in this paragraph affects the validity of an order under paragraph 3(2).

Detention following lapse of cash forfeiture notice

5C (1) This paragraph applies if –

  (a) a cash forfeiture notice is given in respect of any cash,
  (b) the notice lapses under paragraph 5B(4), and

(c) the period for which detention of the cash was authorised under paragraph 3(2) has expired.

(2) The cash may be detained for a further period of up to 48 hours (calculated in accordance with paragraph 3(1A)).

(3) But if within that period it is decided that neither of the applications mentioned in sub-paragraph (4) is to be made, the cash must be released.

(4) The applications are –

(a) an application for a further order under paragraph 3(2);
(b) an application for forfeiture of the cash under paragraph 6.

(5) If within that period an application is made for a further order under paragraph 3(2), the cash may be detained until the application is determined or otherwise disposed of.

Application to set aside forfeiture

5D (1) A person aggrieved by the forfeiture of cash in pursuance of paragraph 5B(3) may apply to a magistrates' court or (in Scotland) the sheriff for an order setting aside the forfeiture of the cash or any part of it.

(2) The application must be made before the end of the period of 30 days starting with the day on which the period for objecting ended ("the 30-day period").

(3) But the court or sheriff may give permission for an application to be made after the 30-day period has ended if the court or sheriff thinks that there are exceptional circumstances to explain why the applicant –

(a) failed to object to the forfeiture within the period for objecting, and
(b) failed to make an application within the 30-day period.

(4) On an application under this paragraph the court or sheriff must consider whether the cash to which the application relates could be forfeited under paragraph 6 (ignoring the forfeiture mentioned in sub-paragraph (1)).

(5) If the court or sheriff is satisfied that the cash to which the application relates or any part of it could not be forfeited under that paragraph the court or sheriff must set aside the forfeiture of that cash or part.

(6) Where the court or sheriff sets aside the forfeiture of any cash –

(a) the court or sheriff must order the release of that cash, and
(b) the cash is to be treated as never having been forfeited.

Release of cash subject to cash forfeiture notice

5E (1) This paragraph applies while any cash is detained under paragraph 5B or 5C.

(2) The person from whom the cash was seized may apply to a magistrates' court or (in Scotland) the sheriff for the cash to be released.

(3) On an application under sub-paragraph (2), the court or sheriff may direct the release of the cash or any part of it if not satisfied that the cash to be released is terrorist cash.

(4) An authorised officer may release the cash or any part of it if satisfied that the detention of the cash to be released is no longer justified.

Application of cash forfeited under cash forfeiture notice

5F (1) Cash forfeited in pursuance of paragraph 5B(3), and any accrued interest on it –

  (a) if first detained in pursuance of an order under paragraph 3(2) made by a magistrates' court or a justice of the peace, is to be paid into the Consolidated Fund;
  (b) if first detained in pursuance of an order under paragraph 3(2) made by the sheriff, is to be paid into the Scottish Consolidated Fund.

 (2) But it is not to be paid in –

  (a) before the end of the period within which an application under paragraph 5D may be made (ignoring the possibility of an application by virtue of paragraph 5D(3)), or
  (b) if an application is made within that period, before the application is determined or otherwise disposed of."

(5) In paragraph 7(4) (release of cash on appeal against decision in forfeiture proceedings), after "of" insert "the whole or any part of".

(6) In paragraph 9 (victims), after sub-paragraph (3) insert –

"(4) If sub-paragraph (5) applies, the court or sheriff may order the cash to be released to the applicant or to the person from whom it was seized.

 (5) This sub-paragraph applies where –

  (a) the applicant is not the person from whom the cash claimed was seized,
  (b) it appears to the court or sheriff that the cash belongs to the applicant,
  (c) the court or sheriff is satisfied that the release condition is met in relation to the cash, and
  (d) no objection to the making of an order under sub-paragraph (4) has been made by the person from whom the cash was seized.

 (6) The release condition is met –

  (a) in relation to cash detained under paragraph 3, if the conditions in that paragraph for the detention of the cash are no longer met,
  (b) in relation to cash detained under paragraph 5B or 5C, if the cash is not terrorist cash, and
  (c) in relation to cash detained pending the conclusion of proceedings in pursuance of an application under paragraph 6, if the court or sheriff decides not to make an order under that paragraph in relation to the cash."

(7) In paragraph 19 (general interpretation), in sub-paragraph (1), at the appropriate places insert –

""cash forfeiture notice" has the meaning given by paragraph 5A(3),";
""senior officer" (in Part 2A) has the meaning given by paragraph 5A(10),".

39 Forfeiture of certain personal (or moveable) property

Schedule 3 contains amendments to the Anti-terrorism, Crime and Security Act 2001 which enable the forfeiture of certain personal (or moveable) property which –

(a) is intended to be used for the purposes of terrorism,
(b) consists of resources of a proscribed organisation, or
(c) is, or represents, property obtained through terrorism.

40 Forfeiture of money held in bank and building society accounts

Schedule 4 contains amendments to the Anti-terrorism, Crime and Security Act 2001 which enable the forfeiture of money held in a bank or building society account which –

(a) is intended to be used for the purposes of terrorism,
(b) consists of resources of a proscribed organisation, or
(c) is, or represents, property obtained through terrorism.

Counter-terrorism financial investigators

41 Extension of powers to financial investigators

(1) The Terrorism Act 2000 is amended in accordance with subsections (2) to (5).
(2) After section 63E insert –

"Counter-terrorism financial investigators

63F Counter-terrorism financial investigators

(1) The metropolitan police force must provide a system for the accreditation of financial investigators ("counter-terrorism financial investigators").
(2) The system of accreditation must include provision for –

(a) the monitoring of the performance of counter-terrorism financial investigators,
(b) the withdrawal of accreditation from any person who contravenes or fails to comply with any condition subject to which he or she was accredited, and
(c) securing that decisions under that system which concern –

(i) the grant or withdrawal of accreditations, or
(ii) the monitoring of the performance of counter-terrorism financial investigators, are taken without regard to their effect on operations by the metropolitan police force or any other person.

(3) A person may be accredited if he or she is –

(a) a member of the civilian staff of a police force in England and Wales (including the metropolitan police force), within the meaning of Part 1 of the Police Reform and Social Responsibility Act 2011;
(b) a member of staff of the City of London police force;
(c) a member of staff of the Police Service of Northern Ireland.

(4) A person may be accredited –

(a) in relation to this Act;

APPENDIX: CRIMINAL FINANCES ACT 2017

(b) in relation to the Anti-terrorism, Crime and Security Act 2001;
(c) in relation to particular provisions of this Act or of the Anti- terrorism, Crime and Security Act 2001.

(5) But the accreditation may be limited to specified purposes.
(6) A reference in this Act or in the Anti-terrorism, Crime and Security Act 2001 to a counter-terrorism financial investigator is to be construed accordingly.
(7) The metropolitan police force must make provision for the training of persons in –

(a) financial investigation,
(b) the operation of this Act, and
(c) the operation of the Anti-terrorism, Crime and Security Act 2001."

(3) In Part 1 of Schedule 5 (terrorist investigations: information: England and Wales and Northern Ireland) –

(a) in paragraph 5 –

(i) in sub-paragraph (1) for "A constable" substitute "An appropriate officer";
(ii) after sub-paragraph (1) insert –

"(1A) Where the appropriate officer is a counter-terrorism financial investigator, the officer may apply for an order under this paragraph only for the purposes of a terrorist investigation so far as relating to terrorist property.";

(iii) in sub-paragraph (3)(a) for "a constable" substitute "an appropriate officer";
(iv) in sub-paragraph (3)(b) for "a constable" substitute "an appropriate officer";
(v) after sub-paragraph (5) insert –

"(6) "Appropriate officer" means –

(a) a constable, or
(b) a counter-terrorism financial investigator.";

(b) in paragraph 6 after sub-paragraph (3) insert –

"(4) In the case of an order sought by a counter-terrorism financial investigator, the first condition is satisfied only to the extent that the terrorist investigation mentioned in sub-paragraph (2)(a) and (b) relates to terrorist property.";

(c) in paragraph 7(2)(a) for "constable" substitute "appropriate officer (as defined in paragraph 5(6))";
(d) in paragraph 13 after sub-paragraph (1) insert –

"(1A) A counter-terrorism financial investigator may apply to a Circuit Judge or a District Judge (Magistrates' Courts) for an order under this paragraph requiring any person specified in the order to provide an

APPENDIX: CRIMINAL FINANCES ACT 2017

explanation of any material produced or made available to a counter-terrorism financial investigator under paragraph 5."

(4) In paragraph 1 of Schedule 6 (financial information orders) –

    (a) in sub-paragraph (1) after "constable" insert "or counter-terrorism financial investigator";

    (b) in sub-paragraph (2)(a) after "constable" insert "or counter-terrorism financial investigator".

(5) In Schedule 6A (account monitoring orders) –

    (a) in paragraph 1 after sub-paragraph (4)(a) insert –

        "(aa) a counter-terrorism financial investigator, in England and Wales or Northern Ireland;";

    (b) after paragraph 3(3) insert –

        "(4) If the application was made by a counter-terrorism financial investigator, the description of information specified in it may be varied by a different counter-terrorism financial investigator.";

    (c) after paragraph 4(2) insert –

        "(2A) If the application for the account monitoring order was made by a counter-terrorism financial investigator, an application to discharge or vary the order may be made by a different counter-terrorism financial investigator."

(6) In Schedule 1 to the Anti-terrorism, Crime and Security Act 2001 (forfeiture of terrorist cash) –

    (a) after paragraph 10(7) insert –

        "(7A) If the cash was seized by a counter-terrorism financial investigator, the compensation is to be paid as follows –

            (a) in the case of a counter-terrorism financial investigator who was –

                (i) a member of the civilian staff of a police force (including the metropolitan police force), within the meaning of Part 1 of the Police Reform and Social Responsibility Act 2011, or

                (ii) a member of staff of the City of London police force, it is to be paid out of the police fund from which the expenses of the police force are met,

            (b) in the case of a counter-terrorism financial investigator who was a member of staff of the Police Service of Northern Ireland, it is to be paid out of money provided by the Chief Constable of the Police Service of Northern Ireland.";

(b) in paragraph 19(1) –

 (i) in the definition of "authorised officer", after "constable" insert ", a counter-terrorism financial investigator";
 (ii) at the appropriate place insert –

 ""counter-terrorism financial investigator" is to be read in accordance with section 63F of the Terrorism Act 2000,".

42 Offences in relation to counter-terrorism financial investigators

(1) After section 120A of the Terrorism Act 2000 insert –

120B Offences in relation to counter-terrorism financial investigators
 (1) A person commits an offence if the person assaults a counter-terrorism financial investigator who is acting in the exercise of a relevant power.
 (2) A person commits an offence if the person resists or wilfully obstructs a counter-terrorism financial investigator who is acting in the exercise of a relevant power.
 (3) A person guilty of an offence under subsection (1) is liable –

 (a) on summary conviction in England and Wales, to imprisonment for a term not exceeding 51 weeks, or to a fine, or to both;
 (b) on summary conviction in Northern Ireland, to imprisonment for a term not exceeding 6 months, or to a fine not exceeding level 5 on the standard scale, or to both.

 (4) A person guilty of an offence under subsection (2) is liable –

 (a) on summary conviction in England and Wales, to imprisonment for a term not exceeding 51 weeks, or to a fine not exceeding level 3 on the standard scale, or to both;
 (b) on summary conviction in Northern Ireland, to imprisonment for a term not exceeding 1 month, or to a fine not exceeding level 3 on the standard scale, or to both.

 (5) In this section "relevant power" means a power exercisable under Schedule 5 (terrorist investigations: information) or Part 1 of Schedule 5A (terrorist financing investigations in England and Wales and Northern Ireland: disclosure orders).
 (6) In relation to an offence committed before the coming into force of section 281(5) of the Criminal Justice Act 2003 (alteration of penalties for certain summary offences: England and Wales) –

 (a) the reference to 51 weeks in subsection (3)(a) is to be read as a reference to 6 months;
 (b) the reference to 51 weeks in subsection (4)(a) is to be read as a reference to 1 month."

(2) After paragraph 10Z7 of Schedule 1 to the Anti-terrorism, Crime and Security Act 2001 (inserted by Schedule 4 to this Act) insert –

PART 4C

OFFENCES

Offences in relation to counter-terrorism financial investigators

10Z8(1) A person commits an offence if the person assaults a counter-terrorism financial investigator who is acting in the exercise of a power under this Schedule.

(2) A person commits an offence if the person resists or wilfully obstructs a counter-terrorism financial investigator who is acting in the exercise of a power under this Schedule.

(3) A person guilty of an offence under sub-paragraph (1) is liable –

(a) on summary conviction in England and Wales, to imprisonment for a term not exceeding 51 weeks, or to a fine, or to both;

(b) on summary conviction in Northern Ireland, to imprisonment for a term not exceeding 6 months, or to a fine not exceeding level 5 on the standard scale, or to both.

(4) A person guilty of an offence under sub-paragraph (2) is liable –

(a) on summary conviction in England and Wales, to imprisonment for a term not exceeding 51 weeks, or to a fine not exceeding level 3 on the standard scale, or to both;

(b) on summary conviction in Northern Ireland, to imprisonment for a term not exceeding 1 month, or to a fine not exceeding level 3 on the standard scale, or to both.

(5) In relation to an offence committed before the coming into force of section 281(5) of the Criminal Justice Act 2003 (alteration of penalties for certain summary offences: England and Wales) –

(a) the reference to 51 weeks in sub-paragraph (3)(a) is to be read as a reference to 6 months;

(b) the reference to 51 weeks in sub-paragraph (4)(a) is to be read as a reference to 1 month."

Enforcement in other parts of United Kingdom

43 Enforcement in other parts of United Kingdom

After section 120B of the Terrorism Act 2000 (inserted by section 42 above) insert –

120C Enforcement of orders in other parts of United Kingdom

(1) Her Majesty may by Order in Council make provision for an investigatory order made in one part of the United Kingdom to be enforced in another part.

(2) In subsection (1) "investigatory order" means any of the following kinds of order –

    (a) an order under section 22B (further information orders);

    (b) an order under paragraph 5 of Schedule 5 (production orders: England and Wales and Northern Ireland) that is made in connection with a terrorist investigation in relation to terrorist property;

    (c) an order under paragraph 13(1)(b) of that Schedule that is made in connection with material produced or made available as a result of an order within paragraph (b) of this subsection;

    (d) an order under paragraph 22 of Schedule 5 (production orders: Scotland) that is made in connection with a terrorist investigation in relation to terrorist property;

    (e) an order under paragraph 30(1)(b) of that Schedule that is made in connection with material produced or made available as a result of an order within paragraph (d) of this subsection;

    (f) an order under paragraph 9 of Schedule 5A (disclosure orders: England and Wales and Northern Ireland);

    (g) an order under paragraph 19 of that Schedule (disclosure orders: Scotland);

    (h) an order under paragraph 1 of Schedule 6 (financial information orders);

    (i) an order under paragraph 2 of Schedule 6A (account monitoring orders).

(3) An Order under this section may apply (with or without modifications) any provision of or made under –

    (a) an Act (including this Act),

    (b) an Act of the Scottish Parliament, or

    (c) Northern Ireland legislation.

(4) An Order under this section –

    (a) may make different provision for different purposes;

    (b) may include supplementary, incidental, saving or transitional provisions.

(5) Rules of court may make whatever provision is necessary or expedient to give effect to an Order under this section.

(6) A statutory instrument containing an Order under this section is subject to annulment in pursuance of a resolution of either House of Parliament."

PART 3

CORPORATE OFFENCES OF FAILURE TO PREVENT FACILITATION OF TAX EVASION

Preliminary

44 Meaning of relevant body and acting in the capacity of an associated person

(1) This section defines expressions used in this Part.

(2) "Relevant body" means a body corporate or partnership (wherever incorporated or formed).

(3) "Partnership" means –

   (a) a partnership within the meaning of the Partnership Act 1890, or
   (b) a limited partnership registered under the Limited Partnerships Act 1907, or a firm or entity of a similar character formed under the law of a foreign country.

(4) A person (P) acts in the capacity of a person associated with a relevant body (B) if P is –

   (a) an employee of B who is acting in the capacity of an employee,
   (b) an agent of B (other than an employee) who is acting in the capacity of an agent, or
   (c) any other person who performs services for or on behalf of B who is acting in the capacity of a person performing such services.

(5) For the purposes of subsection (4)(c) the question whether or not P is a person who provides services for or on behalf of B is to be determined by reference to all the relevant circumstances and not merely by reference to the nature of the relationship between P and B.

Failure of relevant bodies to prevent tax evasion facilitation offences by associated persons

45 Failure to prevent facilitation of UK tax evasion offences

(1) A relevant body (B) is guilty of an offence if a person commits a UK tax evasion facilitation offence when acting in the capacity of a person associated with B.

(2) It is a defence for B to prove that, when the UK tax evasion facilitation offence was committed –

   (a) B had in place such prevention procedures as it was reasonable in all the circumstances to expect B to have in place, or
   (b) it was not reasonable in all the circumstances to expect B to have any prevention procedures in place.

(3) In subsection (2) "prevention procedures" means procedures designed to prevent persons acting in the capacity of a person associated with B from committing UK tax evasion facilitation offences.

(4) In this Part "UK tax evasion offence" means –

   (a) an offence of cheating the public revenue, or
   (b) an offence under the law of any part of the United Kingdom consisting of being knowingly concerned in, or in taking steps with a view to, the fraudulent evasion of a tax.

(5) In this Part "UK tax evasion facilitation offence" means an offence under the law of any part of the United Kingdom consisting of –

(a) being knowingly concerned in, or in taking steps with a view to, the fraudulent evasion of a tax by another person,

(b) aiding, abetting, counselling or procuring the commission of a UK tax evasion offence, or

(c) being involved art and part in the commission of an offence consisting of being knowingly concerned in, or in taking steps with a view to, the fraudulent evasion of a tax.

(6) Conduct carried out with a view to the fraudulent evasion of tax by another person is not to be regarded as a UK tax evasion facilitation offence by virtue of subsection (5)(a) unless the other person has committed a UK tax evasion offence facilitated by that conduct.

(7) For the purposes of this section "tax" means a tax imposed under the law of any part of the United Kingdom, including national insurance contributions under –

(a) Part 1 of the Social Security Contributions and Benefits Act 1992, or

(b) Part 1 of the Social Security Contributions and Benefits (Northern Ireland) Act 1992.

(8) A relevant body guilty of an offence under this section is liable –

(a) on conviction on indictment, to a fine;

(b) on summary conviction in England and Wales, to a fine;

(c) on summary conviction in Scotland or Northern Ireland, to a fine not exceeding the statutory maximum.

46 Failure to prevent facilitation of foreign tax evasion offences

(1) A relevant body (B) is guilty of an offence if at any time –

(a) a person commits a foreign tax evasion facilitation offence when acting in the capacity of a person associated with B, and

(b) any of the conditions in subsection (2) is satisfied.

(2) The conditions are –

(a) that B is a body incorporated, or a partnership formed, under the law of any part of the United Kingdom;

(b) that B carries on business or part of a business in the United Kingdom;

(c) that any conduct constituting part of the foreign tax evasion facilitation offence takes place in the United Kingdom; and in paragraph (b) "business" includes an undertaking.

(3) It is a defence for B to prove that, when the foreign tax evasion facilitation offence was committed –

(a) B had in place such prevention procedures as it was reasonable in all the circumstances to expect B to have in place, or

(b) it was not reasonable in all the circumstances to expect B to have any prevention procedures in place.

(4) In subsection (3) "prevention procedures" means procedures designed to prevent persons acting in the capacity of a person associated with B from committing foreign tax evasion facilitation offences under the law of the foreign country concerned.

(5) In this Part "foreign tax evasion offence" means conduct which –

(a) amounts to an offence under the law of a foreign country,
(b) relates to a breach of a duty relating to a tax imposed under the law of that country, and
(c) would be regarded by the courts of any part of the United Kingdom as amounting to being knowingly concerned in, or in taking steps with a view to, the fraudulent evasion of that tax.

(6) In this Part "foreign tax evasion facilitation offence" means conduct which –

(a) amounts to an offence under the law of a foreign country,
(b) relates to the commission by another person of a foreign tax evasion offence under that law, and
(c) would, if the foreign tax evasion offence were a UK tax evasion offence, amount to a UK tax evasion facilitation offence (see section 45(5) and (6)).

(7) A relevant body guilty of an offence under this section is liable –

(a) on conviction on indictment, to a fine;
(b) on summary conviction in England and Wales, to a fine;
(c) on summary conviction in Scotland or Northern Ireland, to a fine not exceeding the statutory maximum.

Guidance about prevention procedures

47 Guidance about preventing facilitation of tax evasion offences

(1) The Chancellor of the Exchequer ("the Chancellor") must prepare and publish guidance about procedures that relevant bodies can put in place to prevent persons acting in the capacity of an associated person from committing UK tax evasion facilitation offences or foreign tax evasion facilitation offences.

(2) The Chancellor may from time to time prepare and publish new or revised guidance to add to or replace existing guidance published by the Chancellor under this section.

(3) The Chancellor must consult the Scottish Ministers, the Welsh Ministers and the Department of Justice in Northern Ireland when preparing any guidance to be published under this section.

(4) Guidance prepared and published under this section does not come into operation except in accordance with regulations made by the Chancellor by statutory instrument.

(5) A statutory instrument containing such regulations is subject to annulment in pursuance of a resolution of either House of Parliament.

(6) Where for the purposes of subsection (5) a copy of a statutory instrument containing such regulations is laid before Parliament the Chancellor must also lay a copy of the guidance to which the regulations relate.

(7) The Chancellor may approve guidance prepared by any other person if it relates to any matters within the scope of subsection (1).

(8) Approval under subsection (7) –

   (a) must be given in writing, and
   (b) may only be given on the condition that the person who prepared it publishes the approved guidance while it remains in operation as approved guidance.

(9) The Chancellor may withdraw approval under subsection (7) by a notice given to the person who prepared the guidance.

Offences: general and supplementary provision

48 Offences: extra-territorial application and jurisdiction

(1) It is immaterial for the purposes of section 45 or 46 (except to the extent provided by section 46(2)) whether –

   (a) any relevant conduct of a relevant body, or
   (b) any conduct which constitutes part of a relevant UK tax evasion facilitation offence or foreign tax evasion facilitation offence, or
   (c) any conduct which constitutes part of a relevant UK tax evasion offence or foreign tax evasion offence, takes place in the United Kingdom or elsewhere.

(2) Proceedings for an offence under section 45 or 46 may be taken in any place in the United Kingdom.

(3) If by virtue of subsection (2) proceedings for an offence are to be taken in Scotland, they may be taken in such sheriff court district as the Lord Advocate may determine.

(4) In subsection (3) "sheriff court district" is to be read in accordance with section 307(1) of the Criminal Procedure (Scotland) Act 1995.

49 Consent to prosecution under section 46

(1) In this section "proceedings" means proceedings for an offence under section 46.

(2) No proceedings may be instituted in England and Wales except by or with the consent of the Director of Public Prosecutions or the Director of the Serious Fraud Office.

(3) No proceedings may be instituted in Northern Ireland except by or with the consent of the Director of Public Prosecutions for Northern Ireland or the Director of the Serious Fraud Office.

(4) The Director of Public Prosecutions and the Director of the Serious Fraud Office must each exercise any function of giving consent under subsection (2) or (3) personally unless –

   (a) the Director concerned is unavailable, and

APPENDIX: CRIMINAL FINANCES ACT 2017

    (b)   there is another person designated in writing by the Director concerned acting personally as the person who is authorised to exercise the function when the Director is unavailable.

(5)   In that case the other person may exercise the function but must do so personally.

(6)   No proceedings may be instituted in Northern Ireland by virtue of section 36 of the Justice (Northern Ireland) Act 2002 (delegation of functions of the DPP for Northern Ireland to persons other than the Deputy Director) except with the consent of the Director of Public Prosecutions for Northern Ireland to the institution of the proceedings.

(7)   The Director of Public Prosecutions for Northern Ireland must exercise personally any function of giving consent under subsection (3) or (6) unless the function is exercised personally by the Deputy Director of Public Prosecutions for Northern Ireland by virtue of section 30(4) or (7) of that Act.

50 Offences by partnerships: supplementary

(1)   Proceedings for an offence under section 45 or 46 alleged to have been committed by a partnership must be brought in the name of the partnership (and not in the name of any of the partners).

(2)   For the purposes of such proceedings –

    (a)   rules of court relating to the service of documents have effect as if the partnership were a body corporate, and

    (b)   the following provisions (which concern procedure in relation to offences by bodies corporate) apply as they apply to a body corporate –

        (i)   section 33 of the Criminal Justice Act 1925 and Schedule 3 to the Magistrates' Courts Act 1980, and

        (ii)   section 18 of the Criminal Justice Act (Northern Ireland) 1945 (c. 15 (N.I.)) and Schedule 4 to the Magistrates' Courts (Northern Ireland) Order 1981 (S.I. 1981/1675 (N.I. 26)).

(3)   A fine imposed on a partnership on its conviction for an offence under section 45 or 46 is to be paid out of the partnership assets.

Consequential amendments and interpretation

51 Consequential amendments

(1)   In section 61(1) of the Serious Organised Crime and Police Act 2005 (offences to which investigatory powers etc apply) after paragraph (h) insert –

    "(i)   any offence under section 45 or 46 of the Criminal Finances Act 2017 (failure to prevent the facilitation of UK tax evasion offences or foreign tax evasion offences)."

(2)   In Schedule 1 to the Serious Crime Act 2007 (serious offences) –

    (a)   in Part 1 (serious offences in England and Wales), in the heading before paragraph 8 insert "etc" at the end and in paragraph 8 at the end insert –

"(6) An offence under section 45 or 46 of the Criminal Finances Act 2017 (failure to prevent the facilitation of UK tax evasion offences or foreign tax evasion offences).";

(b) in Part 1A (serious offences in Scotland) in the heading before paragraph 16G insert "etc" at the end and in paragraph 16G at the end insert –

"(5) An offence under section 45 or 46 of the Criminal Finances Act 2017 (failure to prevent the facilitation of UK tax evasion offences or foreign tax evasion offences).";

(c) in Part 2 (serious offences in Northern Ireland) in the heading before paragraph 24 insert "etc" at the end and in paragraph 24 at the end insert –

"(6) An offence under section 45 or 46 of the Criminal Finances Act 2017 (failure to prevent the facilitation of UK tax evasion offences or foreign tax evasion offences)."

(3) In Part 2 of Schedule 17 to the Crime and Courts Act 2013 (offences in relation to which a deferred prosecution agreement may be entered into) after paragraph 26A insert –

"26B An offence under section 45 or 46 of the Criminal Finances Act 2017 (failure to prevent the facilitation of UK tax evasion offences or foreign tax evasion offences)."

52 Interpretation of Part 3

(1) In this Part –

"conduct" includes acts and omissions;
"foreign country" means a country or territory outside the United Kingdom;
"foreign tax evasion facilitation offence" has the meaning given by section 46(6);
"foreign tax evasion offence" has the meaning given by section 46(5); "partnership" has the meaning given by section 44(3);
"relevant body" has the meaning given by section 44(2);
"tax" includes duty and any other form of taxation (however described); "UK tax evasion facilitation offence" has the meaning given by section 45(5) and (6);
"UK tax evasion offence" has the meaning given by section 45(4).

(2) References in this Part to a person acting in the capacity of a person associated with a relevant body are to be construed in accordance with section 44(4).

Part 4

GENERAL

53 Minor and consequential amendments

Schedule 5 contains minor and consequential amendments.

54 Power to make consequential provision

(1) The Secretary of State may by regulations made by statutory instrument make provision in consequence of any provision made by or under Part 1 or 2.

(2) The Scottish Ministers may by regulations make provision in consequence of section 29 or any provision made by or under Part 1 or 2 that extends only to Scotland.

(3) The Department of Justice in Northern Ireland may by regulations make provision in consequence of any provision made by or under Part 1 or 2 that extends only to Northern Ireland.

(4) Regulations under subsections (1) to (3) may include transitional, transitory or saving provision.

(5) Regulations under subsections (1) to (3) may repeal, revoke or otherwise amend any provision of primary or subordinate legislation (including legislation passed or made on or before the last day of the session in which this Act is passed).

(6) Regulations under subsection (2) or (3) may not include provision of the kind mentioned in subsection (5) unless the provision is within legislative competence.

(7) For this purpose, a provision of regulations is within legislative competence if –

   (a) in the case of regulations made by the Scottish Ministers, it would fall within the legislative competence of the Scottish Parliament if included in an Act of that Parliament;

   (b) in the case of regulations made by the Department of Justice in Northern Ireland, it deals with a transferred matter.

(8) In this section and in section 55 – "primary legislation" means –

   (a) an Act;
   (b) an Act of the Scottish Parliament;
   (c) a Measure or Act of the National Assembly for Wales;
   (d) Northern Ireland legislation; "subordinate legislation" means –
   (a) subordinate legislation within the meaning of the Interpretation Act 1978;
   (b) an instrument made under an Act of the Scottish Parliament;
   (c) an instrument made under a Measure or Act of the National Assembly for Wales;
   (d) an instrument made under Northern Ireland legislation; "transferred matter" has the meaning given by section 4(1) of the Northern Ireland Act 1998.

55 Section 54: procedural requirements

(1) Before making regulations under section 54(1) the Secretary of State must –

   (a) if the regulations contain provision that would fall within the legislative competence of the Scottish Parliament if included in an Act of that Parliament, consult the Scottish Ministers;

   (b) if the regulations contain provision that deals with a transferred matter, consult the Department of Justice in Northern Ireland;

(c) if the regulations contain provision that would fall within the legislative competence of the National Assembly for Wales if included in an Act of that Assembly, consult the Welsh Ministers.

(2) Before making regulations under section 54(2) the Scottish Ministers must consult the Secretary of State.

(3) Before making regulations under section 54(3) the Department of Justice in Northern Ireland must consult the Secretary of State.

(4) A statutory instrument containing (whether alone or with other provision) regulations under section 54 made by the Secretary of State that repeal, revoke or otherwise amend any provision of primary legislation is not to be made unless a draft of the instrument has been laid before, and approved by a resolution of, each House of Parliament.

(5) Any other statutory instrument containing regulations under that section made by the Secretary of State is subject to annulment in pursuance of a resolution of either House of Parliament.

(6) Regulations under section 54 made by the Scottish Ministers that repeal, revoke or otherwise amend any provision of primary legislation are subject to the affirmative procedure (see Part 2 of the Interpretation and Legislative Reform (Scotland) Act 2010 (asp 10)).

(7) Any other regulations under that section made by the Scottish Ministers are subject to the negative procedure (see Part 2 of that Act).

(8) Regulations under section 54 made by the Department of Justice in Northern Ireland that repeal, revoke or otherwise amend any provision of primary legislation are not to be made unless a draft of the instrument has been laid before, and approved by a resolution of, the Northern Ireland Assembly.

(9) Any other regulations under that section made by the Department of Justice in Northern Ireland are subject to negative resolution (within the meaning of section 41(6) of the Interpretation Act (Northern Ireland) 1954).

(10) A power of the Department of Justice in Northern Ireland to make regulations under section 54 is exercisable by statutory rule for the purposes of the Statutory Rules (Northern Ireland) Order 1979 (S.I. 1979/1573 (N.I. 12)).

56 Financial provision

The following are to be paid out of money provided by Parliament –

(a) any expenditure incurred under or by virtue of this Act by a Minister of the Crown or a government department, and

(b) any increases attributable to this Act in the sums payable under any other Act out of money so provided.

57 Extent

(1) Except as provided by subsections (2) to (6), this Act extends to England and Wales, Scotland and Northern Ireland.

APPENDIX: CRIMINAL FINANCES ACT 2017

(2) The following provisions extend to England and Wales only –

   (a) section 17, so far as relating to paragraphs 3 to 6 of Schedule 1, and those paragraphs;
   (b) section 26;
   (c) section 31(2);
   (d) section 32(2) and (3);
   (e) section 34(2) and (11);
   (f) section 51(3).

(3) The following provisions extend to England and Wales and Northern Ireland only –

   (a) sections 1 to 3;
   (b) section 7;
   (c) section 17, so far as relating to paragraphs 24 and 25 of Schedule 1, and those paragraphs;
   (d) section 18(4)(c);
   (e) section 19(3);
   (f) section 20(3) to (6);
   (g) section 22;
   (h) section 23;
   (i) paragraph 3 of Schedule 2;
   (j) section 41(3);
   (k) section 42.

(4) The following provisions extend to Scotland only –

   (a) sections 4 to 6;
   (b) section 8;
   (c) section 18(2), (3) and (4)(d);
   (d) section 28;
   (e) section 30;
   (f) section 32(4);
   (g) section 34(3);
   (h) paragraph 4 of Schedule 2.

(5) The following provisions extend to Northern Ireland only –

   (a) section 17, so far as relating to paragraphs 7 to 10 of Schedule 1, and those paragraphs;
   (b) section 27;
   (c) section 31(3);
   (d) section 32(5) and (6);
   (e) section 34(4).

(6) An amendment made by Schedule 5 has the same extent as the provision amended.

58 Commencement

(1) Except as provided by subsections (2) to (6), this Act comes into force on whatever day or days the Secretary of State appoints by regulations made by statutory instrument.

(2) The following provisions come into force on whatever day or days the Scottish Ministers appoint by regulations after consulting the Secretary of State –

   (a) section 28;
   (b) section 30;
   (c) section 32(4);
   (d) section 34(3).

(3) The following provisions come into force on whatever day or days the Department of Justice in Northern Ireland appoints by regulations after consulting the Secretary of State –

   (a) section 27;
   (b) section 31(3);
   (c) section 32(5) and (6);
   (d) section 34(4).

(4) The following provisions come into force two months after the day on which this Act is passed –

   (a) section 9;
   (b) section 18;
   (c) section 41;
   (d) section 42.

(5) Part 3 comes into force on whatever day or days the Treasury appoints by regulations made by statutory instrument.

(6) The following provisions come into force on the day on which this Act is passed –

   (a) sections 54 to 57;
   (b) this section;
   (c) section 59;
   (d) any other provision of this Act so far as necessary for enabling the exercise on or after the day on which this Act is passed of any power to make provision by subordinate legislation (within the meaning of the Interpretation Act 1978).

(7) Regulations under subsection (1), (2), (3) or (5) may appoint different days for different purposes or areas.

(8) The Secretary of State may by regulations made by statutory instrument make transitional, transitory or saving provision in connection with the coming into force of any provision of this Act other than –

   (a) the provisions mentioned in subsections (2) and (3), and
   (b) Part 3.

(9) The Scottish Ministers may by regulations make transitional, transitory or saving provision in connection with the coming into force of a provision mentioned in subsection (2).

(10) The Department of Justice in Northern Ireland may by regulations make transitional, transitory or saving provision in connection with the coming into force of a provision mentioned in subsection (3).

(11) The Treasury may by regulations made by statutory instrument make transitional, transitory or saving provision in connection with the coming into force of Part 3.

(12) No regulations may be made under subsection (1) bringing into force any of the following provisions, so far as they extend to Scotland, unless the Secretary of State has consulted the Scottish Ministers –

   (a) sections 4 and 5;
   (b) section 8;
   (c) section 14;
   (d) section 15;
   (e) section 16;
   (f) section 25;
   (g) section 29;
   (h) section 33;
   (i) section 34(10).

(13) No regulations may be made under subsection (1) bringing into force any of the following provisions, so far as they extend to Northern Ireland, unless the Secretary of State has consulted the Department of Justice in Northern Ireland –

   (a) sections 1 and 2;
   (b) section 7;
   (c) section 14;
   (d) section 15;
   (e) section 16;
   (f) section 17 and Schedule 1;
   (g) sections 19 and 20;
   (h) sections 22 to 25;
   (i) section 33;
   (j) section 34(10).

(14) Consultation for the purposes of this section may be, or include, consultation before the day on which this Act is passed.

(15) The power to make regulations under subsections (8) to (11) includes power to make different provision for different purposes.

(16) The power of the Department of Justice in Northern Ireland to make regulations under subsection (3) or (10) is exercisable by statutory rule for the purposes of the Statutory Rules (Northern Ireland) Order 1979 (S.I. 1979/1573 (N.I. 12)).

59 Short title

This Act may be cited as the Criminal Finances Act 2017.

APPENDIX: CRIMINAL FINANCES ACT 2017

Schedules

Schedule 1   Section 17

Powers of members of staff of Serious Fraud Office

1   The Proceeds of Crime Act 2002 is amended as follows.

2   (1) Section 2C (prosecuting authorities) is amended as follows.

   (2) In subsection (2) after "Part" insert "2, 4,".
   (3) In subsection (3) after "Part" insert "2, 4,".

3   In section 47A (meaning of "appropriate officer" for purposes of search and seizure powers under Part 2 of that Act), in subsection (1) –

   (a) omit "or" at the end of paragraph (b), and
   (b) after that paragraph insert –

   "(ba) an SFO officer, or".

4   In section 47G (meaning of "appropriate approval" for purposes of section 47C etc), in subsection (3) after paragraph (ab) insert –

   "(ac) in relation to the exercise of a power by an SFO officer, the Director of the Serious Fraud Office,".

5   In section 47M (further detention in other cases where property is detained under section 47J), in subsection (3) after paragraph (b) insert –

   "(ba) an SFO officer,".

6   In section 47S (codes of practice), after subsection (2) insert –

   "(2A) The Secretary of State must also consult the Attorney General about the draft in its application to the exercise of powers by SFO officers and the Director of the Serious Fraud Office."

7   In section 195A (meaning of "appropriate officer" for purposes of search and seizure powers under Part 4 of that Act), in subsection (1) –

   (a) omit "or" at the end of paragraph (b), and
   (b) after that paragraph insert –

   "(ba) an SFO officer, or".

8   In section 195G (meaning of "appropriate approval" for purposes of section 195C etc), in subsection (3) after paragraph (ab) insert –

   "(ac) in relation to the exercise of a power by an SFO officer, the Director of the Serious Fraud Office,".

9   In section 195M (further detention in other cases where property is detained under section 195J), in subsection (3) after paragraph (b) insert –

   "(ba) an SFO officer,".

10 (1) Section 195S (codes of practice: Secretary of State) is amended as follows.
   (2) In subsection (1) –
      (a) in paragraph (a) for "and immigration officers" substitute ", immigration officers and SFO officers", and
      (b) in paragraph (c) after "immigration officers" insert ", SFO officers".
   (3) In subsection (1A), after paragraph (b) insert –
      "(c) the Director of the Serious Fraud Office."
   (4) After subsection (2) insert –
      "(2A) The Secretary of State must also consult the Attorney General about the draft in its application to the exercise of powers by SFO officers and the Director of the Serious Fraud Office."

11 (1) Section 289 (searches) is amended as follows.
   (2) In subsection (1) after "constable" insert ", an SFO officer".
   (3) In subsection (1A) –
      (a) in paragraph (a) after "constable" insert ", an SFO officer";
      (b) in paragraph (b) –
         (i) after "officer" insert "of Revenue and Customs";
         (ii) after "constable" insert ", SFO officer".
   (4) In subsection (1C) –
      (a) after "constable", in both places where it occurs, insert ", SFO officer";
      (b) after "officer", in the second place where it occurs, insert "of Revenue and Customs".
   (5) In subsection (1D) –
      (a) after "constable", in both places where it occurs, insert ", SFO officer";
      (b) after "officer", in the second place where it occurs, insert "of Revenue and Customs".
   (6) In subsection (2) after "constable" insert ", an SFO officer".
   (7) In subsection (3) after "constable" insert ", SFO officer".
   (8) In subsection (4) after "constable" insert ", SFO officer".
   (9) In subsection (5), in paragraph (c) after "an" insert "SFO officer or".

12 (1) Section 290 (prior approval) is amended as follows.
   (2) In subsection (4), after paragraph (a) insert –
      "(aa) in relation to the exercise of a power by an SFO officer, the Director of the Serious Fraud Office,".
   (3) In subsection (6), after "constable" insert ", SFO officer."

13 In section 291 (report on exercise of powers), in subsection (2) after "constable" insert ", SFO officer".

APPENDIX: CRIMINAL FINANCES ACT 2017

14 (1) Section 292 (code of practice) is amended as follows.

   (2) In subsection (1) after "Customs" insert ", SFO officers".
   (3) After subsection (2) insert –

   "(2A) The Secretary of State must also consult the Attorney General about the draft in its application to the exercise of powers by SFO officers and the Director of the Serious Fraud Office."

   (4) In subsection (6) after "Customs," insert "an SFO officer,".

15 (1) Section 294 (seizure of cash) is amended as follows.
   (2) In subsection (1) after "constable" insert ", an SFO officer".
   (3) In subsection (2) after "constable" insert ", an SFO officer".
   (4) In subsection (4) after "by" insert "an SFO officer or".

16 (1) Section 295 (detention of seized cash) is amended as follows.
   (2) In subsection (1) after "constable" insert ", SFO officer".
   (3) In subsection (4)(a) after "constable" insert ", an SFO officer".

17 In section 296 (interest), in subsection (2) after "constable" insert ", SFO officer".

18 In section 297 (release of detained cash), in subsection (4) after "constable" insert ", SFO officer".

19 In section 297A (forfeiture notice), in subsection (6) –

   (a) omit "or" at the end of paragraph (b), and
   (b) after that paragraph insert –

   "(ba) the Director of the Serious Fraud Office, or".

20 In section 297D (detention following lapse of notice), in subsection (3) after "constable" insert ", an SFO officer".

21 In section 297F (release of cash subject to forfeiture notice), in subsection (4) after "constable" insert ", SFO officer".

22 In section 298 (forfeiture), in subsection (1)(a) for "or a constable" substitute ", a constable or an SFO officer".

23 In section 302 (compensation), after subsection (7) insert –

   "(7ZA) If the cash was seized by an SFO officer, the compensation is to be paid by the Director of the Serious Fraud Office."

24 In section 377A (code of practice of Attorney General etc), in subsection (1)(a) after "Prosecutions" insert ", SFO officers".

25 (1) Section 378 (appropriate officers and senior appropriate officers for the purposes of investigations under Part 8 of that Act) is amended as follows.

   (2) In subsection (1) after paragraph (c) insert – "(ca)   an SFO officer;".
   (3) In subsection (2) after paragraph (b) insert –
      "(ba) the Director of the Serious Fraud Office;".
   (4) In subsection (3A) after paragraph (a) insert – "(aa) an SFO officer;".
   (5) In subsection (3AA) after paragraph (a) insert –
      "(aa) the Director of the Serious Fraud Office;".

(6) In subsection (4) after paragraph (b) insert – "(ba) an SFO officer;".

(7) In subsection (6) after paragraph (a) insert –

"(aa) the Director of the Serious Fraud Office;".

26 After section 454 insert –

454A Serious Fraud Office

For the purposes of this Act "SFO officer" means a member of staff of the Serious Fraud Office."

SCHEDULE 2   Section 35

DISCLOSURE ORDERS

1 The Terrorism Act 2000 is amended as follows.
2 After section 37 insert –

37A Disclosure orders in relation to terrorist financing investigations

Schedule 5A (terrorist financing investigations: disclosure orders) has effect."

3 After Schedule 5 insert –

"SCHEDULE 5A

TERRORIST FINANCING INVESTIGATIONS: DISCLOSURE ORDERS

PART 1

ENGLAND AND WALES AND NORTHERN IRELAND

Interpretation

1 This paragraph applies for the purposes of this Part of this Schedule.
2 A disclosure order is an order made under paragraph 9.
3 A judge is –

(a) in England and Wales, a judge entitled to exercise the jurisdiction of the Crown Court;
(b) in Northern Ireland, a Crown Court judge.

4 A terrorist financing investigation is a terrorist investigation into –

(a) the commission, preparation or instigation of an offence under any of sections 15 to 18, or
(b) the identification of terrorist property or its movement or use.

5 An appropriate officer is –

(a) a constable, or

APPENDIX: CRIMINAL FINANCES ACT 2017

    (b) a counter-terrorism financial investigator.

6   A senior police officer is a police officer of at least the rank of superintendent.
7   "Document" means anything in which information of any description is recorded.
8   "Excluded material" –

    (a) in relation to England and Wales, has the same meaning as in the Police and Criminal Evidence Act 1984;
    (b) in relation to Northern Ireland, has the same meaning as in the Police and Criminal Evidence (Northern Ireland) Order 1989 (S.I. 1989/1341 (N.I. 12)).

Disclosure orders

9 (1) A judge may, on the application of an appropriate officer, make a disclosure order if satisfied that each of the requirements for the making of the order is fulfilled.
    (2) The application must state that a person or property specified in the application is subject to a terrorist financing investigation and the order is sought for the purposes of the investigation.
    (3) A disclosure order is an order authorising an appropriate officer to give to any person the officer considers has relevant information notice in writing requiring the person to do any or all of the following with respect to any matter relevant to the terrorist financing investigation concerned –

        (a) answer questions, either at a time specified in the notice or at once, at a place so specified;
        (b) provide information specified in the notice, by a time and in a manner so specified;
        (c) produce documents, or documents of a description, specified in the notice, either at or by a time so specified or at once, and in a manner so specified.

    (4) Relevant information is information (whether or not contained in a document) which the appropriate officer concerned considers to be relevant to the investigation.
    (5) A person is not bound to comply with a requirement imposed by a notice given under a disclosure order unless evidence of authority to give the notice is produced.
    (6) An appropriate officer may not make an application under this paragraph unless the officer is a senior police officer or is authorised to do so by a senior police officer.

Requirements for making of disclosure order

10 (1) These are the requirements for the making of a disclosure order.
    (2) There must be reasonable grounds for suspecting that a person has committed an offence under any of sections 15 to 18 or that the property specified in the application is terrorist property.
    (3) There must be reasonable grounds for believing that information which may be provided in compliance with a requirement imposed under the order is likely to be of substantial value (whether or not by itself) to the terrorist financing investigation concerned.

(4) There must be reasonable grounds for believing that it is in the public interest for the information to be provided, having regard to the benefit likely to accrue to the investigation if the information is obtained.

Offences

11 (1) A person commits an offence if without reasonable excuse the person fails to comply with a requirement imposed under a disclosure order.

(2) A person guilty of an offence under sub-paragraph (1) is liable –

(a) on summary conviction in England and Wales, to imprisonment for a term not exceeding 51 weeks, or to a fine, or to both;

(b) on summary conviction in Northern Ireland, to imprisonment for a term not exceeding 6 months, or to a fine not exceeding level 5 on the standard scale, or to both.

(3) A person commits an offence if, in purported compliance with a requirement imposed under a disclosure order, the person –

(a) makes a statement which the person knows to be false or misleading in a material particular, or

(b) recklessly makes a statement which is false or misleading in a material particular.

(4) A person guilty of an offence under sub-paragraph (3) is liable –

(a) on conviction on indictment, to imprisonment for a term not exceeding 2 years, or to a fine, or to both;

(b) on summary conviction in England and Wales, to imprisonment for a term not exceeding 12 months, or to a fine, or to both;

(c) on summary conviction in Northern Ireland, to imprisonment for a term not exceeding 6 months, or to a fine not exceeding the statutory maximum, or to both.

(5) In relation to an offence committed before the coming into force of section 281(5) of the Criminal Justice Act 2003 (alteration of penalties for certain summary offences), the reference in sub- paragraph (2)(a) to 51 weeks is to be read as a reference to 6 months.

(6) In relation to an offence committed before the coming into force of section 282 of the Criminal Justice Act 2003 (increase in maximum sentence on summary conviction of offence triable either way), the reference in sub-paragraph (4)(b) to 12 months is to be read as a reference to 6 months.

Statements

12 (1) A statement made by a person in response to a requirement imposed under a disclosure order may not be used in evidence against that person in criminal proceedings.

APPENDIX: CRIMINAL FINANCES ACT 2017

(2) Sub-paragraph (1) does not apply –

  (a) in the case of proceedings under this Part of this Act (including paragraph 11(1) or (3)),
  (b) on a prosecution for an offence under section 5 of the Perjury Act 1911 or Article 10 of the Perjury (Northern Ireland) Order 1979 (S.I. 1979/1714 (N.I. 19)) (false statements), or
  (c) on a prosecution for some other offence where, in giving evidence, the person makes a statement inconsistent with the statement mentioned in sub-paragraph (1).

(3) A statement may not be used by virtue of sub-paragraph (2)(c) against a person unless –

  (a) evidence relating to it is adduced, or
  (b) a question relating to it is asked, by or on behalf of the person in the proceedings arising out of the prosecution.

Further provisions

13 (1) A disclosure order does not confer the right to require a person –

  (a) to answer any privileged question,
  (b) to provide any privileged information, or
  (c) to produce any privileged document or other material, except that a lawyer may be required to provide the name and address of a client.

(2) For the purposes of sub-paragraph (1) –

  (a) a privileged question is a question which the person would be entitled to refuse to answer on grounds of legal professional privilege in proceedings in the High Court;
  (b) privileged information is any information which the person would be entitled to refuse to provide on grounds of legal professional privilege in proceedings in the High Court;
  (c) a privileged document or other material is any document or material which the person would be entitled to refuse to produce on grounds of legal professional privilege in proceedings in the High Court.

(3) A disclosure order does not confer the right to require a person to produce excluded material.

(4) A disclosure order has effect in spite of any restriction on the disclosure of information (however imposed).

(5) An appropriate officer may take copies of any documents produced in compliance with a requirement to produce them imposed under a disclosure order.

(6) The documents may be retained for so long as it is necessary to retain them (as opposed to a copy of them) in connection with the terrorist financing investigation for the purposes of which the order was made.

APPENDIX: CRIMINAL FINANCES ACT 2017

(7) But if an appropriate officer has reasonable grounds for believing that –

(a) the documents may need to be produced for the purposes of any legal proceedings, and

(b) they might otherwise be unavailable for those purposes, they may be retained until the proceedings are concluded.

(8) An appropriate officer may retain documents under sub- paragraph (7) only if the officer is a senior police officer or is authorised to do so by a senior police officer.

Supplementary

14 (1) An application for a disclosure order may be made without notice to a judge in chambers.

(2) Rules of court may make provision as to the practice and procedure to be followed in connection with proceedings relating to disclosure orders.

(3) An application to discharge or vary a disclosure order may be made to the Crown Court by –

(a) the person who applied for the order;
(b) any person affected by the order.

(4) The Crown Court may –

(a) discharge the order;
(b) vary the order.

(5) An application to discharge or vary a disclosure order need not be made by the same appropriate officer that applied for the order.

(6) References to a person who applied for a disclosure order are to be construed accordingly.

(7) An appropriate officer may not make an application to discharge or vary a disclosure order unless the officer is a senior police officer or is authorised to do so by a senior police officer."

4 After Part 1 of Schedule 5A (as inserted by paragraph 3 above) insert –

"PART 2

SCOTLAND

Interpretation

15 This paragraph applies for the purposes of this Part of this Schedule.
16 A disclosure order is an order made under paragraph 19.
17 A terrorist financing investigation is a terrorist investigation into –

(a) the commission, preparation or instigation of an offence under any of sections 15 to 18, or
(b) the identification of terrorist property or its movement or use.

18 "Document" means anything in which information of any description is recorded.

APPENDIX: CRIMINAL FINANCES ACT 2017

Disclosure orders

19 (1)   The High Court of Justiciary may, on the application of the Lord Advocate, make a disclosure order if satisfied that each of the requirements for the making of the order is fulfilled.
   (2)   The application must state that a person or property specified in the application is subject to a terrorist financing investigation and the order is sought for the purposes of the investigation.
   (3)   A disclosure order is an order authorising the Lord Advocate to give to any person the Lord Advocate considers has relevant information notice in writing requiring the person to do any or all of the following with respect to any matter relevant to the terrorist financing investigation concerned –

   (a)   answer questions, either at a time specified in the notice or at once, at a place so specified;
   (b)   provide information specified in the notice, by a time and in a manner so specified;
   (c)   produce documents, or documents of a description, specified in the notice, either at or by a time so specified or at once, and in a manner so specified.

   (4)   Relevant information is information (whether or not contained in a document) which the Lord Advocate considers to be relevant to the investigation.
   (5)   A person is not bound to comply with a requirement imposed by a notice given under a disclosure order unless evidence of authority to give the notice is produced.

Requirements for making of disclosure order

20   (1) These are the requirements for the making of a disclosure order.

Offences

   (2)   There must be reasonable grounds for suspecting that a person has committed an offence under any of sections 15 to 18 or that the property specified in the application is terrorist property.
   (3)   There must be reasonable grounds for believing that information which may be provided in compliance with a requirement imposed under the order is likely to be of substantial value (whether or not by itself) to the terrorist financing investigation concerned.
   (4)   There must be reasonable grounds for believing that it is in the public interest for the information to be provided, having regard to the benefit likely to accrue to the investigation if the information is obtained.
21   (1) A person commits an offence if without reasonable excuse the person fails to comply with a requirement imposed under a disclosure order.
   (2)   A person guilty of an offence under sub-paragraph (1) is liable on summary conviction to –

   (a)   imprisonment for a term not exceeding 6 months,
   (b)   a fine not exceeding level 5 on the standard scale, or
   (c)   both.

(3) A person commits an offence if, in purported compliance with a requirement imposed under a disclosure order, the person –

   (a) makes a statement which the person knows to be false or misleading in a material particular, or
   (b) recklessly makes a statement which is false or misleading in a material particular.

(4) A person guilty of an offence under sub-paragraph (3) is liable –

   (a) on summary conviction, to imprisonment for a term not exceeding 12 months or to a fine not exceeding the statutory maximum or to both, or
   (b) on conviction on indictment, to imprisonment for a term not exceeding two years or to a fine or to both.

Statements

22 (1) A statement made by a person in response to a requirement imposed under a disclosure order may not be used in evidence against that person in criminal proceedings.

  (2) Sub-paragraph (1) does not apply –

   (a) in the case of proceedings under this Part of this Act (including paragraph 21(1) or (3)),
   (b) on a prosecution for perjury, or
   (c) on a prosecution for some other offence where, in giving evidence, the person makes a statement inconsistent with the statement mentioned in sub-paragraph (1).

  (3) A statement may not be used by virtue of sub-paragraph (2)(c) against a person unless –

   (a) evidence relating to it is adduced, or
   (b) a question relating to it is asked, by or on behalf of the person in the proceedings arising out of the prosecution.

Further provisions

23 (1) A disclosure order does not confer the right to require a person –

   (a) to answer any question,
   (b) to provide any information, or
   (c) to produce any document, which the person would be entitled to refuse to answer, provide or produce on grounds of legal privilege.

  (2) A disclosure order has effect in spite of any restriction on the disclosure of information (however imposed).
  (3) The Lord Advocate may take copies of any documents produced in compliance with a requirement to produce them imposed under a disclosure order.
  (4) The documents may be retained for so long as it is necessary to retain them (as opposed to a copy of them) in connection with the terrorist financing investigation for the purposes of which the order was made.

APPENDIX: CRIMINAL FINANCES ACT 2017

(5) But if the Lord Advocate has reasonable grounds for believing that –

  (a) the documents may need to be produced for the purposes of any legal proceedings, and
  (b) they might otherwise be unavailable for those purposes, they may be retained until the proceedings are concluded.

Supplementary

24 (1) An application for a disclosure order may be made without notice to a judge of the High Court of Justiciary.
(2) Provision may be made in rules of court as to the discharge and variation of disclosure orders.
(3) An application to discharge or vary a disclosure order may be made to the High Court of Justiciary by –

  (a) the Lord Advocate;
  (b) any person affected by the order.

(4) The High Court of Justiciary may –

  (a) discharge the order;
  (b) vary the order."

SCHEDULE 3   Section 39

FORFEITURE OF CERTAIN PERSONAL (OR MOVEABLE) PROPERTY

1 Schedule 1 to the Anti-terrorism, Crime and Security Act 2001 (forfeiture of terrorist cash) is amended as follows.
2 After paragraph 10 insert –

"PART 4A

FORFEITURE OF TERRORIST ASSETS

Definition of "listed asset"

10A (1) In this Part of this Schedule, a "listed asset" means an item of property that falls within one of the following descriptions of property –

  (a) precious metals;
  (b) precious stones;
  (c) watches;
  (d) artistic works;
  (e) face-value vouchers;
  (f) postage stamps.

(2) The Secretary of State may by regulations made by statutory instrument amend sub-paragraph (1) –

    (a) by removing a description of property;
    (b) by adding a description of tangible personal (or corporeal moveable) property.

(3) A statutory instrument containing regulations under sub- paragraph (2) may not be made unless a draft of the instrument has been laid before and approved by a resolution of each House of Parliament.

(4) In this paragraph –

    (a) "precious metal" means gold, silver or platinum (whether in an unmanufactured or a manufactured state);
    (b) "artistic work" means a piece of work falling within section 4(1)(a) of the Copyright, Designs and Patents Act 1988;
    (c) "face-value voucher" means a voucher in physical form that represents a right to receive goods or services to the value of an amount stated on it.

Seizure of listed assets

10B (1) An authorised officer may seize any item of property if the authorised officer has reasonable grounds for suspecting that –

    (a) it is a listed asset, and
    (b) it is within subsection (1)(a) or (b) of section 1 or it is property earmarked as terrorist property.

(2) An authorised officer may also seize any item of property if –

    (a) the authorised officer has reasonable grounds for suspecting the item to be a listed asset,
    (b) the authorised officer has reasonable grounds for suspecting that part of the item is within subsection (1)(a) or (b) of section 1 or is property earmarked as terrorist property, and
    (c) it is not reasonably practicable to seize only that part.

Initial detention of seized property

10C (1) Property seized under paragraph 10B may be detained for an initial period of 48 hours.

(2) Sub-paragraph (1) authorises the detention of property only for so long as an authorised officer continues to have reasonable grounds for suspicion in relation to that property as described in paragraph 10B(1) or (2) (as the case may be).

(3) In calculating a period of hours for the purposes of this paragraph, no account shall be taken of –

    (a) any Saturday or Sunday,
    (b) Christmas Day,

APPENDIX: CRIMINAL FINANCES ACT 2017

(c) Good Friday,
(d) any day that is a bank holiday under the Banking and Financial Dealings Act 1971 in the part of the United Kingdom within which the property is seized, or
(e) any day prescribed under section 8(2) of the Criminal Procedure (Scotland) Act 1995 as a court holiday in a sheriff court in the sheriff court district within which the property is seized.

Further detention of seized property

10D (1) The period for which property seized under paragraph 10B, or any part of that property, may be detained may be extended by an order made –

(a) in England and Wales or Northern Ireland, by a magistrates' court;
(b) in Scotland, by the sheriff.

(2) An order under sub-paragraph (1) may not authorise the detention of any property –

(a) beyond the end of the period of 6 months beginning with the date of the order, and
(b) in the case of any further order under this paragraph, beyond the end of the period of 2 years beginning with the date of the first order.

(3) A justice of the peace may also exercise the power of a magistrates' court to make the first order under sub-paragraph (1) extending a particular period of detention.

(4) An application to a magistrates' court, a justice of the peace or the sheriff to make the first order under sub-paragraph (1) extending a particular period of detention –

(a) may be made and heard without notice of the application or hearing having been given to any of the persons affected by the application or to the legal representatives of such a person, and
(b) may be heard and determined in private in the absence of persons so affected and of their legal representatives.

(5) An application for an order under sub-paragraph (1) may be made –

(a) in relation to England and Wales and Northern Ireland, by the Commissioners for Her Majesty's Revenue and Customs or an authorised officer;
(b) in relation to Scotland, by a procurator fiscal.

(6) The court, sheriff or justice may make the order if satisfied, in relation to the item of property to be further detained, that –

(a) it is a listed asset, and
(b) condition 1, condition 2 or condition 3 is met.

(7) Condition 1 is that there are reasonable grounds for suspecting that the property is intended to be used for the purposes of terrorism and that either –

(a) its continued detention is justified while its intended use is further investigated or consideration is given to bringing (in the United Kingdom or elsewhere) proceedings against any person for an offence with which the property is connected, or

(b) proceedings against any person for an offence with which the property is connected have been started and have not been concluded.

(8) Condition 2 is that there are reasonable grounds for suspecting that the property consists of resources of an organisation which is a proscribed organisation and that either –

(a) its continued detention is justified while investigation is made into whether or not it consists of such resources or consideration is given to bringing (in the United Kingdom or elsewhere) proceedings against any person for an offence with which the property is connected, or
(b) proceedings against any person for an offence with which the property is connected have been started and have not been concluded.

(9) Condition 3 is that there are reasonable grounds for suspecting that the property is property earmarked as terrorist property and that either –

(a) its continued detention is justified while its derivation is further investigated or consideration is given to bringing (in the United Kingdom or elsewhere) proceedings against any person for an offence with which the property is connected, or
(b) proceedings against any person for an offence with which the property is connected have been started and have not been concluded.

(10) Where an application for an order under sub-paragraph (1) relates to an item of property seized under paragraph 10B(2), the court, sheriff or justice may make the order if satisfied that –

(a) the item of property is a listed asset,
(b) condition 1, 2 or 3 is met in respect of part of the item, and
(c) it is not reasonably practicable to detain only that part.

(11) An order under sub-paragraph (1) must provide for notice to be given to persons affected by it.

Testing and safekeeping of property seized under paragraph 10B

10E (1) An authorised officer may carry out (or arrange for the carrying out of) tests on any item of property seized under paragraph 10B for the purpose of establishing whether it is a listed asset.

(2) An authorised officer must arrange for any item of property seized under paragraph 10B to be safely stored throughout the period during which it is detained under this Part of this Schedule.

Release of detained property

10F (1) This paragraph applies while any property is detained under this Part of this Schedule.

(2) A magistrates' court or (in Scotland) the sheriff may direct the release of the whole or any part of the property if satisfied, on an application by the person from whom the property was seized, that the conditions in paragraph 10C or

10D (as the case may be) for the detention of the property are no longer met in relation to the property to be released.

(3) An authorised officer or (in Scotland) a procurator fiscal may, after notifying the magistrates' court, sheriff or justice under whose order property is being detained, release the whole or any part of it if satisfied that the detention of the property to be released is no longer justified.

(4) But property is not to be released under this paragraph –

(a) if an application for its release under paragraph 10O is made, until any proceedings in pursuance of the application (including any proceedings on appeal) are concluded;

(b) if (in the United Kingdom or elsewhere) proceedings are started against any person for an offence with which the property is connected, until the proceedings are concluded.

See also paragraph 10G(7).

Forfeiture

10G (1) While property is detained under this Part of this Schedule, an application for the forfeiture of the whole or any part of it may be made –

(a) to a magistrates' court, by the Commissioners for Her Majesty's Revenue and Customs or an authorised officer;

(b) to the sheriff, by the Scottish Ministers.

(2) The court or sheriff may order the forfeiture of the property or any part of it if satisfied that –

(a) the property is a listed asset, and

(b) what is to be forfeited is within subsection (1)(a) or (b) of section 1 or is property earmarked as terrorist property.

(3) An order under sub-paragraph (2) made by a magistrates' court may provide for payment under paragraph 10N of reasonable legal expenses that a person has reasonably incurred, or may reasonably incur, in respect of –

(a) the proceedings in which the order is made, or

(b) any related proceedings under this Part of this Schedule.

(4) A sum in respect of a relevant item of expenditure is not payable under paragraph 10N in pursuance of provision under sub- paragraph (3) unless –

(a) the person who applied for the order under sub-paragraph (2) agrees to its payment, or

(b) the court has assessed the amount allowed in respect of that item and the sum is paid in respect of the assessed amount.

(5) For the purposes of sub-paragraph (4) –

(a) a "relevant item of expenditure" is an item of expenditure to which regulations under section 286B of the Proceeds of Crime Act 2002 would apply if the order under sub-paragraph (2) had instead been a recovery order made under section 266 of that Act;

(b) an amount is "allowed" in respect of a relevant item of expenditure if it would have been allowed by those regulations;

(c) if the person who applied for the order under sub-paragraph (2) was an authorised officer, that person may not agree to the payment of a sum unless the person is a senior officer or is authorised to do so by a senior officer.

(6) Sub-paragraph (2) ceases to apply on the transfer of an application made under this paragraph in accordance with paragraph 10J(1)(a) or (b).

(7) Where an application for the forfeiture of any property is made under this paragraph, the property is to be detained (and may not be released under any power conferred by this Part of this Schedule) until any proceedings in pursuance of the application (including any proceedings on appeal) are concluded.

(8) Where the property to which the application relates is being detained under this Part of this Schedule as part of an item of property, having been seized under paragraph 10B(2), sub-paragraph (7) is to be read as if it required the continued detention of the whole of the item of property.

(9) For the purposes of sub-paragraph (5)(c), a "senior officer" means –

(a) in relation to an application made by a constable or a counter-terrorism financial investigator, a senior police officer;

(b) in relation to an application made by an officer of Revenue and Customs, such an officer of a rank designated by the Commissioners for Her Majesty's Revenue and Customs as equivalent to that of a senior police officer;

(c) in relation to an application made by an immigration officer, such an officer of a rank designated by the Secretary of State as equivalent to that of a senior police officer.

(10) In sub-paragraph (9), a "senior police officer" means a police officer of at least the rank of superintendent.

Associated and joint property

10H (1) Paragraphs 10I and 10J apply if –

(a) an application is made under paragraph 10G in respect of property detained under this Part of this Schedule,

(b) the court or sheriff is satisfied that the property is a listed asset,

(c) the court or sheriff is satisfied that all or part of the property is within subsection (1)(a) or (b) of section 1 or is property earmarked as terrorist property, and

(d) there exists property that is associated with the property in relation to which the court or sheriff is satisfied as mentioned in paragraph (c).

(2) Paragraphs 10I and 10J also apply in England and Wales and Northern Ireland if –

(a) an application is made under paragraph 10G in respect of property detained under this Part of this Schedule,

(b) the court is satisfied that the property is a listed asset,
(c) the court is satisfied that all or part of the property is property earmarked as terrorist property, and
(d) the property in relation to which the court or sheriff is satisfied as mentioned in paragraph (c) belongs to joint tenants and one of the tenants is an excepted joint owner.

(3) In this paragraph and paragraphs 10I and 10J "associated property" means property of any of the following descriptions that is not itself the forfeitable property –

(a) any interest in the forfeitable property;
(b) any other interest in the property in which the forfeitable property subsists;
(c) if the forfeitable property is a tenancy in common, the tenancy of the other tenant;
(d) if (in Scotland) the forfeitable property is owned in common, the interest of the other owner;
(e) if the forfeitable property is part of a larger property, but not a separate part, the remainder of that property.

References to property being associated with forfeitable property are to be read accordingly.

(4) In this paragraph and paragraphs 10I and 10J the "forfeitable property" means the property in relation to which the court or sheriff is satisfied as mentioned in sub-paragraph (1)(c) or (2)(c) (as the case may be).

(5) For the purposes of this paragraph and paragraphs 10I and 10J –

(a) an excepted joint owner is a joint tenant who obtained the property in circumstances in which it would not (as against him or her) be earmarked, and
(b) references to the excepted joint owner's share of property are to so much of the property as would have been his or hers if the joint tenancy had been severed.

Agreements about associated and joint property

10I (1) Where –

(a) this paragraph applies, and
(b) the person who applied for the order under paragraph 10G (on the one hand) and the person who holds the associated property or who is the excepted joint owner (on the other hand) agree, the magistrates' court or sheriff may, instead of making an order under paragraph 10G(2), make an order requiring the person who holds the associated property or who is the excepted joint owner to make a payment to a person identified in the order.

(2) The amount of the payment is (subject to sub-paragraph (3)) to be the amount which the persons referred to in sub-paragraph (1)(b) agree represents –

(a) in a case where this paragraph applies by virtue of paragraph 10H(1), the value of the forfeitable property;

(b) in a case where this paragraph applies by virtue of paragraph 10H(2), the value of the forfeitable property less the value of the excepted joint owner's share.

(3) The amount of the payment may be reduced if the person who applied for the order under paragraph 10G agrees that the other party to the agreement has suffered loss as a result of the seizure of the forfeitable property and any associated property under paragraph 10B and its subsequent detention.

(4) The reduction that is permissible by virtue of sub-paragraph (3) is such amount as the parties to the agreement agree is reasonable, having regard to the loss suffered and any other relevant circumstances.

(5) An order under sub-paragraph (1) may, so far as required for giving effect to the agreement, include provision for vesting, creating or extinguishing any interest in property.

(6) An order under sub-paragraph (1) made by a magistrates' court may provide for payment under sub-paragraph (11) of reasonable legal expenses that a person has reasonably incurred, or may reasonably incur, in respect of –

(a) the proceedings in which the order is made, or
(b) any related proceedings under this Part of this Schedule.

(7) A sum in respect of a relevant item of expenditure is not payable under sub-paragraph (11) in pursuance of provision under sub- paragraph (6) unless –

(a) the person who applied for the order under paragraph 10G agrees to its payment, or
(b) the court has assessed the amount allowed in respect of that item and the sum is paid in respect of the assessed amount.

(8) For the purposes of sub-paragraph (7) –

(a) a "relevant item of expenditure" is an item of expenditure to which regulations under section 286B of the Proceeds of Crime Act 2002 would apply if the order under sub- paragraph (1) had instead been a recovery order made under section 266 of that Act;
(b) an amount is "allowed" in respect of a relevant item of expenditure if it would have been allowed by those regulations.

(9) If there is more than one item of associated property or more than one excepted joint owner, the total amount to be paid under sub- paragraph (1), and the part of that amount which is to be provided by each person who holds any such associated property or who is an excepted joint owner, is to be agreed between both (or all) of them and the person who applied for the order under paragraph 10G.

(10) If the person who applied for the order under paragraph 10G was an authorised officer, that person may enter into an agreement for the purposes of any provision of this paragraph only if the person is a senior officer or is authorised to do so by a senior officer.

"Senior officer" has the same meaning in this sub-paragraph as it has in paragraph 10G(5)(c).

(11) An amount received under an order under sub-paragraph (1) must be applied as follows –

    (a) first, it must be applied in making any payment of legal expenses which, after giving effect to sub-paragraph (7), are payable under this sub-paragraph in pursuance of provision under sub-paragraph (6);

    (b) second, it must be applied in payment or reimbursement of any reasonable costs incurred in storing or insuring the forfeitable property and any associated property whilst detained under this Part of this Schedule;

    (c) third, it must be paid –

        (i) if the order was made by a magistrates' court, into the Consolidated Fund;

        (ii) if the order was made by the sheriff, into the Scottish Consolidated Fund.

Associated and joint property: default of agreement

10J (1) Where this paragraph applies and there is no agreement under paragraph 10I, the magistrates' court or sheriff –

    (a) must transfer the application made under paragraph 10G to the relevant court if satisfied that the value of the forfeitable property and any associated property is £10,000 or more;

    (b) may transfer the application made under paragraph 10G to the relevant court if satisfied that the value of the forfeitable property and any associated property is less than £10,000.

(2) The "relevant court" is –

    (a) the High Court, where the application under paragraph 10G was made to a magistrates' court;

    (b) the Court of Session, where the application under paragraph 10G was made to the sheriff.

(3) Where (under sub-paragraph (1)(a) or (b)) an application made under paragraph 10G is transferred to the relevant court, the relevant court may order the forfeiture of the property to which the application relates, or any part of that property, if satisfied that –

    (a) the property is a listed asset, and

    (b) what is to be forfeited is within subsection (1)(a) or (b) of section 1 or is property earmarked as terrorist property.

(4) An order under sub-paragraph (3) made by the High Court may include provision of the type that may be included in an order under paragraph 10G(2) made by a magistrates' court by virtue of paragraph 10G(3).

(5) If provision is included in an order of the High Court by virtue of sub-paragraph (4) of this paragraph, paragraph 10G(4) and (5) apply with the necessary modifications.

(6) The relevant court may, as well as making an order under sub-paragraph (3), make an order –

    (a) providing for the forfeiture of the associated property or (as the case may be) for the excepted joint owner's interest to be extinguished, or

APPENDIX: CRIMINAL FINANCES ACT 2017

(b) providing for the excepted joint owner's interest to be severed.

(7) Where (under sub-paragraph (1)(b)) the magistrates' court or sheriff decides not to transfer an application made under paragraph 10G to the relevant court, the magistrates' court or sheriff may, as well as making an order under paragraph 10G(2), make an order –

  (a) providing for the forfeiture of the associated property or (as the case may be) for the excepted joint owner's interest to be extinguished, or
  (b) providing for the excepted joint owner's interest to be severed.

(8) An order under sub-paragraph (6) or (7) may be made only if the relevant court, the magistrates' court or the sheriff (as the case may be) thinks it just and equitable to do so.

(9) An order under sub-paragraph (6) or (7) must provide for the payment of an amount to the person who holds the associated property or who is an excepted joint owner.

(10) In making an order under sub-paragraph (6) or (7), and including provision in it by virtue of sub-paragraph (9), the relevant court, the magistrates' court or the sheriff (as the case may be) must have regard to –

  (a) the rights of any person who holds the associated property or who is an excepted joint owner and the value to that person of that property or (as the case may) of that person's share (including any value that cannot be assessed in terms of money), and
  (b) the interest of the person who applied for the order under paragraph 10G in realising the value of the forfeitable property.

(11) If the relevant court, the magistrates' court or the sheriff (as the case may be) is satisfied that –

  (a) the person who holds the associated property or who is an excepted joint owner has suffered loss as a result of the seizure of the forfeitable property and any associated property under paragraph 10B and its subsequent detention, and
  (b) the circumstances are exceptional, an order under sub-paragraph (6) or (7) may require the payment of compensation to that person.

(12) The amount of compensation to be paid by virtue of sub-paragraph (11) is the amount the relevant court, the magistrates' court or the sheriff (as the case may be) thinks reasonable, having regard to the loss suffered and any other relevant circumstances.

(13) Compensation to be paid by virtue of sub-paragraph (11) is to be paid in the same way that compensation is to be paid under paragraph 10P.

Paragraphs 10G to 10J: appeals

10K (1) Any party to proceedings for an order for the forfeiture of property under paragraph 10G may appeal against –

  (a) the making of an order under paragraph 10G;

(b) the making of an order under paragraph 10J(7);
(c) a decision not to make an order under paragraph 10G unless the reason that no order was made is that an order was instead made under paragraph 10I;
(d) a decision not to make an order under paragraph 10J(7). Paragraphs (c) and (d) do not apply if the application for the order under paragraph 10G was transferred in accordance with paragraph 10J(1)(a) or (b).

(2) Where an order under paragraph 10I is made by a magistrates' court, any party to the proceedings for the order (including any party to the proceedings under paragraph 10G that preceded the making of the order) may appeal against a decision to include, or not to include, provision in the order under sub-paragraph (6) of paragraph 10I.

(3) An appeal under this paragraph lies –

(a) in relation to England and Wales, to the Crown Court;
(b) in relation to Scotland, to the Sheriff Appeal Court;
(c) in relation to Northern Ireland, to a county court.

(4) An appeal under this paragraph must be made before the end of the period of 30 days starting with the day on which the court makes the order or decision.

(5) Sub-paragraph (4) is subject to paragraph 10L.

(6) The court hearing the appeal may make any order it thinks appropriate.

(7) If the court upholds an appeal against an order forfeiting property, it may order the release of the whole or any part of the property.

Extended time for appealing in certain cases where deproscription order made

10L (1) This paragraph applies where –

(a) a successful application for an order under paragraph 10G relies (wholly or partly) on the fact that an organisation is proscribed,
(b) an application under section 4 of the Terrorism Act 2000 for a deproscription order in respect of the organisation is refused by the Secretary of State,
(c) the property forfeited by the order under paragraph 10G was seized under this Part of this Schedule on or after the date of the refusal of that application,
(d) an appeal against that refusal is allowed under section 5 of the Terrorism Act 2000,
(e) a deproscription order is made accordingly, and
(f) if the order is made in reliance on section 123(5) of the Terrorism Act 2000, a resolution is passed by each House of Parliament under section 123(5)(b) of that Act.

(2) Where this paragraph applies, an appeal under paragraph 10K against the making of an order under paragraph 10G, and against the making (in addition) of any order under paragraph 10J(7), may be brought at any time before the end of the period of 30 days beginning with the date on which the deproscription order comes into force.

(3) In this paragraph a "deproscription order" means an order under section 3(3)(b) or (8) of the Terrorism Act 2000.

APPENDIX: CRIMINAL FINANCES ACT 2017

Realisation of forfeited property

10M (1) If property is forfeited under paragraph 10G or 10J, an authorised officer must realise the property or make arrangements for its realisation.

(2) But the property is not to be realised –

(a) before the end of the period within which an appeal may be made (whether under paragraph 10K or otherwise), or

(b) if an appeal is made within that period, before the appeal is determined or otherwise disposed of.

(3) The realisation of property under sub-paragraph (1) must be carried out, so far as practicable, in the manner best calculated to maximise the amount obtained for the property.

Proceeds of realisation

10N (1) The proceeds of property realised under paragraph 10M must be applied as follows –

(a) first, they must be applied in making any payment required to be made by virtue of paragraph 10J(9);

(b) second, they must be applied in making any payment of legal expenses which, after giving effect to paragraph 10G(4) (including as applied by paragraph 10J(5)), are payable under this sub-paragraph in pursuance of provision under paragraph 10G(3) or, as the case may be, 10J(4);

(c) third, they must be applied in payment or reimbursement of any reasonable costs incurred in storing or insuring the property whilst detained under this Part of this Schedule and in realising the property;

(d) fourth, they must be paid –

(i) if the property was forfeited by a magistrates' court or the High Court, into the Consolidated Fund;

(ii) if the property was forfeited by the sheriff or the Court of Session, into the Scottish Consolidated Fund.

(2) If what is realised under paragraph 10M represents part only of an item of property seized under paragraph 10B and detained under this Part of this Schedule, the reference in sub-paragraph (1)(c) to costs incurred in storing or insuring the property is to be read as a reference to costs incurred in storing or insuring the whole of the item of property.

Victims

10O (1) A person who claims that any property detained under this Part of this Schedule, or any part of it, belongs to him or her may apply for the property or part to be released.

(2) An application under sub-paragraph (1) is to be made –

(a) in England and Wales or Northern Ireland, to a magistrates' court;

(b) in Scotland, to the sheriff.

APPENDIX: CRIMINAL FINANCES ACT 2017

(3) The application may be made in the course of proceedings under paragraph 10D or 10G or at any other time.

(4) The court or sheriff may order the property to which the application relates to be released to the applicant if it appears to the court or sheriff that –

(a) the applicant was deprived of the property to which the application relates, or of property which it represents, by criminal conduct,

(b) the property the applicant was deprived of was not, immediately before the applicant was deprived of it, property obtained by or in return for criminal conduct and nor did it then represent such property, and

(c) the property belongs to the applicant.

(5) If sub-paragraph (6) applies, the court or sheriff may order the property to which the application relates to be released to the applicant or to the person from whom it was seized.

(6) This sub-paragraph applies where –

(a) the applicant is not the person from whom the property to which the application relates was seized,

(b) it appears to the court or sheriff that the property belongs to the applicant,

(c) the court or sheriff is satisfied that the release condition is met in relation to the property, and

(d) no objection to the making of an order under sub- paragraph (5) has been made by the person from whom the property was seized.

(7) The release condition is met –

(a) in relation to property detained under paragraph 10C or 10D, if the conditions in paragraph 10C or (as the case may be) 10D for the detention of the property are no longer met, and

(b) in relation to property detained under paragraph 10G, if the court or sheriff decides not to make an order under that paragraph in relation to the property.

Compensation

10P (1) If no order under paragraph 10G, 10I or 10J is made in respect of any property detained under this Part of this Schedule, the person to whom the property belongs or from whom it was seized may make an application for compensation.

(2) An application under sub-paragraph (1) is to be made –

(a) in England and Wales or Northern Ireland, to a magistrates' court;

(b) in Scotland, to the sheriff.

(3) If the court or sheriff is satisfied that the applicant has suffered loss as a result of the detention of the property and that the circumstances are exceptional, the court or sheriff may order compensation to be paid to the applicant.

(4) The amount of compensation to be paid is the amount the court or sheriff thinks reasonable, having regard to the loss suffered and any other relevant circumstances.

APPENDIX: CRIMINAL FINANCES ACT 2017

(5) If the property was seized by an officer of Revenue and Customs, the compensation is to be paid by the Commissioners for Her Majesty's Revenue and Customs.

(6) If the property was seized by a constable, the compensation is to be paid as follows –

　(a) in the case of a constable of a police force in England and Wales, it is to be paid out of the police fund from which the expenses of the police force are met;

　(b) in the case of a constable of the Police Service of Scotland, it is to be paid by the Scottish Police Authority;

　(c) in the case of a police officer within the meaning of the Police (Northern Ireland) Act 2000, it is to be paid out of money provided by the Chief Constable of the Police Service of Northern Ireland.

(7) If the property was seized by a counter-terrorism financial investigator, the compensation is to be paid as follows –

　(a) in the case of a counter-terrorism financial investigator who was –

　　(i) a member of the civilian staff of a police force (including the metropolitan police force), within the meaning of Part 1 of the Police Reform and Social Responsibility Act 2011, or

　　(ii) a member of staff of the City of London police force, it is to be paid out of the police fund from which the expenses of the police force are met;

　(b) in the case of a counter-terrorism financial investigator who was a member of staff of the Police Service of Northern Ireland, it is to be paid out of money provided by the Chief Constable of the Police Service of Northern Ireland.

(8) If the property was seized by an immigration officer, the compensation is to be paid by the Secretary of State.

(9) If an order under paragraph 10G, 10I or 10J is made in respect only of a part of any property detained under this Part, this paragraph has effect in relation to the other part.

(10) This paragraph does not apply if the court or sheriff makes an order under paragraph 10O."

3　In paragraph 19 (general interpretation), in sub-paragraph (1), at the appropriate place insert –

""listed asset" has the meaning given by paragraph 10A,".

SCHEDULE 4　　　　　　　　　　　　　　　　　　　　　　　　　　　　　Section 40

FORFEITURE OF MONEY HELD IN BANK AND BUILDING SOCIETY ACCOUNTS

1　Schedule 1 to the Anti-terrorism, Crime and Security Act 2001 (forfeiture of terrorist cash) is amended as follows.

2　After paragraph 10P (inserted by Schedule 3 above) insert –

APPENDIX: CRIMINAL FINANCES ACT 2017

"**PART 4B**

FORFEITURE OF TERRORIST MONEY HELD IN BANK AND BUILDING SOCIETY ACCOUNTS

Application for account freezing order

10Q (1) This paragraph applies if an enforcement officer has reasonable grounds for suspecting that money held in an account maintained with a bank or building society –

    (a) is within subsection (1)(a) or (b) of section 1, or
    (b) is property earmarked as terrorist property.

(2) Where this paragraph applies the enforcement officer may apply to the relevant court for an account freezing order in relation to the account in which the money is held.

(3) But –

    (a) an enforcement officer may not apply for an account freezing order unless the officer is a senior officer or is authorised to do so by a senior officer, and
    (b) the senior officer must consult the Treasury before making the application for the order or (as the case may be) authorising the application to be made, unless in the circumstances it is not reasonably practicable to do so.

(4) For the purposes of this Part of this Schedule –

    (a) an account freezing order is an order that, subject to any exclusions (see paragraph 10U), prohibits each person by or for whom the account to which the order applies is operated from making withdrawals or payments from the account;
    (b) an account is operated by or for a person if the person is an account holder or a signatory or identified as a beneficiary in relation to the account.

(5) An application for an account freezing order may be made without notice if the circumstances of the case are such that notice of the application would prejudice the taking of any steps under this Part of this Schedule to forfeit money that is within subsection (1)(a) or (b) of section 1 or is property earmarked as terrorist property.

(6) The money referred to in sub-paragraph (1) may be all or part of the credit balance of the account.

(7) In this Part of this Schedule –

"bank" has the meaning given by paragraph 10R;
"building society" has the same meaning as in the Building Societies Act 1986;
"enforcement officer" means –

    (a) a constable, or
    (b) a counter-terrorism financial investigator; "relevant court" –

APPENDIX: CRIMINAL FINANCES ACT 2017

    (a) in England and Wales and Northern Ireland, means a magistrates' court, and

    (b) in Scotland, means the sheriff;

"senior officer" means a police officer of at least the rank of superintendent.

Meaning of "bank"

10R (1) "Bank" means an authorised deposit-taker, other than a building society, that has its head office or a branch in the United Kingdom.

   (2) In sub-paragraph (1), "authorised deposit-taker" means –

     (a) a person who has permission under Part 4A of the Financial Services and Markets Act 2000 to accept deposits;

     (b) a person who –

       (i) is specified, or is within a class of persons specified, by an order under section 38 of that Act (exemption orders), and

       (ii) accepts deposits;

     (c) an EEA firm of the kind mentioned in paragraph 5(b) of Schedule 3 to that Act that has permission under paragraph 15 of that Schedule (as a result of qualifying for authorisation under paragraph 12(1) of that Schedule) to accept deposits.

   (3) A reference in sub-paragraph (2) to a person or firm with permission to accept deposits does not include a person or firm with permission to do so only for the purposes of, or in the course of, an activity other than accepting deposits.

Making of account freezing order

10S (1) This paragraph applies where an application for an account freezing order is made under paragraph 10Q in relation to an account.

   (2) The relevant court may make the order if satisfied that there are reasonable grounds for suspecting that money held in the account (whether all or part of the credit balance of the account) –

     (a) is within subsection (1)(a) or (b) of section 1, or

     (b) is property earmarked as terrorist property.

   (3) An account freezing order ceases to have effect at the end of the period specified in the order (which may be varied under paragraph 10T) unless it ceases to have effect at an earlier or later time in accordance with the provision made by paragraphs 10W(6)(c), 10Y(2) to (7), 10Z2(6) to (8) and 10Z3.

   (4) The period specified by the relevant court for the purposes of sub-paragraph (3) (whether when the order is first made or on a variation under paragraph 10T) may not exceed the period of 2 years, starting with the day on which the account freezing order is (or was) made.

   (5) An account freezing order must provide for notice to be given to persons affected by the order.

APPENDIX: CRIMINAL FINANCES ACT 2017

Variation and setting aside of account freezing order

10T (1) The relevant court may at any time vary or set aside an account freezing order on an application made by –

   (a) an enforcement officer, or
   (b) any person affected by the order.

   (2) But an enforcement officer may not make an application under sub-paragraph (1) unless the officer is a senior officer or is authorised to do so by a senior officer.

   (3) Before varying or setting aside an account freezing order the court must (as well as giving the parties to the proceedings an opportunity to be heard) give such an opportunity to any person who may be affected by its decision.

   (4) In relation to Scotland, the references in this paragraph to setting aside an order are to be read as references to recalling it.

Exclusions

10U (1) The power to vary an account freezing order includes (amongst other things) power to make exclusions from the prohibition on making withdrawals or payments from the account to which the order applies.

   (2) Exclusions from the prohibition may also be made when the order is made.

   (3) An exclusion may (amongst other things) make provision for the purpose of enabling a person by or for whom the account is operated –

   (a) to meet the person's reasonable living expenses, or
   (b) to carry on any trade, business, profession or occupation.

   (4) An exclusion may be made subject to conditions.

   (5) Where a magistrates' court exercises the power to make an exclusion for the purpose of enabling a person to meet legal expenses that the person has incurred, or may incur, in respect of proceedings under this Schedule, it must ensure that the exclusion –

   (a) is limited to reasonable legal expenses that the person has reasonably incurred or that the person reasonably incurs,
   (b) specifies the total amount that may be released for legal expenses in pursuance of the exclusion, and
   (c) is made subject to the same conditions as would be the required conditions (see section 286A of the Proceeds of Crime Act 2002) if the order had been made under section 245A of that Act (in addition to any conditions imposed under sub-paragraph (4)).

   (6) A magistrates' court, in deciding whether to make an exclusion for the purpose of enabling a person to meet legal expenses in respect of proceedings under this Schedule –

   (a) must have regard to the desirability of the person being represented in any proceedings under this Schedule in which the person is a participant, and

(b) must disregard the possibility that legal representation of the person in any such proceedings might, were an exclusion not made –

(i) be made available under arrangements made for the purposes of Part 1 of the Legal Aid, Sentencing and Punishment of Offenders Act 2012, or
(ii) be funded by the Northern Ireland Legal Services Commission.

(7) The sheriff's power to make exclusions may not be exercised for the purpose of enabling any person to meet any legal expenses in respect of proceedings under this Schedule.

(8) The power to make exclusions must, subject to sub-paragraph (6), be exercised with a view to ensuring, so far as practicable, that there is not undue prejudice to the taking of any steps under this Part of this Schedule to forfeit money that is within subsection (1)(a) or (b) of section 1 or is property earmarked as terrorist property.

Restriction on proceedings and remedies

10V (1) If a court in which proceedings are pending in respect of an account maintained with a bank or building society is satisfied that an account freezing order has been applied for or made in respect of the account, it may either stay the proceedings or allow them to continue on any terms it thinks fit.

(2) Before exercising the power conferred by sub-paragraph (1), the court must (as well as giving the parties to any of the proceedings concerned an opportunity to be heard) give such an opportunity to any person who may be affected by the court's decision.

(3) In relation to Scotland, the reference in sub-paragraph (1) to staying the proceedings is to be read as a reference to sisting the proceedings.

Account forfeiture notice

10W (1) This paragraph applies while an account freezing order has effect. In this paragraph the account to which the order applies is "the frozen account".

(2) A senior officer may give a notice for the purpose of forfeiting money held in the frozen account (whether all or part of the credit balance of the account) if satisfied that the money –

(a) is within subsection (1)(a) or (b) of section 1, or
(b) is property earmarked as terrorist property.

(3) A notice given under sub-paragraph (2) is referred to in this Part of this Schedule as an account forfeiture notice.

(4) An account forfeiture notice must –

(a) state the amount of money held in the frozen account which it is proposed be forfeited,
(b) confirm that the senior officer is satisfied as mentioned in sub-paragraph (2),
(c) specify a period for objecting to the proposed forfeiture and an address to which any objections must be sent, and

(d) explain that the money will be forfeited unless an objection is received at that address within the period for objecting.

(5) The period for objecting must be at least 30 days starting with the day after the notice is given.

(6) If no objection is made within the period for objecting, and the notice has not lapsed under paragraph 10Y –

(a) the amount of money stated in the notice is forfeited (subject to paragraph 10Z),

(b) the bank or building society with which the frozen account is maintained must transfer that amount of money into an interest-bearing account nominated by an enforcement officer, and

(c) immediately after the transfer has been made, the account freezing order made in relation to the frozen account ceases to have effect.

(7) An objection may be made by anyone (whether a recipient of the notice or not).

(8) An objection means a written objection sent to the address specified in the notice; and an objection is made when it is received at the address.

(9) An objection does not prevent forfeiture of the money held in the frozen account under paragraph 10Z2.

Giving of account forfeiture notice

10X (1) The Secretary of State must by regulations made by statutory instrument make provision about how an account forfeiture notice is to be given.

(2) The regulations may (amongst other things) provide –

(a) for an account forfeiture notice to be given to such person or persons, and in such manner, as may be prescribed;

(b) for circumstances in which, and the time at which, an account forfeiture notice is to be treated as having been given.

(3) The regulations must ensure that where an account forfeiture notice is given it is, if possible, given to every person to whom notice of the account freezing order was given.

(4) A statutory instrument containing regulations under this paragraph is subject to annulment in pursuance of a resolution of either House of Parliament.

Lapse of account forfeiture notice

10Y (1) An account forfeiture notice lapses if –

(a) an objection is made within the period for objecting specified in the notice under paragraph 10W(4)(c),

(b) an application is made under paragraph 10Z2 for the forfeiture of money held in the frozen account, or

(c) an order is made under paragraph 10T setting aside (or recalling) the relevant account freezing order.

(2) If an account forfeiture notice lapses under sub-paragraph (1)(a), the relevant account freezing order ceases to have effect at the end of the period of 48 hours starting with the making of the objection ("the 48-hour period").
This is subject to sub-paragraphs (3) and (7).

(3) If within the 48-hour period an application is made –

   (a) for a variation of the relevant account freezing order under paragraph 10T so as to extend the period specified in the order, or
   (b) for forfeiture of money held in the frozen account under paragraph 10Z2,
   the order continues to have effect until the relevant time (and then ceases to have effect).

(4) In the case of an application of the kind mentioned in sub-paragraph (3)(a), the relevant time means –

   (a) if an extension is granted, the time determined in accordance with paragraph 10S(3), or
   (b) if an extension is not granted, the time when the application is determined or otherwise disposed of.

(5) In the case of an application of the kind mentioned in sub-paragraph (3)(b), the relevant time is the time determined in accordance with paragraph 10Z2(6).

(6) If within the 48-hour period it is decided that no application of the kind mentioned in sub-paragraph (3)(a) or (b) is to be made, an enforcement officer must, as soon as possible, notify the bank or building society with which the frozen account is maintained of that decision.

(7) If the bank or building society is notified in accordance with sub-paragraph (6) before the expiry of the 48-hour period, the relevant account freezing order ceases to have effect on the bank or building society being so notified.

(8) In relation to an account forfeiture notice –

   (a) "the frozen account" is the account in which the money to which the account forfeiture notice relates is held;
   (b) "the relevant account freezing order" is the account freezing order made in relation to the frozen account.

(9) In calculating a period of 48 hours for the purposes of this paragraph no account is to be taken of –

   (a) any Saturday or Sunday,
   (b) Christmas Day,
   (c) Good Friday, or
   (d) any day that is a bank holiday under the Banking and Financial Dealings Act 1971 in the part of the United Kingdom in which the account freezing order was made.

APPENDIX: CRIMINAL FINANCES ACT 2017

Application to set aside forfeiture

10Z (1) A person aggrieved by the forfeiture of money in pursuance of paragraph 10W(6)(a) may apply to the relevant court for an order setting aside the forfeiture of the money or any part of it.

(2) The application must be made before the end of the period of 30 days starting with the day on which the period for objecting ended ("the 30-day period").

(3) But the relevant court may give permission for an application to be made after the 30-day period has ended if it thinks that there are exceptional circumstances to explain why the applicant –

(a) failed to object to the forfeiture within the period for objecting, and
(b) failed to make an application within the 30-day period.

(4) On an application under this paragraph the relevant court must consider whether the money to which the application relates could be forfeited under paragraph 10Z2 (ignoring the forfeiture mentioned in sub-paragraph (1)).

(5) If the relevant court is satisfied that the money to which the application relates or any part of it could not be forfeited under that paragraph it must set aside the forfeiture of that money or part.

(6) Where the relevant court sets aside the forfeiture of any money –

(a) it must order the release of that money, and
(b) the money is to be treated as never having been forfeited.

(7) Where money is released by virtue of sub-paragraph (6)(a), there must be added to the money on its release any interest accrued on it whilst in the account referred to in paragraph 10W(6)(b).

Application of money forfeited under account forfeiture notice

10Z1(1) Money forfeited in pursuance of paragraph 10W(6)(a), and any interest accrued on it whilst in the account referred to in paragraph 10W(6)(b) –

(a) if, before being forfeited, the money was held in an account in relation to which an account freezing order made by a magistrates' court had effect, is to be paid into the Consolidated Fund;
(b) if, before being forfeited, the money was held in an account in relation to which an account freezing order made by the sheriff had effect, is to be paid into the Scottish Consolidated Fund.

(2) But it is not to be paid in –

(a) before the end of the period within which an application under paragraph 10Z may be made (ignoring the possibility of an application by virtue of paragraph 10Z(3)), or
(b) if an application is made within that period, before the application is determined or otherwise disposed of.

Forfeiture order

10Z2(1) This paragraph applies while an account freezing order has effect. In this paragraph the account to which the account freezing order applies is "the frozen account".

(2) An application for the forfeiture of money held in the frozen account (whether all or part of the credit balance of the account) may be made –

   (a) to a magistrates' court, by an enforcement officer, or
   (b) to the sheriff, by the Scottish Ministers.

(3) The court or sheriff may order the forfeiture of the money or any part of it if satisfied that the money or part –

   (a) is within subsection (1)(a) or (b) of section 1, or
   (b) is property earmarked as terrorist property.

(4) But in the case of property earmarked as terrorist property which belongs to joint tenants, one of whom is an excepted joint owner, an order by a magistrates' court may not apply to so much of it as the court thinks is attributable to the excepted joint owner's share.

(5) For the purposes of sub-paragraph (4) –

   (a) an excepted joint owner is a joint tenant who obtained the property in circumstances in which it would not (as against him or her) be earmarked, and
   (b) references to the excepted joint owner's share of property are to so much of the property as would have been his or hers if the joint tenancy had been severed.

(6) Where an application is made under sub-paragraph (2), the account freezing order is to continue to have effect until the time referred to in sub-paragraph (7)(b) or (8).
But sub-paragraphs (7)(b) and (8) are subject to paragraph 10Z3.

(7) Where money held in a frozen account is ordered to be forfeited under sub-paragraph (3) –

   (a) the bank or building society with which the frozen account is maintained must transfer that amount of money into an interest-bearing account nominated by an enforcement officer, and
   (b) immediately after the transfer has been made the account freezing order made in relation to the frozen account ceases to have effect.

(8) Where, other than by the making of an order under sub-paragraph (3), an application under sub-paragraph (2) is determined or otherwise disposed of, the account freezing order ceases to have effect immediately after that determination or other disposal.

Continuation of account freezing order pending appeal

10Z3(1) This paragraph applies where, on an application under sub- paragraph (2) of paragraph 10Z2 in relation to an account to which an account freezing order applies, the court or sheriff decides –

   (a) to make an order under sub-paragraph (3) of that paragraph in relation to part only of the money to which the application related, or

APPENDIX: CRIMINAL FINANCES ACT 2017

(b) not to make an order under sub-paragraph (3) of that paragraph.

(2) The person who made the application under paragraph 10Z2(2) may apply without notice to the court or sheriff that made the decision referred to in sub-paragraph (1)(a) or (b) for an order that the account freezing order is to continue to have effect.

(3) Where the court or sheriff makes an order under sub-paragraph

(2) the account freezing order is to continue to have effect until –

(a) the end of the period of 48 hours starting with the making of the order under sub-paragraph (2), or
(b) if within that period of 48 hours an appeal is brought under paragraph 10Z4 against the decision referred to in sub-paragraph (1)(a) or (b), the time when the appeal is determined or otherwise disposed of.

(4) Sub-paragraph (9) of paragraph 10Y applies for the purposes of sub-paragraph (3) as it applies for the purposes of that paragraph.

Appeal against decision under paragraph 10Z2

10Z4(1) Any party to proceedings for an order for the forfeiture of money under paragraph 10Z2 who is aggrieved by an order under that paragraph or by the decision of the court not to make such an order may appeal –

(a) from an order or decision of a magistrates' court in England and Wales, to the Crown Court;
(b) from an order or decision of the sheriff, to the Sheriff Appeal Court;
(c) from an order or decision of a magistrates' court in Northern Ireland, to a county court.

(2) An appeal under sub-paragraph (1) must be made before the end of the period of 30 days starting with the day on which the court makes the order or decision.
(3) Sub-paragraph (2) is subject to paragraph 10Z5.
(4) The court hearing the appeal may make any order it thinks appropriate.
(5) If the court upholds an appeal against an order forfeiting the money, it may order the release of the whole or any part of the money.
(6) Where money is released by virtue of sub-paragraph (5), there must be added to the money on its release any interest accrued on it whilst in the account referred to in paragraph 10Z2(7)(a).

Extended time for appealing in certain cases where deproscription order made

10Z5(1) This paragraph applies where –

(a) a successful application for an order under paragraph 10Z2 relies (wholly or partly) on the fact that an organisation is proscribed,

APPENDIX: CRIMINAL FINANCES ACT 2017

(b) an application under section 4 of the Terrorism Act 2000 for a deproscription order in respect of the organisation is refused by the Secretary of State,

(c) the money forfeited by the order under paragraph 10Z2 was made subject to an account freezing order on or after the date of the refusal of that application,

(d) an appeal against that refusal is allowed under section 5 of the Terrorism Act 2000,

(e) a deproscription order is made accordingly, and

(f) if the order is made in reliance on section 123(5) of the Terrorism Act 2000, a resolution is passed by each House of Parliament under section 123(5)(b) of that Act.

(2) Where this paragraph applies, an appeal under paragraph 10Z4 against the making of an order under paragraph 10Z2 may be brought at any time before the end of the period of 30 days beginning with the date on which the deproscription order comes into force.

(3) In this paragraph a "deproscription order" means an order under section 3(3)(b) or (8) of the Terrorism Act 2000.

Application of money forfeited under account forfeiture order

10Z6(1) Money forfeited by an order under paragraph 10Z2, and any interest accrued on it whilst in the account referred to in sub- paragraph (7)(a) of that paragraph –

(a) if forfeited by a magistrates' court, is to be paid into the Consolidated Fund, and

(b) if forfeited by the sheriff, is to be paid into the Scottish Consolidated Fund.

(2) But it is not to be paid in –

(a) before the end of the period within which an appeal under paragraph 10Z4 may be made, or

Compensation

(b) if a person appeals under that paragraph, before the appeal is determined or otherwise disposed of.

10Z7(1) This paragraph applies if –

(a) an account freezing order is made, and

(b) none of the money held in the account to which the order applies is forfeited in pursuance of an account forfeiture notice or by an order under paragraph 10Z2.

(2) Where this paragraph applies a person by or for whom the account to which the account freezing order applies is operated may make an application to the relevant court for compensation.

(3) If the relevant court is satisfied that the applicant has suffered loss as a result of the making of the account freezing order and that the circumstances are exceptional, the relevant court may order compensation to be paid to the applicant.
(4) The amount of compensation to be paid is the amount the relevant court thinks reasonable, having regard to the loss suffered and any other relevant circumstances.
(5) If the account freezing order was applied for by a constable, the compensation is to be paid as follows –

(a) in the case of a constable of a police force in England and Wales, it is to be paid out of the police fund from which the expenses of the police force are met;
(b) in the case of a constable of the Police Service of Scotland, it is to be paid by the Scottish Police Authority;
(c) in the case of a police officer within the meaning of the Police (Northern Ireland) Act 2000, it is to be paid out of money provided by the Chief Constable of the Police Service of Northern Ireland.

(6) If the account freezing order was applied for by a counter- terrorism financial investigator, the compensation is to be paid as follows –

(a) in the case of an investigator who was –

(i) a member of the civilian staff of a police force (including the metropolitan police force), within the meaning of Part 1 of the Police Reform and Social Responsibility Act 2011, or
(ii) a member of staff of the City of London police force, it is to be paid out of the police fund from which the expenses of the police force are met;

(b) in the case of an investigator who was a member of staff of the Police Service of Northern Ireland, it is to be paid out of money provided by the Chief Constable of the Police Service of Northern Ireland."

3 (1) Paragraph 19 (general interpretation) is amended as follows.
  (2) In sub-paragraph (1), at the appropriate places insert –

""account forfeiture notice" (in Part 4B) has the meaning given by paragraph 10W(3),";
""account freezing order" (in Part 4B) has the meaning given by paragraph 10Q(4)(a),";
""bank" (in Part 4B) has the meaning given by paragraph 10R,";
"building society" (in Part 4B) has the meaning given by paragraph 10Q(7),";
""enforcement officer" (in Part 4B) has the meaning given by paragraph 10Q(7),";
"relevant court" (in Part 4B) has the meaning given by paragraph 10Q(7),";
""senior officer" (in Part 4B) has the meaning given by paragraph 10Q(7),".

  (3) After sub-paragraph (6) insert –

"(7) References (in Part 4B) to an account being operated by or for a person are to be read in accordance with paragraph 10Q(4)(b)."

APPENDIX: CRIMINAL FINANCES ACT 2017

Schedule 5   Section 53

Minor and consequential amendments

Prescription and Limitation (Scotland) Act 1973 (c. 52)

1   In section 19B of the Prescription and Limitation (Scotland) Act 1973 (actions for recovery of property obtained through unlawful conduct etc), after subsection (4) insert –

"(4A) Subsection (4) is subject to section 13(5) of the Criminal Finances Act 2017 (which provides that, in the case of property obtained through unlawful conduct relating to a gross human rights abuse or violation, proceedings cannot be brought after the end of the period of 20 years from the date on which the conduct constituting the commission of the abuse or violation occurs)."

Limitation Act 1980 (c. 58)

2   (1) Section 27A of the Limitation Act 1980 (actions for recovery of property obtained through unlawful conduct etc) is amended as follows.

(2) After subsection (4) insert –

"(4A) Subsection (4) is subject to section 13(5) of the Criminal Finances Act 2017 (which provides that, in the case of property obtained through unlawful conduct relating to a gross human rights abuse or violation, proceedings cannot be brought after the end of the period of 20 years from the date on which the conduct constituting the commission of the abuse or violation occurs)."

(3) In subsection (8), after paragraph (d) insert –

"(e) Her Majesty's Revenue and Customs, or
(f)   the Financial Conduct Authority."

Civil Jurisdiction and Judgments Act 1982 (c. 27)

3   (1) Section 18 of the Civil Jurisdiction and Judgments Act 1982 (enforcement of UK judgments in other parts of UK) is amended as follows.

(2) In subsection (2)(f), at the end insert "or an unexplained wealth order made under that Part (see sections 362A and 396A of that Act)".

(3) In subsection (2)(g) –

(a) after "investigation" insert ", a detained property investigation or a frozen funds investigation";
(b) for "meaning" substitute "meanings".

(4) In subsection (3) for "and (4ZA)" substitute ", (4ZA) and (4ZB)".

(5) After subsection (4ZA) insert –

"(4ZB) This section applies to the following orders made by a magistrates' court in England and Wales or Northern Ireland –

(a) an account freezing order made under section 303Z3 of the Proceeds of Crime Act 2002;

(b) an order for the forfeiture of money made under section 303Z14 of that Act;

(c) an account freezing order made under paragraph 10S of Schedule 1 to the Anti-terrorism, Crime and Security Act 2001;

(d) an order for the forfeiture of money made under paragraph 10Z2 of that Schedule."

(6) In subsection (5)(d), for the words after "measure" substitute "other than an order of any of the following kinds –

(i) a freezing order of the kind mentioned in paragraph

or (c) of subsection (4ZB) made (in Scotland) by the sheriff (in addition to such orders made by a magistrates' court in England and Wales or Northern Ireland);

(ii) an order for the making of an interim payment;

(iii) an interim order made in connection with the civil recovery of proceeds of unlawful conduct;

(iv) an interim freezing order under section 362J of the Proceeds of Crime Act 2002;

(v) an interim freezing order under section 396J of that Act."

Criminal Justice Act 1987 (c. 38)

4   In section 1 of the Criminal Justice Act 1987 (establishment of the Serious Fraud Office), in subsection (6A) –

(a) for "Part 5" substitute "Part 2, 4, 5, 7";

(b) for the words in brackets substitute "confiscation proceedings in England and Wales and Northern Ireland, civil recovery proceedings, money laundering and investigations".

Limitation (Northern Ireland) Order 1989 (S.I. 1989/1339 (N.I. 11))

5   In Article 72A of the Limitation (Northern Ireland) Order 1989 (actions for recovery of property obtained through unlawful conduct etc), after paragraph (4) insert –

"(4A) Paragraph (4) is subject to section 13(5) of the Criminal Finances Act 2017 (which provides that, in the case of property obtained through unlawful conduct relating to a gross human rights abuse or violation, proceedings cannot be brought after the end of the period of 20 years from the date on which the conduct constituting the commission of the abuse or violation occurs)."

Data Protection Act 1998 (c. 29)

6   The Data Protection Act 1998 is amended as follows.

7   In Schedule 2 (conditions relevant for purposes of the first principle: processing of any personal data), after paragraph 6 insert –

"7   The processing is necessary for the purposes of making a disclosure in good faith under a power conferred by –

(a) section 21CA of the Terrorism Act 2000 (disclosures between certain entities within regulated sector in relation to suspicion of commission of terrorist financing offence or for purposes of identifying terrorist property), or

(b) section 339ZB of the Proceeds of Crime Act 2002 (disclosures between certain entities within regulated sector in relation to money laundering suspicion)."

8   In Schedule 3 (conditions relevant for purposes of the first principle: processing of sensitive personal data), after paragraph 7A insert –

"7B   The processing is necessary for the purposes of making a disclosure in good faith under a power conferred by –

(a) section 21CA of the Terrorism Act 2000 (disclosures between certain entities within regulated sector in relation to suspicion of commission of terrorist financing offence or for purposes of identifying terrorist property), or

(b) section 339ZB of the Proceeds of Crime Act 2002 (disclosures within regulated sector in relation to money laundering suspicion)."

Terrorism Act 2000 (c. 11)

9   The Terrorism Act 2000 is amended as follows.

10   In section 21G (tipping off: other permitted disclosures) –

(a) omit "or" at the end of paragraph (a);

(b) after that paragraph insert –

"(aa) made in good faith by virtue of section 21CA (disclosures within the regulated sector); or".

11   In section 115 (officers' powers) –

(a) for "sections 25 to 31" substitute "Schedule 1 to the Anti-terrorism, Crime and Security Act 2001 (forfeiture of terrorist property)";

(b) after "Schedule 7" insert "to this Act (port and border controls)".

12 In section 121 (interpretation), insert at the appropriate place –

"" "counter-terrorism financial investigator" is to be read in accordance with section 63F;".

13 In Schedule 14 (exercise of officers' powers) –

(a) for "terrorist cash", in each place, substitute "terrorist property";
(b) in paragraph 1(a), after "provisions" insert "(including when referred to in those provisions as an "enforcement officer" or a "senior officer")".

Anti-terrorism, Crime and Security Act 2001 (c. 24)

14 The Anti-terrorism, Crime and Security Act 2001 is amended as follows.
15 (1) Section 1 (forfeiture of terrorist cash) is amended as follows.
(2) In the heading, for "cash" substitute "property".
(3) In subsection (1), in the words before paragraph (a), for "cash" substitute "property".
(4) In subsection (2) –

(a) for "any cash" substitute "property";
(b) for "the cash" substitute "the property".

16 (1) Schedule 1 (forfeiture of terrorist cash) is amended as follows.
(2) In the heading of the Schedule, for "cash" substitute "property".
(3) In the heading of Part 1, after "Introductory" insert ": forfeiture of terrorist cash".
(4) In paragraph 1(1), after "Schedule" insert "(other than Parts 4A and 4B)".
(5) In the heading of Part 2, after "Detention" insert "of terrorist cash".
(6) In paragraph 3(3A), in the words before paragraph (a), after "application to" insert "a magistrates' court,".
(7) In paragraph 5, in sub-paragraph (1), for "this Schedule" substitute "any provision of this Schedule other than Part 2A".
(8) In that paragraph, omit sub-paragraph (4).
(9) In the heading of Part 3, after "Forfeiture" insert "of terrorist cash".
(10) In paragraph 8(1), for "this Schedule" substitute "paragraph 6".
(11) In the heading of Part 4, after "Miscellaneous" insert ": terrorist cash".
(12) After paragraph 9 insert – "*Restrictions on release*

9A Cash is not to be released under any power or duty conferred or imposed by this Schedule (and so is to continue to be detained) –

(a) if an application for its forfeiture under paragraph 6, or for its release under paragraph 9, is made, until any proceedings in pursuance of the application (including any proceedings on appeal) are concluded;
(b) if (in the United Kingdom or elsewhere) proceedings are started against any person for an offence with which the cash is connected, until the proceedings are concluded."

(13) In paragraph 10, in sub-paragraph (1) after "Schedule," insert "and the cash is not otherwise forfeited in pursuance of a cash forfeiture notice,".

(14) In that paragraph, after sub-paragraph (8) insert –

"(8A) If any cash is detained under this Schedule and part only of the cash is forfeited in pursuance of a cash forfeiture notice, this paragraph has effect in relation to the other part."

(15) After paragraph 10Z8 (inserted by section 42) insert –

"PART 4D

PROCEEDINGS UNDER THIS SCHEDULE

Powers for prosecutors to appear in proceedings

10Z9(1) The Director of Public Prosecutions or the Director of Public Prosecutions for Northern Ireland may appear for a person mentioned in sub-paragraph (2) in proceedings under this Schedule if the Director –

(a) is asked by, or on behalf of, the person to do so, and
(b) considers it appropriate to do so.

(2) The persons referred to in sub-paragraph (1) are –

(a) a constable;
(b) a counter-terrorism financial investigator;
(c) the Commissioners for Her Majesty's Revenue and Customs;
(d) an officer of Revenue and Customs;
(e) an immigration officer.

(3) The Director of Public Prosecutions may authorise a person (generally or specifically) to carry out the functions of the Director under sub-paragraph (1) if the person is –

(a) a member of the Director's staff;
(b) a person providing services under arrangements made by the Director.

(4) The Director of Public Prosecutions and the Director of Public Prosecutions for Northern Ireland may charge fees for the provision of services under this paragraph."

Proceeds of Crime Act 2002 (c. 29)

17 The Proceeds of Crime Act 2002 is amended as follows.

18 (1) Section 2A (contribution to the reduction of crime) is amended as follows.

(2) In subsection (2) –

(a) omit "or" before paragraph (e);
(b) after paragraph (e) insert –

"(f) Her Majesty's Revenue and Customs, or
(g) the Financial Conduct Authority."

(3) In subsection (3) –

    (a) omit "and" at the end of paragraph (b);
    (b) after paragraph (c) insert ", and
    (d) in the case of Her Majesty's Revenue and Customs or the Financial Conduct Authority, the Treasury."

19 (1) Section 2C (prosecuting authorities) is amended as follows.
(2) In subsection (2), after "5," insert "7".
(3) In subsection (3A), after "302A" insert ", 303X or 303Z19".

20 In section 7 (recoverable amount for purposes of confiscation order in England and Wales), in subsection (4) –

    (a) in paragraph (b), after "section 297A" insert "or an account forfeiture notice under section 303Z9";
    (b) omit "and" at the end of paragraph (b);
    (c) in paragraph (c), after "298(2)" insert ", 303O(3), 303R(3) or 303Z14(4)";
    (d) after paragraph (c) insert ", and
    (d) any property which is the forfeitable property in relation to an order under section 303Q(1)."

21 In section 47G (appropriate approval for exercise of search and seizure powers in England and Wales), in subsection (3)(c), after "investigator", in the first place it occurs, insert "who does not fall within any of the preceding paragraphs".

22 (1) Section 82 (meaning of free property for purposes of Part 2) is amended as follows.
(2) In subsection (2)(f), for "or 298(2)" substitute ", 298(2), 303L(1), 303O(3), 303R(3), 303Z3 or 303Z14(4)".
(3) In subsection (3) –

    (a) in paragraph (a), after "section 297A" insert "or an account forfeiture notice under section 303Z9";
    (b) in paragraph (b) (as amended by section 34(2) of this Act), for "or 298(4)" substitute ", 298(4) or 303O(9)";
    (c) after paragraph (b) insert –

        "(c) it is the forfeitable property in relation to an order under section 303Q(1)."

23 In section 93 (recoverable amount for purposes of confiscation order in Scotland), in subsection (4) –

    (a) in paragraph (b), after "section 297A" insert "or an account forfeiture notice under section 303Z9";
    (b) omit "and" at the end of paragraph (b);
    (c) in paragraph (c), after "298(2)" insert ", 303O(3), 303R(3) or 303Z14(4)";
    (d) after paragraph (c) insert ", and
    (d) any property which is the forfeitable property in relation to an order under section 303Q(1)."

APPENDIX: CRIMINAL FINANCES ACT 2017

24 (1) Section 148 (meaning of free property for purposes of Part 3) is amended as follows.

(2) In subsection (2)(f), for "or 298(2)" substitute ", 298(2), 303L(1), 303O(3), 303R(3), 303Z3 or 303Z14(4)".

(3) In subsection (3) –

(a) in paragraph (a), after "section 297A" insert "or an account forfeiture notice under section 303Z9";

(b) in paragraph (b) (as amended by section 34(3) of this Act), for "or 298(4)" substitute ", 298(4) or 303O(9)";

(c) after paragraph (b) insert –

"(c) it is the forfeitable property in relation to an order under section 303Q(1)."

25 In section 157 (recoverable amount for purposes of confiscation order in Northern Ireland), in subsection (4) –

(a) in paragraph (b), after "section 297A" insert "or an account forfeiture notice under section 303Z9";

(b) omit "and" at the end of paragraph (b);

(c) in paragraph (c), after "298(2)" insert ", 303O(3), 303R(3) or 303Z14(4)";

(d) after paragraph (c) insert ", and

(d) any property which is the forfeitable property in relation to an order under section 303Q(1)."

26 In section 195G (appropriate approval for exercise of search and seizure powers in Northern Ireland), in subsection (3)(c), after "investigator", in the first place it occurs, insert "who does not fall within any of the preceding paragraphs".

27 (1) Section 230 (meaning of free property for purposes of Part 4) is amended as follows.

(2) In subsection (2)(f), for "or 298(2)" substitute ", 298(2), 303L(1), 303O(3), 303R(3), 303Z3 or 303Z14(4)".

(3) In subsection (3) –

(a) in paragraph (a), after "section 297A" insert "or an account forfeiture notice under section 303Z9";

(b) in paragraph (b) (as amended by section 34(4) of this Act), for "or 298(4)" substitute ", 298(4) or 303O(9)";

(c) after paragraph (b) insert –

"(c) it is the forfeitable property in relation to an order under section 303Q(1)."

28 In section 240 (general purpose of Part 5), in subsection (1)(b) –

(a) for "cash" substitute "property";

(b) at the end insert "and, in certain circumstances, to be forfeited by the giving of a notice".

APPENDIX: CRIMINAL FINANCES ACT 2017

29   In section 241 ("unlawful conduct"), in subsection (3)(b), for "cash" substitute "property".

30 (1) Section 278 (limit on recovery) is amended as follows.

    (2) In subsection (6A) –

        (a) in paragraph (a), after "section 297A" insert "or an account forfeiture notice under section 303Z9";

        (b) in the words after paragraph (b), for "forfeiture notice" substitute "notice".

    (3) In subsection (7) –

        (a) in paragraph (a), after "section 298" insert ", 303O or 303Z14";

        (b) in the words after paragraph (b), for "section 298" substitute "that section".

    (4) After subsection (7) insert – "(7A) If –

        (a) an order is made under section 303Q instead of an order being made under section 303O for the forfeiture of recoverable property, and

        (b) the enforcement authority subsequently seeks a recovery order in respect of related property, the order under section 303Q is to be treated for the purposes of this section as if it were a recovery order obtained by the enforcement authority in respect of the property that was the forfeitable property in relation to the order under section 303Q."

31   In section 289 (searches), in subsection (5)(b) for "a customs officer" substitute "an officer of Revenue and Customs".

32 (1) Section 290 (prior approval) is amended as follows.

(2) In subsection (4)(c), after "investigator", in the first place it occurs, insert "who does not fall within any of the preceding paragraphs".

(3) After subsection (6) insert –

    "(6A) But the duty in subsection (6) does not apply if, during the course of exercising the powers conferred by section 289, the relevant officer seizes property by virtue of section 303J and the property so seized is detained for more than 48 hours (calculated in accordance with section 303K(5))."

33   In section 302 (compensation), in subsection (7A), for "or a constable" substitute ", a constable, an SFO officer or a National Crime Agency officer".

34 (1) Section 311 (insolvency) is amended as follows.

    (2) After subsection (2) insert –

        "(2A) An application for an order for the further detention of any property to which subsection (3) applies may not be made under section 303L unless the appropriate court gives leave.

        (2B) An application for the making of an account freezing order under section 303Z3 in respect of an account in which is held money to which subsection (3) applies, or an application under section 303Z4 for the extension of the period specified in such an order, may not be made unless the appropriate court gives leave."

(3) In subsection (4), after "recovery order" insert ", or to apply for an account freezing order under section 303Z3,".

35 In section 312 (performance of functions of Scottish Ministers by constables in Scotland: excluded functions), in subsection (2), after paragraph (j) insert –

"(k) section 303B(3) (listed asset);
(l) section 303H(1) (code of practice);
(m) section 303O(1)(b) (forfeiture);
(n) section 303Y(3) (minimum value);
(o) section 303Z8(3) (minimum amount);
(p) section 303Z14(2)(b) (forfeiture)."

36 (1) Section 316 (general interpretation of Part 5) is amended as follows.
(2) In subsection (1) –

(a) in the definition of "associated property", after "property"" insert "(in Chapter 2)";
(b) in the definition of "court", for "Chapter 3" substitute "Chapters 3, 3A and 3B";
(c) at the appropriate places insert –

""account forfeiture notice" (in Chapter 3B) has the meaning given by section 303Z9(3),";
""account freezing order" (in Chapter 3B) has the meaning given by section 303Z1(3)(a),";
""bank" (in Chapter 3B) has the meaning given by section 303Z7,";
""building society" (in Chapter 3B) has the meaning given by section 303Z1(6),";
""enforcement officer" (in Chapter 3B) has the meaning given by section 303Z1(6),";
""listed asset" (in Chapter 3A) has the meaning given by section 303B,";
""the minimum amount" (in Chapter 3B) has the meaning given by section 303Z8,";
""the minimum value" (in Chapter 3A) has the meaning given by section 303Y,";
""relevant court" (in Chapter 3B) has the meaning given by section 303Z1(6),";
""relevant officer" (in Chapter 3A) has the meaning given by section 303C(9),";
""senior officer" (in Chapter 3B) has the meaning given by section 303Z2(4),".

(3) After subsection (9) insert –

"(10) References (in Chapter 3B) to an account being operated by or for a person are to be read in accordance with section 303Z1(3)(b)."

37 (1) Section 333D (tipping off: other permitted disclosures) is amended as follows.
(2) In subsection (1) –

(a) omit "or" at the end of paragraph (a);

APPENDIX: CRIMINAL FINANCES ACT 2017

  (b) after that paragraph insert –

    "(aa) for the purposes of proceedings under section 336A (power of court to extend moratorium period);

    (ab) made in good faith by virtue of section 339ZB (disclosures within the regulated sector); or".

(3) After subsection (1) insert –

"(1A) Where an application is made to extend a moratorium period under section 336A, a person does not commit an offence under section 333A if –

 (a) the disclosure is made to a customer or client of the person,

 (b) the customer or client appears to the person making the disclosure to have an interest in the relevant property, and

 (c) the disclosure contains only such information as is necessary for the purposes of notifying the customer or client that the application under section 336A has been made.

"Moratorium period" and "relevant property" have the meanings given in section 336D."

38 In section 340 (Part 7: interpretation), after subsection (14) insert –

"(15) "Further information order" means an order made under section 339ZH."

39 (1) Section 341 (investigations for purposes of Part 8) is amended as follows.

  (2) In subsection (3) –

   (a) omit "or" at the end of paragraph (c);

   (b) in paragraph (d), after "295" insert ", 303K or 303L";

   (c) at the end of paragraph (d) insert ", or

   (e) property held in an account in relation to which an account freezing order made under section 303Z3 has effect."

  (3) After subsection (3A) insert –

"(3B) For the purposes of this Part a detained property investigation is an investigation for the purposes of Chapter 3A of Part 5 into –

 (a) the derivation of property detained under that Chapter, or a part of such property, or

 (b) whether property detained under that Chapter, or a part of such property, is intended by any person to be used in unlawful conduct.

(3C) For the purposes of this Part a frozen funds investigation is an investigation for the purposes of Chapter 3B of Part 5 into –

 (a) the derivation of money held in an account in relation to which an account freezing order made under section 303Z3 has effect (a "frozen account") or of a part of such money, or

(b) whether money held in a frozen account, or a part of such money, is intended by any person to be used in unlawful conduct."

40 In section 342 (offences of prejudicing investigation), in subsection (1), after "a detained cash investigation" insert ", a detained property investigation, a frozen funds investigation".

41 In section 343 (judges), in subsection (2), for "or a detained cash investigation" substitute ", a detained cash investigation, a detained property investigation or a frozen funds investigation".

42 In section 344 (courts), in paragraph (a), for "or a detained cash investigation" substitute ", a detained cash investigation, a detained property investigation or a frozen funds investigation".

43 In section 345 (production orders), in subsection (2)(b), for "or a detained cash investigation" substitute ", a detained cash investigation, a detained property investigation or a frozen funds investigation".

44 In section 346 (requirements for making of production order), in subsection (2), after paragraph (bb) insert –

"(bc) in the case of a detained property investigation into the derivation of property, the property the application for the order specifies as being subject to the investigation, or a part of it, is recoverable property;

(bd) in the case of a detained property investigation into the intended use of property, the property the application for the order specifies as being subject to the investigation, or a part of it, is intended by any person to be used in unlawful conduct;

(be) in the case of a frozen funds investigation into the derivation of money held in an account in relation to which an account freezing order made under section 303Z3 has effect (a "frozen account"), the property the application for the order specifies as being subject to the investigation, or a part of it, is recoverable property;

(bf) in the case of a frozen funds investigation into the intended use of money held in a frozen account, the property the application for the order specifies as being subject to the investigation, or a part of it, is intended by any person to be used in unlawful conduct;".

45 In section 350 (government departments), in subsection (5)(a), for "or a detained cash investigation" substitute ", a detained cash investigation, a detained property investigation or a frozen funds investigation".

46 In section 351 (production orders: supplementary), for subsection (5) substitute –

"(5) An application to discharge or vary a production order or an order to grant entry need not be made by the same appropriate officer that applied for the order (but must be made by an appropriate officer of the same description).

(5A) If the application for the order was, by virtue of an order under section 453, made by an accredited financial investigator of a particular description, the reference in subsection (5) to an appropriate officer of the same description is to another accredited financial investigator of that description."

47 (1) Section 352 (search and seizure warrants) is amended as follows.

(2) In subsection (2)(b), for "or a detained cash investigation" substitute ", a detained cash investigation, a detained property investigation or a frozen funds investigation".

(3) In subsection (5) –

    (a) at the beginning of paragraph (b) insert "a Financial Conduct Authority officer,";

    (b) in that paragraph, after "National Crime Agency officer" insert ", an officer of Revenue and Customs";

    (c) in paragraph (c), after "constable," insert "an SFO officer,";

    (d) after paragraph (c) insert –

"(ca) a constable, an SFO officer, an accredited financial investigator or an officer of Revenue and Customs, if the warrant is sought for the purposes of a detained property investigation;

(cb) a constable, an SFO officer, an accredited financial investigator or an officer of Revenue and Customs, if the warrant is sought for the purposes of a frozen funds investigation;".

(4) In subsection (7), for "paragraph (c)" substitute "paragraphs (c), (ca) and (cb)".

48 (1) Section 353 (requirements where production order not available) is amended as follows.

(2) In subsection (2), after paragraph (bb) insert –

"(bc) in the case of a detained property investigation into the derivation of property, the property specified in the application for the warrant, or a part of it, is recoverable property;

(bd) in the case of a detained property investigation into the intended use of property, the property specified in the application for the warrant, or a part of it, is intended by any person to be used in unlawful conduct;

(be) in the case of a frozen funds investigation into the derivation of money held in an account in relation to which an account freezing order made under section 303Z3 has effect (a "frozen account"), the property specified in the application for the warrant, or a part of it, is recoverable property;

(bf) in the case of a frozen funds investigation into the intended use of money held in a frozen account, the property specified in the application for the warrant, or a part of it, is intended by any person to be used in unlawful conduct;".

(3) In subsection (5)(a), after "(7B)" insert ", (7C), (7D), (7E), (7F)".

(4) After subsection (7B) insert –

"(7C) In the case of a detained property investigation into the derivation of property, material falls within this subsection if it cannot be identified at the time of the application but it –

    (a) relates to the property specified in the application, the question whether the property, or a part of it, is recoverable property or any other question as to its derivation, and

APPENDIX: CRIMINAL FINANCES ACT 2017

(b) is likely to be of substantial value (whether or not by itself) to the investigation for the purposes of which the warrant is sought.

(7D) In the case of a detained property investigation into the intended use of property, material falls within this subsection if it cannot be identified at the time of the application but it –

(a) relates to the property specified in the application or the question whether the property, or a part of it, is intended by any person to be used in unlawful conduct, and

(b) is likely to be of substantial value (whether or not by itself) to the investigation for the purposes of which the warrant is sought.

(7E) In the case of a frozen funds investigation into the derivation of money held in a frozen account, material falls within this subsection if it cannot be identified at the time of the application but it –

(a) relates to the property specified in the application, the question whether the property, or a part of it, is recoverable property or any other question as to its derivation, and

(b) is likely to be of substantial value (whether or not by itself) to the investigation for the purposes of which the warrant is sought.

(7F) In the case of a frozen funds investigation into the intended use of money held in a frozen account, material falls within this subsection if it cannot be identified at the time of the application but it –

(a) relates to the property specified in the application or the question whether the property, or a part of it, is intended by any person to be used in unlawful conduct, and

(b) is likely to be of substantial value (whether or not by itself) to the investigation for the purposes of which the warrant is sought."

(5) In subsection (10) –

(a) at the beginning of paragraph (b) insert "a Financial Conduct Authority officer,";
in that paragraph, after "National Crime Agency officer" insert ", an officer of Revenue and Customs";

(c) in paragraph (c), after "constable," insert "an SFO officer,";

(d) after paragraph (c) insert –

"(ca) a constable, an SFO officer, an accredited financial investigator or an officer of Revenue and Customs, if the warrant is sought for the purposes of a detained property investigation;

(cb) a constable, an SFO officer, an accredited financial investigator or an officer of Revenue and Customs, if the warrant is sought for the purposes of a frozen funds investigation;".

(6) In subsection (11), for "paragraph (c)" substitute "paragraphs (c), (ca) and (cb)".

49 (1) Section 355 (further provisions: confiscation and money laundering) is amended as follows.
 (2) In the heading, for "and money laundering" substitute ", money laundering, detained cash, detained property and frozen funds investigations".
 (3) In subsection (1)(a), for "or a detained cash investigation" substitute ", a detained cash investigation, a detained property investigation or a frozen funds investigation".

50 In section 356 (further provisions: civil recovery), in the heading, at the end insert "and exploitation proceeds investigations".

51 (1) Section 357 (disclosure orders) is amended as follows.
 (2) In subsection (2), after "detained cash investigation" insert ", a detained property investigation or a frozen funds investigation".
 (3) In subsection (7), in paragraph (b) –
   (a) after "investigation," insert "a Financial Conduct Authority officer,";
   (b) after "National Crime Agency officer" insert ", an officer of Revenue and Customs".

52 In section 363 (customer information orders), in subsection (1A), at the end insert ", a detained property investigation or a frozen funds investigation".

53 (1) Section 369 (customer information orders: supplementary) is amended as follows.
 (2) For subsection (5) substitute –

   "(5) An application to discharge or vary a customer information order need not be made by the same appropriate officer that applied for the order (but must be made by an appropriate officer of the same description).
   (5A) If the application for the order was, by virtue of an order under section 453, made by an accredited financial investigator of a particular description, the reference in subsection (5) to an appropriate officer of the same description is to another accredited financial investigator of that description."

 (3) In subsection (7) –
   (a) after "National Crime Agency officer," insert "a Financial Conduct Authority officer,";
   (b) after "constable" insert ", an SFO officer".

54 In section 370 (account monitoring orders), in subsection (1A), at the end insert ", a detained property investigation or a frozen funds investigation".

55 In section 375 (account monitoring orders: supplementary), for subsection (4) substitute –

   "(4) An application to discharge or vary an account monitoring order need not be made by the same appropriate officer that applied for the order (but must be made by an appropriate officer of the same description).
   (4A) If the application for the order was, by virtue of an order under section 453, made by an accredited financial investigator of a particular description, the

APPENDIX: CRIMINAL FINANCES ACT 2017

reference in subsection (4) to an appropriate officer of the same description is to another accredited financial investigator of that description."

56 (1) Section 375A (evidence overseas) is amended as follows.
   (2) In subsection (1), after "detained cash investigation" insert ", a detained property investigation, a frozen funds investigation".
   (3) In subsection (5), after paragraph (b) insert –

   "(ba) in relation to an application or request made for the purposes of a detained property investigation, evidence as to a matter described in section 341(3B)(a) or (b);
   (bb) in relation to an application or request made for the purposes of a frozen funds investigation, evidence as to a matter described in section 341(3C)(a) or (b);".

57 In section 375B (evidence overseas: restrictions on use), in subsection (3), after paragraph (b) insert –

   "(ba) if the request was made for the purposes of a detained property investigation, proceedings under Chapter 3A of Part 5 of this Act arising out of the investigation;
   (bb) if the request was made for the purposes of a frozen funds investigation, proceedings under Chapter 3B of Part 5 of this Act arising out of the investigation;".

58 (1) Section 377 (code of practice of Secretary of State) is amended as follows.
   (2) In subsection (1) after paragraph (f) insert – "(g) Financial Conduct Authority officers."
   (3) After subsection (2) insert –

   "(2A) The Secretary of State must also consult the Treasury about the draft in its application to functions that Financial Conduct Authority officers have under this Chapter."

   (4) In subsection (3) for "subsection (2)" insert "subsections (2) and (2A)".

59 In section 378 (officers), after subsection (3B) insert –

   "(3C) In relation to a detained property investigation these are appropriate officers –

   (a) a constable;
   (b) an SFO officer;
   (c) an accredited financial investigator who falls within a description specified in an order made for the purposes of this paragraph by the Secretary of State under section 453;
   (d) an officer of Revenue and Customs.

   (3D) In relation to a detained property investigation these are senior appropriate officers –

   (a) a police officer who is not below the rank of inspector;
   (b) the Director of the Serious Fraud Office;

(c) an accredited financial investigator who falls within a description specified in an order made for the purposes of this paragraph by the Secretary of State under section 453;

(d) an officer of Revenue and Customs who is not below such grade as is designated by the Commissioners for Her Majesty's Revenue and Customs as equivalent to the police rank of inspector.

(3E) In relation to a frozen funds investigation these are appropriate officers –

(a) a constable;
(b) an SFO officer;
(c) an accredited financial investigator who falls within a description specified in an order made for the purposes of this paragraph by the Secretary of State under section 453;
(d) an officer of Revenue and Customs.

(3F) In relation to a frozen funds investigation these are senior appropriate officers –

(a) a police officer who is not below the rank of inspector;
(b) the Director of the Serious Fraud Office;
(c) an accredited financial investigator who falls within a description specified in an order made for the purposes of this paragraph by the Secretary of State under section 453;
(d) an officer of Revenue and Customs who is not below such grade as is designated by the Commissioners for Her Majesty's Revenue and Customs as equivalent to the police rank of inspector."

60 In section 380 (production orders), in subsections (2) and (3)(b), for "or a detained cash investigation" substitute ", a detained cash investigation, a detained property investigation or a frozen funds investigation".

61 In section 381 (requirements for making of production order), in subsection (2), after paragraph (bb) insert –

"(bc) in the case of a detained property investigation into the derivation of property, the property the application for the order specifies as being subject to the investigation, or a part of it, is recoverable property;

(bd) in the case of a detained property investigation into the intended use of property, the property the application for the order specifies as being subject to the investigation, or a part of it, is intended by any person to be used in unlawful conduct;

(be) in the case of a frozen funds investigation into the derivation of money held in an account in relation to which an account freezing order made under section 303Z3 has effect (a "frozen account"), the property the application for the order specifies as being subject to the investigation, or a part of it, is recoverable property;

(bf) in the case of a frozen funds investigation into the intended use of money held in a frozen account, the property the application for the order specifies as being subject to the investigation, or a part of it, is intended by any person to be used in unlawful conduct;".

APPENDIX: CRIMINAL FINANCES ACT 2017

62 In section 385 (Government departments), in subsection (4)(b), for "or a detained cash investigation" substitute ", a detained cash investigation, a detained property investigation or a frozen funds investigation".

63 In section 386 (production orders: supplementary), in subsection (3)(b), for "or a detained cash investigation" substitute ", a detained cash investigation, a detained property investigation or a frozen funds investigation".

64 In section 387 (search warrants), in subsections (2) and (3)(b), for "or a detained cash investigation" substitute ", a detained cash investigation, a detained property investigation or a frozen funds investigation".

65 (1) Section 388 (requirements where production order not available) is amended as follows.

(2) In subsection (2), after paragraph (bb) insert –

"(bc) in the case of a detained property investigation into the derivation of property, the property specified in the application for the warrant, or a part of it, is recoverable property;

(bd) in the case of a detained property investigation into the intended use of property, the property specified in the application for the warrant, or a part of it, is intended by any person to be used in unlawful conduct;

(be) in the case of a frozen funds investigation into the derivation of money held in an account in relation to which an account freezing order made under section 303Z3 has effect (a "frozen account"), the property specified in the application for the warrant, or a part of it, is recoverable property;

(bf) in the case of a frozen funds investigation into the intended use of money held in a frozen account, the property specified in the application for the warrant, or a part of it, is intended by any person to be used in unlawful conduct;".

(3) In subsection (5)(a), after "(7B)" insert ", (7C), (7D), (7E), (7F)".

(4) After subsection (7B) insert –

"(7C) In the case of a detained property investigation into the derivation of property, material falls within this subsection if it cannot be identified at the time of the application but it –

(a) relates to the property specified in the application, the question whether the property, or a part of it, is recoverable property or any other question as to its derivation, and

(b) is likely to be of substantial value (whether or not by itself) to the investigation for the purposes of which the warrant is sought.

(7D) In the case of a detained property investigation into the intended use of property, material falls within this subsection if it cannot be identified at the time of the application but it –

(a) relates to the property specified in the application or the question whether the property, or a part of it, is intended by any person to be used in unlawful conduct, and

APPENDIX: CRIMINAL FINANCES ACT 2017

(b) is likely to be of substantial value (whether or not by itself) to the investigation for the purposes of which the warrant is sought.

(7E) In the case of a frozen funds investigation into the derivation of money held in a frozen account, material falls within this subsection if it cannot be identified at the time of the application but it –

(a) relates to the property specified in the application, the question whether the property, or a part of it, is recoverable property or any other question as to its derivation, and

(b) is likely to be of substantial value (whether or not by itself) to the investigation for the purposes of which the warrant is sought.

(7F) In the case of a frozen funds investigation into the intended use of money held in a frozen account, material falls within this subsection if it cannot be identified at the time of the application but it –

(a) relates to the property specified in the application or the question whether the property, or a part of it, is intended by any person to be used in unlawful conduct, and

(b) is likely to be of substantial value (whether or not by itself) to the investigation for the purposes of which the warrant is sought."

66 (1) Section 390 (further provisions: confiscation, civil recovery, detained cash and money laundering) is amended as follows.

(2) In the heading, after "detained cash" insert ", detained property, frozen funds".

(3) In subsection (1), after "detained cash investigations" insert ", detained property investigations, frozen funds investigations".

(4) In subsections (5), (6) and (7), for "or a detained cash investigation" substitute ", a detained cash investigation, a detained property investigation or a frozen funds investigation".

67 In section 391 (disclosure orders), in subsection (2), after "detained cash investigation" insert ", a detained property investigation or a frozen funds investigation".

68 In section 397 (customer information orders), in subsection (1A), at the end insert ", a detained property investigation or a frozen funds investigation".

69 In section 404 (account monitoring orders), in subsection (1A), at the end insert ", a detained property investigation or a frozen funds investigation".

70 (1) Section 408A (evidence overseas) is amended as follows.

(2) In subsection (1), for "or a detained cash investigation" substitute ", a detained cash investigation, a detained property investigation or a frozen funds investigation".

(3) In subsection (5), after paragraph (b) insert –

"(c) in relation to an application or request made for the purposes of a detained property investigation, evidence as to a matter described in section 341(3B)(a) or (b);

APPENDIX: CRIMINAL FINANCES ACT 2017

(d) in relation to an application or request made for the purposes of a frozen funds investigation, evidence as to a matter described in section 341(3C)(a) or (b);".

71 In section 408B (evidence overseas: restrictions on use), in subsection (3), after paragraph (b) insert –

"(c) if the request was made for the purposes of a detained property investigation, proceedings under Chapter 3A of Part 5 of this Act arising out of the investigation;
(d) if the request was made for the purposes of a frozen funds investigation, proceedings under Chapter 3B of Part 5 of this Act arising out of the investigation;".

72 In section 412 (interpretation), in paragraph (b) of the definitions of "appropriate person" and "proper person", for "or a detained cash investigation" substitute ", a detained cash investigation, a detained property investigation or a frozen funds investigation".

73 In the title of Chapter 4 of Part 8, before "Interpretation" insert "Supplementary and".

74 Before section 413 (in Chapter 4 of Part 8), insert –

"412A Power to vary monetary amounts

(1) In order to take account of changes in the value of money, the Secretary of State may by regulations substitute another sum for the sum for the time being specified in –

(a) section 362B(2)(b) (minimum value of property for purposes of making unexplained wealth order in England and Wales or Northern Ireland), and
(b) section 396B(2)(b) (minimum value of property for purposes of making unexplained wealth order in Scotland).

(2) The Secretary of State must consult the Department of Justice in Northern Ireland and the Scottish Ministers before making regulations under subsection (1)."

75 In section 414 (property), in subsection (3) before paragraph (a) insert – "(za) property is held by a person if he holds an interest in it;".

76 (1) Section 416 (Part 8: other interpretative provisions) is amended as follows.

(2) In subsection (1), after the entry for "detained cash investigation" insert – "detained property investigation: section 341(3B)frozen funds investigation: section 341(3C)".

(3) In subsection (2), at the appropriate places in the list insert – "enforcement authority: section 362A(7)";

"interim freezing order: section 362J(3)"; "unexplained wealth order: section 362A(3)".

(4) In subsection (3), at the appropriate places in the list insert – "interim freezing order: section 396J(3)";

"unexplained wealth order: section 396A(3)".

(5) After subsection (3A) insert –

"(3B) In relation to an order in England and Wales or Northern Ireland that is an interim freezing order or an unexplained wealth order, references to the enforcement authority are to the enforcement authority that is seeking, or (as the case may be) has obtained, the order."

(6) In subsection (7), after "Recovery order," insert "property freezing order".

(7) After subsection (7) insert –

"(7ZA) "Settlement" has the meaning given by section 620 of the Income Tax (Trading and Other Income) Act 2005."

77 (1) Section 435 (use of information by certain Directors) is amended as follows.

(2) In the heading for "Directors" substitute "authorities".

(3) In subsection (1) –

(a) for "the Director" substitute "a relevant authority";
(b) for "his", in each place, substitute "the authority's";
(c) for "him" substitute "the authority".

(4) In subsection (2) –

(a) for "the Director" substitute "a relevant authority";
(b) for "his", in each place, substitute "the authority's";
(c) for "him" substitute "the authority".

(5) In subsection (4) –

(a) in the words before paragraph (a), for ""the Director"" substitute ""relevant authority"";
(b) omit "or" at the end of paragraph (b);
(c) after paragraph (c) insert –
"(d) Her Majesty's Revenue and Customs; or
(e) the Financial Conduct Authority."

(6) The amendments made by this paragraph apply to information obtained before, as well as to information obtained after, the coming into force of this paragraph.

78 (1) Section 436 (disclosure of information to certain Directors) is amended as follows.

(2) In the heading for "Directors" substitute "authorities".

(3) In subsection (1) –

(a) for "the Director", in the first place it occurs, substitute "a relevant authority";
(b) for "the Director", in the second place it occurs, substitute "the authority";
(c) for "his" substitute "the authority's".

APPENDIX: CRIMINAL FINANCES ACT 2017

(4) In subsection (5), after paragraph (h) insert –

"(i) the Financial Conduct Authority."

(5) In subsection (10) for ""the Director"" substitute ""relevant authority"".
(6) The amendments made by this paragraph apply to information obtained paragraph.

(1) Section 437 (further disclosure) is amended as follows.

(2) In subsection (2), in paragraph (a) for "the Director's" substitute "a relevant authority's".

(3) In subsection (6) –

(a) for "the Director", in the first place it occurs, substitute "a relevant authority";
(b) for "the Director", in the second place it occurs, substitute "the authority".

(4) In subsection (7) for ""the Director"" substitute ""relevant authority"".

(1) Section 438 (disclosure of information by certain Directors) is amended as follows.
(2) In the heading for "Directors" substitute "authorities".
(3) In subsection (1) –

(a) in the words before paragraph (a) –

(i) for "the Director" substitute "a relevant authority";
(ii) for "his" substitute "the authority's";
(iii) for "him" substitute "the authority";

(b) in paragraph (c) for "Director's" substitute "authority's";
(c) in paragraph (e) after "Part 5" insert "or 8";
(d) in paragraph (f) –

(i) for "or a constable" substitute ", a constable or an SFO officer";
(ii) after "Chapter 3" insert ", 3A or 3B";

(e) in paragraph (fa) for "Director" substitute "relevant authority".

(4) In subsection (5) –

(a) for "the Director" substitute "a relevant authority";
(b) for "he", in each place, substitute "the authority".

(5) In subsection (10) for ""the Director"" substitute ""relevant authority"".
(6) The amendments made by this paragraph apply to information obtained before, as well as to information obtained after, the coming into force of this paragraph.

81 (1) Section 439 (disclosure of information to Lord Advocate and to Scottish Ministers) is amended as follows.
(2) In subsection (1), after "Part 5" insert "or 8".

277

(3) In subsection (5), after paragraph (h) insert –
"(i) the Financial Conduct Authority."
(4) The amendments made by this paragraph apply to information obtained before, as well as to information obtained after, the coming into force of this paragraph.

82 (1) Section 441 (disclosure of information by Lord Advocate and by Scottish Ministers) is amended as follows.
(2) In subsection (1), after "Chapter 3" insert "or 3A".
(3) In subsection (2) –

(a) in the words before paragraph (a), after "5" insert "or 8";
(b) in paragraph (d), after "5" insert "or 8";
(c) in paragraph (fa), for the words from "functions" to "Ireland" substitute "functions of a relevant authority, as defined by section 435(4),";
(d) in paragraph (g) –

(i) omit "a customs officer or";
(ii) after "Chapter 3" insert ", 3A or 3B".

83 In section 443 (enforcement in different parts of the United Kingdom), in subsection (1) after paragraph (c) insert –

"(ca) for an order made by a court under Part 7 in one part of the United Kingdom to be enforced in another part;".

84 In section 445 (external investigations), omit subsection (3).

85 In section 450 (pseudonyms: Scotland), in subsection (1)(a), for "or a detained cash investigation" substitute ", a detained cash investigation, a detained property investigation or a frozen funds investigation".

86 In section 453A (certain offences in relation to financial investigators), in subsection (5), at the end of paragraph (d) (before the "or") insert –

"(da) section 303C (powers to search for a listed asset); (db) section 303J (powers to seize property);
(dc) section 303K (powers to detain seized property);".

87 (1) Section 459 (orders and regulations) is amended as follows.
(2) In subsection (3A), at the end insert "or regulations under section 131ZA(7)".
(3) In subsection (4), after paragraph (a) insert –
"(aza) regulations under section 303B(2), 303G(5), 303W(10), 303Y(2), 303Z8(2) or 303Z18(10);".
(4) In subsection (5), in paragraph (a) –

(a) after "other than" insert "regulations under section 131ZA(7) or";
(b) after "293(4)," insert "303H(4),".

(5) In subsection (6)(b), after "293(4)," insert "303H(4),".
(6) After subsection (6) insert –

"(6ZA) No regulations may be made by the Scottish Ministers under section 131ZA(7) unless a draft of the regulations has been laid before and approved by a resolution of the Scottish Parliament.

APPENDIX: CRIMINAL FINANCES ACT 2017

(6ZB) No regulations may be made by the Secretary of State under section 303B(2), 303G(5), 303W(10), 303Y(2), 303Z8(2) or 303Z18(10) unless a draft of the regulations has been laid before Parliament and approved by a resolution of each House."

(7) In subsection (6A), after "302(7B)" insert "or of regulations under section 303W(10) or 303Z18(10)".

(8) In subsection (7A) –

(a) after "302(7B)," insert "303I(4),";
(b) at the end insert "or regulations under section 303W(10) or 303Z18(10)".

(9) In subsection (7B), after "302(7B)," insert "303I(4),".

(10) After subsection (7B) insert –

"(7BA) No regulations may be made by the Department of Justice under section 303W(10) or 303Z18(10) unless a draft of the regulations has been laid before, and approved by a resolution of, the Northern Ireland Assembly."

(11) In subsection (7D), after "(7B)" insert ", (7BA)".

88   In section 460 (finance), in subsection (3) –

(a) omit "and" at the end of paragraph (a);
(b) after paragraph (b) insert ", and
(c) any sums received by the Financial Conduct Authority in consequence of this Act are to be paid into the Consolidated Fund."

Homelessness etc. (Scotland) Act 2003 (asp 10)

89   In section 11 of the Homelessness etc. (Scotland) Act 2003 (notice to local authority of proceedings for possession etc.), in subsection (5), after paragraph (f) insert –

"(fa) section 245ZA(2) of the Proceeds of Crime Act 2002 (notice to local authority of application for decree of removing and warrant for ejection),".

Bankruptcy and Diligence etc. (Scotland) Act 2007 (asp 3)

90   The Bankruptcy and Diligence etc. (Scotland) Act 2007 is amended as follows.

91   (1) Section 214 (expressions used in Part 15) is amended as follows.

(2) In subsection (1) –

(a) omit "and" after the definition of "a decree for removing from heritable property", and
(b) after the definition of "an action for removing from heritable property" insert –

""defender", in relation to a decree for removing from heritable property of the type mentioned in subsection (2)(l), means any person against whom the decree is enforceable."

(3) In subsection (2) –

 (a) omit "and" at the end of paragraph (j), and
 (b) after paragraph (k) insert "; and (l) a decree of removing and warrant for ejection granted under section 266(8ZA) of the Proceeds of Crime Act 2002."

92 In section 216 (service of charge before removing) –

 (a) in subsection (1), in paragraph (a), for "14 days" substitute "the appropriate period", and
 (b) after that subsection insert –

 "(1A) In subsection (1)(a), "the appropriate period" means –

 (a) in the case of a decree for removing from heritable property of the type mentioned in paragraph (l) of section 214(2), 28 days,
 (b) in the case of a decree for removing from heritable property of the type mentioned in any other paragraph of that section, 14 days."

93 In section 218 (preservation of property left in premises), after subsection (2) insert –

 "(3) In the application of this section to the granting of a decree for removing from heritable property of the type mentioned in section 214(2)(l), "pursuer" means the trustee for civil recovery who is responsible by virtue of section 267(3)(ba) of the Proceeds of Crime Act 2002 for enforcing the decree."

Crown copyright 2017

Printed and published in the UK by The Stationery Office Limited under the authority and superintendence of Carol Tullo, Controller of Her Majesty's Stationery Office and Queen's Printer of Acts of Parliament.

INDEX

account freezing: bank 6.31; building society 6.32; challenges 6.29; estimated use 6.30; forfeiture, and 6.27, 6.37–6.38; order 6.34–6.36; terrorist financing 7.91–7.93

application for extending moratorium period: application notice 1.30–1.39; application to withhold specified information 1.36–1.37; costs 1.38; hearing 1.25–1.29; interested person 1.22; notice 1.21; order, the 1.35; procedure 1.20–1.38; respondents' notice 1.34; specified information 1.23–1.24; subsequent 1.19; timing 1.16–1.18; tipping off 1.39–1.40; who 1.15

application to vary and discharge unexplained wealth orders: code of practice 5.7; compliance impossible 5.8; contentious areas 5.3–5.9; costs 5.14; process 5.1; reasonable cause 5.6; requirements 5.3; reverse onus 5.2; variation 5.9

appropriate consent 1.2

authorised disclosure 1.2; diligence 1.09, 1.11; expeditiousness 1.11

bank account monitoring order 6.9

banks and building societies: terrorist money 7.89–7.90; unexplained wealth orders 6.31–6.33; 6.37–6.38

cash: administrative forfeiture 6.25, 7.78–7.83; definition 6.17–6.18; forfeiture 6.20, 7.72–7.73; previous loophole 6.16; terrorist 7.71–7.83

civil recovery: administrative forfeiture 7.94; anti-terrorism 7.3, 7.67–7.70; application to set aside 7.80–7.83; cash 6.16–6.20; cash forfeiture notice 7.75–7.76; objections 7.78–7.79; power to commence 6.10, 6.11; reasonable suspicion 7.74; terrorist cash 7.71–7.83; property 7.84–7.86

companies 4.17–4.18; holding property 4.22–4.23; prosecution 9.7; risks 9.18–9.21

compulsion to produce documents 6.9

confidentiality: joint reporting 3.24–3.27; terrorist financing 7.52

confiscation of criminal benefit 6.4

consent regime 1.2: problems 1.3

corporate offences 8.1; application 8.4; companies and partnerships 9.7; criminal prosecution 9.5–9.10; defence 9.2–9.4 *see also* prevention procedures defence; liability 8.5; penalties 9.10; policy 9.5–9.6; purpose 8.3

criminal suspects and connected persons: investigation 4.16; person reasonably suspected 4.14; serious crime 4.13; standard 4.15

cryptocurrency 6.18

customer information order 6.9

disclosure orders 7.3, 7.5–7.6; effect of written notice 7.25–7.26; giving reasons 7.8; making application 7.7–7.14; procedural requirements 7.9; public interest 7.17, 7.36–7.37; relevant information 7.18–7.20; requirements for making 7.15–7.17; responding to written notice 7.27 - 7.32; scope 7.7; terrorism 7.11–7.12; terrorist property 7.13–7.14; variation and discharge 7.33–7.37; written notice 7.21–7.26

failure to prevent model of liability 9.1

Financial Conduct Authority: civil recovery investigation, power to commence 6.11; extension of powers 6.3

foreign tax evasion: additional conditions for liability 8.42–8.43; consent 9.8, 9.9; facilitation 8.48–8.49; jurisdiction 8.50–8.51; offence 8.44–8.47; UK, and 8.41 *see also* UK tax evasion

fraud: aiding terrorism 7.2; cheating revenue 4.16, 8.17–8.19; false invoicing 8.18; income tax 4.16, 8.35; intent 8.28; IR35 8.29; serious crime 4.14; VAT 8.34

further information orders 2.4–2.5, 7.53–7.54: appeals 2.18, 7.65–7.66; application

2.6–2.12, 7.56–7.62; conditions 7.60–7.62; effect 7.63–7.64; introduction of 7.3; procedure 2.13, 7.57

gambling documents 6.19
gross human rights abuse or violation: conditions 6.43; examples 6.49; public official 6.46; material assistance 6.47; standard 6.48; torture or cruel, inhuman and degrading treatment 6.44; treatment in consequence of exposing illegal activity 6.45

HM Revenue & Customs: extension of powers 6.3; new powers 6.9–6.10; offences against 6.13; previous powers 6.8

immigration officers: extension of powers 6.3; offences against 6.13; powers 6.12
incriminatory evidence 2.14–2.16
information sharing: anti-terrorism 7.3; channels 3.4; confidentiality 7.52; conditions 7.41–7.46; detail 7.44; duty to report 7.50–7.51; importance 3.1, 3.3; joint reporting 7.47–7.49; notification 7.43; unexplained wealth orders 5.23; voluntary disclosure *see* voluntary disclosure
insufficient means: challenging 5.6; known sources of lawful income 4.26–4.28; market value 4.31; obtain property, to 4.25–4.31; trusts 4.29–4.30
interim freezing order 4.36–4.38; compensation 5.13; discharging 5.11–5.13; timing 4.43–4.45; varying 5.10

Joint Money Laundering Intelligence Taskforce (JMLIT) 3.2, 3.4
joint reporting: impact on duty 3.21–3.23, 7.50–7.51; limit 3.23; period 3.20; required notification 3.22, 7.43–7.45; requirements 3.19; terrorist legislation 7.47–7.49

listed assets 6.22–6.23; administrative forfeiture 6.25; estimated use 5.26; procedural safeguards 6.24
London Anti-Corruption Summit 3.3

money laundering: duty to report 3.14; partnership working 3.2
moratorium period, extending: application 1.15–1.40 *see also* application for extending moratorium period; commencement 1.8; court 1.14; criteria for making order 1.9–1.14; impact assessment 1.6, 1.7; police resources and criteria 1.12; power discretionary 1.110; procedure for extending 1.5; proposals 1.4; purpose 1.2; renewability 1.3; significance 1.1; standard of proof 1.13

National Crime Agency: disclosure request notification 3.13, 3.16; extending moratorium period 1.2, 1.15; further information orders 7.56; investigative assistance 2.2; joint suspicious activity reports 3.4; request for further information 2.2–2.4

politically exposed person 4.9–4.12; challenging 5.4
prevention procedures defence: application 9.11; communication 9.26; due diligence 9.20, 9.25; evidence 9.24; guidance 9.12–9.13; guiding principles 9.16–9.29; monitoring and review 9.28–9.29; onus of proof 9.14; proportionality 9.22–9.29; risk assessment 9.18; scope 9.15; top-level commitment 9.23; training 9.27
privilege: disclosure order notice 7.30–7.31; further information order 2.17; self-incrimination 4.3, 5.19, 7.64; waiving 51.5
prohibited act: appropriate consent 1.2; authorised disclosure 1.2; handling of criminal property 1.1; liability 2.11
property: challenging relationship 5.5; company or trust-held 4.22–4.23; definition 4.20; effective control 4.21; forfeiture 4.4; holding 4.19–4.24; insufficient means to obtain 4.25–4.31; potential beneficiary 4.23; timing 4.24
public interest: anti-terrorism 7.17, 7.36–7.37; foreign tax evasion 8.41, 9.8; unexplained wealth order 4.6, 4.48, 5.7
public revenue 8.31–8.32; cheating 8.17–8.19

regulated sector 2.11, 7.40
request for further information: appeals 2.18; application 2.6–2.12; background 2.3; domestic cases 2.8; evidential status 2.14–2.17; foreign cases 2.9; incriminatory evidence 2.14–2.16; legally privileged material 2.17; non-compliance 2.19–2.20; order *see* further information order; procedure 2.13; power 2.1, 2.2; regulated sector 2.11; substantial value 2.12
response to unexplained wealth orders: financial gifts and gambling wins 5.18; information 5.16; satisfactory explanation 5.17; truthfulness 5.15; use of explanation 5.19–5.24
restraint of assets 6.4
risks 9.18–9.19; communication 9.26; customer due diligence 9.20–9.21, 9.25; monitoring

and review 9.28–9.29; top level commitment 9.23; training 9.27
rules of court: extending moratorium period 1.5, 1.25–1.38; further information order 2.13

search and seizure powers: HM Revenue & Customs 6.9; non-conviction 6.6; Serious Fraud Office 6.4–6.5
Serious Fraud Office: confiscation of a criminal benefit 6.4; extension of powers 6.3; offences against 6.13; previous powers 6.5; restraint of assets 6.4; search and seizure powers 6.5–6.7
suspicious activity report 2.1, 2.3, 2.15: account freezing 5.28; domestic 7.60; foreign 7.61–7.62; joint 3.18–3.20; review 3.2; terrorist financing 7.1, 7.43

tax evasion: avoidance, and 8.20–8.30; foreign *see* foreign tax evasion; individual liability 8.52; responsibility 8.2; UK *see* UK tax evasion
terrorism 7.11–7.12
terrorist property 7.3, 7.13–7.14
terrorist-financing: cross-border enforceability 7.99–7.102; importance 7.1; investigation 7.10; joint reporting 7.47–7.49 *see also* information sharing; joint suspicious activity reports, and 2.1, 7.1; legislation 2.1; powers 7.95–7.98; regulated sector 7.40
trusts: insufficient means to obtain 4.29–4.30; property held by 4.22–4.23; respondents 4.34

UK tax evasion 8.14; avoidance or evasion 8.20–8.30; causation 8.12; cheating the public revenue 8.17–8.19; facilitation of 8.6, 8.39–8.40; fraudulent 8.33–8.35; offence 8.15–8.35; person acting in association 8.8 - person's status 8.9; partnership 8.10; proving 8.36–8.38; public revenue 8.31–8.32; relevant body 8.7; scope 8.11, 8.13

unexplained wealth orders: application to vary and discharge *see* application to vary and discharge unexplained wealth orders; civil enforcement proceedings 5.21; companies 4.17–4.18; criminal suspects and connected persons 4.13–4.16; criminal investigations 5.20, 5.22; development 4.1; effect 4.32–4.35; extra-territoriality 4.45–4.50; failure to respond 4.4; framework 4.2; holding property 4.19–4.24; insufficient means to obtain property 4.25–4.31 *see also* insufficient means; investigative value 4.3; non-compliance 4.39–4.42; policy 4.48; politically exposed person 4.9–4.12; providing explanation 4.35; reasonable excuse 4.42; recoverability presumption 4.41; requirements 4.5–4.7; respondent 4.8–4.18, 4.34 *see also* response to unexplained wealth orders; standard 4.5; timing 4.43–4.45; use 5.25–5.26
unlawful conduct 6.42; expansion 6.39; gross human rights abuse or violation 6.43–6.50; previous definition 6.41; purpose of amendment 6.40

voluntary disclosure 3.6, 3.7; anti-terrorism 7.39; conditions 3.8–3.17; confidentiality 3.24–3.27; impact on duty to report 3.21–3.23, 7.50–7.51; incentive 3.17; joint reporting 3.18–3.20; notification requirement 3.10, 3.13; privacy 3.24–3.27; request 3.11; respondent 2.12; standard required 3.9; suspicion 3.15

written notice: copies 7.32; effect 7.25–7.26; efficiency of 7.23; legal privilege 7.30–7.31; length 7.22; responding to 7.27–7.32; service 7.21; scope 7.24